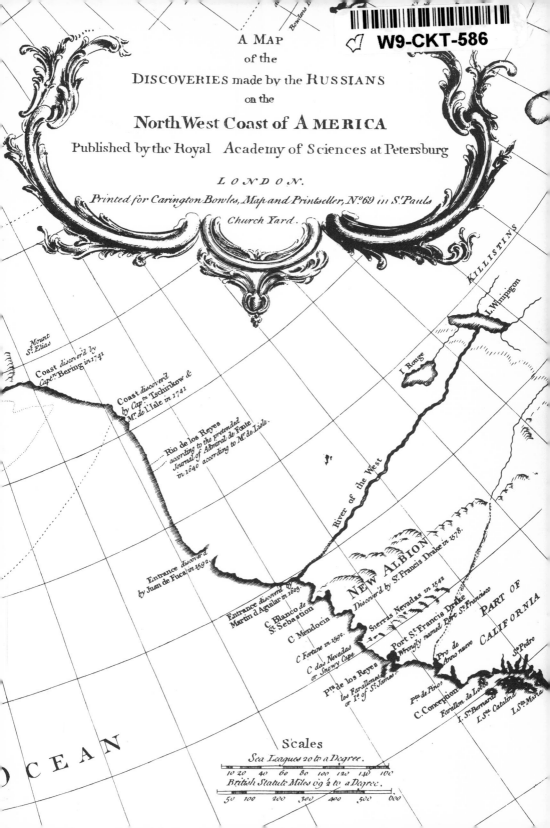

Alaska and Its History

ALASKA AND ITS HISTORY

EDITED BY MORGAN B. SHERWOOD

UNIVERSITY OF WASHINGTON PRESS

Seattle and London

Copyright © 1967 by the University of Washington Press
Library of Congress Catalog Card Number 67-13108
Printed in the United States of America
Designed by Adrian Wilson

In memory of Hector Chevigny,
who did so much to interest Americans
in the history of Alaska

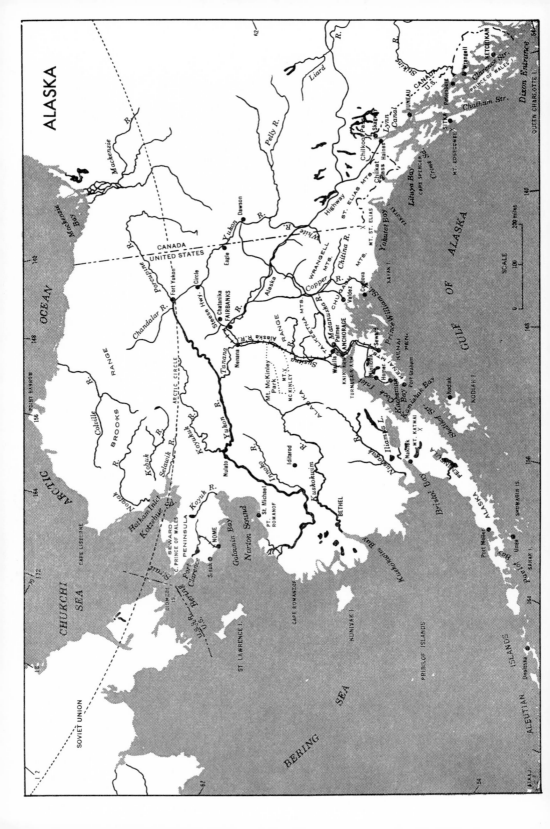

Contents

PART **II** *THE TRANSITION*

PART III · THE AMERICAN PERIOD

Illustrations

Introduction

Alaska's history has regional, national, and international dimensions. An understanding of Alaska's prehistory is crucial to an understanding of the origin of all the native peoples on the continent. Alaska was the outpost of Russian eastward expansion and Alaska's past is therefore closely related to Russian and Far Eastern history. Russian America had a role in the history of the whole Pacific Ocean area. Alaska was the westward continental limit of United States territorial expansion, and therefore deserves the attention of historians of the American westward movement. Both Russian Alaskan and American Alaskan history merges with the history of Canada. Alaska's purchase, its boundaries and fisheries have played an important part in the diplomatic history of the United States. As the first noncontiguous territory of the United States, Alaska's past is an area for the study of American colonial practices. Alaska's large area, ample resources, but small population pose a problem for students of economic growth. A part of the country's past is a notable chapter in the history of American science and exploration. And Alaska itself is a living laboratory for study of Frederick Jackson Turner's frontier hypothesis.[1]

Though Alaska's history is entwined with the history of other regions and with some of the great issues in man's social evolution, and despite the cascade of words in print about Alaska,

[1] "The Significance of the Frontier in American History," in *The Frontier in American History* (New York: Henry Holt, 1950; published originally in 1893).

xiii

the country has not received the steady attention of many professional historians. At best, only a dozen broad, solid, scholarly books of Alaskan history have appeared in English.

The most enduring general work is H. H. Bancroft's *History of Alaska*, published in 1886 as one part of the author's multivolumed history of the American West.[2] Since then, much of what has been written about the Russian period, in the uncountable travel and "inside Alaska" books, is little more than a rewriting of Bancroft.

In 1906, following the lead of his fellow scientist William Dall, Alfred Hulse Brooks outlined the history of Alaskan exploration, both maritime and continental, during the Russian period, and he calendared the work of Americans since the purchase. The sketch appeared in a U.S. Geological Survey Professional Paper entitled *The Geography and Geology of Alaska*.[3] This and other essays written by Brooks received scant attention from historians at the time, though Brooks' treatment of Russian inland exploration revealed a sophistication that any professional historian would envy. In extenuation, history as a profession was still young when the book and articles appeared. (The American Historical Association was chartered in 1884.)

Around the second decade of the twentieth century, two scholars focused on the far northwestern limits of the continent. Frank A. Golder published his *Russian Expansion in the Pacific* in 1914, and edited *Bering's Voyages*, published in 1922 and 1925.[4] Golder maintained a lively and critical interest in Russian America, publishing articles and establishing a firm foundation for future work. About the same time, Jeannette Paddock Nichols wrote her *Alaska*, covering the first fifty years of United States rule. Professor Nichols' volume remains unchallenged as the classic analysis of the early political history of American

[2] See J. W. Caughey, *Hubert Howe Bancroft: Historian of the West* (Berkeley and Los Angeles: University of California Press, 1946).

[3] See also, A. H. Brooks, *Blazing Alaska's Trails* (Caldwell, Idaho: University of Alaska and Arctic Institute of North America, 1953).

[4] For books by the authors in this anthology, please see the Contributors' Bibliography.

Alaska. Golder died in 1929, and Nichols turned her attention to other national subjects.

The book void was filled temporarily by Clarence L. Andrews, a self-taught historian and friend of Alaska. He learned Russian and probed the primary sources to produce two useful volumes. Also in the Thirties, Victor J. Farrar built his reputation as an expert on the purchase of Alaska by the United States.[5] Other researchers, in books that were not written about Alaska exclusively, filled in a few gaps, for example, such eminent historians as Thomas A. Bailey and Samuel Eliot Morison. But it was a professional writer, not a professional historian, who quickened the interest of Americans in Alaskan history. Hector Chevigny's *Lost Empire* and *Lord of Alaska*, biographies of Nikolai Rezanov and Aleksandr Baranov, were popular and exciting; though admittedly, for the scholar, the books were occasionally too imaginative. Chevigny capped his remarkable career in 1965 with *Russian America*. His last book is thoughtful, interpretive, and also a tale well told.

Alaska has been plagued by nonhistories. By nonhistory is meant a book that purports to be all or part history, but was written from two or three secondary accounts — if that — and from no primary sources. Over the years, the literature of Alaskan history has been inundated by such thin, stale, and unreliable volumes. The nonhistories of Alaska continue to come off the presses, but in the last twenty years a few rays of scholarly light have penetrated the gloom. Stuart Ramsay Tompkins' short *Alaska: Promyshlennik and Sourdough* (1945) is well written, judicious, carefully researched, and contains an excellent bibliography. Ernest Gruening, who is a writer and scholar as well as a statesman, used government documents extensively in his fine political history, *The State of Alaska* (1954), which brought Nichols' subject up to date. And in 1951, an English translation of S. B. Okun's *Russian-American Company* was published in the United States.

[5] For example, see V. J. Farrar, *The Annexation of Russian America to the United States* (Washington: 1937).

This is not a complete list of worthwhile Alaskan history books, only the highlights. There are other excellent volumes on narrower topics. Nevertheless, a comprehensive inventory of reliable books, both general and specific, would be comparatively short. For additional sound, secondary work, the investigator must turn to the articles in professional journals. Here too, the literature is limited when compared with that on other subjects. A few Alaskan topics have been investigated thoroughly in the quarterlies. Some topics, such as the purchase of Alaska, have perhaps received too much attention, given the wide gaps in our knowledge and considered as a matter of priority.[6] Others, such as the importation of reindeer, have been popular out of all proportion to even their regional historical significance.[7] The topical imbalance can be explained by the normal desire of researchers to investigate novel subjects or episodes closely related to national and international, rather than parochial affairs.

An explanation of the relatively limited quantity of scholarly articles hinges also, in part, on the preference for broader topics. Furthermore, Alaska is a geographical freak and is in so many ways an anachronism in U.S. and Russian history, that very often the editors of learned journals and scholars in general simply do not know what to make of it. There is, for example, an erroneous belief that the sources for Alaska historical research are obscure and slim. To find the documents may require effort, but rich archival materials are available, and some good Alaskan history on important subjects can still be written from printed primary sources alone.

John Wesley Powell once said that scholarship breeds scholarship. The converse is equally true. When few historians write Alaskan history and too little responsible scholarship exists,

[6] The editor has played the game. His only alibi is that George Davidson's expedition was also an episode in the history of American exploration and science.

[7] To qualify this harsh observation, a recent article hints that much of what was written earlier about the reindeer might have been more valuable if the authors had used archival sources; see, D. J. Ray, "Sheldon Jackson and the Reindeer Industry of Alaska," *Journal of Presbyterian History*, XLIII (June, 1965), 71–99.

professors who direct the research of students and editors who accept and reject manuscripts have no adequate yardsticks with which to determine what should be researched or published. The *Mississippi Valley Historical Review* (now the *Journal of American History*) and the *American Historical Review* have featured Alaskan articles, but very few. A happy departure from this bleak scene is the record of two old and honorable American journals, the *Pacific Northwest Quarterly* (formerly the *Washington Historical Quarterly*) and the *Pacific Historical Review*. The former is a regional journal, but covers a wide region indeed. It would be misleading to call the latter regional, because it concentrates on the whole Pacific Ocean area. Both journals have published a substantial number of reliable essays on Alaskan history. A new quarterly, the *Journal of the West*, has displayed an active interest in the Far Northwest.

Despite the weaknesses of Alaskan historiography (and not all have been mentioned), the available articles represent a body of scholarship that is almost unknown to the Alaskan history buff or to scholars working in other areas of specialization. One reason for the book in hand is to introduce both amateurs and professionals to the monographic literature in article form.

Not all of the essays in this anthology were written by professional historians, not all of the geographical settings are Alaskan, and not all of the selections appeared originally in history journals. In addition to historians, the collection contains articles by a geologist, a librarian, a U.S. senator, a museum curator, and a professional writer. In the studies that follow, the reader will visit California, Siberia, London, Hawaii, and Canada, among other places. Eleven periodicals are represented in the collection:

American Slavic and East European Review
California Historical Society Quarterly
Canadian Geographical Journal
Canadian Historical Review
Journal of the West
Mississippi Valley Historical Review
Pacific Historical Review

Pacific Northwest Quarterly
Russian Orthodox Journal (a revised reprint)
Scientific Monthly
Slavonic and East European Review.

For various reasons, it was necessary to use essays from three books: Andrews' *Sitka* (Caldwell, Idaho: Caxton Printers, 1945); Brooks' *Geography and Geology of Alaska*; and Chevigny's *Russian America* (New York: Viking Press, 1965). I acknowledge gratefully the reprint permission granted by each publisher.

I have also attempted to make the collection representative by covering Alaskan history chronologically and by including as many important topics as possible, as many productive scholars as possible, as many kinds of sources and topics as possible — all without duplicating information. Because of the criteria, the space limitation, and topical imbalance in the general literature, obviously something had to give way. The anthology is not chronologically complete. Not all the topics are of great moment in the history of Russia or of America, or even always of Alaska. A pivotal article by William A. Dunning on the purchase of Alaska is not included because it duplicated, in part, another more recent selection that makes mention of the Dunning essay. The Klondike Rush is represented by a single essay. Much has been written about the Klondike, but not many articles by careful investigators.[8] Some highly competent scholars are not represented. Moreover, the essays reprinted below are not necessarily the best examples of any particular author's work. Though "Mining in Alaska before 1867" is an original subject, Golder's research on Russian expansion and his essays on Russo-American relations at the time of the Cession have been more influential. And I would hesitate to say which of Bailey's articles was more important, his essay on the boundary controversy, reproduced here, or his "Why the United States Purchased Alaska," in the *Pacific Historical Review* (1934).

Two other things were kept in mind during the selection proc-

[8] For an excellent book on the Klondike, see Pierre Berton, *The Klondike Fever* (New York: Alfred A. Knopf, 1958).

ess. First, I tried to avoid primary sources. It was easy enough to eliminate edited documents from the collection (though some editing is so thorough that it constitutes an original contribution to the secondary sources).[9] It was not easy to eliminate primary sources altogether, because the old primary-secondary classification breaks down in Alaskan historiography. A great deal of Alaskan history has been written by individuals who have since become historical figures. William Dall and Alfred Brooks wrote the history of Alaskan exploration; both were explorers. How they interpreted the progress of exploration may reveal their own subjective involvement in the subject. In the same way, the work of Ernest Gruening is at once history and of historical interest. Gruening's *The State of Alaska* can be read as a plea for Alaskan statehood, yet his writing of early Alaskan history is both thoughtful and scholarly.

Second, I tried to include recent scholarship whenever possible. Given the other selection criteria, the goal was not always attainable. The most recent essay is dated 1965, the oldest 1906. The reader should not accept as final all the conclusions that follow. The progress of scholarship is merciless. Subsequent research has already modified some of the interpretations and some of the detail in the essays. A few of the revisions will be obvious from assertions in the more recent articles, and the editor has made notations along the way. But the serious beginning student of Alaskan history will want to check all the relevant sources mentioned in the footnotes. A Contributors' Bibliography is appended for the same purpose, and to help overcome other pitfalls in the selection of articles.

Although a handful of obvious, minor typographical errors have been corrected and one or two ellipses included, the essays are reproduced as they appeared originally. I did not tamper with grammar, syntax, spelling, transliteration of Russian names, or note style. Biographical information about the authors was obtained from the journals in which the articles appeared,

---

[9] For an example, see J. W. VanStone, "Russian Exploration in Interior Alaska, An Extract from the Journal of Andrei Glazunov," *Pacific Northwest Quarterly*, L (April, 1959), 37–47.

from obituaries in the *American Historical Review* and the *Pacific Northwest Quarterly*, from *Who's Who* and the *Directory of American Scholars*, and from correspondence with the authors.

My good wife, Jeanie, helped me through the numerous proof readings which a work of this kind requires. Most of all, as an historian and as an Alaskan, I want to thank the scholars who researched and wrote the articles. This is their book, not mine.

M.B.S.

University of California, Davis

PART I

THE RUSSIAN PERIOD

Professor Robert J. Kerner reminded the scholarly world that Russia had a frontier tradition too, but it was an eastward movement rather than westward expansion as in the American experience. Russian America was the far reach of Ivan's eastward grasp and the westward continental limit of Uncle Sam's. In this article from the Pacific Historical Review, *XVII (May, 1948), 135–48, Kerner indicates the relevance of Siberian history to Alaskan history, not only before discovery and during the Russian period, but also up to the present. Kerner (1887–1956) received his doctorate from Harvard in 1914. He was Sather Professor of History at the University of California, Berkeley, and served as the first director of the Institute of Slavic Studies at the University.*

The Russian Eastward Movement: Some Observations on Its Historical Significance

ROBERT JOSEPH KERNER

The Russian eastward movement carried a European people across the vast expanse of Asia to the Pacific, where they joined the descendants of the Spanish and the Anglo-Saxons among populations that will always be preponderantly Asiatic. It made the Russian people, numerically the largest and fastest-growing European nation, neighbors of the largest and fastest-growing Asiatic people, the Chinese, and created at the same time the longest land frontier in the world. More recently it brought into this intimate contact of cultures and races a rapid industrialization based upon European technology and abundant natural resources and propagated with an expansive revolutionary ideology. One does not have to be a prophet to foresee that this historical development will produce still greater changes in the future than it has already achieved. The role of Russia in Asia and on the Pacific will be a very important one, to say the least. Whether it will be the dominant one in the next century will depend in existing circumstances on the future power and the foreign policy of the United States.

The greatest of Russian historians, V. O. Klyuchevsky, maintained that "the history of Russia is the history of a country in the process of colonization." It was, therefore, a country where the frontier continually played a prominent, if not dominant, role. The Russian people have been and still are a nation in movement. They utilized their unique river systems to reach the seas, and nowhere was the opportunity so inviting as beyond the Urals in Siberia. Hence colonization in one river basin after the other and an advance eastward from one river system over easy portages to the next were the chief characteristics of the Russian movement of exploration and acquisition from the Urals to the Pacific. The Ob', Enisei, and Lena, whose main streams flowed north, but whose great branches flowed east and west, and the eastward-flowing Amur gave speed to the advance to the Pacific, which the great land highway — the *Veliky Trakt* — and then the Trans-Siberian Railway eventually took over for the most part.

The earliest background of the eastward movement across the Urals is to be found in the fur-trading enterprise of Novgorod. Daring merchants and trappers from Novgorod exploited the lower reaches of the Ob' from about the fourteenth century by portaging from the tributaries of the Pechora. They and the Muscovites, who carried out expeditions in 1465, 1483, and 1499, raided the inhabitants beyond the Urals for the purpose of obtaining tributes of furs, of which there was a diminishing supply in European Russia. The Russian raids were often followed by counterraids of Siberian natives, which endangered the security of the Ural frontier. It was the latter which especially concerned Tsar Ivan the Dread. He received news that the Volga pirate Yermak, who was wanted for offenses against the laws of tsardom, had, in the employ of the Novgorodian family of the Stroganovs, raided beyond the Urals. The tsar, in fact, ordered the Stroganovs to bring him back for trial. He feared the Ural frontier would be overrun by the tribesmen of the Tatar khan, Kuchum. Yermak's success in capturing Sibir, the capital of Siberia, caused the tsar to change his intentions in regard to Yermak; instead of beheading him he gave Yermak his blessing and a real coat of armor. Incidentally, it was this heavy accoutrement that caused Yermak to lose his life by drowning.

Moscow took over in 1583 and ended the practice of raids. It initiated a planned domination of rivers and portages through the building of blockhouses, called *ostrogs* in Russian. This was in line with centuries of Russian tradition in Europe. The original motive for the advance into Siberia was the acquisition of furs. Moscow sought to add to it the search for gold and silver. The conquest of the Tatar khanate gave security to the Ural frontier and created a base for further expansion. Thus from its origins to the present day, Russian rule in Asia was planned and regimented from Moscow.

The first Russians in Siberia were fur merchants and trappers, government officials, Cossacks, and Orthodox priests. The advance was rapid, once the khanate had been subdued. Within a decade and a half after Yermak's death the basin of the Ob' had become a Russian possession with the ostrog of Tobolsk on the Irtysh, founded in 1587, as the key, but with ostrogs guarding the route to it from Russia and others built on the lower reaches of the Ob' and the upper reaches of its tributaries. The pattern set in the Ob' basin was followed, in the years 1607–1625, in that of the Enisei, directly to the east with its center at Eniseisk (1618). The basin of the Lena was occupied between 1630 and 1648, with its center at Yakutsk, an ostrog founded in 1632. The Russians reached the Pacific in 1639. Their occupation of the Lake Baikal and Amur region, with its center at Irkutsk (1652), followed in the 'fifties and 'sixties. Forced out of the Amur River region by the Chinese under the Manchu emperor Kang-hsi by the negotiations which resulted in the Treaty of Nerchinsk (1689), the Russians lost the base of an adequate supply of grain and vegetables. This was to make their hold on eastern Siberia precarious for nearly two centuries. Even more than that, they lost easy access to the Pacific, which they did not regain until 1858–1860.

A century before Bering, the Cossack Dezhnev sailed down the Kolyma in northeastern Siberia and rounded the northeastern shores north of Kamchatka in 1648. He proved that Asia and North America were separated by a body of water; but this knowledge, then of little significance, was soon forgotten. The occupation of Kamchatka followed, with great difficulty, more than half a century later, and that of the Aleutians and the shores of Alaska by another half century. The process, however, remained much the same. In the expansion to North America, "the sea was like a river; the key island, guarding passages between islands or dominating chains of islands (or the coast), was an ostrog." Thus the ostrogs of Unalaska, Kodiak, and Sitka (Novo-Arkhangelsk) were founded. Russian power in Alaska was exercised from these island ostrogs and not from the mainland of North America.

The historian deals with unique situations involving men, events, and other human factors, but he also deals with processes, which, unlike the unique, recur again and again. Yermak, Poyarkov, Khabarov, Atlasov, Bering, and Baranov were a few of the rugged and fearless men who, so to speak, forged Russia's route to the Pacific over the long and lonesome trails of northern Asia and across the fogbound and stormy North Pacific. In most ways they and what they did were unique. Yet they operated through and in a process, which remained very much the same from the Volga to the Yukon — a process the preponderant and persistent motive of which was the acquisition of furs. It was a process as old as Russia, and beyond that, as old as the Vikings or Varangians, who most probably introduced it into the Russian river system.

The Russian government was the chief fur trader, for it collected from the natives the tribute or tax in furs called *yasak*. It levied a tax of 10 per cent, collected from the best furs obtained by private fur traders and trappers. It also exercised the right to buy their best furs. It created a monopoly on the sables and black foxes sold to China. It engaged in the business of selling furs. In this way Russia became and has remained to this day the leading source of supply of furs in the world. The revenue from furs in the seventeenth century was an important item in the income of a state as poor as that of Russia. It showed a profit over and above the expenses which Siberia caused to the treasury. Whenever the supply of fur-bearing animals diminished in one region and another offered easier yields, the hunter and trader moved on. This determined the speed and tempo of Russian eastward expansion — it had been the original cause of expansion across the Urals. Out of it all, Siberia became a colony and "a big business enterprise" of the Muscovite government.

This government-owned and government-managed enterprise had developed at a time of great internal turmoil inaugurated by Ivan the Dread, who, through a system of terror, half destroyed political feudalism by exterminating many of the prominent families of the old nobility who might compete with the crown for political control. However, the economic and social features of the medieval structure were left intact. Thus it was that Russian peasants, facing complete enserfment, fled in vast numbers from central Russia to the south toward the Black Sea, and to the north to the White Sea, almost depopulating the region they left, and certainly causing a lack of easily accessible manpower for the wars which Ivan waged at the gates of the Baltic.

The management of the Siberian enterprise was put in the hands of an office called the Siberian Prikaz, controlled by Muscovite bureaucracy, which, apart from supporting the territorial expansion involved, was concerned essentially with fair treatment of the natives as a steady and rich source of fur through the yasak, and with securing a continuous supply of grain through peasant colonization for officials and soldiers who ruled Siberia. Because the flight of peasants before complete enserfment led to many measures to hold them where they were for labor on the great landed estate of the *pomeshchiks*, the government had to offer many liberal inducements to peasants to go to Siberia at this time. They, however, would go only as free peasants, because they could remain where they were as serfs.

Thus serfdom, as practiced in European Russia, was not introduced in Siberia; and because there were no serfs in that sense in Siberia, the nobles, as great landowners, did not go to Siberia, where all land was owned by the state or by the imperial household. Hence, the serving nobles, who went to Siberia as officials, returned to Russia after their assignments ended. The church, which would have created large landholdings and was in the process of doing so during the first half century of Siberia's occupation, was restricted in this by the government. Large landed estates, therefore, did not become a feature of the Siberian landscape. The dominant characteristic of Siberia, from the point of view of land tenure, was the free peasant's holding as much land as he could personally clear and cultivate, from whence came the hardy, independent Siberian — the Sibiryak, known for his prowess on the battlefield. Siberian regiments won for Russia many a battle that would have been lost had they not been thrown in. Their fighting at Stalingrad saved that important city from the Nazi armies.

The research that has been directed to the study of the colonization of Siberia has brought out so much detail that only a few of the main trends can be touched upon in this account. It may be stated that, until the building of the Trans-Siberian Railway was begun in 1892, the aim of the government was to hold or to secure its possession of Siberia against possible seizure or invasion from without. The economic and social development of that region was not its primary aim. With the building of that railway, economic development became a prime motive. That change of policy coincides approximately with the beginning of the industrial revolution in Russia. Hence the 'nineties of the last century were a turning point, not only as regards internal Siberian development and Russian development as a whole, but of Russian foreign policy in Asia and on the Pacific.

In the period down to 1892 the government was not interested in opening Siberia for free entry and rapid development. Its objective — to secure its possession of this territory — was much more limited. There were a number of reasons for this. The great landowners feared so great a depletion of manpower that they would be unable to cultivate their extensive domains, and the government feared it could not hold the loyalty of the large number of serfs that would become free peasants on going to far-off Siberia. Another factor was the fear of the officials that "naked" peasants, i.e., peasants without the necessary financial support and agricultural equipment, would produce a disaster if they returned disappointed. The government, therefore, intended to keep a firm grip on Siberia both from within and without. How far it fell short of achieving the aim of regimentation is not known. The number of persons who emigrated to Siberia of their own free will and who went illegally, in defiance of the government's regulations, was always much greater than the number of free persons and convicts who were sent there. The historic Russian wanderlust could not be kept down, especially if it meant free land and freedom. After the emancipation of the serfs in 1861–1863, the numbers increased by leaps and bounds. In fact, the migration became elemental. The government issued decrees and regulations uselessly and, so to speak, after the event. Belatedly it tried to introduce some order into the "human rush" and, if possible, to foresee its effect upon the land problem, living conditions, and political development. It worked to direct a flood it could not dam up, by encouraging settlement into the Far Eastern regions, along the Amur, and in the Altai and Kirghiz country. It was generally agreed, if the government could enforce it, that each peasant should receive not more than 38 acres (15 hectares) nor less than 25 acres (10 hectares) of arable land for use for an undetermined term. He could not sell this land nor incur debt on it in any way. For it, after three years, he paid rent or other government levies. In Siberia, however, use meant property in the ordinary sense of the word. In course of time the *mir*, with its periodical repartition, appeared in Siberia, only to be almost dissolved by the Stolypin land reform in the decade between the revolutions. Under the Bolsheviks there followed, after 1930, the organization of the landholdings into collective farms. Because people of all nationalities and races poured in from European Russia, and because in Siberia they lived among many others, Siberia became the melting pot of Russia.

As already indicated, the building of the Trans-Siberian Railway from 1892 on was a decisive conjuncture of events. The railroad itself was the result of both internal and international developments. The Veliky Trakt, the great land road, was no longer able to serve even the most elementary economic needs of a region so fast-developing as Siberia, not to say anything of the vital importance communications had assumed in an age of railroad building. With the awakening of Japan and its rise as a power, Siberia with a single, poor land road could not be defended, because troops in sufficient number could not be transported over what in many places was barely a trail without adequate bridges and which, during certain seasons, was not always passable. The Committee on the Trans-Siberian Railway became a force for the economic development of a region which had been held back by lack of communications and by the brakes applied by officials to control the migration. It meant also for Siberia the first real impulse to the spread of the industrial revolution and, at the same time, the revival and expansion of mining.

For the first time in Russian history, Asia and the Pacific began to play an important and even a decisive role in Russian foreign policy. Much that was happening was foreseen by the only Russian statesman in more than two centuries who understood Russia's position in Asia and the Far East. It was only natural that his views were not immediately appreciated. Count N. N. Muravyev — later called Count Muravyev-Amursky, because he more than anyone was responsible for obtaining for Russia the north bank of the Amur and the region in which Vladivostok was to be built — sketched the fundamentals of a sound Russian policy. In a series of reports in the 1850's he emphasized that Russia's access to the Pacific was the main objective. To secure it and to defend it should be the chief purpose of Russian policy. Russia should consolidate her possessions on the Asiatic mainland by relinquishing Alaska to the United States to prevent its falling into the hands of the British. Muravyev indicated, something that few believed at the time, that China's internal difficulties need give little trouble to Russia. But he was the first to point to the need of preventing other powers from driving a wedge between Russia and China through Korea, Manchuria, Mongolia, and Sinkiang; Russia must not permit any other power to gain influence in these regions, because this would endanger Russia's easiest access to the sea, along the Veliky Trakt and the Amur River. As conceived by Muravyev this was purely a defensive conception, and it has always been so in the minds of those who planned Russian foreign policy, even when they ventured beyond these fundamentals.

There were, of course, other good and adequate reasons besides those indicated by Count Muravyev-Amursky for the ultimate sale of Alaska in 1867 to the United States. These are well known and need not be recounted here. From the point of view of this account of the Russian eastward movement, which here spilled over an ocean to reach another continent, a few observations may be made. In spite of the useful studies which have been written on the Russian-American Company, relatively insufficient attention has thus far been given to the fact that Russian Alaska was really a direct extension of the Russian eastward movement, where many of its traditions and practices were applied. Here may be seen the postulate that the land belonged to the Russian state, that yasak was to be collected from the native, that the native as a source of state income was to be well treated in order to remain productive, and that the church should accompany the Russians to guard their souls and morals and to welcome the natives if they cared to join. The Russian government, owning the land and its appurtenances, could grant the exercise of its power to a company to do what the British East India Company had been doing for nearly two centuries. In the early years of the seventeenth century European governments dared not exploit regions and peoples in the way that chartered companies could. Only Russia came into the field nearly two centuries later, and then only because the Siberian merchants and trappers, having exhausted the easily available huge quantities of furs in Siberia, impelled the Russian government to engage in this overseas extension of Siberian activities. That the entire enterprise was based on this conception is proved by the fact that it folded up commercially when the sea-otter catch declined to an uncommercial basis and the original Aleut population had been almost destroyed.

After the relinquishment of Alaska, an agreement between Russia and Japan in 1875 called for Russia's giving up claims to the Kuril Islands and Japan to that of Sakhalin. The possession of Sakhalin protected Russia's access to the Pacific down the Amur because that island guards the mouth of that river. The Treaty of St. Petersburg in 1881 which ended the Kuldja or Ili Affair gave Russia priority in trade in Mongolia and what is now known as Sinkiang.

The building of the Trans-Siberian Railway inspired fantasy, particularly when it became evident that its eastern section might have to be built across Manchuria or even across China. Nebulous projects of one kind or another sprang up. The Buryat Mongolian Tibetan doctor, Badmayev, conceived the idea of dominating China by acquiring preponderance for Russia in its Mongolian and Tibetan hinterland. The tsar was to be the political protector of the Buddhist Church through an arrangement with the Tibetan Dalai Lama. Japan struck back by driving China out of Korea in 1895 and by seeking to gain a foothold in Manchuria. This led to the secret Russo-Chinese Alliance of 1896, whereby Russia obtained the right to continue the Trans-Siberian as the Chinese Eastern Railway through northern Manchuria. Thus Russian predominance was established in Manchuria, which, in addition to Mongolia and Sinkiang, was crucial to the defense of Russian access to the Pacific. The naval base of Vladivostok was frozen for six months in the year, making it necessary for the Russian fleet to spend the winter in the ports of Japan which were nearest to its shores. Hence the lease of the naval base of Port Arthur and of Dalny (Dairen) as a commercial harbor — both warm water ports — seemed the logical development of the urge to the sea and of the trend that began with the economic upsurge of Siberia consequent upon the building of the Trans-Siberian Railway. These dreams in large part vanished in the Russo-Japanese War, as a result of which the first attempt by Russia to monopolize the fate of China failed.

Out of the debris Russia managed to salvage her former predominance in northern Manchuria, Outer Mongolia, and Sinkiang. The Chinese Revolution which began in 1911 gave the Mongols an opportunity to free themselves from the Chinese, and they became lodged under the protection of the Russians. The First World War and the Bolshevik Revolution gave Japan its first chance since the sixteenth century to control the destiny of China and to occupy the Russian Far East. It was the vigorous stand of the United States at the Washington Conference (1920–1921) that caused the Japanese to evacuate Russian territory and that was to give China, in the shadow of Japanese predominance, an opportunity to develop into an independent nation.

The Communists of Soviet Russia were the only ones to help Dr. Sun Yat-sen in his revolutionary struggle. As a result of agreement in 1924 between him and the Soviet envoy A. Joffe, Chinese Communists were admitted into the Kuomintang on the condition that they were to obey Kuomintang principles and discipline and not "turn the Kuomintang into a Communist party." The course of events in the successful national Chinese Revolution which followed indicated that the Chinese Communists under the leadership of their Russian advisers sought to capture the Chinese Revolution and were expelled in 1927. This ended the second attempt of Russia to monopolize the fate of China and hence the destiny of Asia and the Pacific. Incidentally, the failure of the Communists to seize power in Germany by 1923 and in China in 1927 ended the first wave of the world revolution as conceived by the Russian leaders of the Third International.

When, in 1931, Japan embarked on the Manchurian venture which was to develop in a decade into the Greater East Asia Co-Prosperity Sphere — in other words, into the second Japanese attempt to monopolize the fate of China and secure control of Asia and the Pacific — the reaction in the Soviet Union was decisive. To avoid war with Japan, if possible, by selling the Russian share of the Chinese Eastern Railway in 1935 and to enter into a neutrality pact in 1941, in which they pledged each other respect for Manchukuo and Mongolia, were manifestations in Soviet foreign policy. Soviet internal policy was decisively influenced. Although the First Five-Year Plan, begun in 1928, called for investment in industry in Siberia, it was seen at once that industry in Russian Asia would have to be developed with a much more rapid tempo in order to be able to supply Russian armies and war materials for defense against Japan, which with Nazi Germany might decide to attack the Soviet Union.

The Soviet Union Conference of Productive Forces, after a thorough survey by geologists and engineers, in 1931 had reached the conclusion that Soviet Asia (exclusive of the Caucasus) included 80.5 per cent of the energy resources of the entire Soviet Union. These were named as coal, shale, oil, turf, gas, wood, and water power. It was estimated that this region possessed 28 to 40 per cent of the known iron resources, 87 to 97 per cent of the copper, 95 per cent of the zinc, 95 per cent of the rare metals, 60 per cent of the area suitable for wheat cultivation, and 72 per cent of the yearly growth of forest. In other words, the region from the Urals to Lake Baikal might well become the industrial backbone of the Soviet Union.

As a result of this information and because of the danger of attack by Japan and Nazi Germany, from that time to the present one of the principal objectives has been to create this second metallurgical base extending from the Urals eastward. To illustrate: in the Fourth Five-Year Plan (1946–1950) at least 36 per cent of the total capital investment called for will be expended in this region, in spite of the fact that the main objective of this plan is to reconstruct the regions in European Russia totally devastated in the Second World War. According to Soviet estimates the share of Soviet Asia in the total industrial output of the Soviet Union in 1950 is to be 60 per cent of the coal, iron, and steel production and between 36 and 50 per cent of the oil production. It is, therefore, clear that, if the plans of the Soviet Union succeed, the center of its basic industrial production will shift eastward out of European Russia into the Urals and beyond. If the same policy is successfully followed during the course of the next decade or two, the economic center of the Soviet Union will be in Siberia. This development was hastened when many industries were moved across the Urals during the Second World War to avoid destruction at the hands of the Nazis.

It is possible to conclude that this basic change of economic center appears inevitable both by reason of resources and of security in war. In this way the Soviet Union is destined to become the strongest industrial power in Asia in our generation. With peace-treaty limitations on the war industries of Japan and Japan's loss of control of resources on the Asiatic continent and with the relative industrial backwardness of China and India, this will certainly be a possibility for some time to come. Thus the Russian eastward movement seems destined to pull the economic center of Russia with it.

The significance of this fundamental shift in Soviet Russia's economic basis from Europe to Asia can scarcely be envisaged at this time. It not only increases Russia's military security as a whole in any future conflict, especially in a war that may be chiefly fought out with air power, but it also increases that country's power in Asia and on the Pacific. The pressure created by the Soviet industrial revolution in Siberia will be felt not only along the frontier of six thousand miles, but deep in the heart of Asia and beyond, among Asia's half-awakened hundreds of millions.

One of the features of the Fourth Five-Year Plan calls for "the conversion of the Northern or Siberian Sea Route into a normally working sea-lane by 1950." This route is open spasmodically for about three months in the year and is the route alternate to the present combination of the direct Trans-Siberian Railway and inland river and canal route to the Pacific. The recent acquisition of the Kuril Islands makes possible direct Soviet-controlled sea connections from Murmansk and Archangel in Europe with the naval bases of Petropavlovsk, Vladivostok, and Port Arthur and the commercial port of Dalny (Dairen) in the Far East.

The mention of this strategic sea route in the Soviet Arctic brings to mind a frontier which the Russian eastward movement created and which under Communist direction is being explored, acquired, and exploited with great diligence for both internal reasons and international objectives. It is a subject which can only be mentioned here, but the historical origins of which go back to the sixteenth-century search for the Northeast Passage; to the Russian urge to the sea by way of the Ob', Enisei, Lena, and Kolyma; to the need of cheap transportation to Europe before the First World War for Siberian butter, lumber, and other products; to ice-breakers and airplanes; to revolutionary ideology among polar peoples; and to possible future war in the air by way of the polar regions. No group of scientists and explorers knows as much about the arctic regions — their natural resources, their animal resources, and their peoples — or about the development of regions of permafrost as do the Russians. There are figures to the effect that from 25 to 47 per cent of the area of the Soviet Union is in the permafrost zone. The claims made by Soviet Russia extending to the North Pole clash with the international law that has thus far been developed as regards the freedom of navigation of the high seas and of the air. Suffice it to say that along this unknown frontier — in the knowledge of which the Russians excel all others as to science, organization, and daring — is being written a decisive act of the great drama of the future.

Another factor of great importance in Russia in Asia has been the policy of national autonomy of the Communist leadership of the Soviet Union as contrasted with the policy of Russification or national assimilation of Russia under the tsars. The latter, down to 1917, had led to the point where it was only a matter of time before most of the Asiatic races within Russia would have disappeared through assimilation or extinction.

Soviet Russia in Asia consists of the eastern half of the constituent Union Russian Soviet Federative Socialist Republic, and five other constituent Union republics (Uzbek, Kazakh, Kirghiz, Tadzik, and Turkmen). On both sides of the present frontier there live Iranians (called Takziks in Russia), Turko-Tatars (called Bashkirs, Oirats, Kazakhs, Uzbeks, Turkmen, and Kirghizes in Russia) and Mongols, who in Russia go under the name of Buryats. Inside the Russian Republic, in the heart of eastern Siberia, live the Turko-Tatar Yakuts of Yakutia, to mention only the most important of the Asiatic folk. The cultural autonomy and various degrees of political autonomy granted to these, and the status of constituent republic granted to those mentioned previously — even under the strict and hard ideological rule of the Communists — affect their kinsmen across the border who do not possess this autonomy in Korea, Manchuria, Mongolia, Sinkiang, and Iran. These populations become restless and demand similar autonomous rights or independence, especially if they are propagandized by their Communist kinsmen across the border.

The Bolshevik impact on this back yard of Asia is a powerful one and can scarcely be overestimated. During the Fourth Five-Year Plan the industrial output of the Kazakh and Kirghiz republics is expected to be more than doubled, that of the Uzbek Republic increased 89 per cent, and of the Tadzhik Republic 56 per cent. When the force of economic attraction by the Trans-Siberian and Turk-Sib railways — as the only economic outlets of this region — is added to the political and cultural factors, one can appreciate the prestige and priority the Bolsheviks possess without effective foreseeable competition from non-Asiatic states along these lengthy and lonesome Asiatic frontiers. This merely raises questions without adequate answers.

Suffice it to say that the reasons are clear why Outer Mongolia (otherwise known as the Mongolian Peoples Republic) gravitates toward the Soviet Union and why it has been possible for the Russians first to separate it from China and then to bind it to the Soviet Union, thus preparing it for a fate contrary to the Soviet-Chinese Treaty of August 14, 1945. By the same treaty, most of the rights acquired by Russia in Manchuria before the Russo-Japanese War were restored to the Soviet Union. With the survival, after 1927, of the Chinese Communist party and its great expansion down to the present, the struggle goes on for the monopoly of the fate of China by Moscow. The same is true of Korea.

The Russian eastward movement has thus far resulted in the acquisition of a vast territory about three-fourths of the size of the Soviet Union and including a population of from forty to fifty million people. This is about one-fourth to one-fifth of the total population of that country. Russians now form a majority of the inhabitants in the area from the Urals to the Pacific. The *taiga* — the virgin woodland alternating with swamps — alone has an area of 4,500,000 square miles, i.e., about one and a half times the area of the United States. Under planned settlement it is capable of supporting a huge population. Large cities have grown up. Novosibirsk is reported to have a population of about 700,000. New railroads and highways, air lines, and steamship lines are being developed. Large penal colonies have been put to work.

But Siberia still remains a vast underdeveloped continent. German and Japanese writers and scholars have cast envious eyes upon this second North America, as they call it. Li Hung-chang, the grand old statesman of China, once remarked that "Russia will rue the day that she encroached on China and intervened in that country's internal affairs when she begins to see Siberia will become Chinese." Did he have reference there to a future Chinese westward movement? The Mongols and Turko-Tatars have already taken fright. They have seen the Manchus of Manchuria disappear before the Chinese flood. Perhaps that is one reason they prefer Russian autonomy to future amalgamation with the Chinese. The possibilities of such a development may also have had weight with the Russians when they have sought and now appear to seek control of China in what the leaders in the Kremlin probably believe to be the second way of the world revolution, which has developed since 1945. At any rate, it seems clear that the main emphasis of Russian foreign policy will follow the shift of Russian economic power eastward, and hence Asia and the Pacific will play an increasing, if not a dominant, role in its formulations.

Soviet Russia cannot allow another great power to dominate China, Japan, and Korea without endangering its access to the Pacific or its security. But neither can the United States permit Russia to dominate China, Japan, and Korea. This would mean Russian domination not only of Asia but of the Pacific, and that would endanger the security of the United States.*

*On the subject of Russian eastward movement, see also *Russia's Eastward Expansion*, edited by G. A. Lensen (Englewood Cliffs, N.J.: Prentice-Hall, 1964). — ED. NOTE.

The nature of Ivan's eastward maritime reach for Alaska is detailed in the selection by Alfred Hulse Brooks. Brooks was an explorer, geologist, historian, and general Alaskan expert who served for years as the head of the Alaskan branch of the U.S. Geological Survey. He graduated from Harvard in 1894, studied abroad, and first came north in 1898 to explore for the USGS. He returned to Alaska many times before his death in 1924. During World War I, he was chief geologist in the American Expeditionary Force, and following the war he became an adviser to the American Peace Team at Paris. His Alaskan publications are voluminous. This selection is an abbreviated extract from his Geography and Geology of Alaska *(Washington: USGS Professional Paper No. 45, 1906), 104–14.*

History of Explorations
and Surveys *

ALFRED HULSE BROOKS

Geography as Related to Development

The history of Alaska will be more easily understood if the avenues of approach for explorers and settlers are
briefly discussed. Alaska's peninsular form and irregular shore
line give a coast exposure of great extent. Some of this fronts
upon the frozen sea and adds little to the accessibility of the
country, but much the larger part is washed by waters which
are open to navigation throughout the year, and along this extensive seaboard the first explorations and settlements were
made. An almost unbroken series of ranges — the Pacific Mountain system — lies near the Pacific shore line and offers a bar-

---

*In the first two paragraphs, which are not reproduced here, Brooks apolo-
gized for the lack of documentation, the tentative nature of the sketch, and the
necessity of relying in part on W. H. Dall's *Alaska and Its Resources* (Boston,
1870), Ivan Petroff's *Tenth Census — Alaska*, House Miscellaneous Document
42, Part 8, 47th Congress: 2nd session (2136), and H. H. Bancroft's *History of
Alaska* (San Francisco, 1886). Brooks appended a bibliography to *Geography
and Geology of Alaska*, to which the student may refer. — ED. NOTE.

rier which long prevented inland exploration or settlement; for only within recent years have passes through it been discovered. The broad, depressed interior area lying behind this ridge is again cut off from the coast region on the north and east by another mountain chain, here termed the Rocky Mountain system, which also retarded man's approach, because it interposed a barrier between the interior of Alaska and that extensive system of waterways of northern Canada which enabled the fur traders to find their way across the continent from the Atlantic seaboard. This Central Plateau region, as it has been called, opens out to Bering Sea, into which it pours most of its drainage through two great rivers, the Yukon and Kuskokwim, both of which are navigable and afford easy access to the interior.

Another important geographic feature of Alaska in relation to its development is its juxtaposition to Asia. The westernmost point of its mainland is visible from the Siberian coast across Bering Strait, only 60 miles wide; but as this strait is navigable only in summer, it is of less importance as a route of travel than the Aleutian Islands, which form a chain almost connecting the Asiatic and American continents. These islands are mostly intervisible, so that as soon as the western one had been reached from Asia even the Russian traders, who were usually entirely unskilled in navigation, could follow the archipelago eastward to the mainland.

Main Features of History

A complete history of the discovery and exploration of Alaska would involve a consideration of the history of eastern Asia and western Canada, as well as of the explorations of the northern Pacific and the Arctic region, and is beyond the scope of the present paper. In the few pages here devoted to the subject it is possible only to broadly outline the progress of discovery, calling attention to a few of the more important expeditions which have added to the geographic knowledge of the country and the agencies which were operative in its exploration. During the two centuries which have elapsed since white men first obtained definite tidings of Alaska, exploration and surveys have been carried on spasmodically by various nationalities and un-der various auspices. Though the larger geographic features are now fairly well known, there still remain some unexplored areas, and the topographic mapping is hardly begun.

Explorations of the northwestern corner of America may be said to have been made from three directions — from the west by the Russians, across Siberia and Bering Sea; from the east by the English, through the Mackenzie Valley, and from the south by navigators of various nationalities exploring the eastern shore of the Pacific.

Before the end of the sixteenth century Russian fur traders crossed the Urals, gradually extended their operations eastward across northern Asia, and established themselves on the shores of Bering Sea. During this time the French voyageurs and their successors of English blood had been making their way west-ward from the Atlantic coast. Reaching the Rocky Mountain barrier they were there held in check for over a hundred years, but before the middle of the nineteenth century they had sur-mounted this obstacle and established trading posts on rivers tributary to the Pacific and the Bering Sea. Meanwhile the Rus-sians crossed Bering Sea and had taken possession of Alaska. By the beginning of the nineteenth century the fur trade which had been developed by these two nationalities had left the hands of individuals and in both cases had come under the control of a strong company. The two rival fur-trading interests, which had been moving toward each other for upward of two cen-turies, after practically encircling the globe finally came into competition in Alaska. These facts are recited here because the desire to obtain control of and exploit the fur trade was directly or indirectly the prime motive for the early explorations of the territory.

Early Russian Explorations

Less than a century after the discovery of the American Con-tinent Yermac Timofeief and a band of Cossack adventurers crossed the low barrier of the Ural Mountains and began that series of conquests in Siberia which was to make Russia an Asiatic power. While the western nations of Europe were exploring the east coast of North America, and almost before they had obtained a foothold on its shores, the Russian Cossacks had crossed northern Siberia and in 1638 reached the sea of Okhotsk. Step by step these Cossack adventurers made their way across the great lowlands of northern Siberia, traveling with horses by land and skin boats by water. The comparatively peaceful character of the natives and the absence of mountain barriers greatly facilitated the work of conquest.

After reaching salt water it was but natural that the Cossacks should extend their explorations along the coast. In 1648 Deshnef sailed eastward from the mouth of the Kolyma on the Arctic, rounded East Cape, passed through the body of water afterwards named Bering Strait, and wintered at the Anadir River. More than half a century elapsed before this exploration was extended by another Cossack, Popof, who, in 1711, was sent to East Cape to induce the natives to pay tribute. The warlike Chuckchees, who inhabited that part of the Siberian coast, refused to acknowledge the sovereignty of Russia, but Popof brought back an account of the Diomede Islands in Bering Strait and rumors of a continent said to lie to the east.

In course of time news of this discovery was transmitted to St. Petersburg, and the reigning sovereign, Peter the Great, was quick to realize its importance. Spurred on, no doubt, by the knowledge he had of the discoveries and settlements made by the western nations of Europe in the New World, Peter ordered the organization of an expedition which should verify Popof's statements and extend his explorations. Vitus Bering, a Dane and fleet captain in the Russian navy, was placed in charge of the expedition. Peter did not live to see his plans executed, dying soon after signing Bering's orders; but his successor, the Empress Catharine, actively carried out the purpose of her husband. Bering's command, after crossing Siberia, built two small vessels at Okhotsk. In July, 1728, he sailed northward along the coast of Siberia as far as East Cape, passing through the strait which bears his name. From East Cape he stood to the northeast for a day and then returned to his port of embarkation without having sighted the American Continent.

While Bering himself believed that his short voyage definitely proved the absence of an eastern connection of Asia with North America, yet so meager was his evidence that most geographers refused to accept it, and it was not until Cook's voyage, half a century later, that convincing proof was obtained. Bering did, however, discover and name St. Lawrence Island, and may therefore be regarded as the first white man to look upon any part of what is now Alaska.

Three years later a vessel in command of a Cossack named Gwosdef, one of a small fleet sent to subdue the Chuckchees, was blown onto the American coast by a storm, probably somewhere in Norton Sound. The records of this voyage, vague as they are, contain the first reference to the mainland of Alaska based upon the actual observations of white men. In the following year (1729) Bering made a second voyage, which was even less fruitful of results.

The interest excited by these discoveries led to the organization at St. Petersburg of another expedition, of which Bering was again put in command. Such were the difficulties of travel that six years were spent in transporting the party and outfit across Siberia, which at that time afforded nothing except game, fish, and furs, so that all supplies, including the iron work and tools necessary for the construction of ships, had to be brought from Europe. Finally, in 1741, the expedition sailed from Okhotsk in two vessels, one commanded by Bering himself and the other by Chirikof. These soon became separated, and Bering, sailing eastward, on July 18 fell in with the American coast near Mount St. Elias, which he named, and a few days later landed on what was probably Kayak Island.

With this discovery Bering seemed to consider that his mission was fulfilled, and after a very cursory examination became impatient to return to Asia. The expedition, which had taken years of preparation, turned westward without attempting surveys or investigations and without even making a landing on the mainland of the newly discovered continent. Sailing southwest they discovered the Shumagin Islands, and named them after a member of the crew who was buried there.

Bering's haste to return to Asia again prevented him from making an adequate exploration. He continued westward along the line of the Aleutian Islands, some of which he sighted, but without gaining more than a very superficial knowledge of them. Scurvy broke out among the crew, and the entire party seems to have been bewildered. They sailed hither and yon, now heading for the American, now for the Asiatic coast, at last wrecking their vessel upon Bering Island of the Commander group, now belonging to Siberia. Of those that reached the shore many died, among them Bering, a disheartened and despairing man. The cross over his grave was the first emblem marking the extension of Russian sovereignty eastward of Siberia. The survivors of the ill-fated expedition built a small vessel of the wreckage and returned to Kamchatka.

Chirikof's voyage was even less successful. After becoming separated from Bering he sailed eastward, and on July 15 sighted the continent, probably near Cross Sound. An attempt to land ended disastrously, for both boats were lost, and nearly a third of the crew were killed by the natives. Chirikof hastily put to sea and returned to the Asiatic coast, sighting some of the Aleutian Islands in his passage.

The explorations made by these two navigators, while not fruitful of results commensurate with the elaborateness of the preparations, were yet of the utmost importance from a geographic standpoint. Two points on the American Continent were fixed with a fair degree of accuracy and the location of some of the Aleutian Islands approximately established. These islands, which are part of the broken chain connecting the Asiatic and North American continents, were to become an important factor in the early development of the fur trade of Alaska.

The reports by Bering's crew of the existence of valuable furs in the newly discovered islands east of Kamchatka soon led the hardy Siberian fur hunters, called promyshleniki, to brave the perils of an unknown sea. The first of these was Bassof, who two years after Bering's return reached Bering Island in a small vessel. The rich harvest of furs with which he returned after a year's absence induced him to make a second, and later a third voyage. He was but the forerunner of a swarm of promyshleniki who gradually pushed their way eastward along the Aleutian chain of islands to the mainland of Alaska.*

These Siberian fur hunters had up to this time but little knowledge of deep-sea navigation, an ignorance which fitted them in a measure for the task which they had undertaken, for experienced seamen would have refused to take part in such utterly hazardous and foolhardy enterprises. As all iron for shipbuilding on the Bering Sea had to be transported across Siberia to Kamchatka, the result was that a species of vessel was devised which could be constructed without iron, the planks being sewed together with thongs of rawhide in lieu of nailing. Provisions also were scarce in Kamchatka, and these roving traders depended largely on such food as could be obtained from the sea.

In these crude crafts, manned by crews which knew little of seamanship, and usually but ill-equipped and provisioned, these intrepid fur traders boldly pushed out into unknown stormy seas. Many lives were lost by wrecks, starvation, and scurvy, and many of the adventurers met deserved death at the hands of the outraged natives. The risks were great, but when the expeditions were successful the profits were enormous, and the necessary capital for such enterprises was easily procured among the merchants of eastern Siberia.

This vanguard of civilization was made up of men who had no virtues other than valor and intrepidity. Their gradual mastery of the Aleutian Islands, which led to Russia's becoming a North American power, is a tale of blood and rapine, of murder and outrage. Under plea of exacting tribute from the natives they took their furs by force and not by barter, practically reducing the natives to slavery. Their firearms gave them an in-

---

*This phase of Russian expansion is examined in an excellent, detailed study of Peter Simon Pallas' contribution to the history of Russian exploration: J. R. Masterson and H. Brower, *Bering's Successors, 1745–1780* (Seattle: University of Washington Press, 1948). — ED. NOTE.

calculable advantage over these people, whose arrows and spears were still tipped with bone. The Aleuts, at first friendly to the strangers, only too soon learned their true character; and though not so warlike as the true Eskimos to the north, or the Haidas and Thlinkets of southeastern Alaska, with whom the Russians later came in conflict, did not give up without resistance. Many a bloody and well-deserved reprisal did they inflict on their oppressors. The struggle was, however, hopeless; ravages of the barbaric Siberian fur traders during the half century succeeding Bering's discoveries threatened to exterminate the indigenous population of the Aleutian Islands. While the outrages were largely the work of private individuals they received a certain sanction from the Russian Government, which allowed the traders to plunder and murder the natives at will, but was ready enough to exact tribute on the ill-gotten furs. The cry of the murdered and outraged Aleut did not reach St. Petersburg, or if it did was not heeded.

It was through this murderous crew of traders that the civilized world learned of the Aleutian Islands and the adjacent mainland. Russia was to owe her American colony to the initiation and enterprise of private individuals, for the Court of St. Petersburg paid little heed to its American possessions for more than half a century after Bering's last voyage. But two attempts at official investigation were made, both more or less abortive. In 1767 Lieutenant Synd, of the Russian Navy, was sent out to explore the American coast, and though his results were meager and his statements unreliable, there seems no reason to doubt that he landed on the southern coast of Seward Peninsula. About the same time Captain Krenitzin reached the Alaska Peninsula on a similar mission.

When the Spanish and English first appeared on this coast Russia had no permanent settlement in Alaska. Bering's expedition had discovered a new continent; yet though a third of a century had passed during which private enterprise had developed a lucrative fur trade in the adjacent islands, no effective attempt had been made to extend his discoveries or to exploit the resources of the main continent. The trading voyages had approximately established the relative location and configuration of the Aleutian Islands and Kodiak. Krenitzin had astronomically determined a few positions in the eastern part of the chain and along the southern coast of the Alaska Peninsula. These, together with Bering's discovery, and a less definite knowledge of the mainland lying adjacent to Bering Strait, comprised Russia's investigations in North America previous to the advent of other nations.

Exploration by Rival Nationalities

While the Russian influence was extending over Alaska from the west the Spaniards were approaching it from the south, where they had established themselves on the coast of California. Reports of these Russian encroachments led the viceroy of Mexico to send out several successive expeditions to explore the coast and where they found it uninhabited to plant the arms of Spain. Perez, a Spanish ensign, discovered the Queen Charlotte Islands in 1774, and the following year Lieutenant Quadra explored as far north as Cross Sound.

The first important systematic survey of any part of what is now known as Alaska was made by Captain Cook, the great English navigator. Cook sailed from England with two vessels in 1776. His first landfall on the Alaskan coast was in May, 1778, near Mount Edgecumbe, previously discovered by Bodega y Quadra. Thence he sailed westward, exploring Prince William Sound and Cook Inlet as far as Unalaska, where he was received very kindly by a band of Russian traders. It is of interest to note that an American in Cook's vessel, John Ledyard, was the first to interview the Russians.

Cook now entered Bering Sea and continued his surveys of the coast toward the north, through Bristol Bay, Norton Sound, and Bering Strait, until he was checked by the Arctic ice pack. This he skirted westward to where it impinged on the Siberian mainland at a point which he named Cape North, whence he returned to the south along the Siberian coast. The winter was spent in the Hawaiian Islands, and there the famous navigator met his death. The following year his vessels set out again under the command of Clerke, in an attempt to extend the surveys farther north, but the ice pack again interfered before they had penetrated much farther than before.

Cook had been unsuccessful in finding the water passage to Hudson Bay which he sought, but in the course of a single summer he had accomplished many times as much as all previous explorers. His voyage outlined the larger coastal features of Alaska, from about latitude 58° to 70°; definitely established the fact that there was no land connection between America and Asia, and convinced the navigator himself of the futility of seeking a waterway to the Atlantic, a conclusion which was in part based on Hearne's exploration in 1771 from Hudson Bay to the mouth of the Coppermine River. This last result was not generally acknowledged, and it remained for one of Cook's officers, Vancouver, to bring the final proof — not even then accepted by the theoretical geographers — about fifteen years later.

Great as was Cook's contribution to the geography of the Alaskan coast, perhaps of still more lasting importance was his inauguration of a new era in the explorations of the Alaskan seaboard. The vague and haphazard reports of the previous explorers were replaced by concise charts and accurate observations, many of which have stood the test of more detailed investigation. Several officers who accompanied Cook and were trained in his methods returned in later years to the Alaskan coast and continued the work of exploration.

Though some of the promyshleniki had reached Kodiak as early as 1762, it was not until after Cook's voyage that, finding the sea otters were becoming relatively scarce among the Aleutians and the voyages less profitable, they began to seek new hunting grounds to the northeast. Up to this time the fur gathering had been in the hands of individuals or small, weak companies, and hence but little concerted effort had been made. In 1781 a company of eastern Siberian merchants was formed for exploiting the American fur trade. The leader of this organization was Gregor Ivanovich Shelikof, who, with Ivan Golikof, controlled a majority of the shares. Under Shelikof's leadership an expedition was sent out, which, in 1783, founded a colony at Three Saints Bay, near the southern end of Kodiak Island. This was the first settlement within the limits of Alaska and was the pioneer of the Russian occupation, which was to last for three-quarters of a century, until the territory was transferred to the United States.

In the year this colony was founded a group of trading vessels, under the command of Potan Zaikof, reached Prince William Sound. He attempted the same high-handed proceedings which had been so successful among the Aleuts, but found to his cost that he was dealing with a fierce, warlike population, and the expedition ended disastrously. The event was noteworthy, as it was the first time the Russian traders are definitely known to have reached the mainland. Nagaief, a member of this party, discovered the Copper River and ascended it a short distance.

In the meantime the published account of Cook's voyage had aroused other nations to the fact that the rich fur trade in the northwestern extremity of the American continent was rapidly passing into the hands of the Russians. The English traders were the first to follow it up. In 1785 James Hanna visited the west coast of Vancouver Island, in British Columbia, and in the succeeding years made several voyages to the coast of what is now Alaska. Similar trips were made by English and American trading vessels and ships of other nationalities. The published logs and track charts of a number of these vessels added to the general knowledge of the northwest coast. All of these the Russians regarded as unlawful intruders, and many petitions were sent to St. Petersburg protesting against foreign ships engaging in this trade.

While merchants and traders of various nationalities were struggling for commercial supremacy in Alaskan waters, their home governments were not unmindful of the political side of the controversy. The English, Spanish, and French governments showed a desire to wrest some of these new discoveries from the Russians. The Spaniards claimed the coast, because it was a northern extension of their California possessions, and also by right of the discoveries of Bodega y Quadra. The English claim rested on Cook's discoveries.

The Spanish claims were strengthened by an expedition led by Arteaga, with Quadra as second in command, which sailed northward from Mexico in 1779, and visited and surveyed Port Bucareli on the west side of Prince of Wales Island. Later they entered Prince William Sound and, in obedience to their instructions, took formal possession of what they believed were newly discovered lands. They little realized that Cook in the previous year had gone through the same ceremony in the name of the British sovereign almost at the same spot. After extending their explorations to the southwest as far as the southern end of the Kenai Peninsula they returned to Mexico.

The French had no part in the discovery or in the exploitations of the new country; but to gain a valid claim, La Perouse, a naval officer, was dispatched to the northwest coast in 1785. In the following year he landed at Lituya Bay, of which he made a detailed examination and took formal possession. Then, ignoring his instructions to survey the Aleutian Islands, he sailed southward without landing again on the Alaskan coast.

The Spaniards, apparently satisfied that Arteaga's explorations established their territorial claims, took no further action for several years. The publication of Cook's voyages and the report of the numerous trading vessels that visited the northwest coast, however, aroused them again from their lethargy. In 1788, two vessels, commanded by Estevan Martinez and Gonzalez Haro, were dispatched northward to gain further information. While Martinez explored Prince William Sound, Haro visited the Russian establishments on Kodiak Island, and obtained full knowledge of the Russian occupation. Delarof, the director of the colony, took pains to impress the Spaniard with the wide extent and importance of the Russian settlements, of which at that time there were only six. After visiting Unalaska and going through the absurd performance of taking possession in the name of His Most Catholic Majesty of an island which contained a Russian colony and had been under Muscovite influence for upward of a quarter of a century, the expedition sailed for Mexico.

Martinez's report of the Russian occupation showed the viceroy of Mexico that Spanish claims to the northwest coast must be enforced by more decisive action. Both vessels were therefore again dispatched to take immediate possession of Nootka Sound on the west side of Vancouver Island, which had been discovered by Cook and had been used as a rendezvous by English, American, and Portuguese traders. The Spaniards did not molest the American ships, but warned off all those flying English colors. This high-handed action led to an immediate protest by the British Government, and commissioners were appointed by both governments to come to an understanding. The first meeting at Nootka led to a disagreement; but subsequently the Spaniards receded from their position and withdrew their forces, leaving the region in the possession of the traders and natives.

In 1791 Malaspina, an Italian navigator, in command of two Spanish corvettes, engaged in a scientific exploration which was to encircle the globe. He was sent to the northwest coast to explore for a northwest passage, rumors of which were again gaining credence. He made landfall near Mount Edgecumbe, and tracing the coast to the northwest entered Yakutat Bay, then known as Port Mulgrave. The ceremony of taking possession of the newly discovered land was not omitted, though Portlock and Dixon had surveyed and published a chart of the bay some years before, and the Russians had long used it as a rendezvous in their fur-trading expeditions. Malaspina made a cursory examination of Prince William and Cross sounds, and then turned southward.

George Vancouver, one of Cook's midshipmen, was the English representative in the Nootka dispute, and while his conferences with the Spaniards had no immediate result, his later explorations were of the utmost importance. He received orders to survey the coast between the thirty-fifth and sixtieth parallels of latitude, a task which he faithfully executed with his two vessels in 1793 and 1794. In the course of two seasons he accurately delineated thousands of miles of the coast line of southeastern Alaska, and supplemented the work of previous explorers westward as far as Cook Inlet. Not an indentation of the mainland, hardly a break in the shore line of the numerous islands, escaped his notice. His would have been a difficult task even in the days of steam, and to thread the intricate waterways of the Alexander Archipelago and make such surveys as he did within so short a period was little short of marvelous. He was a worthy successor of the great Cook, under whom he had learned navigation and geodesy. After his task was completed the general features of the entire coast line of the mainland of Alaska from Dixon Entrance as far north as Cape Belcher were charted with a fair degree of accuracy.[*]

While the Russians and the Spaniards were attempting to dispossess all other nations of commercial and territorial rights in the coastal zone of Alaska, the English, their most aggressive rivals, were steadily approaching the region from the east. The French pioneers, following the route of the Great Lakes, had crossed half of the American continent long before the Russians had knowledge of the Aleutian Islands, and about the time of Bering's discovery of the mainland of Alaska, Verandrye had reached the foothills of the Rockies near the headwaters of the Missouri. Ten years later another pioneer trader established a post at the present sight of Calgary (Alberta), at the very base of the Rocky Mountains and only 500 miles from the Pacific waters. This post, with many others, was abandoned when Canada passed into the hands of the English.

Henceforth the English fur trade gradually expanded into the region which had been pioneered by the French. The Rocky Mountain barrier for a long time marked the limits of this western fur trade. It remained for Alexander Mackenzie to surmount this barrier, and to introduce a new factor in the development of Alaska. Mackenzie, who was a member of the Northwestern Fur Company, the great rival of the Hudson Bay Company, ascended the Peace River from Lake Athabasca, crossed the Rocky Mountains, then traversed the headwaters of the Fraser, and after crossing the Coast Range reached Pacific waters in

---

[*]Vancouver's career is discussed in Bern Anderson, *Surveyor of the Sea* (Seattle: University of Washington Press, 1960). — ED. NOTE.

the latitude of Queen Charlotte Sound. This journey, which was the first made across the continent north of Mexico, was accomplished in 1793, at the same time that Vancouver was surveying adjacent waters. It was the forerunner of the fierce rivalry which was to spring up between the two great competitors in the fur trade, the Russian-American and Hudson Bay companies.

In spite of the small degree of success achieved by previous official explorations, the authorities at St. Petersburg in 1785 determined on another. This was placed in charge of Joseph Billings, who seems to have been chosen more because he had been attached to one of Cook's vessels than because of any particular merit or experience. Billings sailed from Kamchatka in 1789, and passing through Bering Strait penetrated the Arctic Ocean to about latitude 69° and then returned to Kamchatka. In 1790 he made a second start, and the two vessels of the expedition, stopping at Unalaska and Kodiak, reached Prince William Sound, and then again returned to the point of debarkation. In the following year a third start was made and Billings once more reached Unalaska, whence he sailed northward, touching at Pribilof Islands, Seward Peninsula, and St. Lawrence Island. Billings himself afterwards landed on the Chuckchee Peninsula, Siberia, where he made a hazardous but apparently bootless journey inland. The two vessels wintered at Iliuliuk, Unalaska Island, and the following year returned to Kamchatka. The expedition, which in its preparation and execution had cost seven years of time and large sums of money, accomplished almost nothing beyond gaining some information regarding the abuse of the natives by Russian traders.

Russian Occupation

The last two decades of the eighteenth century were to witness important changes in the Russian fur trade. The Shelikof Company, after its settlement on Kodiak in 1783, gradually extended the sphere of its trading operations to the neighboring islands and mainland. In 1788 an imperial ukase granted to this company the exclusive control of the regions actually occupied by its agents. In 1792 an important step was taken in appointing Alexander Andreivich Baranof, chief director of the company's American interests. Baranof, who held this post for twenty-five years, showed himself to be a far-sighted, energetic man, though coarse and unscrupulous. The early years of his administration were a fitting introduction to the stormy ones to follow. At Cook Inlet rival traders had established themselves, who for some time quarreled and fought among themselves, but finally united to oppose their common enemy, the Shelikof Company. At length Baranof was forced to assume authority which he did not legally possess, and restored some measure of peace by arresting and imprisoning the ringleader.

In the meantime Baranof was energetically looking after the interests of the company in other directions. A shipyard was established on Prince William Sound,* and attempts were made at agriculture at Kodiak and Yakutat Bay, while the fur trade was pushed vigorously. The first Greek Catholic missionaries arrived from Siberia in 1794, and at the same time the first convicts were imported and settled at Yakutat.

At the close of the century the court at St. Petersburg was beginning to be moved by reports of the disorders and outrages committed by the irresponsible fur traders, and was becoming weary of the quarrels of the rival companies. It was, moreover, desirous of maintaining Russian prestige in America by a responsible representation. Thus it happened that the Shelikof Company, with the aid of financial backing, was able to obtain a new charter under the name of the Russian-American Company. The imperial ukase which established this company was dated 1799, and granted exclusive privileges of trade and occupation of northwestern America, lying north of latitude 55° and including the Aleutian Islands. The original grant was for twenty years, but two extensions placed Alaska in the hands of this company for sixty years. From this time on the history of Alaska up to its transfer to the United States is practically the history of this company which controlled this great monopoly. The region being now definitely in the hands of the Russians, the

*Resurrection Bay. — ED. NOTE.

limits of whose possessions were determined by treaty with England in 1825, other nations discontinued their explorations.*

. . .

When Captain Golofnin of the Russian Navy was sent out by the home government in 1810, and a second time in 1818, for the purpose of investigating the affairs of the company and the status of the natives, some contribution was again made to geographic knowledge, though only incidentally.

The most important exploring voyage of this period was undertaken in the brig *Rurik* by Otto von Kotzebue, of the Russian navy. His purpose was the general advancement of scientific knowledge, including the discovery of a northeast waterway, in the existence of which many geographers still obstinately believed. Sailing from Kronstadt in 1815, Kotzebue reached Kamchatka the following year, whence he headed for Bering Strait. He touched at St. Lawrence Island, rounded Cape Prince of Wales, and coasting along the north side of the Seward Peninsula entered and surveyed the great sound which bears his name. On his return passage he visited Unalaska. After wintering in the Hawaiian Islands Kotzebue made a second trip to Alaska, but did not extend his former surveys.

No systematic explorations or surveys had been attempted under Baranof, but a change came about when the directorship of the Russian-American colony was transferred to naval officers, several of whom were men of scientific tastes and training and did much to foster geographic investigations. Other sciences were not neglected: systematic meteorologic records were kept at Sitka for many years, and a magnetic station was also maintained. Of the directors of the colony Baron F. P. von Wrangell was most prominent. Coming to his post fresh from Arctic explorations, he naturally looked with favor on all geographic investigations, and it was under his regime that the most important of the explorations carried on by the company were undertaken. This work was actively furthered by one of Wrangell's

* A history of the Russian-American Company by the Soviet scholar, S. B. Okun, is available in translation: *The Russian-American Company*, translated by Carl Ginsburg (Cambridge, Mass.: Harvard University Press, 1951). — ED. NOTE.

successors, Capt. Michael D. Tebenkof, who was also an explorer. Tebenkof's atlas of the northwestern coast of America, comprising a summary of all previous investigations, is the most important contribution to the geography of Alaska made during the entire Russian occupation.

In 1826 began the most valuable coastal exploration made by the Russian-American Company. This expedition, under the direction of Kramchenko, Etolin, and Vasilief, spent two years in examining the shore line of Bristol Bay and Norton Sound. In the following year Captain Lütke, sent out by the authorities at St. Petersburg, visited Unalaska and the Pribilof Islands and made a careful survey of the northern coast of the Alaska Peninsula. The southern coast of the Alaska Peninsula was mapped a few years later by Vasilief.

Among the lesser expeditions made under the direction of the company may be mentioned the explorations of the Bristol Bay and Kuskokwim regions by Korsakof, Vasilief, and Kolmakof from 1818 to 1832, and Malakof's exploration of the Sushitna in 1834. A more important expedition was one in charge of a creole by the name of Andrei Glasunof, who crossed from the Russian post at St. Michael, Norton Bay, to the Yukon and thence to the Kuskokwim. This, with Malakof's trip up the Yukon as far as Nulato, paved the way for the exploitation of the fur trade of the Yukon River.

By far the most fruitful of the Russian inland explorations was that made by Lieutenant Zagoskin, of the Imperial navy, in 1842–43. Zagoskin ascended the Yukon as far as the mouth of the Tanana and explored the lower stretches of the Koyukuk. Under his auspices a post was built at Nulato. He also traversed the Innoko, an easterly tributary of the lower Yukon, and made his way eastward to Kuskokwim waters. As far as time and means would permit, Zagoskin made track surveys and astronomic determinations of position, meanwhile taking careful notes on the native population and the resources of the region traversed. In the light of subsequent developments it is of interest to note his statement that the Yukon, or Kwickpack as he called it, was not navigable above the mouth of the Tanana.

In the meantime activity in Arctic exploration once more drew the attention of English navigators to the northwest coast. In 1789 Alexander Mackenzie had followed to the Arctic Ocean the great river which bears his name. In 1826 Sir John Franklin had traversed the Arctic coast westward, from the mouth of the Mackenzie as far as Return Reef on the north Alaskan coast; and Capt. F. W. Beechey, of H. M. S. *Blossom*, who had been dispatched to cooperate with Franklin, carefully charted the southern coast of the Seward Peninsula to Cape Prince of Wales, and added many details to the work of Kotzebue in Kotzebue Sound, extending his surveys northward until blocked by ice. A boat expedition under Beechey's mate Elson succeeded in reaching Point Barrow, which, it was hoped, Franklin would be able to reach from the east. But as Franklin was blocked by the ice 100 miles east of Point Barrow, this part of the coast line represented a hiatus in the charts for ten years.

In 1837 Peter Warren Dease and Thomas Simpson, of the Hudson Bay Company, descended the Mackenzie and followed the coast westward. Like Franklin, they, too, were stopped by the ice, but Simpson continued on foot and in native boats. He reached Point Barrow August 4, 1837, thus completing the exploration of the entire coast line of the mainland of Alaska, which was begun by Bering about one hundred years before.

Another impetus to Alaskan exploration was given by the series of Franklin relief expeditions which were sent out by the British Government between 1848 and 1853. While the primary purpose of these expeditions was to find and bring relief to Franklin, yet the commanders incidentally accomplished considerable exploration and charting. An added stimulus was the hope of finding a northwest passage, which geographers were loath to give up. In 1849 Capt. Thomas E. L. Moore in H. M. S. *Plover*, Capt. Henry Kellett in H. M. S. *Herald*, and the yacht *Nancy Dawson*, reached Kotzebue Sound. A boat expedition under Lieutenant Pullen was sent northward, and rounding Point Barrow proceeded eastward to the Mackenzie River, which it ascended to a Hudson Bay post. A second expedition from these vessels explored the Buckland River. Other minor explorations were made by the crew of the *Plover* while she wintered in Kotzebue Sound. Thus Lieut. Bedford Pim crossed the eastern end of Seward Peninsula to the Russian post at St. Michael, and Simpson, surgeon of the expedition, explored the Selawik River and made the first mention of the Kobuk River. The *Plover* spent the two following winters at Point Barrow, from which she continued to send out exploring parties.

In 1850 Commander Robert S. M. McClure, in H. M. S. *Investigator*, sailed eastward past Point Barrow and beyond the mouth of the Mackenzie until he was stopped by the ice. His vessel was never brought through, but eventually his crew, by walking over the solid ice, was the first to make the northwest passage. The following year Capt. Richard Collinson, in H. M. S. *Enterprise*, also passed Point Barrow, and subsequently wintered at Walker Bay, on the north coast of Alaska. In 1853 H. M. S. *Rattlesnake*, Commander Trollope, wintered at Port Clarence, on the south side of the Seward Peninsula, which some of the crew crossed during the winter.

The surveys of these Arctic expeditions were very carefully executed and are still the bases for most of the charts of the regions they cover. The accounts of the voyages are full and contain much valuable information, which up to very recent times was all that was available concerning Arctic Alaska.

In 1848 the American whaler *Superior*, commanded by Captain Roys, ventured through Bering Strait, and was amply rewarded by a good catch. This example was followed by many others in succeeding years. The whaling industry along the Arctic coast of Alaska has continued to be an important one up to the present day, though it received a serious setback during the civil war by the ravages committed by the Confederate privateer *Shenandoah*, which captured and destroyed many vessels of the American whaling fleet. Stations are now maintained by the whaling companies at Point Barrow and Herschel Island, east of the international boundary. The experienced seamen who usually commanded these whalers added not a little to the geographical knowledge of the Arctic coastal region of Alaska.

The only other important American contribution during the

period of Russian control was furnished by Lieut. William Gibson, U. S. Navy, who, in command of the schooner *Fenimore Cooper*, of the Rodgers United States Northern Pacific Exploring Expedition, made surveys and explorations among the Aleutian Islands in 1855. Some of the other vessels of the same fleet passed through Bering Strait and into the Arctic Ocean.

Many years elapsed after Mackenzie made his explorations to the Pacific before the English fur trade was to establish itself near the bounds of what is now known as Alaska. Though the Hudson Bay Company was incessantly pushing its outposts to the west, it did not reach the drainage basins of rivers which emptied into the sea through the Russian American possessions until toward the middle of the nineteenth century. Campbell established a Hudson Bay post in 1840 on the headwaters of the Pelly, a branch of the Yukon, and eight years later (1848) built Fort Selkirk, at the mouth of the Pelly. In the previous year, however, Fort Yukon had been built at the mouth of the Porcupine by A. H. Murray, another Hudson Bay agent. The English traders of these posts soon learned through the natives that the Russians were in possession of the lower river, and, probably about 1850, some of them made a trip down the Yukon to the mouth of the Tanana, which was the uppermost point reached by the Russians in their trading expeditions. This was also the point reached by the explorer Zagoskin in his ascent of the river in 1843.* It can therefore be stated that the preliminary exploration of the main Yukon by white men was completed by this journey of the Hudson Bay traders, though its first mapping remained to be done by the members of the scientific corps of the Western Union Telegraph Expedition.

In 1834 the Hudson Bay Company had by high-handed proceedings attempted to establish itself within Russian America, in what is now called southeastern Alaska, but it was promptly ejected by the Russian Company. After a conference this coastal belt was, in 1837, leased by the Russians to the Hudson Bay Company for a term of ten years. The Hudson Bay Company, from its two posts in the Yukon drainage basin, controlled the

---

*The exact point reached by Zagoskin is debatable. — Ed. Note.

fur trade of the upper river, while the Russian-American Company controlled the trade on the lower river.

One other expedition needs mention — the last of the Russian official surveys in America. In 1863, word having been received at Sitka that American prospectors had found gold on the Stikine River, it was decided to send out an expedition to find out whether these discoveries were in Russian territory. This party, in command of Commander Bassarguine, of the Imperial navy, and accompanied by the American geologist, William P. Blake, made a reconnaissance survey of the lower part of the Stikine.

In 1863 the Western Union Telegraph Company determined to build an overland telegraph line from the western coast of the United States through British Columbia and what was then known as Russian America to Bering Strait. This line was to be connected by cable with a trans-Siberian line, and thus telegraphic communication was to be established between America and Europe. This project, first conceived by Perry M. D. Collins,* was a daring one, for it contemplated the building and maintaining of a telegraph line through thousands of miles of almost unexplored territory in America and Asia. The first essential to the project was preliminary exploration of the proposed route. The success of the Atlantic cable led to an abandonment of the enterprise only three years after its organization, but even in that short time important contributions were made to a geographic knowledge of Alaska and adjacent portions of Canadian territory. The explorations in Siberia were also fruitful of important results.

The task which confronted the Western Union Telegraph survey in Russian America was not an easy one. The region to be explored was several thousand miles distant from the nearest port of the United States. While there were some Russian trading posts on Bering Sea and along the lower Yukon, they were widely separated and the Russian knowledge of the interior was practically limited to the lower part of the Yukon and the Kuskokwim. Moreover, the Russian outposts were small and

*Perry McDonough Collins. — ED. NOTE.

ill equipped, so that practically all supplies had to be taken from the Pacific coast ports of the United States.

Robert Kennicott was chosen as head of the scientific corps, serving under Capt. Charles S. Buckley, engineer in chief of the expedition. Kennicott was a fortunate choice, as he was an able and enthusiastic worker and his previous expedition into the far northwest, in 1860–61, when he had reached Fort Yukon by following the Hudson Bay Company route from the Mackenzie, had fitted him well for the undertaking. He did not live to see the execution of his comprehensive plans, for he died at Nulato in 1866, his death being brought about by the incessant toil and exposure to which he had been subjected. William H. Dall, who took the leadership of the scientific corps, continued alone his researches on Norton Sound and the lower Yukon after the telegraph survey party was disbanded. His book, based on these investigations, and the reports which he wrote later under the auspices of the Coast Survey, are still the standard works on Alaska.

In 1865 Robert Kennicott, Frank Ketchum, and Michael Lebarge had started up the Yukon. After Kennicott's death at Nulato in 1866 Ketchum and Lebarge pushed on up the river to Fort Yukon. In the following year they continued their explorations as far as Fort Selkirk, at the junction of the Lewes and Pelly rivers. Dall and Frederick Whymper reached Fort Yukon in the summer of 1867, after making the first survey of the lower Yukon. In the meanwhile, in 1865, Baron Otto von Bendeleben and W. H. Ennis, also of the telegraph survey, made an exploration from Golofnin Bay to Port Clarence, and J. T. Dyer and Richard D. Cotter crossed overland from Norton Bay to the mouth of the Koyukuk, while Capt. E. E. Smith carried on surveys in the delta of the Yukon.

The geographical results of this survey in Alaska are a map of the Yukon River, definitely establishing the identity of the Yukon of the Hudson Bay Company with the Kwikpak of the Russians, and important additions to the knowledge of the Yukon Delta, Seward Peninsula, and the Norton Bay region. It is interesting to note that the route which these first explorers selected has been practically adopted by the telegraph lines which are now being constructed in Alaska and in Canadian territory. Of still greater importance even than the actual surveys was the more or less exact information which the telegraph survey explorers were able to furnish the American public during and after the negotiations by which Russian America became an American possession.

Clarence Andrews (1862–1948) was born in Ohio and reared in Oregon. He worked as a postal clerk, rancher, teacher, and as a customs collector in Sitka, Skagway, and Eagle, Alaska. In 1897 he was with the Mt. St. Elias expedition of the Duke of the Abruzzi. After his retirement, he edited and published the periodical Eskimo, *from 1936 to 1947. The early days of Sitka are described in this selection, which is reproduced with permission from* Sitka *(Caldwell, Idaho: Caxton Printers, 1945) 26–38.*

Settlement of Sitka

CLARENCE L. ANDREWS

The sea otter, a marine animal about four feet in length when fully grown, with soft, long black pelage of silky texture, is one of the most valued of fur bearers. It was found abundantly all the way along the northwest coast, and especially in the passages about Sitka. It is now nearly extinct.

The Russians had been gathering the skins of the sea otter in the northern waters for years, ever since Chirikov made his voyage to Sitka, and they were truly an El Dorado in fur to the traders who plied their trade along the coasts. Captain Cook and his sailors, when on their voyage in these waters, bought skins for mere trifles, some for a handful of iron nails. These same skins sold for as much as sixty dollars each in China where the adventurers visited on their way home. The story of the furs went over the world, and English, French, and American traders thronged to these waters to sail their ships into the straits and barter for the rich pelts.

A profit of fifty thousand dollars on a voyage was not unusual. . . . The French ship *Solide,* sailed from France in 1791 to gather a portion of the harvest. Her captain, Etienne Marchand, anchored in Sitka Bay, and called it "Tchinkitinay," as he declares it was known to the natives. To his ship flocked the painted and skin-clad natives with their peltries for barter. On their persons he saw articles of European manufacture, showing that other ships had visited there, and in the ears of one young savage were hanging pendant two copper coins of the colony of Massachusetts. His success in trade was not such as he might have wished, so he sailed away, remarking that, "The modern Hebrews would, perhaps, have little to teach these people in the art of trade."

On March 31, 1799, the Yankee skipper, Cleveland, of the merchant ship *Caroline*, sailed into the bay, dropped anchor, and fired a cannon shot as a signal. He was one of those shrewd, lean traders, skilled in navigation, who sailed from Boston round the Horn, with their bucko mates, who could drive a tack with the prow of a ship, so to speak, and in those days there were no corners of the earth where they might not be found seeking profit. He was wise to the ways of the sharp-trading canoe-men of these waters, and their aggressive proclivities, so he prepared his ship to meet all possible contingencies. Around it as a bulwark he stretched a barrier of dry bulls' hides brought from the California coast. At the stern was a place prepared for trading. Forward on the deck were planted cannon shotted with shrapnel, aimed to rake the afterdeck, and beside each was a gunner's match.

On the first day, for two hundred yards of broadcloth he purchased a hundred prime sea-otter skins, worth fifty dollars each in Canton. Barter was going merrily on, when a scream from amidships startled the crew. The Tlingits sprang to their boats. The squaws backed the canoes away from the ship's sides. Arrows were fitted to bowstrings, spears were poised, and muskets primed. On the ships the sailors lighted the cannon matches and stood by ready to fire. A fight was imminent when the cause of the disturbance was discovered. An inquisitive Tlingit pried between the bull hides opposite the cook's galley, and the cook had saluted him with a ladle of hot water. In his surprise he upset his canoe, and his family were struggling in the sea. His baby was rescued by a seaman, amends were made to his injured feelings, and the barter proceeded as before.

The waters were filled with ships. In a stay of a month the *Caroline* spoke to the ships *Hancock, Despatch, Ulysses,* and *Eliza* — all of Boston; and to the English ship *Cheerful.* All were trading for furs among the Sitkan Islands.

The Russians, in their colony on Kodiak Island, were jealous of the intrusion on what they considered their domain. Gregory Ivanovich Shelekhov, a Siberian merchant, one of the wealthiest and most farseeing of the leaders in the Aleutian Islands, conceived the plan of combining the whole of the fur trade in one great monopoly. He worked to this end till his death in 1795. Following him, his widow, Natalya, and his son-in-law, Nikolay Petrovich Rezanov, succeeded in procuring a charter from Emperor Paul in 1799, under the name of the Russian American Company, which gave the exclusive right to all profits to be derived from every form of resource in the Russian possessions in America for a period of twenty years. To the management of his business in the colony, established on Kodiak Island, he appointed Aleksandr Andreyevich Baranov, a Siberian trader of great ability and experience. Baranov, the wise and farsighted ruler of the Russian American Company, at his factory in St. Paul Harbor on Kodiak Island, had long planned the extension of his settlements to the southeast. The sea-otter catch of the Russians was made by brigades of Aleuts from the western islands, who went along the shores and as far as twenty miles to sea, while hunting in their wonderful skin boats, called "bidarkas." When a sea otter lifted its head from the water to breathe within sight of a detachment of Aleut hunters, it seldom escaped.

The passages between the islands about Sitka were called the "Straits" by the Russians, and in them the sea-otter skins were taken by the thousands. It was not unusual for a Russian hunting party consisting of a hundred bidarkas to take on one expedition, two thousand skins of the *morskikh bobrov,* as they called the sea otter.

The animals were becoming scarce in the seas about the western islands and Baranov was compelled to replenish his trade by hunting in the southeastern waters. In 1795 he sent one of his ships as far south as the Queen Charlotte Islands, and it visited Sitka on the way. Two thousand skins were secured by the hunters while on this voyage. In the same year Baranov himself paid Sitka a visit, coming through the strait from the north in his little schooner *Olga,* a forty-foot boat, and he named the passage for his craft, Olga Strait. On the shore near his anchorage he erected a cross; the bay he named Krestov Bay, and he then selected the locality of his future settlement.

In the spring of 1799, Baranov sent orders to the chiefs of the tribes on the islands around Kodiak to assemble the hunters. Five hundred and fifty bidarkas, each manned by two or three Aleut paddlers, came in answer to his call, and with two convoying ships he set sail for Sitka Sound. On July 7, he landed at a bay six miles north of the present town of Sitka, purchased a tract of land from Skayeutlelt, a local chief, and began the construction of a post which he named Redoubt St. Michael. The building was done under great difficulties. Rain fell incessantly. There were but thirty Russian workmen, since most of the Aleuts returned to Kodiak, hunting as they went. Of the men who remained, ten had to stand guard constantly, for the Tlingits were not to be trusted. Barracks, storehouses, and quarters for the commanding officer were constructed; a bathhouse also, for the Russian must have his bath; and the whole was surrounded by a stockade and strengthened by blockhouses. Their troubles were not all with the elements, for during the winter the scarcity of provision and other causes brought scurvy to add to their discomfort. Their food was mostly *yukali* (dried salmon), but during the winter the hunters took forty sea lions, and in the spring many seals were killed in the bay by the Aleuts.

The natives, called "Tlingits" at the present, were known as the "Kolosh" by the Russians. They were divided among themselves in their feelings toward the new settlers in their midst. Some looked with extreme disfavor upon the establishment, while others were friendly. The young and turbulent warriors were hostile. A messenger was sent to invite them to a *prazdnik* (holiday) at the fort. He was taken prisoner by them and detained until Baranov landed in their midst with an armed force and demanded his release. Then they set him free and ridiculed the incident. At a dance at the fort many of the Kolosh came with long knives concealed under their cloaks. Their treachery was detected and their design frustrated. The courage and caution of Baranov held them in check until spring when he departed for Kodiak, leaving strict instructions about the precautions to be observed during his absence. After his departure the discipline grew more lax and the Kolosh became more bold. The watchful savages at last saw an opportunity to rid themselves of their new neighbors.

On a June day of 1802 (the exact date is not recorded), a horde of painted savages burst from the forest, clad in all the paraphernalia of war masks and barbaric armor. A fleet of war canoes landed warriors on the beach in front of the redoubt. In the attack that followed the stockade and buildings were reduced to smoking ruins, the magazines were robbed of rich stores of furs; most of the defenders died on the spears of the Kolosh or were tortured till death relieved their sufferings, and the women and children were made slaves. Skayeutlet, the false friend of Baranov, directed the battle from a near-by knoll, and his nephew, Katlean, was one of the principal actors in the bloody tragedy. A few survivors who were hunting in their bidarkas or were in the forest escaped to the ships of the English and American traders which were in the bay.

Captain John Ebbets on the American ship *Alert* and Captain Henry Barber of the British ship *Unicorn* were in the harbor. Some of the survivors on reaching these ships asked them to rescue their countrymen. Captain Ebbets ransomed several prisoners, but Captain Barber adopted a more effective course. Chief Katlean and Chief Skayeutlelt came on board his ship to trade. He at once put them in irons and threatened to hang them to the yardarm of the ship if the captives remaining in the hands of the natives and also the plundered sea-otter skins were not immediately surrendered to him. The threat was effective; the greater part of the sea-otter furs and several captives were brought on the ship and delivered to him. He then took the ransomed captives from the other ships and sailed for Kodiak, where he demanded a ransom of fifty thousand rubles from Baranov. After forcing Barber to reduce the amount to ten thousand rubles, Baranov paid the ransom.

Two years passed. . . . English and American captains sailed their ships into the harbor and gathered the furs which Baranov had endeavored to garner in the storehouses of the Russian American Company. In the summer of 1804, Baranov gathered at Kodiak a force with which to cross the Gulf of Alaska to re-establish his post. There were 150 bearded *promyshleniki*,[1] or fur hunters, and over five hundred Aleuts in their skin bidarkas. With him were the ships, *Aleksander, Ekaterina, Yermak* and *Rostislaf*. When they reached Sitka they found there, to help them recapture the post, one of the first Russians to encircle the globe, Captain Lisiansky of the Imperial Russian Navy, with his ship *Neva*.

The Indian village of Sitka was almost in the same place as the present town grouped around the Baranov hill which was called by the Russians a *"kekoor."* On the top of the *kekoor* was a redoubt, and a stronger fort was near the mouth of the Indian River, or *Kolosh Reka*.

On the morning of September 20, the Russian ships moved to a point opposite the village, the *Neva* being towed by a hundred bidarkas. The Sitkans abandoned their village and the fort on the hill and withdrew to the stronger fortification near the river. Baranov landed a force and occupied the *kekoor*, planted cannon on the top, then opened negotiations for the surrender of the other fort, but his overtures were rejected by the Indians.

---

[1] The *promyshleniki* of the Russian American Company were generally a hard lot, recruited in the dives of Okhotsk. They were of much the same class as the whalers signed on for the Arctic cruise in sailors' boardinghouses of San Francisco during the worst days of the whaling trade in the North. The name was derived from the Russian *promshlyat'* (to trade). Dr. Langsdorff describes them in his *Voyages and Travels* (London, 1813), where he says: "Our crew was composed of drunkards, adventurers, bankrupt traders and mechanics, or branded criminals in search of fortune."

Among them were some excellent men, mechanics and others. All worked for a share of the fur trade transacted by the Company.

The ships were brought near the river fort and the cannon were trained on it. The fort was built of thick logs in the shape of an irregular square, with portholes on the side next to the sea, and inside the breastworks were fourteen "barabaras," or native houses.

The walls were of such thickness that the cannon shot from the *Neva* made but little impression on the structure. Baranov was impatient and urged an attack. Reinforcements were landed from the ships under command of Lieutenants Arbusov and Polavishin. The hunters, sailors, and Aleuts flung themselves against the fortifications but, meeting a murderous fire, they were driven back in disorder and only saved from disaster by the protection of the ship's guns. Ten men were killed and twenty-six wounded; among the latter was Baranov.

Captain Lisiansky then took command and moved his ships nearer the shore. A canoe with reinforcements and a supply of powder for the Indians approached the island, but a shot from the *Neva* struck it, the powder exploded, and the Indians who were saved from the wreck were taken on board the Russian ship. The bombardment continued steadily until October 6, when the Kolosh proposed to surrender. A parley was held, but during the night the Kolosh evacuated the fort and went over the mountains to the north. In the fort were left, besides the bodies of thirty warriors, also those of five children who had been killed to pevent their cries from making the retreat known to the Russians. The only remaining survivors were two old women and a little boy. A few straggling warriors remained lurking about, seeking revenge, and a few days later they killed eight Aleuts who were fishing on Jamestown Bay.

How the Kolosh went over the mountains was long a mystery to the Russians. They reached the shore of Peril Strait and crossing to the north shore erected a fort near the entrance to Sitkoh Bay — one stronger than their old fort at Indian River — where more than one thousand people had gathered. A tradition among the old Indians says that the fugitives first went to Old Sitka, then over the mountains to the northeastern side of the island. On the way they suffered extremely from fatigue and hunger, and one Sitka Indian who lives on Peril Strait relates that his father was a child at the time of the exodus. His father carried him till, exhausted, he abandoned him; his mother then took him up and carried him the remainder of the way.

The property left in the fort by the Kolosh was taken out, the fortification was burned, and the canoes on the beach were broken to pieces. There was enough left of the structure that some of the remains of the foundation may yet be seen in the forest which has sprung up around it in the Indian River Park, although more than a century has since elapsed.

Then began the restoration of the post on the present site of Sitka, and with energy and despatch the building of a new Russian settlement proceeded. Around the *kekoor* the native houses were removed, and along with them more than a hundred burial houses with the ashes of the bodies which had been burned. The great tribal houses, or "barabaras," as they are called in the Russian accounts, were spacious, some measuring fifty feet in width and eighty feet in length.[2] In their place rose the town of New Archangel (*Novo Arkhangelsk*), and on the *kekoor* was built a redoubt. This was the official name and generally recognized by the Russians, but the name Sitka was early used by them. Baranov frequently used the term Sitka in his letters, and in the letter of the Minister of Finance to the Minister of Marine, from St. Petersburg, April 9, 1820, Sitka is used in several places. The name Sitka, or "Sheetkah," in the Tlingit language, means "in this place," "this is the place," or "the best place," implying superiority over all other places.

All winter there was cutting of logs in the forest, and by the spring of 1805 there were eight substantial buildings. Space for fifteen kitchen gardens had been cleared, the livestock brought from the ships were thriving, and an air of prosperity pervaded the place.[3] Surveys of the harbor were made by Captain Lisi-

---

[2] In Wrangell, and at a few other places in Alaska, may yet be seen some of these old tribal houses, built, for the most part, as in primitive days. The beams and planks were fashioned with an adze, and the evenness of the workmanship in hewing them is marvelous.

[3] The livestock taken to Sitka in 1804 consisted of "four cows, two calves,

ansky who, after making the first ascent of Mt. Edgecumbe, sailed for Kronstadt, Russia, by way of Canton, with a cargo of furs valued at four hundred and fifty thousand rubles, for the China trade.[4]

three bulls, three goats, a ewe and a ram, with many swine and fowls." — Lisiansky, *Voyage Round the World, 1803–1806*, p. 218.

[4] Lisiansky made the surveys and named the islands of the archipelago which had not been charted by Vancouver, of which he says, "By our survey it appears that amongst the group of islands, which in my chart I have denominated the Sitka Islands, from the inhabintants, who call themselves Sitka-hans, or Sitka people, are four principal ones, viz: Jacobi, Kruze, Baranof, and Chichagof." — *Ibid.*, p. 235.

*Hector Chevigny (1904–1965) began a radio career in Seattle
after attending Gonzaga University in Spokane, Washington.
A few years later he moved to Los Angeles, California,
where he wrote for radio, motion pictures, and national
magazines. Altogether he wrote more than 1,500 radio shows.
He was national president of the Radio Writer's Guild.
Shortly after Chevigny moved to New York City in 1943,
he lost his sight. He continued to work. His first two Alaskan
books are perhaps better known than any other histories of
the region:* Lost Empire *(1937) and* Lord of Alaska *(1942).
The following episode is from his last book,* Russian America:
The Great Alaskan Venture, 1741–1867 *(New York: The
Viking Press, 1965). One reviewer has said correctly that*
Russian America *was "written as a good history should be—
by a storyteller with perspective."*

The Tragedy of Anna Petrovna

HECTOR CHEVIGNY

he exploring expedition which set out from New
Archangel in the fall of 1808 for the purpose of locating a site
for a fort in the Columbia River region was under the command
of a naval officer by the name of Nikolai Bulygin. With him was
his young and attractive wife. Anna Petrovna Bulygin was to
have the distinction of being the first white woman to set foot on
New Albion, the name, borrowed from the English, by which
the Russians denoted the vast stretch of coast between California and Russian America.

The leader of the promyshlenniki assigned to the expedition
was Timofei Tarakanov, one of Baranov's most experienced
men. Tarakanov was probably born in eastern Siberia, a descendant of the old promyshlenniki, and had been in the colony
at least ten years. He was with the garrison of the first fort built
at Sitka in 1799 and was one of the few not killed on the spot
at the massacre in 1802. Captured, taken to a Tlingit village, he
witnessed the death by torture of two of his comrades. He was
the last man to be rescued by Captains Ebbets and Barber.

Unfazed by the experience, he made himself one of the colony's foremost dealers with the Tlingits, whose speech he learned. He had an ear for the speech of all the natives, who generally respected him highly, the Aleuts in particular. When the practice of poaching otter along California was instituted, he went on a number of the voyages as foreman of the Aleut crews, having the respect and liking also of the American skippers. He was inventive and resourceful, having great skill with his hands. Though classed as a hunter, he could have qualified as a carpenter or metal-worker. He could also, as he had demonstrated, center a target with a Moscow musket at two hundred feet. He went with the Columbia River expedition in the capacity of supercargo. He would have charge of activities such as trading and other dealings with the Indians.

The expedition departed New Archangel at virtually the same time that Kuskov and his men set out for the purpose of reconnoitering the region just north of California. Neither party was to build a fort. They were both to return and report before final action would be taken. The Columbia-bound vessel, commanded by Nikolai Bulygin, was the *Saint Nicholas*, a fine little brig acquired from the Yankees. Aboard were twenty people: seventeen men, four of them Aleuts, and three women, Aleuts with the exception of Anna Petrovna, whom Bulygin "loved more than himself," in the words of Tarakanov, who was to give a first-person account of what occurred. His narrative was preserved for publication, thanks to the interest in history taken by a ranking naval officer.*

Bulygin, who had been in the colony about two years, was better liked than most of the naval men. He had proved himself able and was considerate of others. The indications all are that he and Anna Petrovna had not been married long. She was popular, was probably about eighteen, and plainly had a zest for adventure. What Tarakanov may have thought of having

* Here Chevigny refers the reader to a bibliographical entry: Vasilii Tarakanov, "Krushenie Rossiiskago-Amerikanskoi Kompanii sudna 'Sviatoi Nikolai'. . . ." ("Wreck of the R-A Co. ship *Saint Nicholas*. . . ."). In V. M. Golovnin's *Opisaniia primechatel'nykh korablekrushenii* (St. Petersburg, 1853) Vol. 4. — ED. NOTE.

her on such an expedition, his narrative does not say. He had no words of criticism for superiors. In the event of shipwreck a young white woman was likely to create special problems. Much of the coast they were to survey was rocky; all of it was wild, beset by fog and rain and peopled by savages known to take slaves. But Bulygin obviously had entire confidence in his skill as a navigator. Besides, the *Saint Nicholas* was taut and strong, and they had Vancouver's excellent charts. And, should some accident befall them, according to plan they would make for Gray's Harbor and await Kuskov, who was scheduled to meet them there with his party in December.

They traded as they went, at the Queen Charlotte Islands and down Vancouver Island. Every Company operation, including exploring, was expected to pay for itself. As of old, the men were on shares; what they made depended on the year's take of furs. They lay to and fired a gun when totem poles showing above the dark, wet forest indicated a village. As many as a hundred canoes at a time would put out from shore, bringing otter. Since the Americans often visited these parts, the natives had guns. Tarakanov would allow only three of them aboard at a time.

Their progress was further delayed by storms alternating with periods of no winds at all. They were becalmed for four days off the Strait of Juan de Fuca, which they did not try to enter, repelled, no doubt, by the dense fog forever shrouding the entrance. Few vessels ventured in, despite Vancouver's clear indication of the passage. On a night late in October they anchored near Destruction Island, so named as a memento of the experiences of previous mariners with the Indians of the adjacent mainland, the Olympic Peninsula of the present State of Washington.

Disaster struck with dumfounding suddenness. Everything went wrong at once. Bulygin had thrown out three anchors to hold the *Saint Nicholas* against a strong sea current, but a stiff southeaster came up, adding so much pull on the cables that they snapped, one after the other, cut by sharp submerged rocks. A foreyard broke, ending hope of maneuvering the brig against the wind. On the morning of November 1 she was on the mainland rocks. So precarious was her situation that Bulygin ordered her evacuated and camp made on the beach, despite the rain, which at that season at that place comes in off the ocean in torrents, drawn inland by the high, cold Olympic Mountains.

Guns were issued as the tents went up, Tarakanov telling everyone to keep a sharp lookout for Indians. Enslavement at their hands was to him a fate "a hundredfold worse than death itself." Indians were not long in coming out of the thick forest fringing the beach, "a multitude" of them suddenly appearing, half naked and barefoot. To Tarakanov's relief they had no guns, only spears, which showed how seldom this section of the coast was visited by traders. These were Quillayute Indians, unrelated to the Tlingits and more primitive, but speaking a language sufficiently close to those known to Tarakanov for him to understand it.

They were merely curious, not hostile. They had a village nearby, as Tarakanov learned from the chief, who was affable. On learning that whites were in the vicinity, they had come running over to have a look. Their curiosity was unbounded. They were all over the camp, examining everything, fingering whatever attracted them. They tried to make off with some objects, provoking tussles. "Bear with them," Tarakanov advised. "Get them out of here peacefully." But someone lost his temper, perhaps hitting one of the Indians. They backed off, offended, throwing spears and stones, felling Tarakanov and drawing blood from Bulygin. Guns began going off. Three of the Indians were killed before the others withdrew into the forest.

The rest of the day passed in futile attempts to salvage the *Saint Nicholas*. In the morning Bulygin announced that without further delay they would start walking to Gray's Harbor, which lay less than seventy miles to the south. They should be there in plenty of time to meet Kuskov in December. The warmest parkas and the best sealskin mukluks were issued. Every man was given two muskets to carry and a pistol. Slings were made, in which to carry kegs of powder, bags of shot, axes and other tools of the kind, provisions, trade goods, and the most valued of their personal belongings. Because the Quillayutes were likely to loot the brig, everything which might serve them as a weapon was thrown into the water. Then they set out, at their heels the dog who was the pet of the expedition. One who no doubt relished this as adventure was Fillipp Kotelnikov, a youthful student who had come on the voyage.

As events were to show, the Quillayutes had been holding angry council at their village, debating how to avenge the three deaths and the wounds inflicted on them. They had not failed to notice how the whites protected that woman of theirs who had blue eyes and yellow hair. She would fetch a fine price from some wealthy tribe. When the sentinels appointed to watch the movements of the whites ran in with word they were on the march, fifty warriors ran after them to see where they were going and to harry them with spears and stones. The word went out all over the peninsula; Indians came running from miles around. In view of the direction the whites were taking, they would presently come to the Hoh River, which they would find too deep to wade. It was decided to set a trap for them there.

The heaviness of the constant rain gave Tarakanov and his companions one of their greatest problems as they slogged on, hugging the shoreline and avoiding, as much as they could, the forest with its hidden throwers of spears and stones. Loaded down as they were, it was difficult to see that the firing mechanisms of their muskets were kept dry at all times. The rain was coming down in sheets when, on November 7, they reached the Hoh River, which they soon saw would take boats to cross.

On the opposite shore stood a village made up of a number of large huts with dugout canoes moored nearby. Also there, watching intently, were some two hundred Indians. Only later was Tarakanov to realize that a quarter of them had been his party's pursuers. After a parley he conducted through cupped hands, two of the canoes were brought over, one large enough to carry nine in addition to the paddlers, and a smaller, for four passengers. Several trips would have to be made to get everyone and all the baggage across, but that was as well. They should not all be on the water at the same time.

Bulygin was giving the orders. He and Tarakanov would be among the last to cross. The ladies would go first, Anna and the two Aleut women. They, the student Filipp Kotelnikov, and the Indian paddler shoved off in the small canoe. The nine men who followed in the larger had their muskets at the ready to give protection when the women reached the opposite shore. But in midstream their paddlers unplugged holes that had been cut in the bottom and jumped overboard, leaving them to a hail of spears and arrows from the Indians ashore. Their muskets were too drenched to shoot back. They could use them only as paddles in a frantic effort to get back to safety, at the same time stopping the upwelling water with their feet. Meanwhile Anna and those with her were paddled across and whisked out of sight.

Bulygin could only rave and curse. In the sluicing rain he had allowed his musket to get too wet to spark shots, and so had all the men on his side of the river, including Tarakanov. They could give no cover to the men trying to paddle clear of the spears and arrows. When their canoe was pulled in, not one of them was unwounded. The Indians, having heard no shots, concluded that they could wipe out the whites and moved upstream to cross over for the purpose. By the time the attackers were on them, Tarakanov and the others had their arms dried and cleaned. Even so it took an hour to drive back the Indians, two of whom had guns. Manifestly this exposed position on the riverbank had to be abandoned. Carrying the seriously wounded in their arms, leaving behind much of their equipment, including the tools for repairing guns, they set out for higher ground.

When they had gone only a little way, one of the wounded begged simply to be set down in the brush. He could not endure the pain, said Khariton Sobachnikov, who was dying of the arrowhead in his belly. It had to be as he asked. All wept as they laid him down in a secluded place, bade him farewell, and prayed God to have mercy on his soul.

For nearly a week they plunged on through the forest in in-

creasingly disorganized fashion, finding no campsite that offered an adequate food supply. They had used up their provisions; they lived on the few mushrooms they could find and on
tree fungi. Finally they were constrained to kill and eat the dog.
Meanwhile another of the wounded had died. Bulygin was no
fit leader in a situation such as this. He was so unacquainted
with woodcraft he did not know how to use an ax or shoot down
a bird. And the thought of what might be happening to his
wife had him in such a state that "it was impossible to look on
him without compassionate tears." At length he asked Tarakanov to take command, confessing that he knew not how to
get them out of their desperate situation.

Tarakanov asked to have the request in writing and, scrupu-
lously following promyshlennik practice, had the men vote on
it. He was unanimously elected leader. Taking the necessary
risk of exposing the fact they were still in the vicinity, he led a
raid on a small Indian village for its dried fish. The harrying
they received after that decided Tarakanov to abandon the
coast region. They would, he told the men, go up the Hoh River
and into the mountains. There they would winter and think
out what to do next. It was too late even to think of resuming the
attempt to make Gray's Harbor. Kuskov could not now be met
in time.

They had not gone far up the Hoh when two chiefs caught up
with them. Presenting a mass of whale blubber for sale, they
asked also how much would be paid for the white woman. Bulygin, when this question was translated for him, "was beside himself with joy." He contributed even his epaulets to the pile of
trade goods and the personal valuables given up by all the
men, the Aleuts included. But the chiefs were unsatisfied. They
also wanted four guns. Tarakanov's reply to that was that they
had to see Anna first. The chiefs had to concede it was only
reasonable to prove they would not be selling a dead body.

Anna was brought from the opposite shore of the river in a
canoe, but only about halfway. Bulygin had to talk to her across
several yards of water. They "were drowned in tears and could
hardly speak. She tried to comfort him, saying she had been well

treated and had met with no harm." Her words were no doubt belied by her appearance. Those who had been captives of the Quillayutes for any length of time were usually gaunt, exhasuted, and filthy. The chiefs now resumed negotiations, repeating their demand for four guns. When Tarakanov conceded no more than one broken musket, they ordered Anna taken away and they departed.

Bulygin, when he understood what had been said, was beside himself with anger. Ignoring the fact he had given up the leadership, he ordered the men to pay the price. Tarakanov tried to reason with him, pointing out that that meant giving up a quarter of their usable guns. Owing to their lack of tools for the making of repairs, they were now all down to one good musket apiece, and more were bound to go out of commission. Besides, any guns given away would be used against them. Bulygin only repeated his orders, adding a tearful plea. Tarakanov then sharply told the men that any who complied need no longer consider him their comrade. He prevailed. In bitter silence the march up river was resumed.

Some ten weeks later, in February of 1809, they came back down the Hoh in a crude boat with a friendly Indian as their pilot. Tarakanov, who had pulled them through the winter with no further casualties, had proposed they build the boat in the hope of making it out to sea. They should be able to reach Destruction Island, where passing ships could be signaled, or they might even attain the Columbia, which was being visited by the Americans. They would see how things went when they reached salt water.

Bulygin was again in command. When the proposal to build the boat was made he came out of the stupor that had possessed him and asked to be reinstated. Tarakanov had been agreeable. They would need his skill as a navigator. Bulygin seemed wholeheartedly of the opinion they should now all devote themselves to getting back to civilization, until they neared the village on the lower river where they had been tricked. He then announced he intended making an effort to find out what had become of his wife.

The men were angry. This was foolhardy. No longer did they have enough guns or ammunition to risk battle. But Tarakanov persuaded them to obey, and luck seemed with them for a change. Two Indians were easily captured and held on the boat in wait for their people to make the next move. One of the two was a woman whose husband proved to be of tribal importance. Very concerned about his wife, he begged for four days' time, during which he would try to bring back the white woman, who had, he said, been given in tribute to a chief of the Makahs, a tribe living on the Strait of Juan de Fuca.

Bulygin decided to do his waiting where his two hostages would not be easily taken from him. Leaving the boat pulled up on the riverbank, he made camp on a cliff a mile distant. There, together with the men and the captives, he waited eight days. Word then came that a delegation of Makahs had arrived and were at the river, waiting to parley. To ascertain the truth of this, Bulygin sent Tarakanov, who went well armed with several men. It was all as reported. The Makahs were there, waiting, fifteen of them, headed by an obviously wealthy old chief named Utra-Makah, who wore a European shirt, trousers, and a fur cap. All of them seemed prosperous and above most of the natives thereabouts. And with them, "to our joy," was Anna Petrovna.

She was not the woebegone girl they had last seen the previous fall. Indeed her appearance was a great surprise. She looked healthy; she was clean; she was warmly garbed in good fur clothing and moccasins. And she had a different air. She was a person of power and influence among the Makahs. Though Tarakanov did not later say so in as many words, clearly she had become a favorite wife of the chief who had acquired her. What she had to say, when the greetings and expressions of surprise were over, "struck us all like thunder. . . . We listened with horror and bitterness. . . ."

Speaking "decisively and firmly," she refused to leave her present situation only to go wandering again in search of escape with no certainty of finding it, enduring more privations and dangers. What they should do, she told Tarakanov, was join her, voluntarily give themselves over to the Makahs, a kindly people who would treat them as well as she was treated. She could give assurance on the point; she had made the arrangement. They would be at villages on Juan de Fuca Strait, where two ships had of late put in, she had heard. When another appeared they would not be hindered from asking the captain to take them home. Tarakanov told her he would have to go talk to Bulygin.

It took Bulygin some time to believe the story and when he did "he was like a madman. He seized a gun and rushed away with the intention of shooting his wife." But he could not go through with it. He halted, burst into tears, asked Tarakanov to go talk again to Anna, who was to be told how close she had come to getting shot.

Her comment was sharp. "Tell my husband I have only contempt for his threat." Death did not frighten her, she said. What did was the risk of enslavement "by an evil and barbarous people." Having offered an arrangement by which they would all be safe and perhaps soon find their way home, she had no more to say.

Again Tarakanov hiked the mile back to the cliff and reported to Bulygin, who listened closely, stood a moment in thought, then collapsed. He was put to bed, crying helplessly and saying he wanted to die. The men wanted to get back to the boat, be on their way. Only Tarakanov gave thought to Anna's proposal. It was eminently worth considering, in view of her information that ships were now visiting the strait. As for the treatment they would be accorded, Anna should know what she was talking about. All things considered, joining her seemed a safer gamble than trusting themselves to that boat they had built. That evening he told the assembled company that he for one wished to surrender himself to the Makahs.

A rancorous discussion ensued, some charging Anna with the intention of betraying them, for love of her chief, apparently. In vain they were reminded that, after all, she was a Russian. The majority, from Ivan Bolotov to Savva Zuev and Kasian Zyrianov, voted to continue on with the boat. Only four sided with

Tarakanov: his close friend Kozma Ovchinnikov, two of the Aleuts, and Bulygin, who was evidently letting his thinking be done for him. It was agreed that the party should split, though not in enmity. They would all pray for the safety of one another. Next day Tarakanov took the two Indian captives back to their people and conferred with the trousered Makah chief, who assured him that everything would be as Anna had promised.

When she and those who had chosen to go with her had departed for the Strait, the others relaunched the boat, their destination Destruction Island. They came to grief at once, the boat striking a rock and sinking when barely past the river's mouth. They all made it back to shore but had lost all their arms and ammunition. They were quickly captured by the Quillayutes, who sold two of them, an Aleut and a Russian, as far away as the Columbia. The Makahs bought some of the others, who thus rejoined their former companions.

The Makahs lived in wooden communal dwellings which provided no privacy and forever smelled of stale smoke and rancid fish oil, but by comparison to their neighbors to the south they lived richly, and their hospitality was at first all that Anna had said it would be. Tarakanov and Bulygin were made the property of the kindly Utra-Makah, who treated them entirely as guests, not slaves. His village, to Tarakanov's gratification, had a clear view of the Strait to the fog-shrouded entrance. Vessels venturing in would immediately be seen. Anna was at another village until her owner obligingly bought Bulygin, whereupon they were together again, in a manner of speaking. The captives scattered through the various villages included one John Williams, though who he was and how he got there, Tarakanov's narrative does not say.

Spring wore into summer; no ships appeared. The Indians, whose mood could change quickly, tired of maintaining so many captives in what, to them, was luxury, and put them increasingly to work. They also began to "pass us from hand to hand," by sale or as gifts to friends and relatives. Even Anna found herself sold to someone else at another village. Again she and her husband were apart. Presently the captives were nothing but slaves, made to work interminably in all weather and given the worst of the food, usually revoltingly unfresh fish. Only Tarakanov appears to have been retained by his first owner. He managed it by making himself too useful and interesting to Utra-Makah to be got rid of. With tools he made himself, he fashioned dishes of wood and toys for the children and invented a device with which to signal in time of war.

In August Anna Petrovna died, apparently a suicide. Tarakanov, who details how others met death, in this case was laconic, stating only the fact and the month. She had reason to despair. August was the last month when a ship could reasonably be expected that year. None knew better than she how hideous was the situation into which she had led her husband and compatriots. Her last owner "was such a barbarian he would not permit her body to be buried and had it simply thrown into the forest." Bulygin gave up trying to live after that. He "went into a decline," succumbed to an infection of some sort, and died in February. Dead too was Tarakanov's close friend, Ovchinnikov. They might all be dead if no ship came this year either.

The season was approaching when the ships sailing to New Archangel would be passing not many miles out from that cursed fog hugging the entrance to the Strait. Tarakanov put his inventive mind on the problem of signaling those ships. A kite! A kite would rise well above that fog and be judged the work of only a European. He made one of some thin material stretched over a wooden frame. His string was twisted gut. The Indians marveled, saying that he had found a way to reach the sun. There was even talk of making him a chief.

Tarakanov, a pious man, surely dropped to his knees when, in May of that year of 1810, a vessel materialized out of the fog. And she was one he knew, the Boston brig *Lydia*, commanded by Captain J. Brown. And when Tarakanov was aboard, who should clasp him in his arms but Afanasii Valgusov, whom the Quillayutes had sold to the natives on the Columbia, where Brown had ransomed him. As for the Aleut sold down the Columbia, he had been rescued the previous year by Captain George Ayers of the *Mercury*.

After some haggling, Brown offered the Makahs for each of their captives, including John Williams, five blankets, twelve yards of cloth, a saw, a mirror, two knives, five bags of powder, and five of shot. Word of the price went out over the Olympic Peninsula so quickly that in four days the gaunt survivors were being brought in from as far away as the Quinault River. Some owners of captives tried to hold out for more than the standard price, but Brown put a stop to that by seizing one of them and putting him in the *Lydia's* brig. Counting Williams, Brown rescued thirteen souls, including the two Aleut women, all who had survived the expedition, with the exception of the young student Kotelnikov, who was known to be alive but was at some place too distant for the Indians to trouble to find him. Seven were dead of the twenty who had sailed with the *Saint Nicholas*.

The rescued saw New Archangel again on June 9, 1810. They had been away twenty-one months, fifteen of them in captivity. To the clerk assigned to him for the purpose, for he was illiterate, Tarakanov began dictating the report telling of the fate of the first white woman to set foot on the shores of the Pacific Northwest.

Under Baranov, Russian activity in the western Pacific was not confined to the Alaskan coast. The Russian-American Company extended its operations south to the California coast in pursuit of the sea otter and other resources, and Alaskan-based Russian commerce looked southwest into the Pacific. A complicated story of early Russian intrigue and international competition in Hawaii is clarified in the following article, which also illustrates the character and limitations of Russian power in the Pacific.

An historian of Russia, Richard Pierce received his Ph.D. from the University of California, Berkeley, in 1956. He now teaches at Queens University in Kingston, Ontario, Canada. Among the new students of Alaskan history, probably no one knows the Russian archival sources better than Professor Pierce. The article is from the Pacific Historical Review, *XXXII (November 1963) 397–405. Pierce is the author of a larger study of the same subject:* Russia's Hawaiian Adventure, 1815–1817 (Berkeley and Los Angeles: University of California Press, 1965).

Georg Anton Schäffer, Russia's Man in Hawaii, 1815-1817

RICHARD A. PIERCE

The attempt by the German surgeon, Georg Anton Schäffer (or Egor Antonovich Scheffer, as he was known in Russia), to engineer Russian annexation of the Hawaiian Islands is generally known.[1] However, gaps and errors exist in the

[1] The main source was for a long time the account supplied by the company historian, P. Tikhmenev, in *Istoricheskoe obozrenie obrazovanie Rossiisko-Amerikanskoi Kompanii* (Historical review of the origin of the Russian-American Company), 2 vols. (St. Petersburg, 1861–1863). It was drawn upon by H. H. Bancroft, *History of Alaska, 1730–1885* (San Francisco, 1886), and by W. D. Alexander, "The Proceedings of the Russians on Kauai, 1814–1816," Hawaiian Historical Society *Papers*, No. 6 (Honolulu, 1894). F. A. Golder, "Proposals for Russian occupation of the Hawaiian Islands," in A. P. Taylor and R. S. Kuykendall, eds., *The Hawaiian Islands* (Honolulu, 1930), 39–49, contributed material drawn from earlier work in the Russian archives.

The only publication of primary material has been in S. B. Okun's "Tsarskaia Rossiia i Gavaiskie Ostrova" (The Tsarist Government and the Hawaiian Islands), *Krasnyi Arkhiv*, LXX (1936), 161–186, comprising eight documents. These form the core of Klaus Mehnert's *The Russians in Hawaii* (Honolulu, 1938), which includes translations of several of the documents, and of Anatole

record of the venture so far available, and very little has been known about Schäffer himself. Additional materials reveal new facts about this fast-working interloper, who for a short time disturbed the torpor of pre-missionary Hawaii.[2]

Schäffer was born in Münnerstadt, Bavaria, on January 27, 1779, the son of a miller. He was baptised in the Catholic church, received a good education, and was set up as an apothecary. He pursued his profession as far afield as Hungary and Galicia. In 1804, he passed the "Surgeons' Examination" at St. Julius Hospital in Würzburg, and became eligible to practice medicine. Invited to go to Russia in 1808, he served in the army as a staff physician, and in 1812 took part in an abortive project for construction of balloons to watch Napoleon's invading army. In 1813, he signed on with the Russian-American Company in St. Petersburg as surgeon on the ship *Suvorov*, about to make a round-the-world voyage to Alaska.

During the voyage Schäffer quarrelled with the ship's commander, Lt. M. P. Lazerev. When Lazerev departed hastily from the port of Novo-Arkhangel'sk (Sitka) after an altercation with A. A. Baranov, chief manager of the company's North American holdings, he left Schäffer behind.

Schäffer's antipathy to Lazarev recommended him to Baranov, as did his education and background, unique in the rough outpost. For lack of anyone else, Baranov entrusted the newcomer with a mission to the Hawaiian (then Sandwich) Islands.

Baranov had long desired closer relations with the islands as a means of enhancing the food supply of Russian America. Now he sought satisfaction for the seizure by natives of the island of Kauai of a cargo of furs from the company brig *Bering*

G. Mazour, "Egor Scheffer: Dreamer of a Russian Empire in the Pacific," *Pacific Historical Review*, VI (1937), 15–20.

[2] This account is based mainly upon copies of unpublished Russian documents which are in the Bancroft Library, Berkeley, California, and biographical data furnished by Prof. Enrico Schaeffer of Sao Paulo, Brazil, collateral descendant of G. A. Schäffer. Prof. Schaeffer is the author of "De velhas cronicas de familias: O Cavalheiro Georg Anton de Schaeffer," *Revista Genealogica Latina* (Sao Paulo, 1959), and "Aus alten Familien-Chroniken: Georg Anton Ritter von Schaeffer, Seelenverkaeufer und Freund der brasilian. Kaiserin," *Revista Suedamerika* (Buenos Aires, 1960).

(the former American vessel *Atahualpa*, Captain James Bennett), wrecked there on January 31, 1815.[3]

Sailing for the islands on October 17, 1815, on the American ship *Isabella*, Schäffer bore orders from Baranov instructing him to appear as a naturalist until company ships could be sent to back him up. By using "tact and diplomacy" he was to win the favor of King Kamehameha, and then get the latter's help in securing return of the *Bering's* cargo or compensation for it in sandalwood. He was also to try to obtain trading privileges and a monopoly on sandalwood within Kamehameha's domains.

Arriving at the island of Hawaii a month later, Schäffer found tact and diplomacy of little help. The elderly British seaman, John Young, Kamehameha's chief advisor, suspected the visitor's motives. John and Richard Ebbets, William Heath Davis, Nathan Winship, and other American traders feared encroachment on their privileges. These adversaries alarmed Kamehameha with tales of Russian designs. Schäffer's journal and reports refer frequently to their "intrigues," and "abuse and slander."

By medical aid and personal assurances Schäffer finally managed to mollify the King so that the latter ordered a house built for him, and agreed to grant land to the company and to permit establishment of a factory on the island of Oahu. However, provisions were supplied irregularly, Schäffer's movements were circumscribed, and some of the King's advisors even urged that he be killed.

These conditions caused Schäffer to petition Kamehameha for permission to move to Oahu. The King finally consented, though adhering to his usual policy of prohibiting foreigners to build permanent structures, he assigned him one of his own warehouses at Honolulu for a factory.

Transported to Oahu on the American ship *Beverly*, Schäffer took possession of the lands which he had purchased. Then, on May 3 the company ship *Otkrytie* (Lt. Podushkin) arrived from Sitka, and soon after it another company vessel, the brig *Il'mena*. The *Il'mena* was unexpected; its American captain,

---

[3] See F. W. Howay, "The last days of the *Atahualpa*, alias *Behring*," Hawaiian Historical Society, *Annual Reports*, No. 41 (1933), 70–80.

William Wadsworth, had made an unauthorized detour to the islands after leaving the Russian port of Rumiantsev (Bodega) in California en route to Sitka. Reinforced by several Russians and over forty Aleut hunters off the *Il'mena*, Schäffer left the factory at Honolulu in charge of a subordinate and sailed on the *Otkrytie* for Kauai, to settle accounts there.

Arriving at Kauai on May 28, Schäffer found conditions far more agreeable than in Kamehameha's nominally friendly domains. Kaumualii, King of Kauai and Niihau, and claimant to the remainder of the islands, told Schäffer the same story he had told earlier visitors (including the Russians Lisianskii in 1806 and Hagenmeister in 1809), complaining of Kamehameha's usurpation and indicating his readiness to assent to anything which would gain him an ally.

Schäffer eagerly grasped what seemed a great opportunity for the company and himself alike. On the deck of the *Otkrytie* one glorious day, June 2, 1816, he achieved all of his original aims and a great deal more. Besides restoring what remained of the *Bering's* cargo, Kaumualii pledged allegiance to the Emperor Alexander I, and promised to trade exclusively with the Russian-American Company, to supply it with cargoes of sandalwood, to allow it to establish factories anywhere in his domains, to supply men to aid in the erection of buildings and in the development of plantations, and to furnish provisions for Russian ships. In return Schäffer promised the protection of the Russian Empire, and to provide the King with a fully armed ship when the first cargo of sandalwood was ready. He bestowed on the King a silver medal, and had him don the uniform of an officer in the Imperial Russian Navy.

By a secret treaty concluded July 1, still wider commitments were made. Kaumualii agreed to send an army of 500 men, under Schäffer's command, to reconquer the islands held by Kamehameha, and to aid in construction of a Russian fort on each of the islands, the forts "to be placed in charge of Russian commanders, as in the case of the fort at Honolulu." (Schäffer was evidently deceiving Kaumualii here, for elsewhere he refers to the establishment on Oahu only as a factory.) Kaumualii also promised to give the company one-half of the island of Oahu and strips of land on each of the other islands, all of the sandalwood on the island of Oahu, and to "refuse to trade with citizens of the United States." Schäffer agreed to supply ammunition and ships for the prospective conquest, to supply the King with fish and timber from Russian America (the timber to be cut by islanders sent to Sitka), and, finally, "to introduce a better economy, which will make the natives educated and prosperous."

Schäffer had thus exceeded his original instructions to a degree undreamed of by the careful Baranov. The *Otkrytie* sailed for Sitka in June, but Schäffer had the Russians and Aleuts from the *Il'mena*. With the King's "X" on several agreements, and with the King's subjects busy cutting sandalwood in the mountains and piling lava blocks at Waimea for the construction of a future Fort Elizabeth, to be named after the Empress of Russia, he could feel the exultation of success.

Although able to fend off the King's queries as to when they should declare war on Kamehameha, Schäffer had to make good sooner than expected regarding the promised ship. In August Kaumualii asked for the schooner *Lydia*, owned by Captain Henry Gyzelaar of New York. Schäffer had no choice but to comply, but turned the incident to advantage by giving Gyzelaar a promise of payment from the company, and giving the vessel to Kaumualii in return for the valley and port of Hanalei, on the north shore of Kauai. He next arranged for purchase by the company of yet another American vessel, the ship *Avon*, from Captain Isaac Whittemore for 200,000 piasters, payable in Sitka, Kaumualii to compensate the company with three cargoes of sandalwood, in exchange for the protection and added assurance the *Avon* would afford his expansionist projects.

Completing the ship purchases at Honolulu, Schäffer was reinforced by the old and leaky brig *Kad'iak*, which Baranov had sent from Sitka under Captain George Young, an American in company service.

On Oahu, however, Schäffer clashed with John Young, angry

at the Russian pretensions. Soon after his return to Kauai, word came from Oahu that the natives, allegedly roused by Young and "the American hot heads," had burned the Russian factory, though in an enthusiastic report to St. Petersburg Schäffer mentioned neither this incident nor the financial legerdemain accompanying purchase of the ships.

Taking possession of Hanalei, Schäffer acceded, not unwillingly it would seem, to Kaumualii's wish that he attach his own name to the valley, and that he give Russian names to other localities and to several chiefs. Henceforth in his journal appear references to the Schäffer Valley, the Georgievskaia and Don rivers, and to the chieftains Vorontsov and Platov. He began construction of two new forts, one on each side of the mouth of the Hanalei river, to be named Forts Alexander and Barklay. Schäffer and Kaumualii exchanged cannon salutes at the slightest pretext, and the Russian flag flew over Waimea.

Contemplating his achievements, Schäffer's imagination soared at the prospects ahead. His journal and reports are full of comments on the natural abundance of the islands, the healthful climate, and the prospects for manufactures and trade. The natives, he observed, worked scarcely a tenth of the land. This stemmed partly from natural laziness, partly from the fact that in Kamehameha's domains "not one of them can be master of his own property. If anyone works his own land, or fattens a pig, the men of King Kamehameha take it from him." On Hawaii and Oahu, "there is a great deal of dissatisfaction. . . . Many told me I should ask the great Russian monarch to take over their islands, only leaving them their taro fields. . . . If the Sandwich Islands could have a monarch like Russia's great Alexander, truly the inhabitants could live in a golden age!"

Cotton, Schäffer felt, should be Russia's main object in the islands, as it would yield more from a small expenditure and effort "than all the fur trade on the Northwest Coast." Sandalwood, till then the chief product of the islands, could continue to be profitable, especially if the company held a monopoly and could impose conservation measures. Enough taro and maize could be grown to feed the Russian settlements in America and Okhotska and Kamchatka in Siberia. Sugarcane could be processed into sugar and rum. Oil nuts could be grown and sold for medicinal purposes. Grapes could yield wine equal to the finest Madeira; enough tobacco could be grown to supply Russian needs in the North Pacific and to leave some for foreign sales. Tropical fruits, placed on the Chinese market, could "bring down in one blow the trade of the English and Americans." Stockbreeding, pearl fishing, and sale of supplies to ships could also bring substantial return.

There were equally attractive political advantages.

> Through these holdings Russia will soon obtain able and experienced seamen. The Chinese will have to allow the Russian flag to wave in Canton. The English and Americans will have their trade cut off. . . . The Sandwich Islands must be made a Russian West India and a second Gibraltar. Russia must have these islands at any cost!

Nor could there be any question of title. Kamehameha had ceded the island of Hawaii to England in an agreement concluded with Captain Vancouver in 1794, but England had taken no further action. The other islands belonged to King Kaumualii, a Russian subject, and as King Kamehameha had proclaimed himself an enemy of Kaumualii, Russia could freely intervene. "No power in the world has more right to these islands than Russia!"

But soon the idyll was marred by difficulties. At the end of November, Lt. O. E. Kotzebue, commanding the brig *Rurik* on a voyage of discovery, arrived at the island of Hawaii, placated Kamehameha by assuring him that Schäffer was backed by neither the company nor the Russian government, and left the islands in December without any move to go to Kauai. In January, 1817, Baranov sent word via the American brig *Cossack* (Capt. J. Brown) that he would not honor the agreement to buy the *Avon*, forbidding Schäffer to engage in further speculation, and demanding return of the *Kad'iak* and *Il'mena* and their crews, and an accounting of all of the capital which he had expended.

Schäffer, undeterred, ignored Baranov's orders, placing his hope in arrival of a ship from St. Petersburg. He occupied himself with planting, plans for the future, and tours of the island. Then, during the spring of 1817, rumors reached Kauai of trouble between Russia and the United States. Schäffer obtained additional land grants but noticed that the King no longer flew the Russian flag, nor offered salutes. On May 7, he heard that five boats had arrived from Oahu, with news that the United States and Russia were at war.

Hastening to see Kaumualii, Schäffer found the King amidst an array of a thousand men. He endeavored to withdraw, but was seized by six American sailors and a native chief, placed in a canoe and sent to the *Il'mena* with a warning not to return to shore.

After a futile wait in the harbor at Waimea, watching "a piratical flag" (a blue and white ensign which may be ranked among the earliest Hawaiian flags) raised daily ashore, Schäffer and his men sailed around the island to Hanalei, in hope of making a stand at Fort Alexander. "Everything is in the hands of the Lord," he wrote Baranov, adding that "if I die or am killed, please send word of it to the Frankfurt newspapers. I intend to show that I deserve your confidence and the rank of a Russian staff officer."

But the natives at Hanalei had already run off all the livestock, and had killed two Aleuts. When an order came from Waimea to leave Hanalei or await hostile action, Schäffer blustered but had to comply. Still unwilling to accept defeat, however, he sent the *Il'mena* to Sitka under Captain Young, with tidings of the disaster and pleas for support, while he and the remaining several Russians and forty-odd Aleuts sailed the leaky *Kad'iak* to uncertain sanctuary in Honolulu, where Schäffer hoped to await reinforcements.

Arriving in Honolulu on June 23, they secured grudging permission from the local authorities to beach the *Kad'iak*. Only then did they learn that the "war" which had brought about the revolution on Kauai had been a trumped-up affair, to alarm Kaumualii. Ashore there was uncertainty as to what to do with the unwelcome guests. Finally a friendly American captain, Isaiah Lewis, whom Schäffer had given medical treatment the year before, offered passage to Canton on the brig *Panther*. Probably eager to be rid of him, Schäffer's men urged that he accept, in order that he might make his way to Europe and report directly to the company heads. They were left to get back to Alaska by hiring themselves out to the skipper of another American vessel, paying their passage by poaching for sea otter on the coast of Spanish California.

Reactions to the fiasco in Sitka and St. Petersburg were governed by the slowness of communications of that day. Contrary to the impression given in some accounts, it could only have been a one-man show. Baranov, in Sitka, appears to have heard nothing about the fate of the agent he had sent to the Islands in November, 1815, until the return of the *Otkrytie* the following June. The displeasure and uneasiness he then felt at the turn events had taken could not be communicated for some months. When Whittemore arrived in early October, 1816, with a 200,000 piaster claim for the *Avon* and further evidence of Schäffer's zeal, Baranov could still not communicate with the islands until the departure of the brig *Cossack* in late December. He could not inform St. Petersburg of the situation and of his demands on Schäffer until the brig *Brutus* left for Siberia in the following May, 1817, bearing dispatches to be sent overland via Okhotsk.

The company directors in St. Petersburg, half a world away, were scarcely in the picture at all. They seem to have heard of Schäffer's successes of May, 1816 (via Canton), only in the summer of 1817, after the game was already up and Schäffer had left the islands. Their eagerness for the benefits which would accrue from the unexpected windfall, displayed in the subsequent correspondence with Sitka, was diluted only by the Emperor's wish that caution be followed and actual annexation avoided. They heard of the collapse of the dream only in the summer of 1818, at about the same time that Schäffer arrived in Europe.

After vainly attempting to gain an interview with the Emperor at Aachen, Schäffer reached St. Petersburg at the end of 1818. He submitted lengthy memorials to the Emperor and the company, setting forth the worth of the islands and urging an expedition to regain the lost foothold there. For a time the company gave cautious support, until final evidence of the Emperor's displeasure caused the whole thing to be dropped in May, 1819.

Seeking to repair his fortunes, Schäffer returned to Brazil early in 1821. He had already become acquainted with the Emperor and Empress during a stop at Rio de Janeiro on the outward voyage of the *Suvorov* in May, 1814. From them he received an estate, which he named "Frankenthal," and joined the parvenu nobility of the Brazilian capital as Count von Frankenthal. In 1823 he returned to Europe to recruit German colonists. His book, *Brasilien als unabhängiges Reich, in historischer, mercantilischer und politischer Beziehung* . . . (Altona, 1824), a propaganda effort which helped earn him the sobriquet of "the soul-buyer" because of the hardships suffered by the colonists, is nevertheless one of the best descriptions of the Brazil of that day. About 1827, he returned to Brazil and there remained until his death in 1836.

In evaluating Schäffer, one cannot overlook the opportunism and personal ambition behind his rash disregard of instructions, the vanity which led him into a hopeless predicament, the probable hypocrisy of his too-fervent love for Russia, "my second home," the legalistic mind which caused him to place naive reliance on the symbols of power. Outraged at Kaumualii's fickleness, he lacked the realism which led the native monarch to quickly change sides when the pleasant game of signing treaties and bills of sale, building forts, and giving cannon salutes promised unfavorable results. He had nothing to match the resourcefulness, practicality, and flinty resolve of the Yankee traders, and no understanding of the seapower they represented, upon which he and the Company were dependent at almost every turn.

On the other hand, this ship's surgeon turned empire-builder managed to get surprisingly far on slender resources. Lengthy survey tours of Hawaii, Oahu, and Kauai and his attention to local resources and to planting testify to his zeal and energy. Under watchful supervision he would have made an excellent plantation manager. Could his gains have been taken over by some soberer head, a role Kotzebue might have played, Russia might have salvaged at least a foothold in the islands to the benefit of her possessions in eastern Siberia and Alaska. As it was, Schäffer's fleeting success merely typified Russia's own brief rise in the North Pacific, due largely to the absence of any effective competition. Baranov's forced retirement in 1819, which ended the forward policy he had pursued practically single-handed for the Russian-American Company, the death of Kamehameha and the arrival of the missionaries in Hawaii, and the rapid increase of foreign shipping all signalled a new era in Pacific affairs in which Russia could take only a limited part.

Stuart Ramsay Tompkins was born in Canada and received his doctorate in 1931 from the University of Chicago. He is now an emeritus professor of the University of Oklahoma, where he taught for many years. "Drawing the Alaskan Boundary," which follows, is an excellent example of how Alaskan history was often tied to complex international affairs. The article is from the Canadian Historical Review, *XXVI (March, 1945), 1–24.*

Drawing the Alaskan Boundary[1]

STUART R. TOMPKINS

laska's boundary seems to defy geography and common sense. The clean slash that marks the 141st meridian moves unerring from north to south across the ridges but stops just short of the Pacific. From St. Elias it straggles to the southeast across the mountains, enclosing a long appendage that reaches as far south as Dixon Entrance and bars access to the interior. This anomalous pattern was conceived a little over a century ago by diplomats of three powers called to reconcile competing national claims.

But in 1824 and 1825 the agreements grew in part only out of conflicting territorial claims in these regions. They reflected also the growing rift between Great Britain and Russia in their relation to the concert of Europe and the diplomatic crisis in-

[1] The original Monroe Doctrine emphasized two guiding principles in Europe's relation to the American continent; (1) non-intervention as regards the Latin American states then struggling for independence; (2) non-colonization of unoccupied parts of the continent. Studies of the Monroe Doctrine give scant attention to the second, and general works on the diplomacy of this period are of little help in discussing it.

83

volving Spain's colonies that accompanied French intervention in Spain in 1823. One must therefore set the conflict in north-western America against the general international background. Purely commercial interests, however, precipitated the diplo-matic struggle.

The north-west coast of America had originally been regarded as Spain's under the claims she had established by the Papal Bull of 1493 and the Treaty of 1494 with Portugal. This claim for long was not seriously challenged. But beginning in 1741, Rus-sian explorers had moved from Okhotsk in Siberia across the Pacific Ocean. The chance discovery of the sea-otter, for whose pelts keen demand arose in China, inspired a feverish search for this wealth by companies operating from Okhotsk. Posts were founded on the islands, and even the mainland came under Russian sway. Spain met this challenge by advancing her posts from Mexico northward into upper California and by dispatch-ing maritime expeditions to the north Pacific. She showed only a languid interest in the fur trade, her principal aim being to exclude rivals.[2] But she began shortly to encounter more dan-gerous competitors, the English. Captain Cook's third voyage in 1778 and the wealth in furs disclosed stimulated English interest and enterprise in that region. After 1788 Spain had to face equally formidable rivals — the Yankee traders from Bos-ton. In 1790 she engaged in a test of strength with England for possession of the coast, a struggle in which she came off second best. Thereafter she was gradually eased out of the north Pa-cific.[3]

[2] Regarding Spain's interest in the fur trade see Adele Ogden, *The California Sea Otter Trade, 1784–1848* (University of California Publications in History, XXVI, Berkeley and Los Angeles, 1941).

[3] The convention of the Escurial in 1790 ostensibly settled only the rights of Britain at Nootka Sound and agreed that her ships were free to navigate the waters of the north-west coast. But whatever the wording of the treaty, contem-poraries regarded it as ringing down the curtain on Spain's monopoly and the recognition of England's claims on the coast. See the admission of the Spanish king in 1790 as reported in Floridablanca's letter to Iriarte, November 21, 1790. "English trade and settlements were limited to that part of the coast north of Nootka," William Ray Manning, "The Nootka Sound Controversy" (*Annual Report of the American Historical Association* 1904, 458).

The encroachment of English and American traders threatened Russian interest too, already weakened by feuds between rival companies and in 1799 the Russian government moved to put an end to this chaotic state of affairs by granting a monopoly in the fur trade on the north-west coast of America, the islands, and the coasts of Siberia to the Russian American Company. The charter granted this company the exclusive right to the fur trade on all parts of the American coast north of latitude 55° north. They (the company) were authorized to prosecute their explorations not only within these limits but also, "further to the south, and to occupy the new lands so discovered as Russian possessions, if they have not been previously occupied by, or been dependent on any other nation."[4] The charter was never notified to foreign governments but failure to challenge it later prejudiced the British case. Moreover, the Napoleonic Wars more and more hampered British commerce and by the end of the century the British flag had all but disappeared from the seas. Britain's interests were, however, being advanced from the landward side. Alexander McKenzie of the North West Company, the first explorer to cross the continent in latitudes north of Mexico, had pushed over the mountains to the mouth of the Bella Coola River in 1793. The North West Company had posts to the west of these mountains by 1806 and were in a fair way to reach the sea first had they not been forestalled by John Jacob Astor who planted a trading post at the mouth of the Columbia River in 1810.

American trade with the north-west coast had expanded phenomenally after 1800. This continued encroachment on the Russian monopoly led that government to lodge protests in Washington, particularly against the trade of the Yankee ship-owners

[4] *Proceedings of the Alaska Boundary Tribunal Convened at London . . . under the Treaty concluded at Washington, January 24, 1903. . . .* (Washington, Government Printing Office, 1904, 7 vols., 56–2, Sen. Doc. 162, Ser. 4600), II, App. 23–5; hereinafter cited as *Alaska Boundary Tribunal.* Also *Polnoe Sobranie Zakonov Rossiiskoi Imperii* (Complete Collection of Laws of the Russian Empire) (44 vols., St. Petersburg, 1830), XXV, Text 19, 233. Russia's occupation of Fort Ross near Bodega Bay on the California coast would come under this head.

in liquor and firearms, a deadly combination which imperilled Russia's tenuous control over the natives. These protests were disregarded, but Astor shrewdly sought to play on Russia's fears by a proposal to Baranov to divide the coast between them. While Baranov temporized, the War of 1812 and the loss of Astoria to the English North West Company extinguished Astor's interests. The restoration of Astoria to nominal American sovereignty in 1818 under the terms of the Treaty of Ghent was not intended to affect the claims of either side, though astute use was made of this by Adams to prejudice the claims of Great Britain.[5]

Meanwhile in 1811 the Russian American Company itself had thrown down the gauntlet not only to Spain but to their other rivals, the United States and Great Britain, by moving southward to latitude 38° (approximately) where they established Fort Ross near Bodega Bay, allegedly to supply the northern posts with grain and meat. This foothold was maintained against the protests of Spain in the hope that a favourable turn of events would render it permanent. It was not surrendered until 1841.[6]

[5] See memorandum of H. U. Addington, May 10, 1826, in Edward John Stapleton (ed.), *Some Official Correspondence of George Canning, 1821–1827* (2 vols., London, 1887), II, 113–15. According to Addington, in spite of the admonition of Castlereagh that in restoring Astoria, special reservation was to be made of English rights, such reservation was not made in writing; and "by an equal fatality, the reservation of the territorial claims enjoined by Earl Bathurst on those appointed to deliver Fort Astoria . . . to the Americans in 1818, was omitted in the Publick Act passed on that occasion between the parties."

The only account taken of this by Adams appears in his instructions to Rush, July 22, 1822, "about the time of the conclusion of the Convention of 1818, some vague intimation was given by Mr. Bagot of British claims on the northwest coast. The restoration of the place and the convention of 1818 [on the joint use of the subjects of both countries of the land lying west of the Rocky Mountains] was considered as a final disposition of Mr. Bagot's objections" (*Alaska Boundary Tribunal*, II, App. 55).

[6] The occupation of Fort Ross was the work of the company and could, as a last resort, be disavowed. The persistency with which the post was retained, is a pretty good indication that the government countenanced such retention and would ultimately turn it to account. Muraviev is authority for the statement that in 1823 the government had refused the company's request to take over

The efforts to settle a number of outstanding differences between Great Britain and the United States led to these con-
troversial issues being submitted to the Tsar Alexander for arbitration. The territorial question was, however, dealt with by
a special commission consisting of Frederick J. Robinson and
Henry Goulburn for Great Britain and Richard Rush and Albert Gallatin for the United States. It was found impossible
to agree on a boundary and in lieu of this the Commissioners
decided that all the country lying to the west of the Rocky
Mountains should be open to the citizens of both countries on
equal terms. While claims of both countries were specifically
reserved, the United States rights were recognized for the first
time in the territory north of the 49th parallel — a factor which
was to play a considerable role in later negotiations.[7]

The following year the United States advanced her claim still
further by signing with Spain the Adams-Onis Treaty of 1819
according to the terms of which the northern boundary of
Spain's possessions was fixed at the 42nd parallel of latitude.[8]
The whole situation, therefore, in the north Pacific was in a
state of tension with three powers remaining in the contest —
Russia, Great Britain, and the United States — all with claims
that had to be recognized.

The first charter of the Russian American Company lapsed
on July 8, 1819. On July 31 its privileges were provisionally extended to allow the Ministry of the Interior time (one year spe-

---

California (Ivan Barsukov, *Graf Nikolai Nikolaevich Muraviev-Amurskii*, Moscow, 1891, I, 321).

[7] The instructions to this commission, the negotiations, and the convention
finally agreed on are to be found in *American State Papers, Foreign Relations*,
IV, 370–406.

[8] *Ibid.*, 623–4. The Treaty with Spain provides in Article 3: "The United
States hereby cedes to His Catholic Majesty, and renounces forever all the
rights, claims, and pretensions to the territories lying west and south of the
said line; and in like manner, His Catholic Majesty cedes to the United States all
his rights, claims and pretensions to any territories east and north of the said
line, and, for himself, his heirs, and successors, renounces all claim to the
said territories forever." This somewhat indefinite provision would not seem
to be of much value as a title deed to any special tract of land. It was, however,
later invoked by Adams in his despatch to Rush, July 22, 1823 (*ibid.*, V, 446),
but was never regarded as other than the lawyer's formula "or in the alternative."

cifically) to gather information on the company's operations and to submit to the Emperor recommendations for his action.[9] A committee named for this purpose conducted hearings during the course of the following months and in due time submitted its report which dealt primarily with injury caused to its trade by American and English interlopers. On the basis of this an ukase proclaimed September 4 / 16, 1821, recited in the preamble how, "the trade of our subjects on the Aleutian Islands and on the northwest coast of America, appertaining to Russia, is subject, because of secret and illicit traffic, to oppression and impediments."[10] It specifically reserved to Russian subjects the pursuit of commerce, whaling, fishery, and all other industry within an area extending from Bering Strait to the 51st° of latitude on the American coast and on the Asiatic side, from the Strait to 45° 50′ (the southern tip of Urup Island in the Kuriles). Foreign vessels were not to approach within one hundred Italian miles of the coasts. On September 13 / 25 the new charter was finally issued. In somewhat more precise language the company was granted "the privilege of carrying on to the exclusion of other Russians and of the subjects of foreign states, all industries connected with the capture of wild animals and all fishing industries on the shores of northwestern America which have from time immemorial belonged to Russia, commencing from the northern point of the Island of Vancouver, under 51° north latitude to Bering Straits and beyond them, and on the islands which belong to that coast, as well as on the other situated between it and the eastern shore of Siberia, and also on the Kurile Islands where the Company has carried on industries, as far as the outer tip of the Island of Urup under 45° 50′."[11]

The purpose of this was effectively to exclude American and

[9] *Polnoe Sobranie*, XXXVI, Text 27,906, decree of July 31, 1819.

[10] *Ibid.*, XXXVII, Text 28,747. An English translation containing the essential parts is to be found in *Alaska Boundary Tribunal*, II, App. 25, 26.

[11] *Polnoe Sobranie*, XXXVII, Text 28,756, and *Alaska Boundary Tribunal*, II, App. 27. The word industry (in the sense of craft) is a direct translation of the Russian word "promysl" — a general term applied to hunting, trapping, and fishing. The word "promyshlenniki" — literally craftsmen — are those who carry on such crafts or "industries."

English ships from carrying on trade in furs in the coastal waters of the North Pacific. Instructions went forth at once to the ambassadors abroad to bring this pronouncement to the attention of the respective governments to which they were accredited.

The language of Castlereagh on hearing of this, "that His Britannic Majesty must be understood as hereby reserving all his rights" was the warning growl of the British lion. In Washington the action was less abrupt. "The President . . . has seen with surprise" were the words used by John Quincy Adams. The wheels of diplomacy began to revolve and three world powers prepared for a trial of strength for the possession of the areas bounding the South Seas.[12]

The preliminary negotiations opened at Washington in the early months of 1822. The ill health of Poletika, the Russian ambassador, led to their being interrupted. Meanwhile the Russian government appointed Baron Tuyll as the former's successor. Tuyll delayed his departure, and in the interval the Russian government, finding their position challenged by both Great Britain and the United States, saw the advantages of having negotiations with both powers conducted by the same plenipotentiaries. Since this could be done only at the Russian capital, they were transferred to St. Petersburg. Meanwhile, other more pressing matters tended to crowd the issue in the north Pacific into the background. As a result of the revolt in Greece, and the revolution in Spain, a call went out to the members of the Quadruple Alliance to send representatives to Vienna to consider the threat to Europe's peace.[13] Here, England standing aside, her allies gave France authority to invade Spain and to restore the power of King Ferdinand as absolute monarch. The dispute in the north Pacific was, it is true, broached by the Duke of Wellington,[14] but his somewhat perfunctory protest was met

[12] The Russian government, pending a peaceful settlement wisely decided not to enforce the rules. See footnote 20.

[13] Later moved to Verona.

[14] Named plenipotentiary to take the place of Castlereagh who had just died.

with the suggestion that these matters could better be discussed in St. Petersburg.

The ukase of September 4, 1821, contained two features that were objectionable alike from the British and American point of view; first, the exclusion of all foreign shipping from waters extending one hundred Italian miles from shore; secondly, the extension of Russia's territorial claims as far south as the 51st parallel of latitude.

The powers of a plenipotentiary were issued to Sir Charles Bagot on February 20, 1823, but these made no mention of the territorial dispute and provided solely for discussion with Russia. Before Bagot had been able to launch the negotiations they were, owing to a series of unforeseen complications, practically suspended for six months.

Meanwhile in Washington the recall of Pierre Poletika, the Russian ambassador, who had initiated the discussions, and the arrival of the new ambassador, Baron Tuyll, with a request from the Emperor that Henry Middleton, United States ambassador at St. Petersburg, receive powers as a plenipotentiary, suggested to the Secretary of State, John Quincy Adams, the advantages of acting jointly with England. The upshot was a suggestion to this effect, made to the British ambassador, and by him conveyed to the Foreign Secretary Canning.[15] The invitation which was cordial in tone contained this extraordinary statement, "He [Adams] added that the United States had no territorial claims of their own as high as the 51st degree of latitude. . . ." This was relayed by George Canning to Bagot with this caution: "The part of the question in which the American government is peculiarly desirous of establishing a concert with this country is that which concerns the extravagant assumption of maritime jurisdiction . . . the other part of the question which relates to territorial claims and boundary is perhaps susceptible of separate adjustment."[16] Canning had not been officially approached

---

[15] *Alaska Boundary Tribunal*, II, App. 120–1, Despatch of Mr. Stratford Canning to Mr. George Canning, dated Washington, May 3, 1823 (received June 12).

[16] *Ibid.*, App. 123–4, Despatch of Mr. George Canning to Sir Charles Bagot, July 12, 1823.

by Rush in this matter. Hence the cautious wording of his despatch. Despite this Bagot interpreted this communication as a directive and he informed Nesselrode that he and Middleton would probably act together. "Count Nesselrode being upon the eve of setting out to join the Emperor . . . I have thought it advisable even in the absence of those further instructions which you lead me to expect in your despatch No. 12, of the 12th of last month, to apprise him of the probability of Mr. Middleton and myself being soon instructed to act jointly in negotiating with him some proposition for the definitive settlement of that part at least of the question growing out of the Imperial Ukase of 4th (16th) September, 1821." [17]

Bagot expected further instructions but in the absence of these he adhered to the view that joint action with the United States was to be restricted to the question of "the extravagant assumption of maritime jurisdiction" marking time meanwhile on the territorial question.

The official documents give us an incomplete version of these preliminary discussions.[18] Turning to Bagot's private letters to Canning we find they reflect intense concern over the factors that had delayed negotiations and on which he was imperfectly informed. Moreover, the issues to be settled had not been clearly defined. Hence he asks in a letter of March 1, 1823: is he to negotiate for a line of demarcation, or (2) is he to negotiate for common occupancy; (3) is the virtual declaration of the north Pacific a *mare clausum* to be the subject of negotiation? A letter of June 2, 1823, indicates his impatience at the delay caused by the Russian government. By August 31 he had opened the battle by sounding out Nesselrode (in accordance with Canning's instructions of July 12), in the hope of forestalling his rival Middleton:

[17] *Fur Seal Arbitration, Proceedings of Tribunal of Arbitration convened at Paris* (Washington, Government Printing Office, 1895, 53–2, Sen. Doc. 177, Ser. 3166), part 4, IV, 407–81, Despatch of Sir Charles Bagot to Mr. George Canning, August 19/31, 1823 (received September 23).

[18] Preliminary because neither the American nor the Russian plenipotentiaries had received their powers. Middleton's did not arrive till October, 1823, those of Nesselrode and Poletika were not issued till 1824.

I hope you will not think that I have run too fast in the American question. I have feared that Middleton might any day receive his instructions directly from Washington which might lead him to talk to Nesselrode before I had done so. This would have been inconvenient. As it is I have got hold of Nesselrode first and have put the matter to him in a way for which he is grateful. He hates Middleton and Jonathan *comme de raison*, and he has fairly acknowledged to me that he is delighted to have us to protect him against them and to keep them in order.[19]

Nevertheless he continued (as did Middleton) to assume that in the matter of maritime jurisdiction the two countries would treat jointly with Russia. In the course of these discussions Middleton revealed the negotiations undertaken the previous year (1822) when the first United States protests had been lodged against the ukase.

Middleton now tells me what I was not before aware of, that he had last year by direction of the President, several interviews with Count Nesselrode and Count Capodistrias upon the subject of this ukase and that it was at length agreed that he should inquire officially what were the intentions of the Imperial government in regard to the execution of it, an assurance being previously given that the answer he should receive would be satisfactory. Mr. Middleton has been good enough to furnish me with a copy of this answer, which I now enclose. As however, he considered the communication of the paper as personally confidential, I take the liberty of requesting that no public use be made of it.[20]

[19] Bagot Papers, II, part 3, Letters from Sir Charles Bagot to Mr. George Canning, March 22, June 2, and August 31, 1823. The direct quotation is from the letter of August 31.

The Public Archives of Canada have copies of the private correspondence of Sir Charles Bagot with Canning, carried on while Ambassador at Washington and St. Petersburg.

[20] *Alaska Boundary Tribunal*, II, App. 126, Despatch Sir Charles Bagot to Mr. George Canning, August 19/31, 1823 (received September 23). These negotiations touched not so much on the offending provisions of the ukase with regard to the exclusions of foreign (i.e., non-Russian) shipping, as on their enforcement. To render the atmosphere more favourable for negotiations on this delicate matter, the Russian government agreed for the time being not to attempt to enforce the offending clauses without, however, withdrawing the ukase. Much the same information had been conveyed indirectly to the English. See despatch

Main street of Nome, around the turn of the century. Photograph courtesy of the Bancroft Library

Alaskan volcano seen from English Bay, Cook Inlet. From Dixon's Voyage

Sitka, 1805. From Lisianskii's Voyage

Veniaminov as Metropolitan Innocent.

An artist's depiction of the occasion of the treaty-signing that completed the transfer of Alaska from Russia to the United States. Photograph courtesy Alaska Centennial Commission

C.S.S. Shenandoah. *Photograph from National Archives, courtesy of B. F. Gilbert*

George Davidson. *Photograph courtesy of Bancroft Library*

Sheldon Jackson. *Photograph courtesy of* Pacific Northwest Quarterly

Main street of Chena, Alaska. Photograph courtesy of Bancroft Library
Veniaminov as Metropolitan Innocent

With regard to the territorial dispute, he writes: "I have explained to Count Nesselrode that the United States making no pretensions to territory so high as the 51st degree of north latitude, the question rests between His Majesty and the Emperor of Russia alone, and becomes therefore a matter for separate settlement by their respective governments. . . ."[21] On these assumptions Bagot had begun his preliminary discussions directly with the Russian ministers on the question of boundary, leaving the maritime problem to be the subject of joint negotiations later, a course that was to be fruitful in misunderstandings.

The instructions to him had put the territorial question in the vaguest terms. Bagot himself on his own responsibility challenged Russia's claims south of 59° north latitude.[22] But Canning had suggested 57°.[23] Two considerations made a parallel of latitude an awkward boundary line. One was the general northwest to south-east trend of the coast south of Yakutat Bay; the other was the uncertainty as to how far east such cession should reach. Too great an extent would threaten the trading rights of the Hudson's Bay Company in the Mackenzie River valley as well as in the area between the Rocky Mountains and the sea. During the course of Bagot's discussions with Poletika this became obvious. As he turned the matter over in his mind, it occurred to Bagot that he could meet these difficulties by a novel solution. Still continuing to mark time while waiting for definite word from London, he wrote to Canning:

---

of Middleton to Adams, August 8, 1822, giving account of the former's interview with Capodistrias and the enclosures, letter addressed to Nesselrode (July 27) and the reply (August 1). In his letter to Nesselrode Middleton calls himself "envoy extraordinary and minister plenipotentiary" although his powers were not received till a year later (*ibid.*, App. 42–6).

The same assurance was conveyed to the United States government on his arrival in Washington. See Despatch of Nesselrode to Tuyll, July 13 (o.s.) 1822 ("Correspondence of the Russian Ministers in Washington, 1818–1825," *American Historical Review*, XVIII, Jan. 1913, 335–44).

[21] *Alaska Boundary Tribunal*, II, App. 126, Despatch of Sir Charles Bagot to Mr. George Canning, August 19/31, 1823 (received September 23).

[22] *Ibid.*

[23] *Ibid.*, App. 124.

I have half a mind to exceed my instructions and try if I cannot get a degree of longitude instead of latitude for our line of demarcation. It appears to me that if we take a degree of latitude we leave Russia with undefined pretensions to the eastward and in the interior of the continent, whereas a degree of longitude would describe both the boundary on the coast and within the continent at the same time. I do not know whether Russia would listen to such a proposition but it would, I think, be a great point if we could get somewhere about the 139th degree of west longitude as the line. This would cut the coast about Bering's Bay (Yakutat) to the south of which Russia has in fact no pretensions whatever, to discovery or anything else. This would make the latitude of our boundary about 59½° instead of 57° with which you say you would be contented. If I am to secure 57° it may at all events be as well to begin by claiming something more, and I have some notion of bringing forward this idea. . . . You may depend upon it that the Americans will try to interfere somehow or other in our boundary negotiations as distinguished from the maritime jurisdiction question. Mr. Middleton has already told me clearly that he thinks the United States have an interest in the business and upon what grounds? Because Spain had, by treaty, the right to trade with our coasts in that quarter and that the United States by their last treaty have acquired all the rights in that respect and stand in her shoes. Is not this preposterous? [24]

Still the word so impatiently awaited did not come.

Some days later Bagot's composure was rudely disturbed when he discovered that both he and George Canning had been in the dark as to the real intentions of the United States. This was owing to the facile assurance given by Stratford Canning that the United States had no "territorial pretensions as high as the fifty-first degree of north latitude." [25] Canning had been misled and far from being entirely disinterested in the territorial issue, the United States was prepared to assert equal claims with Great Britain to the whole of the north-west coast. [26]

[24] Bagot Papers, II, part 3, Letter from Sir Charles Bagot to Mr. George Canning, October 5, 1823.

[25] Conveyed in his despatch of May 3, 1823. See footnote 15.

[26] *Alaska Boundary Tribunal*, II, App. 129–30. Confidential despatch from Sir Charles Bagot to Mr. George Canning, October 17/29, 1823.

Even Bagot had allowed his better judgment to be overborne. His disillusionment but strengthened him in his original resolution to pursue the territorial discussions separately. Signs of growing Russian confidence impelled him to endeavour to come to terms with Russia at once before broaching the subject with the United States. But to his great disquiet the home government was showing signs of weakening, as is seen from the following note received from the Foreign Office: "It is probable that since the settlement of Sitka, the Russians may have extended their possessions to the great adjacent island (Baranof). I should think therefore that if latitude 56° which takes in the whole of that island and longitude 225° (or what is the same thing 135° west) were assigned as the Russian limits, Chatham Strait, Lynn Canal, and a line running from the head of the latter in the direction of northwest, would form an unobjectionable boundary. Perhaps a sketch of this part of the chart might accompany Sir Charles Bagot's instructions." [27] But by the time of its receipt Canning's instructions directing him to conduct his entire negotiations apart from his American colleague were on the way.

So far we have followed events in Washington and St. Petersburg, a method which gives an incomplete picture. It was in London that we can see the impact of the various forces that were shaping events. Here the struggle for a few miles of rugged and inhospitable coast was overshadowed by the rise of the new republics in South America and the feverish partisanship that this evoked in the old world. Great Britain had in international affairs been veering from her allies in the Quadruple Alliance in their policy of constituting themselves custodians of Europe's peace and the implacable foes of revolution. In general, England's strong commercial ties, as well as her own revolutionary tradition, evoked sympathy with the constitutional government of Spain and the new states in South America and brought her interests into harmony with those of the United

[27] Bagot Papers, Correspondence Foreign Office, Document dated January 13, (1824 — in pencil). Probably a minute drawn up by a clerk to serve as a basis for instructions to Sir Charles Bagot.

States where public feeling was on the side of Spain's revolting colonies. But it was more or less by chance that this opportunity, fleeting as it was, arose for England and her own emancipated colonies to find a common interest in the cause of freedom.

Shortly after George Canning had become Secretary of State for Foreign Affairs in succession to Castlereagh, John Quincy Adams with his tireless energy had once more addressed himself to clearing up a number of matters that had remained unsettled since the signing of the Treaty of Ghent. He accordingly sent a series of despatches to Richard Rush with instructions that he approach Mr. Canning and initiate negotiations on these problems. The documents reached Rush on July 29, 1823, and he was told that a seventh to follow would deal with the north-west coast.[28] Rush had his first interview with Canning on August 16 on the subjects covered in the first six despatches, omitting to deal with the north-west coast, instructions on which had not then arrived. At the conclusion of this interview Rush referred to still another matter on which he appears to have had some lead from Adams. "The proper object of it [the interview] over, I transiently asked him whether notwithstanding the late news from Spain, we might not still hope that the Spaniards would get the better of their difficulties."

He further suggested that: ". . . Should France ultimately effect her purpose of overthrowing the constitutional government in Spain, there was at least the consolation left, that Great Britain would not allow her to go further and stop the progress of emancipation in the colonies."[29] The words struck a responsive chord in Canning, but for the moment he contented himself with innocuous platitudes and the conference was at an end. Canning, however, carefully weighed Rush's remarks and at his next interview on August 22 returned to the subject of South America. On this occasion he proposed that Great Britain and the United States should issue a joint declaration on the subject

[28] Richard Rush, *Memoranda of a Residence at the Court of London* (Philadelphia, 1845), 396.
[29] *Ibid.*, 399.

of the Spanish-American colonies. Thus negotiations between Rush and Canning took an entirely new direction.

In a subsequent interview (August 27) Rush pressed Canning for recognition by Great Britain "of the independence of the new communities" as a necessary condition of such joint action.[30] But Canning balked at this as he considered recognition by England premature. The matter continued, however, to be discussed in later interviews until November 26 when, an agreement having proved impossible, it was dropped. At this point Canning began to pick up once more the threads of the controversy of the north-west coast not yet included in the agenda of matters to be discussed at London.

On December 12 as he was about to give Bagot final instructions for his guidance in this matter at St. Petersburg, he suggested that Rush communicate to him the views of the United States government on this matter. Canning in the meantime being taken down with gout, the scene is shifted to the sick room in Gloucester Lodge which, on the occasion of their next discussion, became the audience chamber of the Minister of State. There, propped up on pillows, and with his maps spread out before him, Canning listened to Rush explain the demands of the United States to be a party to any territorial settlement between Great Britain and Russia. Whatever his feelings he restrained them and merely murmured, as Rush took his leave, that "our claim seemed much beyond anything England had anticipated."[31]

For two weeks the American ambassador heard nothing. Whether it was the gout, or whether it was the shock of the disclosures that had overtaxed the patient, Canning remained in the seclusion of his home. Then at the end of a fortnight he had sufficiently recovered from both to pen this message to Rush: "What can this intend? Our northern question is with Russia as our southern is with the United States. But do the United States mean to travel north to get between us and Russia?"

[30] The United States had already agreed to recognize the new governments.

[31] The circumstances of the famous interview and of the subsequent correspondence is recounted in Rush, *Memoranda*, 467–9.

Rush's laconic reply that "it was even so" did not spare the sick man. The shock caused by this revelation had scarcely worn off when the text of President Monroe's message to Congress came to hand. The words — "that the American continents . . . are henceforth not to be considered as subjects for future colonization by any European power," [32] directed in the first instance against Russia, were now ostensibly turned against England. Canning, at length recovered, braced himself for the struggle and drew up the final instructions to Bagot which would take account of this new complication.

The long delay of London in coming to some decision on the matter of joint negotiations is only partly to be explained by pre-occupation with other matters. Misunderstanding also played its part. It appears that Adams had intended to reach an agreement with England on the north-west coast before proceeding to joint negotiations in St. Petersburg. The north-west coast was only one among seven different matters which it was proposed to refer to a special commission. Indeed, Adams, in his letter of instructions to Rush, distinctly says, "Among the subjects of negotiation with Great Britain which are pressing upon the attention of this Government is the present condition of the north-west coast of this continent." [33] There was, therefore, no reason why Rush should hurry Canning on this matter since it would be dealt with in due course. But apparently both Canning and Rush were at cross purposes, the former waiting for a fuller communication from Washington while Rush rather leisurely proceeded to gather up the threads of negotiations in London, unconcerned over those proceeding at St. Petersburg. It was only when word had been received back in London from the Russian capital that Canning had approached Rush:

> Upon receipt of Your Excellency's dispatch No. 48 reporting the arrival of Mr. Hughes at St. Petersburg with the instructions

[32] *American State Papers, Foreign Relations*, V, 246, Message of the President of the United States at the commencement of the 1st Session of the Eighteenth Congress, December 2, 1823.

[33] *Alaska Boundary Tribunal*, II, App. 52, Despatch of Mr. Adams to Mr. Rush, July 22, 1823.

of the Government of the United States to Mr. Middleton, I applied to Mr. Rush for information as to the tenor of these instructions. I then found what I had not before been led to expect, that Mr. Rush had himself authority to enter into negotiations with us as to the respective claims of Great Britain and the United States on the northwest coast of America, although he does not appear to have been instructed to invite such negotiation here if we should prefer leaving it to be conducted at St. Petersburg.[34]

Canning had from the beginning been reluctant to reopen England's dispute with the United States since the agreement of 1818 had still five years to run.[35] But in failing to do so he allowed the United States to become, under the terms of the Convention of 1818, a party to settling the boundary between Britain and Russia.[36]

When Adams invited Great Britain to take part in joint negotiations he had casually disclaimed (at least Stratford Canning had so asserted) any interest for the United States beyond the 51st parallel of latitude. In his instructions to his ministers in London and St. Petersburg he gives signs of no such disinterestedness. In a document called "Observations on the Claim of Russia to Territorial Possessions on the Continent of North America," communicated with Mr. Adams's letter of July 22, 1823, to Mr. Middleton we read: "With the exception of the

[34] *Ibid.*, App. 144–9, Despatch of Mr. George Canning to Sir Charles Bagot, January 15, 1824.

[35] *Ibid.*

[36] Stratford Canning had on Christmas Eve, 1823, warned the Foreign Secretary that of the two matters at issue with Russia the maritime could not be adjusted without settling the territorial. To achieve the latter, a prior understanding must be reached with the United States.

He opposed the tri-partite agreement which Canning was considering and strongly recommended coming to terms with the United States essential to a satisfactory settlement with Russia, emphasizing the paramountcy of England's interest in the region of the Columbia River over those to the north. "Is it not primarily by contracting our claws to the north we may hope to obtain a permanent share in the possession of the great wealth of the Columbia"? Canning failed to take this good advice and by attempting to settle with Russia without coming to a prior understanding with the United States, suffered a diplomatic defeat. See Bagot Papers, Correspondence regarding the Russian ukase of 1821, 48, Letter of Mr. Stratford Canning to Mr. George Canning, December 24, 1823, Berkeley Square.

British establishments north of the United States, the remainder of both the American continents must henceforth be
left to the management of American hands . . . the United
States can in no wise admit the right of Russia to exclusive
territorial possession on any part of the continent of North
America south of the 60th degree of north latitude."[37] He instructed Middleton — "With regard to territorial claims . . . we
are willing to agree to the boundary line within which the Emperor Paul granted exclusive privileges to the Russian American Company, that is to say, latitude 55°." A passing reference
to Great Britain's claim and a hint at the possibility of joint negotiations dismisses Britain's case. It is suggested that — "as the
British Ambassador at St. Petersburg is authorized and instructed to negotiate likewise upon this subject, it may be proper
to adjust the interests and claims of the three powers by a joint
convention."[38] He enclosed a project for a treaty between the
United States and Russia setting the 55th parallel of latitude as
their boundary.

Adams's intentions are set forth with greater fullness in his
letter of instructions of the same day to Rush in London. In
these, 55° and 51° assume a slightly different aspect, the one
the British boundary as against Russia in the north, the other
as against the United States to the south. Bagot was partly prepared for the revelation that the United States had extensive
claims north of 51°, but the announcement of President Monroe's message to Congress on December 2 and the decision of
Canning to proceed alone, marked the end of the truce and
brought the two ambassadors at the Russian capital face to face.
"What do you think those original instructions [from Adams to
Middleton] were? Nothing less than to proceed to divide the
whole coast between Her and the United States to our entire
exclusion. . . . Now there does appear to me to be a baseness
in this business on the part of Adams which nobody but
Adams was capable of. But this trick has failed . . . I shall con-

[37] *American State Papers, Foreign Relations,* V, 445–6.
[38] *Alaska Boundary Tribunal,* II, App. 47–51, Letter of Adams to Middleton,
July 22, 1823.

clude certainly speedily, and I think satisfactorily, our separate arrangements and Adams may bellow as much as he pleases." [39] Evidently the period of waiting had resulted in a certain exacerbation of feelings (of which Russia was not slow to avail herself). Finally on February 12, 1824, the Russian plenipotentiaries received their powers. Bagot was now in receipt of his final instructions from Canning and official conferences were opened.

Nor had Middleton been inactive during the interlude. He had submitted his first confidential memorial to the Emperor in December, 1823, and apparently had conversations with Bagot regarding the respective claims of their countries. Of the discussion between them, Bagot had this to say in a private letter to Canning: "This project is, I have no doubt, the modification of that which Mr. Middleton was originally furnished to negotiate about territorial demarcation and everything else, without us and to our exclusion. . . . The duplicity of the American government as it regards us, has, you may depend upon it been extreme and I heartily hope that Squinty Adams may lose his election of it." [40]

The negotiations were thus begun by each country separately and carried on independently with little communication between the British and the American representatives. Middleton, however, at the start served notice on both the Russian government and Sir Charles Bagot "that if any attempt was made to negotiate upon territorial questions without our participation, it would become my duty to protest in the strongest terms." He also asserted the claim of the United States, till then officially unknown to Bagot, that "the said [United] States have concurrent rights, claims and pretensions with Great Britain to whatever point here may be considered to extend." [41] On the first

[39] *Bagot Papers*, II, Part 3, Letter of Sir Charles Bagot to Mr. George Canning, February 17, 1824.

[40] *Ibid.*, Letter of Sir Charles Bagot to Mr. George Canning, February 28, 1824.

[41] *Alaska Boundary Tribunal*, II, App. 70–1, Despatch from Middleton to Adams, April 7/19, 1824. It is questionable whether Middleton's statement is true. For specific terms of the convention see *American State Papers, Foreign Relations*, IV, 406, footnote 8.

point Bagot had already been instructed by Canning to make reservation of the claims of the United States as had been done in the convention of 1818, that "the agreement between the contracting powers should not be taken to affect the claims of any other power or state in any part of the said country."

The conferences of Middleton proceeded without further incident. At the outset, after some preliminary sparring, he offered the Russians in return for abrogation of the offending maritime clause in the ukase of 1821, and for trading privileges along the coast, recognition of the territorial boundary of 55°, thus at the beginning, proposing to buy concessions by a horse trade.[42] With this bait dangled before them the Russian plenipotentiaries made little difficulty and by the first of April they had succeeded in hammering out a convention that was mutually satisfactory. It was agreed that the parallel of 54° 40′ north latitude was to be the southern limit of Russian occupation or settlement, and the northern limit of such by citizens of the United States.[43] All parts of the north Pacific Ocean were to be open to the subjects of both powers without discrimination for purposes of trade or fishing, with the stipulation that they were not to resort to a part of the coast occupied by the other power without permission. For ten years the ships of both powers were to be free to frequent coastal waters. Traffic in firearms and liquor was forbidden.

The conferences between Bagot and the Russian plenipotentiaries opened on February 28 and ran concurrently with those with the United States ambassador. From the beginning there

---

[42] This does not seem to have been lost on Canning, for he wrote: "It does not seem very uncharitable to suppose that the object of the United States in making a selection, otherwise wholly arbitrary, of these two points of limitation for British dominion, was to avoid collision with Russia themselves, and to gratify Russia at the expense of Great Britain" (*Alaska Boundary Tribunal*, II, App. 146, Despatch of Mr. George Canning to Sir Charles Bagot, January 15, 1824).

[43] The boundary was set at 54°40′ instead of 55° since the latter would have cut Prince of Wales Island. It seemed preferable to assign to Russia the whole of the island to do which it was necessary to fix the boundary so that it would pass south of the southern extremity (*American State Papers, Foreign Relations*, V, 459, 465; *Alaska Boundary Tribunal*, II, App. 161).

was a stiffness and lack of cordiality that boded no good. At the outset Bagot submitted a proposal originally suggested by Count Lieven in London on January 21 that, "The question of strict right should be provisionally waived on both sides and that the adjustment of our mutual pretensions should be made upon the sole principle of the respective convenience of both countries." This was accepted.

Two things hampered the British representative from the beginning. First the retention of the 55th° of latitude as an approximate southern boundary was made by the Russians a face-saving issue.[44] The other was that the United States' representative had, despite his assertion of claim of United States rights concurrent with the British as far north as the extreme limit of their claims, already indicated that they were prepared to forget this if they secured the trading concessions which they wished. Moreover Bagot, following Canning's instructions of January 15, had modified his original proposal to take Cross Sound as the line separating Russian from British territory. But the selection of a north and south line dividing Prince of Wales Island from the mainland, would give United States ships access to the coastal waters (in British possession) and so render their exclusion from Russian waters difficult.[45] Bagot therefore was forced by the invincible opposition of the Russian plenipotenti-

[44] The Russian stand was in flat contradiction of the principle of "mutual convenience" which they had accepted. Logic perhaps was against them but the facts were with them. The United States having conceded this boundary, there was no alternative for Britain but to follow suit. The arguments are to be found in the letter of M. Poletika to Count Nesselrode, November 3, 1823 (o.s.) (*Alaska Boundary Tribunal*, II, App. 141) and in the letter from Count Nesselrode to Count Lieven, April 5/17 (*ibid.*, App. 173–5).

[45] This first proposal of Bagot had been made during his preliminary discussions with Poletika at a conference apparently on October 2, 1823. The line would run through Cross Sound and up Lynn Canal and then north along the 135th meridian of longitude, the head of Lynn Canal being slightly west of this meridian. It, of course, had no official validity and was presumably disavowed by Canning to permit Novo-Arkhangel'sk (Sitka) to be given to Russia (*ibid.*, App. 129–31, Letter (confidential) from Sir Charles Bagot to Mr. George Canning, October 17/29, 1823; Letter from M. Poletika to Count Nesselrode, with English translation, November 3 (o.s.), 1823 (received November 7/19, 1823), 132–42; also *ibid.*, U. S. Atlas, Map 3.

aries to agree to an east and west line — "the fifty-fifth degree of latitude as her boundary on the islands" — in order to preserve also an uninterrupted British access to the Pacific Ocean.[46] This necessarily involved imposing some eastward limit. To secure all the coastal waters the frontier must be some distance from the coast, which would give Russia a littoral.[47] This point was reluctantly conceded by Sir Charles but he sought to fix the southern limit of such a coastal strip at the 56th parallel. From the point where this parallel cut the coast the new line was to pass out through Sumner Strait to the ocean so as to assign Sitka and Baranof Island to Russia but Prince of Wales Island to Great Britain. This proposal was rejected by the Russians, however, who returned to their original terms, a frontier that would secure Russia possession of the whole of Prince of Wales Island, then traverse Portland Canal to the summit of the mountains (which were assumed to border the coast), and then pass along the summit of these mountains to the 139th° of longitude. Along this meridian it would proceed to the Arctic Ocean.[48]

This concession Bagot refused as going beyond his original instructions. Negotiations were thereupon broken off and Bagot decided to toss the problem of territorial delimitation back to the Home government. He assumed that the question of maritime jurisdiction could be dealt with. But Nesselrode refused to negotiate on one point till the other was settled and asserted

---

[46] The various stages in the negotiations of Bagot with the Russian plenipotentiaries are set forth in a despatch of March 17/29 from St. Petersburg and received in London, April 13 (*ibid.*, II, App. 153–7). See also *ibid*, U.S. Atlas, Map 3, for various British proposals.

[47] This argument that such a strip was necessary to bar the progress of the Hudson's Bay Company was advanced by Count de Lambert appointed to represent the Russian American Company in a conference with Poletika (*ibid.*, II, 137–8, Letter of M. Poletika to Count Nesselrode, November 3, 1823).

[48] Counter draft by the Russian plenipotentiaries (date as shown in the Russian archives, 12/24 February, 1824) enclosed in a letter from Sir Charles Bagot to Mr. George Canning, March 17/29, 1824 (*Ibid.*, II, App. 158).
The width of this "lisière" as conceived by the Russian American Company was somewhat vague. Admiral Mordvinov claimed for Russia everything up to the Rocky Mountains. Letter of Admiral Mordvinov to Count Nesselrode, 20 February, 3 March, 1824 (*ibid.*, App. 152).

that the offending article in the ukase of September 4, 1821, would stand until Russia's terms were met. Bagot's disappointment and chagrin at his discomfiture came out in his personal letter to Canning:

> They [the Russian government] must be dealt with as you would deal with a horse dealer. Their whole conduct in the late negotiations has been of the most huckstering and peddlarlike character and in my opinion they will not be brought to reason unless they are told roundly that if they will not arrange the matter equitably and according to our mutual present convenience, they shall not be allowed to settle anywhere upon these islands south of their present lowest establishment, viz, Sitca. They [Poletica and Nesselrode] are both under the dominion of the Russian American Company at the head of which is an old Admiral Mordvinoff, an honest man but mighty obstinate who mistakes obstinacy for patriotism.[49]

With matters reaching this complete deadlock Bagot referred the dispute back to Canning.

The secret of the unyielding attitude of Russia which Bagot characterized as that of "a horsetrader" is abundantly clear from the letter which Nesselrode penned to Lieven to guide him in the discussions he was instructed to open with Canning. He had chosen the convention of 1818 with the United States as the weak joint in Britain's armour.[50] By admitting the Americans to an equal share in the exploitation of the region beyond the mountains she had conceded the weakness of her claims to exclusive sovereignty. Russia having further strengthened her case by coming to terms with Britain's partner and rival, there was nothing left for Britain but to acquiesce and to accept the same or a similar boundary. Having now attained her main purpose, a settlement of the long-standing difficulties with the United

---

[49] *Bagot Papers*, II, part 3, Letter from Sir Charles Bagot to Mr. George Canning, March 29, 1824.

[50] This was not an afterthought on Nesselrode's part. He had written to Tuyll from Verona, December 2/14, 1822, that "by the convention of 1818 the territories adjacent to ours are to belong to both England and the United States for ten years" "Letter of Nesselrode to Tuyll" (*American Historical Review*, XVIII, Jan., 1913, 335–44).

States, Russia could afford to sit back and wait for England to come to her terms. To make it more palatable to Englishmen Lieven was to represent Russia's retreat from her extreme pretensions as proof of her moderation.[51] Nesselrode ironically suggested that Britain should compensate herself by an extension of her claims southward into Oregon.

Canning, already struggling in a maze of unsolved problems, was forced to take up this task anew. Caught as he was in a difficult international situation he had no choice but to compromise and on July 12 he forwarded to Bagot a draft convention seasoned to Muscovite taste by the master chef, Lieven himself. All he now hoped to achieve, aside from saving some fragment of self-esteem, was to secure trading privileges at Novo-Arkhangel'sk and along the coast; to restrict within the narrowest limits the Russian American Company's hold on the mainland. But compromise was of little use. Full capitulation was to be the price paid for the treaty. The offer of the right to trade at Novo-Arkhangel'sk without time limit was withdrawn.[52] Liberty to navigate and trade *forever* along the coast of the *lisière* was also refused, as well as the right to frequent other parts of the north-west coast (this refers to the parts of Alaska beyond the area in dispute) though it is only fair to Russia to add that these had not been contained in Russia's original offer. Bagot, therefore, threw up his hands, refused to sign and returned the "proj-

---

[51] *Alaska Boundary Tribunal*, II, App. 172–5, Despatch from Count Nesselrode to Count Lieven, April 5/17, 1824. The fallacy of advancing an extravagant claim and later to cite readiness to yield as proof of a conciliatory spirit was not lost on Bagot. See above private letter from Bagot to Canning. The subtle suggestion with regard to Oregon shows how cleverly Nesselrode played the two rivals off against one another.

[52] It is probable that this change was due to an unguarded statement of Canning's. The offer had originally been conveyed in the counter draft by the Russian plenipotentiaries, February 12/24, 1824 (*ibid.*, App. 158). That Nesselrode had been quite prepared to yield this point is evident from his letter to Lieven on April 5/17, 1824, cited above. But in writing to Count Lieven on May 29, 1824, Canning had said, "It can hardly be expected that we should not also put in our claim for like privileges of trade as are or may be stipulated with Russia by any other nation" (*ibid.*, App. 180). As the rights of the United States in this regard had been restricted to ten years it seems reasonable to suppose that Nesselrode had taken advantage of Canning's slip.

ect" with a "counter project" of the Russians to London for final decision. He rightly saw that the traditional British methods of conciliation and compromise had broken down.

The publication of the convention with the United States had raised a clamour of protests against the supposed sacrifice of Russian interests, Bagot pointed out. "Nesselrode and Poletika are now afraid of signing anything upon the subject in which there are not great and signal advantages secured to Russia. . . . I should like to have been the person to sign a treaty of such magnitude and importance and I should have ended my days here handsomely by doing so. But *Dis aliter visum est.* . . ." [53]

Bagot left St. Petersburg in the summer of 1824 without reaching an understanding with Russia. By early winter the British Cabinet had decided to yield on the major issues and Stratford Canning was sent over to bring negotiations to a conclusion. His instructions were "if the present project is agreeable to Russia we are ready to conclude and sign a treaty." [54] The only point now at issue was the width of the *lisière* to be conceded to Russia along the coast and the methods by which its boundaries should be fixed. Canning was determined to restrict it within the narrowest limits and, with this in mind, preferred to have the frontier run along the base of the mountains, a proposal that was rejected by the Russians for a suggestion that the crest of the range be followed. Canning yielded on this but insisted that it should at no point exceed ten marine leagues in width. This was grudgingly accepted by the Russians and on this sour note the negotiations came to an end. [55] One important concession came to the British more or less as an afterthought. This

[53] *Bagot Papers*, II, part 3, Personal letter from Sir Charles Bagot to Mr. George Canning, August 24, 1824.

[54] *Alaska Boundary Tribunal*, II, App., 212, Letter from Mr. George Canning to Mr. Stratford Canning, December 8, 1824.

[55] It seems strange that so trifling a matter should have called forth a peevish protest from Lieven. "Even before the receipt of that document, I had made it my duty to remark to the Secretary of State how ungracious the refusal of the English Government" (*ibid.*, App. 230, Letter of Count Lieven to Count Nesselrode, May 8/20, 1825).

was the shifting of the line that ran north from Mount St. Elias 2° westward.[56]

A further incident troubled the diplomatic waters. Adams records in his diary that one day in December, 1824, before the treaty could come before the Senate, he received a mysterious call from Baron Tuyll, the Russian ambassador. With evident embarrassment the latter informed him that the Russian government wished, in view of an outcry that had arisen against the clauses admitting United States ships to Russian coasts everywhere in the Pacific, to amend the treaty. Tuyll brought the suggestion that on the occasion of the exchange of ratifications an explanatory note be issued modifying the treaty to the extent of restricting commercial intercourse of Americans in the north Pacific to that part of the American coast south of latitude 57°. Adams at once warned the Russian envoy that such tampering with the treaty would certainly mean its failure to secure ratification in the Senate, but agreed once this was assured to do something to meet Russia's wishes. Hence the curious instructions issued by the Russian American Company to the Governor at Sitka and apparently acquiesced in by the United States, limiting commercial intercourse of Americans to that part of the American coast south of Yakutat (Bering) Bay.[57] In the British

[56] This very substantial set-off which ultimately gave Canada what was to be the Klondike goldfields was secured by Canning's tenacity, but was apparently due originally to the prompting of Sir Charles Bagot. As early as March, 1824, Bagot had written: "If by the cession of Prince of Wales Island . . . some equivalent concession can be obtained in respect of the longitudinal demarcation to the westwards (sic), in the higher latitudes, I may find it advisable to exceed . . . the letter of your instructions. . . ." (*Bagot Papers*, II, part 3, Letter of Sir Charles Bagot to Mr. George Canning, March 10, 1824). The suggestion was not lost sight of for we find Lieven noticing "with pleasure that the English Government entirely renounced the demand which it had recently made with regard to fixing upon a degree of longitude farther to the west than the boundary assigned by our court. . . . and that the boundary shall be formed by . . . the 139th degree of longitude" (*Alaska Boundary Tribunal*, II, App. 186, Despatch from Count Lieven to Count Nesselrode, July 13/25, 1824, received August 7/19). The omission was made good and, on December 8, Stratford Canning was instructed to require that north of latitude 59° the boundary should be altered from the 139th meridian to the 141st (*ibid.*, App. 211, Letter of Instructions from Mr. George Canning to Mr. Stratford Canning, December 8, 1824).

[57] John Quincy Adams, *Memoirs*, edited by Charles Francis Adams (Phila-

treaty this was provided for by Article VII which says, "During the period of ten years, to date from the signing of this convention the vessels of the high powers or those belonging to their respective subjects, shall have equally the right to frequent, without any let or hindrance whatever, all the interior seas, the gulfs, havens and creeks in those parts of the coast mentioned in Article III, in order to carry on fishing and to trade with the natives." [58]

Shortly after Middleton had finished negotiating the treaty he wrote to Adams bewailing the fact that Congress had apparently taken no action toward the occupation of the Pacific coast. Middleton (like Adams) was one with many of his countrymen in regarding the convention of 1818 as but a momentary check in the progress of American expansion. Proposals of this kind made in 1821 had been the subject of a heated protest by Stratford Canning and an equally heated rejoinder by Adams. [59] The proposal in 1821 never got past the committee stage though it did become the subject of diplomatic discussions. But a similar motion made in 1823 by Congressman Floyd "to inquire into the expediency of occupying the Columbia or the Oregon River," emerged in January, 1824, as a bill for the despatch of troops to the west coast, a course supported by the Quartermaster-General Jesup. Fortunately the Senate rejected the bill and thus spared the administration the embarrassment of a move that was inspired by anti-British feelings. [60]

delphia, 1874–7), VI, 435 ff. Further light is thrown on this incident by *Bering Sea Tribunal, Fur Seal Arbitration, Proceedings,* VII, 156 and S. B. Okun, *Rossiisko-Amerikanskaya Kompaniya* (The Russian American Company) (Leningrad, 1939), 108. Two alternative points were suggested as marking the furthest limits of commercial intercourse for U. S. ships — Cross Sound in latitude 57° north or Yakutat Bay, nearly 2° farther north (the latter only if the United States resisted the former). Yakutat Bay was finally decided on (*Alaska Boundary Tribunal,* II, App. 93, Letter of the Minister of Finance to the Board of Directors of the Russian American Company, September 4 (o.s.), 1824, signed by Lieutenant-General Kankrin, Minister of Finance and Yu. Druzhinin, Director [of the company]).

[58] *Ibid.,* II, App. 222.
[59] *Ibid.,* II, App. 92, Letter from Middleton to Adams, August 18/30, 1824.
[60] Floyd, the mover, made no secret of his feelings. The preamble stated that "the Columbia was the only point on the globe where a naval power can reach

The settlement of the dispute over the north-west coast was based neither on any abstract title nor on "mutual convenience." Spain had had the most clear-cut claim but a Papal Bull had no standing with heretics outside the Roman Catholic fold. It was of little use to invoke "mutual convenience" since the governments were ill-informed on actual conditions in these remote regions. None of those participating in the discussions had ever been to the north-west coast. The maps used were imperfect and antiquated. The British placed their reliance on those of Vancouver, who, gazing from the deck of his ship had fancied the serrated peaks forming the eastward horizon were a continuous and well-defined ridge. A group of diplomats sitting around tables on the other side of the globe, working under such handicaps with defective, out-of-date maps could hardly produce satisfactory boundaries. Canning's quip of "bobbing for whale *ipsis in faucibus Beringi*" was mildly satirical of the air of academic unreality that hung over the negotiations. The convention was but one incident of a diplomatic game in which the participants were playing for stakes not always visible on the board.

Considered by itself the issue was less one between the Anglo-Saxon powers and Russia as it seemed to be, than a phase of the struggle between Great Britain and the United States for the possession of the continent. It is questionable whether Russia could ever have made a serious bid for power in the north Pacific against either of her rivals. She had an insecure foothold on the continent. The original Shelekhov-Golikov Company had never penetrated further east and south than Lituya Bay (approximately latitude 59° 30′ north).[61] Baranov had

---

the East India possessions of our eternal enemy, Great Britain" (H. H. Bancroft, *The History of the Northwest Coast*, 2 vols, San Francisco, 1886, I, 353–4; Annals of Congress, 18th Cong., 2nd Sess., 14–27, 36–61). In his message to Congress in 1824 President Monroe actually suggested "the propriety of establishing a military post at the mouth of the Columbia or at some other point in that quarter within our acknowledged limits" (*American State Papers, Foreign Relations*, V, 358).

[61] This was the extreme limit of the concession granted in 1798 when the government sanctioned the merger of the rival companies in the North American trade. The charter of 1799, however, carried the boundary forward 3½°. The

been subsequently instructed to extend his operations to the south and east but when he did so, such extension was made from commercial motives and not out of deference to Russia's political aspirations.[62] Russia's tenure was constantly threatened by native risings. Russian occupation, Baranov continued to regard as provisional.[63] At the very time when negotiations were under way in the capital, the Board of Directors had already authorized abandonment of Sitka, a fact carefully suppressed during the discussions.[64] Moreover, up to 1825, Russia had one by one relinquished most of the mainland posts. The methods by which the Russian American Company obtained their furs tended to exhaust rather than preserve its resources and thus to render their rule transitory.

The "non-colonization" doctrine already foreshadowed by Adams and proclaimed by Monroe played relatively little role in the actual discussions. It was, however, implicit in the attitude of Adams and others, and it did not need to be insisted on to exert an influence on events. Bagot's anger against Adams was perhaps due to the latter's skill in cloaking a policy of ex-

---

so-called Act of Union, August 5, 1798, is given in *Polnoe Sobranie*, 1799, Text 19,030; an English translation of the first chapter is in *Alaska Boundary Tribunal*, II, App. 23. The claim to the American coast as far south as 55° north latitude appeared first in the time of Catherine and was advanced by Müller by virtue of Chirikov's discovery. See *Doklad Komiteta ob Ustroistvye Russkikh Amerikanskikh Kolonii* (2 vols., St. Petersburg, 1863), I, App. 279.

[62] Records of the Russian American Company, Instructions from the Board of Directors, St. Petersburg to the Governor of the Colonies (Baranov), April 18, 1802. These records of the Russian American Company's Sitka office consist for the most part of correspondence exchanged between the Directors at St. Petersburg and the Governor of the colonies at Sitka (or Novo-Arkhangel'sk). They were handed over to the United States by the terms of the Treaty of Cession of March 30, 1867. They remained for years in the custody of the State Department but are now in the National Archives. Files for the years 1802 (except for one or two communications) to 1817 are missing.

[63] Baranov's views are given in a letter on Kodiak to Larionov at Unalaska, March 3, 1798, given in P. Tikhmenev, *Istoricheskoe obozrenie obrazovaniya Ross. Am. Kompanii i dyeistvii eya do nastoyasnago vremeni* (Historical Survey of the Formation of the Russian American Company and its Activity down to the present) (2 vols., St. Petersburg, 1861–3).

[64] Records of the Russian American Company, Letter from the Board of Directors to the Chief Factor of the American Colonies, Muraviev, February 22, 1822.

clusion with the mantle of a righteous crusade against tyranny. Yet Rush believed that this novel "pretension on the part of his Government was intended as a set-off against the maritime pretension of the Russian ukase." [65] The principle had not been adhered to in the settlement with Russia and Adams was probably ready for a deal with Canning. It is apparently this combination of extravagant claims with a show of moderation that explains the inconsistency which Bagot called "duplicity." In the midst of Adams' campaign for the presidency there could be no weakening in the emphasis on "manifest destiny."

[65] *Alaska Boundary Tribunal*, II, App. 147, Despatch Mr. George Canning to Sir Charles Bagot, January 15, 1824.

Interior exploration during the Russian period moved eastward and westward. While the Russians probed inland from the western littoral, British traders with the Hudson's Bay Company explored westward from the Canadian Subarctic. The two giant fur companies — H.B.C. and the Russian-American Company — met head-on at Nukluklayet, near the confluence of the Tanana and Yukon rivers.

Lawrence J. Burpee (1873–1946) was for many years a close student of inland exploration in western Canada. He was a librarian and historian, and served as president of the Royal Society of Canada and president of the Canadian Historical Society. His article is from the Canadian Geographical Journal, *XXX (April, 1945), 200–01.*

Campbell of the Yukon

LAWRENCE J. BURPEE

On a midsummer day in 1840, Robert Campbell, of the Hudson's Bay Company, stood on a high bank and saw "a large river in the distance flowing North-West". He named it the Pelly, and the Pelly it still is, although Sir George Simpson, the Governor of the Company, said that it should bear the name of its explorer. Clambering down to the banks of the river, Campbell, in the flowery language of the period, "drank out of its pellucid water to Her Majesty and the H. B. C.". He then built a raft and floated down the stream a few miles, throwing in a sealed tin with a note of the discovery and the date, "with a request to the finder, if perchance the can should fall into anyone's hands, to make the facts known". Finally he completed the ceremony of taking possession in the name of the Company by carving "H. B. C." with the date on a tree, meanwhile flying the H. B. C. ensign overhead.*

* Campbell narrates his journeys in "The Discovery and Exploration of the Pelly (Yukon) River," *Royal Readers: Fifth Book of Reading Lessons* (Toronto, 1883).—ED. NOTE.

The identity of the river remained in doubt for some time, but there was no uncertainty as to the importance of the discovery. At that time there was keen rivalry between the Hudson's Bay Company and the Russian American Company for the control of the fur trade of the North Pacific coast and the interior country. Much might depend upon whether the Pelly emptied into the Arctic or the Pacific. Thomas Simpson who, three years before, had found the mouth of a large river on the Arctic coast west of the Mackenzie, and named it the Colvile, was convinced that Campbell's Pelly was the Colvile. Sir George Simpson, in his letters to Campbell, develops a variety of theories. In 1841 he thinks "the stream you are upon falls into the Pacific". Two years later he has reached the conclusion that "the river in question is the Tako falling into Lynn's Canal". In 1844 the Governor is hot on the trail. He offers two alternatives, "Pelly River, from what you say of it and from an examination of the chart you have sent me, is either Turnagain or Quikpok". It was not Turnagain, but it was Quikpok, or Kwikhpak, for that was the name by which the Russians knew the Yukon. Campbell himself says that he was always of the opinion that the Pelly and the Yukon were one, but it was not until 1851, when he had explored the river down to the mouth of the Porcupine, that he was convinced that the Pelly was the Yukon.

Meanwhile, having made his original discovery, he returned over the height of land to his trading post on Frances Lake, which he had named Glenlyon House, in memory of his boyhood home in Scotland. Campbell, to whom dangers and discomforts were part of the day's work, describes his journey from the Liard River to Frances Lake and the Pelly in matter-of-fact terms, but that route became so notorious that the Company's men, when they signed their engagements, always tried to have it excluded.

In 1843 the explorer returned to the Pelly, built canoes at the place where he had first seen the river, and paddled downstream until he came to the forks of the Pelly and another large stream which he named the Lewes, the former called after the home Governor of the Hudson's Bay Company, and the latter after

John Lee Lewes, a Chief Factor. On his way down, Campbell gave names to a number of the tributaries of the Pelly, and it is pleasant to recognize their association with his boyhood days in Perthshire (described by Sir Walter Scott as "the fairest portion of the northern kingdom"), and particularly in his native glen. Campbell's map of his discoveries has been lost, but George M. Dawson, in his 1887 Report on the Yukon, provides a map in which he has incorporated much of the information furnished by Campbell to Arrowsmith, including place-names. Here we find such names as Earn, Tummel and Orchy, rivers, lochs and glens that were very dear to this sturdy son of the Campbells of Breadalbane. Remember the lament of the MacGregors:

Glenorchy's proud mountain, Colchurn and her towers,
Glenstrae and Glen Lyon, no longer are ours!

At the forks Campbell met a party of Knife Indians, who had never before seen white men, but were quite friendly. They urged him to go no farther. The tribes below were so savage that they would not only kill him but they would eat him. Campbell, who understood Indian character, and as a matter of fact got along very well with them, was not impressed, but his men were thrown into a panic. However, he was not equipped to go on down the river at this time.

In a letter written in June, 1844, Simpson had suggested the forks of the Pelly and Lewes as a suitable site for a trading post. Conditions in the fur trade stood in the way, and it was not until 1848 that Campbell built Fort Selkirk at the forks. His immediate superior at Fort Simpson, Murdoch McPherson, took a sour view of the Pelly adventure and, while he could not openly oppose a project approved by the Governor, made it very difficult for Campbell to go on with it.

In 1851 the explorer received definite instructions to continue his discoveries. He left about the beginning of June, and, visiting a number of Indian villages on the river below Fort Selkirk, found the natives, as he had expected, neither bloodthirsty nor unfriendly. They were equally astonished at seeing the white men and their boat. "All our accoutrements — even the simplest articles — were a mystery to them." Their only arms were bows and arrows; "their substitute for axe and knife was of bone or stone", their 'kettle' was made of the small fibres of the roots of trees which became waterproof after a time.

Campbell, after he had travelled some distance down the river, was told by the Indians that he was approaching a place where there were white people like himself living in a fort. It proved to be, as he had hoped, Fort Yukon, built by Alexander Hunter Murray at the mouth of the Porcupine in 1847. It had been already established that the Porcupine emptied into the Yukon. "I had thus the satisfaction", says Campbell, "of demonstrating that my conjectures from the first, in which hardly anyone concurred, were correct and that the Pelly and the Youcon were identical."

Campbell travelled up the Porcupine and over the mountains to the Mackenzie, and up the Mackenzie to Fort Simpson at the mouth of the Liard, where he was received with astonishment, the only known route from Fort Selkirk being down the Liard, not up the Mackenzie.

The following year a party of treacherous Chilkat Indians came down the Lewes from the coast. Campbell, who was almost alone at Fort Selkirk, managed to escape, but the post was looted.* The Company decided to abandon the Pelly as too dangerous to be profitable, greatly to Campbell's disappointment, who had planned to explore the Lewes.

*For more information about the incident, see George Davidson, "Explanation of an Indian Map of the River, Lakes, Trails and Mountains, Drawn by the Chilkaht Chief Kohklux, in 1869," *Mazama* (April, 1901), 1–8.—ED. NOTE.

*The Russian Church and the Russian-American Company
were the two most influential institutions in Alaska before
its purchase by the United States. Missionary accomplishment
by the Church was uneven, in part because of the vast size
of the country and the harsh frontier conditions, but churchmen
did bring the Gospel and schooling to many remote native
villages, and did minister to the small and scattered Russian
population. One priest, Father Veniaminov, became a key
figure in the social history of Russian America.*

*Helen Shenitz, of Auke Bay, Alaska, received her several
academic degrees in Russia, at the Sorbonne in Paris, and
at Columbia University in New York City. In 1961 she retired
as librarian of the Alaska State Historical Library in Juneau.
"Alaska's 'Good Father'" is a revised reprint of an article
that appeared in the* Russian Orthodox Journal, XXX
(February, 1957), 6–10.

Alaska's "Good Father"

HELEN A. SHENITZ

eep in the heart of Siberia, in the little village of Anginskoe, situated on the left shore of the clear and fast flowing river Angara, on August 26, 1797, a boy was born into the family of the local sacristan Popov. The boy was named Ivan.*

The outlook for the boy's future was not encouraging. His father was ailing and there were two children in the family besides Ivan. The highest aspiration that the boy's parents could have for him would have been for the boy to become a local priest; even that humble dream had a remote chance to become a reality.

As he grew up, the little boy turned out to be a bright child. At the age of four, Ivan, under the tutoring of his father had

* See also: A. P. Kashevaroff, "Ivan Veniaminov, Innocent, Metropolitan of Moscow and Kolomna: His Life and Work in Alaska, drawn from His Biography in the Russian," *Alaska Magazine*, I (February, 1927), 49–56; I (March, 1927), 145–50; and, I (April, 1927), 217–24. Also, A. W. Shiels, "The Work of Veniaminov in Alaska," *British Columbia Historical Quarterly*, XI (October, 1947), 265–72.—ED. NOTE.

121

started to read and at the time of his father's death in 1803, the boy could read fluently.

Ivan's mother was left with four children to support as meanwhile another boy was born into the family. In order to ease her burden, Ivan's uncle, his father's brother who was the local deacon, took the boy into his family to bring him up as his own. The uncle's family was good to the boy and his uncle continued to train Ivan in reading. At the age of seven, Ivan started to read the Holy Scriptures during the Church services and, according to the records, he read so well that the congregation was pleased with him and prized him highly. It has been the only case on record that a child of that age was able and was permitted to be a church reader of the Holy Scriptures.

Encouraged by Ivan's achievement, the boy's mother tried to place him as a sacristan to fill the vacancy left by his father but all her efforts were in vain.

In 1806, at the age of nine, the boy entered the theological seminary in Irkutsk where he remained for eleven years. According to the seminary records, through all of the eleven years the boy's school marks remained the same: "Eleganter," "egregie," and "exemie," which were equivalent to our present day's "excellent," "superior," and "outstanding."

The academic standards of the seminary were high but the living conditions were deplorably poor. School rooms served also as dormitories and the food was of such a low quality that after Ivan became a priest he often mentioned that only after his graduation had he tasted, for the first time, bread made from pure flour, without any substitutes.

After three years of Ivan's schooling, his mother again tried to obtain for him the job of sacristan and again she failed. Many years later when Ivan Popov became a Church dignitary he often referred to his mother's failure to make a sacristan out of him as a sure sign that he was destined to serve in Alaska.

The early orphanhood and the lack of normal family life reflected upon the boy's emotional make-up. He avoided his schoolmates and their boisterous games and kept mostly his own company. For his lack of sociability, at the beginning, he was much disliked by the other boys and often was the subject of their mockery and ridicule. But this attitude was short-lived.

Studious and reticent Ivan spent his free time in reading and in studying mechanics. When a clockmaker Klim was engaged by the bishop of Irkutsk to construct a clock for the belfry and therefore was given quarters at the bishop's residence, Ivan immediately became a frequent visitor there. When the bishop noticed that a student of the seminary was spending considerable time with the clockmaker, he suspected that the student was playing hooky. The bishop called this supposed delinquency to the attention of the rector of the seminary. Upon investigation the bishop was informed that the student was one of the best students at the seminary and that it was not laziness but intellectual curiosity that prompted the boy to spend so much time with Klim. From then on Ivan was free to visit Klim and Klim in turn was glad to have such an industrious helper.

While faithfully attending classes, doing his homework, and helping Klim, Ivan still found time to read extensively. After reading Prof. Halle's "Secrets of Ancient Magicians" Ivan constructed a water clock. That clock made a great impression on the residents of Irkutsk; it was a great event, especially due to the fact that any clock or watch was a rarity in Irkutsk at that time. Next, Ivan made a pocket sun-watch. Its mechanism was so simple that soon the boy was able to supply his schoolmates with pocket watches. These watches broke the ice and changed his schoolmates' attitude from mockery to friendship and admiration.

Shortly after Ivan entered the seminary his last name was changed by the order of the rector. Popov is a common name and there were many Popovs at the seminary. In order to distinguish them the rector ordered each Popov to take for his last name the name of the place from which he came. Ivan came from the village of Anginskoe, hence he became Ivan Aginskii.

In 1814 the beloved bishop of Irkutsk, Veniamin, passed away. The rector of the seminary decided that the most deserving student should be given the last name of Veniaminov.

And who was the most deserving student? Ivan Anginskii, of course. So, in order to perpetuate the distinguished name, Ivan Popov-Anginskii became Ivan Veniaminov.

In 1817, while still a student at the seminary, Ivan married and became a deacon. His marriage changed considerably the course of events in his life. As one of the best students he was destined upon graduation to be sent to the Theological Academy in Moscow. But according to the regulations only single men were permitted to study at the Academy.

Here is what Ivan Veniaminov told his biographer: "The rector had me in mind as a candidate for the Academy, as he told me personally later on. As to why the rector didn't stop my marriage, the answer is that he was in no position to do so due to a rare occurrence that took place at that time. The river Angara that separated the seminary from the bishop's residence became impassable at the time I decided to marry. The river remained impassable for many days. That gave me an opportunity to marry without the bishop's knowledge, or his permission. If not for this temporary isolation I couldn't have married at that time and therefore would have been sent to the Academy instead of Alaska."

Four years after Ivan Veniaminov became a deacon he was ordained a priest and became Fr. Ioann Veniaminov. At that time his family consisted of wife, son, his mother and his brother.

At the beginning of 1823 the bishop of Irkutsk received an order from the Church administration in St. Petersburg to send a priest to Unalaska. According to the Church regulations no priest could be ordered to serve overseas. A call for volunteers was issued. None was to be found.

At that time there arrived in Irkutsk a visitor from the Aleutian Islands by the name of Kriukov. He had spent quite a few years in Alaska. Being a friend of Fr. Veniaminov he tried to persuade the priest to go to Unalaska. Many stories he told to Father and he strongly emphasized the wealth that Father could accumulate in Alaska. Father was not interested. Happily married, beloved by his congregation, Fr. Veniaminov, according to his own words, could see no reason for leaving his fatherland. But, when on the day of his departure, Kriukov came to the bishop to take his leave, and when in the presence of Fr. Veniaminov he again told the bishop how eagerly the Aleuts were seeking Christianity and what a Christian life those who were baptized were leading, Fr. Veniaminov suddenly felt an urge to go there and serve these people. He astonished the bishop by asking for permission to go to Alaska.

When he came home that day he took his one year old son into his arms, kissed him, and said: "Kenia, Kenia, where are your feet going to tread?" At once his family understood what he meant. He was going to Alaska. In tears they begged him to reconsider. Their pleading fell upon a deaf ear. Fr. Veniaminov's mind was made up.

Fr. Veniaminov arrived in Unalaska on June 24, 1824. Prior to his arrival he had written to the Russian Chief Manager in Sitka in reply to the generous offer of the Russian-American Company to give him the privilege to receive furs from the natives as their contribution to the support of the priest. It was a generous offer indeed, because according to the strict rules established by the Russian-American Company, no one could have in his possession any furs as all furs were the property of the Company.

Wrote Fr. Veniaminov: "From your letter of April 27th, No. 132, it can be seen that I have the right to accept all donations from the parishoners without breaking the rules set up by the Russian-American Company. I voluntarily decline this privilege and will not accept any donations from the Aleuts for the following reasons:

1. Because, besides leading to all the crooked deals, it would be to the contrary to the rules set up for all the Russian employees of the Company, and therefore may cause unpleasantness between myself and the local authorities.
2. To avoid the correspondence which would unavoidably arise between the Church authorities and the administration of the Company which could be very detrimental to me.
3. According to my opinion, a simple, sincere, and without any

remuneration, teaching of Faith would impress people more effectively than the same teaching remunerated by donations. So, according to the above mentioned and other reasons, I refuse to accept the privilege given me by the Russian-American Company and respectfully request that I would be permitted to receive as part of my agreed upon salary, two or three skins or blankets, which I would need for clothing for my family and myself, and which I promise would never fall into the hands of any outsider, not a member of my family.

With this letter Fr. Veniaminov locked and sealed the door which was open for him into the world of material wealth.

When Fr. Veniaminov arrived on Unalaska, there were no accommodations to house the priest and his family. Father's first step was to build a house for his family and to make the furniture for it. This building of the house had given Fr. Veniaminov his first chance to teach the natives carpentry, cabinetmaking, blacksmithing, brickmaking and bricklaying. As soon as enough men had been trained, he started to build the first church on the Aleutian Islands in Unalaska.

July 29th, 1826 the church was consecrated and from then on Fr. Veniaminov devoted his time to the needs of the natives. This required a great deal of hazardous traveling.

Realizing that he couldn't successfully carry his missionary work without being able to speak the native tongue, he started to study the Aleutian-Fox language-dialect, the dialect that was used by the majority of the islanders. At the same time he undertook a careful and methodical study of ethnography of Aleuts and the flora and fauna of the islands. He also started a daily recording of temperature, winds, tides and barometer readings. He opened schools and workshops, writing the school textbooks himself.

Fr. Veniaminov left Unalaska for Sitka at the end of 1834. During his 10 years on the Aleutians he had accomplished more than any other man under similar circumstances would have accomplished in a lifetime. He had spread Christianity all over the islands and through his truly Christian spirit had introduced the Aleuts to Christian democracy. He was the first white man from whom the Aleuts received respect, understanding and good will. He left the Aleuts with a firm belief not only in Christian doctrine but in Christian life as well. He left them with a firm belief in human kindness, cooperation, and the value of knowledge.

During his ten years on Unalaska he had composed the first Aleutian grammar that according to Scott and other renown orientalists, had been the ground stone in further research in Oriental languages. His sermon: "Showing the Way into the Kingdom of God" written on Unalaska in the Aleutian-Fox language has undergone 26 editions in Russian and has been translated into French, German, and the Tlingit languages. He had written the first Aleutian primer, compiled an Aleutian-Fox vocabulary, had translated the catechism and had written a brief ecclesiastic history also in the Aleutian-Fox language. Numerous articles on the Aleutian Islands had appeared in the Russian magazines during that period and had been translated and published in French and German magazines. But his main accomplishment in the field of study and writing as far as we in Alaska and all those who are doing research on Alaska are concerned, was his book, "Notes on the Islands of Unalaska District." A book of 658 pages, it consists of three parts, two parts on the Aleutian Islands and the third part, written in Sitka, on the Tlingit Indians.

In Nouvelle Dictionnaire de Geographie Universelle said Vivien de Saint-Martin: "After Billings there were expeditions of Kotzebue, Lutke and other explorers. Among all published research works the research done by the Russian priest Veniaminov occupies the first place."

William H. Dall, himself an expert on Alaska, in a letter to R. H. Geoghegan, written before the First World War, stated that he considered Veniaminov's "Notes" one of the most important source-books on Alaska and that he was surprised that it never yet had been translated.

In 1956 Aurel Krause's book "The Tlingit Indians" was published in English, translated by Dr. Erna Gunther. The German original, published in 1885, has been considered an excellent study of Tlingit ethnography. Yet, Krause's chief source was Veniaminov's third part of "Notes."

The value of "Notes" is not limited to ethnology. Topography, climate, mineralogy, demography and vital statistics are also well covered; as to the information on botany, fish, and wild life of the Aleutian Islands, I do not believe there is a better source anywhere.

Upon his arrival in Sitka, Fr. Veniaminov started all over again doing exactly the same things and in the same manner that he had been doing on the Aleutians: studying the Tlingit language and ethnography and making friends with Indians which was not an easy task as Indians of that period were militant people. The esteem in which the Tlingits learned to hold Fr. Veniaminov was demonstrated during the epidemic of smallpox in Sitka. It was he who was able to persuade the Indians to accept inoculation against the disease.

He opened schools and workshops and of course, as on the Aleutians, spread Christianity among the Indians.

At the same time he continued his mechanical work. After learning that the Franciscans in California were in need of musical instruments, he made barrel organs for them. The first organ he delivered himself to California, where an historical meeting took place. East met West. Both parties enjoyed the meeting; they had a common language — spirituality, and the common tongue — Latin.

Fr. Veniaminov had a keen sense of humor. For many years after his trip to California, each time that he was called to describe the historical East-West meeting, he always told the following story: For his first organ for the Franciscans he made two rolls. One with Church music and the other with Russian folk songs and folk dance music. First he played the roll with the church music; the Franciscans expressed only mild pleasure. Then he played the song and dance music. The Franciscans were enchanted. They shook and shook his hand, placed the organ in the church and promptly paid what Fr. Veniaminov asked for the organ. With a twinkle in his eyes he invariably added: "I presume those Franciscans are still praying under the Russian song and dance music."

In Sitka, Fr. Veniaminov wrote "Notes on Kolosh and Kodiak languages and other Russian-American languages," which Buschman, a well-known Americanologist used for his book: "Die Spurer den amerikanischen Sprachen in noerdlichen Mexico and hoeherem amerikanischen Norden" to compare the Haida language spoken on Kaigan with the Haida spoken on Queen Charlotte Island.

In 1838, Fr. Veniaminov left for St. Petersburg and Moscow. In both places he was received with open arms by the Church administration, the Russian aristocracy and finally by the Czar. Such a reception of a humble priest from Alaska or from anywhere else had been unheard of, but his personality, his deeds and his writings impressed everyone.

Fr. Veniaminov never came back to Alaska as a priest. In 1841 he returned as the Bishop of Kamchatka, the Kurile and the Aleutian Islands. One hundred years after Bering's discovery, Alaska greeted her first bishop, Bishop Innokentii (Innocent).

For the next six years the new bishop was busier than ever. The necessary travels all over his bishopric consumed a great part of his time. He established new schools for the natives and covered Alaska with new missions. But he remained the same "Good Father," as the natives lovingly called him, and the same inquisitive scholar.

In 1847 he established a separate Indian church in Sitka and in 1848, in Sitka, he consecrated the St. Michael's Cathedral, our Alaskan historical monument. The clock on the belfry of St. Michael's Cathedral that one can see even today, was made by Fr. Veniaminov.[*]

But his Alaska days were numbered. In 1850 he was elevated to the rank of archbishop which necessitated his moving to Yakutsk, his new see. In 1868 he became the Metropolitan of

---

[*]In January 1966, St. Michael's Cathedral was destroyed by fire. Plans are afoot to reconstruct it.—ED. NOTE.

Moscow and Kolomna and therefore the Head of the Russian Church, being chosen for that post by the Emperor himself.

He remained as the Head of the Church until his death which took place on the Saturday before Easter, March 31, 1879. He died totally blind, but until his last day he never stopped working.

In his personal and Christian humility and in his scholarly endeavors he proved himself to be a truly great priest and a truly great man. For years and years to come Fr. Veniaminov, as he is known in Alaska, will live in the hearts of Alaskans and in the minds of those who study Alaska with the help of his books.

Tourists and other travelers of today, when they have an opportunity, frequently enter the humble huts of the Aleuts. When they see the portrait of Metropolitan Innocent proudly displayed at the place of honor, they naturally ask, "Who is that man?" The answer is always the same: "It is Our Good Father."

Before his death, Clarence John Du Four was for many years professor of history and dean at San Francisco State College. The following selection by Du Four describes the events which led to the departure of the Russians from California. The article appeared in the California Historical Society Quarterly, XII (*September, 1933*), 240–49, *along with related documents. The same issue of the* Quarterly *contains several items on the Fort Ross venture.*

The Russian Withdrawal from California

CLARENCE JOHN DU FOUR

Less than three years after the fascinating Rezanoff had sailed through the Golden Gate, leaving to the lovely
Doña Concepcion Argüello only blissful memories and undying
hopes, another Russian sailed along the nearby coast. The newcomer was Ivan Kuskoff on the *Kadiak* from Sitka.

Rezanoff's California venture had given him two new objectives. One was the establishment of permanent trade relations with California and the other the founding of a settlement north of San Francisco Bay which might serve as a trading
and agricultural supply station for the benefit of the Alaskan
colonies. In his report to the Russian American Company Rezanoff eloquently urged the adoption of his two-fold plan,[1] in

---

[1] Tikhmeneff, P., *Historical Review of the Origin of the Russian American
Company*, St. Petersburg, 1861. Translation from the Russian in manuscript
"Russian America," II, Appendix, 267, Bancroft Library, Berkeley, California.
An important interpretative article entitled "Russian Expansion to America: its
Bibliographical Foundations," by Robert J. Kerner was published in 1931 in
the *Papers of the Bibliographical Society of America*, Volume XXV.

which, before leaving Sitka, he succeeded in arousing the interest of Governor * Baranoff.[2] Two years later Kuskoff was sent to examine the coast with a view to the selection of a suitable location for a station.

Kuskoff sailed into Bodega Bay, made some nearby explorations and, upon his return to Sitka in October, reported that he had found a suitable harbor and a wholly satisfactory site for the projected settlement.[3] After another interval he was dispatched to Bodega in 1810 and then again in 1811.[4] His fourth arrival was in March, 1812.[5] It was then that an actual occupation began which was to end with the year 1841 — a span of close to thirty years.

My purpose is not to relate the history of Russian occupation. Instead it is to indicate the major reasons for the abandonment of the region, in the light of failures to realize the original and later objectives, and to furnish the documents that describe the attempts of the Russians to dispose of their holdings — first to Englishmen, next to Californians and finally and successfully to a naturalized Swiss newly established on the Sacramento.

The prime purpose of the Russian American Company in establishing settlements in California was trade. This comprehended an extension of otter hunting to the shores of New Albion and the Farallones[6] and the barter of cloth and iron for wheat and barley, peas, beans, tallow and dried meats for the northern colonies.[7] With the rapid falling off of the otter supply after 1818, the agricultural and stock-raising activities assumed greater and greater importance.[8] Simultaneously and for vari-

*The term "chief manager" is more precise, but because managers of the Russian-American Company exercised quasi-governmental powers, some writers employ the label "governor."—ED. NOTE.

[2] Potechine, W., "Settlement of Ross," Extract from the *Journal of the Department of Manufactures and Trade*, St. Petersburg, 1859, Translation from the Russian in "Russian America," V, Part II, 5.

[3] Potechine, 5.

[4] Tikhmeneff, I, 208.

[5] *Ibid.*, I, 208.

[6] *Ibid.*, I, 210–212.

[7] Potechine, 3.

[8] *Ibid.*, 14–15.

ous reasons the trade relations with California failed to reach satisfactory proportions. Finally the expense of the enterprise appeared disproportionate to the return, and when the last hope of success through expansion was thwarted no incentive remained for maintaining the station. When this was fully recognized and abandonment officially ordered, every effort was made to salvage as much as possible from the wreckage.[9]

At the outset the Spanish Californians appeared to place no obstacle in the way of settlement. José Argüello, *Comandante* at San Francisco, learned of the presence of the Russians in July of 1812 and promptly sent Gabriel Moraga to investigate. Moraga made a thorough survey and before leaving amiably agreed to use his influence to encourage the desired trade relations.[10] He again visited the Russians in January, 1813, and later reported to Argüello on his observations. Governor Arrillaga, duly notified, communicated in turn with the viceroy concerning the visitations of Moraga. No formal trade concessions appear to have been granted, but Russian authorities attest that on Moraga's second journey he brought gifts of cattle and horses [11] and that Kuskoff had no difficulty in exchanging a cargo of supplies for one of foodstuffs to the value of $14,000.[12]

In 1813 the viceroy sent a protest to the Russians which, in 1814, Moraga, on a third visit, conveyed to Kuskoff.[13] The latter indicated that he would lay the matter before Baranoff and the Company and would then await the official decision.[14] Meanwhile Governor Arrillaga died and Argüello filled the executive office ad interim. The acting governor, not so tractable as his predecessor, peremptorily demanded the Russian withdrawal from California.[15] Kuskoff again declared his inability to comply until he received instructions from Baranoff.[16]

---

[9] Tikhmeneff, I, 365–66.
[10] *Ibid.*, I, 212–13.
[11] *Ibid.*, I, 213.
[12] Potechine, 7.
[13] *Ibid.*, 7–8.
[14] Tikhmeneff, I, 214.
[15] *Ibid.*, I, 215.
[16] *Ibid.*, I, 215.

The new governor, Sola, made his own investigation of the
Russian situation and in 1816 summoned Kuskoff to San Francisco. Again the latter temporized [17] and in the following year
Sola wrote to the viceroy that it would be difficult to oust the
intruders.[18] Notwithstanding the fact that in 1818 he was ordered by the viceroy to expel the Russians, Sola declared that
he could not comply because of inadequate soldiery.[19]

With the retirement of Governor Sola, following the establishment of Mexican independence, Don Luis Argüello assumed
temporary charge of the California government. On December
1, 1823, he entered into an agreement with the Russians permitting them to hunt otter for four months to March 31,
1824.[20] An attempted renewal of the contract in 1825 failed,
but the new governor, Echeandia, informally allowed the Russians to hunt in the early months of 1826. The yield was not
more than 468 pelts. A temporary permit in 1828 was even less
fruitful.[21] In three years' hunting the Russian American Company netted but 1181 pelts. The end of otter hunting in California was obviously in sight.

Ship-building for a short time assumed a temporary importance in Russian California, but the wood was "cut in sap" and
used before being thoroughly dried, with disastrous results.[22]

Agriculture and stock-raising also failed to yield an adequate
return. Kuskoff had no training as a farmer but he made a beginning at least.[23] His successor Karl Schmidt, governor or manager at Fort Ross from 1821 to 1826, was chiefly interested in

[17] *Conferencia celebrada en el presidio de San Francisco*, Provincial State
Papers, MS, XX, 29–33. Original in Spanish.

[18] Sola, Governor Pablo Vicente to the Viceroy, Monterey, January 2, 1817,
in Archives of California, Provincial Records, MS, IX, 155–67. Original in
Spanish.

[19] Sola, P. V., to the Viceroy, Monterey, April 3, 1818, summarized in Archives
of California, Provincial Records, MS, IX, 195–96. Original in Spanish.

[20] Khlebnikoff, K., Letters on America, MS, 142. Translation from the Russian
in Russian America, III, Part III, 212.

[21] *Ibid.*, 145.

[22] *Ibid.*, 149.

[23] *Ibid.*, 150.

ship-building. When that industry failed, however, he too tried to do something with agriculture.[24] Schmidt's successor, Paul Shelikoff, 1826 to 1829, did everything he could to develop farming.[25] However, except for the year 1823, the average yield was not over five to one.[26]

Cattle-breeding, begun under Kuskoff and continued under his successors, was figuratively and literally an up-hill struggle. The utilization of pasture land for grain cultivation left only wooded and rough country for the stock.[27] Hence the ratio of receipts to expenditures in this branch of industry fell far short of reasonable expectations.[28]

Sheep-raising proved unprofitable because of the coarse quality of the wool and the inability of the Russians to fabricate it into blankets as did the California missionaries.[29]

Fruits and vegetables brought no revenue to the Company so could not be accounted as valuable.[30]

Trade with the Californians never reached satisfactory proportions and was frequently attended with annoyances due to the suspicions of Californian and Mexican officials. Governors Echeandia, Victoria and Figueroa every now and then disturbed the even tenor of Russian arrangements.

In 1830 Baron Wrangell became governor or general manager of the Russian colonies in America. During his incumbency Figueroa apparently played a double game, encouraging the Russians on the one hand and reporting adversely in regard to them to the superior government in Mexico.[31]

In the course of a visit to Fort Ross in 1833, Baron Wrangell established William E. P. Hartnell as agent for the Russian American Company at Yerba Buena, where he was commis-

[24] *Ibid.*, 151.
[25] *Ibid.*, 152–53.
[26] Potechine, 14–15.
[27] Khlebnikoff, 153.
[28] *Ibid.*, 153–54.
[29] *Ibid.*, 156.
[30] *Ibid.*, 155.
[31] Bancroft, H. H., *History of California*, IV, 162.

sioned to procure produce from the Californians and exemptions from duty payments.[32]

According to a Russian authority the expenditures for the California establishments from 1825 to 1829 totaled 224,171 roubles, while the receipts for the same period amounted only to 43,858 roubles.[33] Hence it is not surprising that Baron Wrangell, soon after his arrival at Sitka, became interested in the business problems of Fort Ross. At first he appeared to regard its agricultural progress as fairly satisfactory but in April, 1834, in his report to the Russian American Company he recommended the foundation of agricultural and cattle-raising settlements to the eastward of the area then occupied. To this end he even advocated the purchase of the missions of San Rafael and Sonoma.[34]

In a letter to Wrangell Governor Figueroa hinted at the desirability of attempting to interest the Tsar in a formal recognition of Mexican independence. Nothing loath, Wrangell readily embodied the suggestion in his report, recommending it as a suitable quid pro quo.[35]

The Company, agreeable to Wrangell's recommendations, brought the whole matter to the attention of the Tsar who positively refused to allow any negotiations involving the question of recognition. Consequently the Company was able to permit Wrangell to negotiate nothing more than a commercial treaty and to arrange, if possible, for the purchase of the lands north of San Francisco Bay.[36]

Baron Wrangell thereupon surrendered his governorship to his successor, Kuprianoff, and late in 1835 sailed for Monterey. Arriving there he was grieved to learn that the friendly Figueroa had recently died. He went on to Mexico, however, in the hope of securing some advantages, but as he really had nothing to

[32] Vallejo, M. G., *Documentos para la historia de California*, MS, XXXI, 21. Bancroft Library. Original in Spanish.

[33] Potechine, 15.

[34] Zavalishin, Dmitry, *Affairs of the Ross Colony*, Moscow, 1866. Translation from the Russian in Russian America, V, Part I, 13–14.

[35] *Tikhmeneff*, I, 362.

[36] *Ibid.*, I, 362.

offer he was unable to accomplish anything other than to receive a courteously worded note from the Mexican government acquainting him with its willingness to conclude a treaty of the character indicated provided the Tsar should have the same desire. In that case the Mexican minister at London would be empowered to conclude such a treaty.[37] With this communication, Baron Wrangell continued his journey to St. Petersburg, submitted it together with his report, and the whole matter was officially reviewed and finally dropped.[38]

The failure of Wrangell's plans marked the beginning of the end of Russian California. The annual deficits continued,[39] hopes for an agricultural expansion were definitely dashed, and the relations with Mexico, never satisfactory, had apparently now reached an impasse. The Russian American Company saw no future advantage in maintaining the settlements and soon decided upon their early abandonment. To this the Tsar gave his formal sanction on April 15, 1839.[40]

All that remained to be done was to dispose of the properties and to that end the colonial representatives of the Company next bent all their efforts. Late in 1839 or early in 1840 a contract was entered into with the Hudson's Bay Company for the annual delivery of foodstuffs to the Alaskan colonies at Sitka.[41] This arrangement removed the last vestige of need for maintaining the California colony.

In April, 1840, Sir James Douglas of the Hudson's Bay Company visited Governor Kuprianoff at Sitka. While there he received an offer of the California properties for the sum of $30,000.[42] This Douglas proposed to report to Doctor John McLoughlin at Fort Vancouver who might open negotiations if interested. Nothing further appears to have been done about it and in the following year the Russians cast their lines elsewhere.

[37] *Ibid.*, I, 364.
[38] *Ibid.*, I, 364.
[39] Potechine, 19.
[40] *Ibid.*, 19; Tikhmeneff, I, 364–67.
[41] Tikhmeneff, I, 351–52.
[42] The Documents referred to are printed in the Appendix to this account.

The year 1840 furnished a dramatic episode in the *Lausanne* affair, in the course of which an American ship captain succeeded in precipitating a quarrel between the Governor of Fort Ross and the Sonoma commandant, Don Mariano Guadalupe Vallejo. Briefly stated the facts of the case are as follows:

Josiah Spalding, captain of the American ship *Lausanne*, coasting south from the Columbia, dropped anchor at Bodega, which he chose to conceive as a Russian free port. He hoped to save anchorage dues and possibly to reap some trade profits. Governor Rotcheff, although doubtless surprised at the unprecedented procedure, interposed no serious objection and set out for Yerba Buena and Monterey without imposing any restrictions upon the captain, crew or passengers. Spalding also departed for Yerba Buena, and in his absence some of the passengers called upon Vallejo at Sonoma and solicited passports permitting them to remain in California. The commandant, thus apprised of the irregular procedure, promptly dispatched an officer with a detail of soldiers to Bodega to order the return of all passengers and crew to the vessel and to prevent any illicit trade.

Captain Spalding visited Vallejo on his return from Yerba Buena and was duly called to account for his anchorage dues. Spalding demurred but was permitted to continue his journey to Bodega. Soon afterward Rotcheff appeared on the scene and engaged in a heated altercation with the officer sent from Sonoma by Vallejo. The officer reported the matter to Vallejo and the latter sent orders to Rotcheff denying his right to travel beyond the Russian area of occupation. These orders the angry Rotcheff refused to receive. Spalding soon after weighed anchor and sailed away, having created trouble enough by his ill-advised action.[43] Rotcheff was still nursing his rage at Vallejo when late in October Kuprianoff, retiring as colonial governor and on his way home from Sitka, paid a visit to the port of San Francisco, where he remained several weeks, chiefly occupied in investigating the *Lausanne* tangle. He succeeded only in losing his temper, however, and finally sailed on his homeland

[43] Bancroft, H. H., *History of California*, IV, 171–73.

journey, in the course of which perhaps the ocean breezes somewhat cooled his indignation.

On the first of January, 1841, Vallejo, advised of the Russians' intention to abandon their California settlements, attributed their decision to his own well-played role in the *Lausanne* drama. Obviously he was unaware of the fact that the order had been given some fifteen months before Captain Spalding dropped anchor in Bodega Bay. Writing to Mexico he reported that the Russians were seeking a purchaser of their properties and recommended that immediate steps be taken to assume possession and to establish a garrisoned colony there.

Peter Kostromitinoff, successor to Hartnell as Russian agent at Yerba Buena, on February 16 formally approached Vallejo on the subject of the purchase of Fort Ross for the sum of 30,000 pesos. He indicated that payment might be made half in cash or in Hudson's Bay Company warrants, or partly in each and half in produce, and he further advised that the Russians also wished to dispose of a launch of twenty-five tons.

Colonel Vallejo, replying to Kostromitinoff on February 19 and evidently playing for time, discussed the offer of the Russian agent and the proposed terms without in the least committing himself. He contrived, however, to hold the matter open for further correspondence and concluded his letter with assurances of "respect and particular appreciation."

The president of Mexico, writing through his secretary to Governor Alvarado under date of March 11, acknowledged receipt of the information of the intention of the Russians to abandon their California settlements and then set down his instructions as to immediate procedures. He authorized the immediate taking over of the properties, expressed some uncertainty in regard to the future district status of the region and prescribed the means whereby acceptable foreigners might acquire residential rights and privileges there. He directed that a careful survey and census should be prepared and that all reports should be forwarded promptly. In conclusion he advised the governor to supplement the official orders with such additional rules and regulations as his good judgment might direct.

Kostromitinoff left the matter of the sale of the property in the air for some weeks and made a journey to Sitka. He returned on the 15th of July, and two days later sent a courteous note to Vallejo notifying him of his arrival. He did not refer to their previous correspondence, but the announcement of his return probably was intended to pave the way for a meeting of the minds.

In the meanwhile it is not unlikely that Kostromitinoff had approached Captain John A. Sutter on the subject of the desire of the Russians to sell out. According to an anonymous publication printed in 1860 Rotcheff on July 26 wrote Sutter a letter in which he reported the arrival of Kostromitinoff from Sitka with instructions to decline Sutter's offer since it contemplated only the purchase of the cattle and not the real estate and other personal property. An alleged copy of the letter appears in the pamphlet.

Under date of July 27 Vallejo indited an exuberant epistle to Governor Alvarado. In it he announced (rather tardily) the forthcoming evacuation of the Russians, mentioned Kostromitinoff's offer to sell him everything including "even the acres of ground that Ross, Bodega and the neighboring ranches contain," and earnestly begged Alvarado to come to Sonoma to help conclude a matter so important to the northern frontier.

Kostromitinoff's inventory and proposed agreement, referred to in Vallejo's letter of July 27, included all the lands, improvements, chattels and livestock of Fort Ross and Bodega and the three ranches in between. The price was not set down but the payments were to be made in drafts on the Hudson's Bay Company, or half in those and the balance in produce. Three years' time was allowed for full settlement. According to the inventory the livestock numbered 3540 head.

In Alvarado's reply to Vallejo's letter he expressed regret that the condition of his health forbade his acceptance of the invitation to make the journey to Sonoma. He added expressions of his own pleasure at the coming departure of the "usurping" Russians but declared that no steps might as yet be taken towards taking possession. Further official correspondence with the governor at Sitka was awaited and likewise additional advices from the president of Mexico before any agreement to purchase might be made. Towards the end of his letter he suggested the desirability of waiting for the Russians to abandon the properties and then as a matter of right to step in and take them.

At some time between July 27 and August 27 Vallejo evidently made a tentative offer of $9,000 for the livestock alone. Pending the settlement of the question of the right of the Russians to sell their real estate and improvements he presumably felt that the acquisition of the livestock was purely a personal matter involving no legal complications. Indeed it is not unlikely that he had never entertained any desire or intention to purchase anything except the livestock. His interest in the Kostromitinoff proposal may have been only concern lest the holdings should become otherwise alienated.

The tone of Captain Sutter's letter of August 10 to Antonio Suñol indicates some resentment towards the Russians. Probably the communication of July 26 from Rotcheff had something to do with it. At any rate this letter of Sutter's offers substantial evidence of the genuineness of that of July 26.

It may be that Alvarado failed to send his reply to Vallejo's letter of July 27 with customary promptness, notwithstanding the fact that the reply bears the date of the 29th. We know that Vallejo ultimately received it and filed it, but on August 11 he wrote the governor and reminded him that his letter remained unanswered. Next he announced that Kostromitinoff, not satisfied with Vallejo's reasons for being unable to consummate a contract of sale, intended calling upon the governor for verification and to justify the Russian rights in the case.

Alvarado's reply is dated August 14. In it he referred to both of Vallejo's letters and agreed with his views denying the Russians' right to sell the real estate or improvements. He expressed the fear that the "barbarians" might burn down their buildings, although such conduct, he declared, would be most reprehensible. He concluded with the promise to clarify the situation in Kostromitinoff's mind when he called.

On August 27 Kostromitinoff, following his call upon the governor at Monterey, wrote to Vallejo that it was quite clear that the Superior Government had not denied the right of the Russians to sell their holdings but had only authorized delay until such time as they should announce their evacuation. Consequently Kostromitinoff argued that no obstacles stood in the way of a sale and that he desired to have Vallejo's immediate acceptance or rejection of the offer.

Vallejo replied the very next day, declaring, in accordance with his previous statement, that because no governmental permission had been given no purchase could be made. He concluded with a renewal of his offer for the cattle. This letter closed the correspondence between the Russian agent and the commandant. Vallejo's brother-in-law, Jacob Leese, was said to have later offered $20,000 for the property, payable $5,000 in cash and the balance in three equal annual installments. No verification of this offer has been unearthed as yet.

Captain Sutter's letter of September 1 to Suñol contained the statement that the Russians had reopened negotiations with him following their failure to "come to an agreement with Mr. Vallejo." He added that he would be "a little more exacting now."

Events henceforth moved rapidly. On September 4 Governor Rotcheff arrived at Sutter's Fort on the schooner *Sacramento*. He urged Sutter to return with him to Bodega for the purpose of meeting some persons who were officially empowered to transact business with him. Despite his declaration of three days before Sutter promptly accepted the invitation and with Rotcheff made all haste to Bodega. Arriving there the purchase of the Russian property for $30,000 was very quickly agreed upon.

In his Reminiscences, dictated to Bancroft in 1877, Sutter painted a colorful picture of the episode and seemed to have quite forgotten that more than three months were to pass before the formal contract was executed. Sutter was empowered however to take immediate possession of the livestock and perhaps other movable property and this he lost no time in doing. He formally notified Vallejo on the 19th of September that he had bought "all the movable and fixed property" of the Russians and that he intended sending some men overland to Fort Ross to "embark" furniture, etc. He requested the courtesy of Vallejo's permission for these men to pass over his domain and concluded with "the sincere expression" of his respect. It is not unlikely that the exuberant Sutter thoroughly enjoyed writing this letter to the *Comandante General.*

In a postscript to a letter written on December 8, Sutter thanked Vallejo for his assistance and advice to the men driving the livestock to Sutter's Fort. The Sonoma magnate had seemingly accepted the situation in a thoroughly sportsmanlike manner. Nevertheless he wrote to the Mexican Minister of War and Marine on December 12 that he had refused the Russian offer as "impertinent" but that Sutter had purchased for 30,000 pesos "all cattle and real property at Ross, Bodega, and the other places that the Russians occupied and *continue to occupy.*" He criticized Sutter's activities at Bodega, sounded a warning note regarding the movements of the Hudson's Bay Company, and expressed apprehension at the continued presence of the Russians and their "noisy statements."

On December 12, 1841, Rotcheff at Fort Ross drew up a bill of sale in which he made declaration as commander of Fort Ross that all the Russian properties both real and personal had been ceded by the Russian American Company to "M. le Capitaine Sutter" for thirty thousand dollars. Just what occasioned this action we have no means of determining. It may have been obligingly taken at the solicitation of Sutter, who perhaps thought it would be of some future value to him. At any rate, it held no important legal significance, as Rotcheff was not vested with any authority in the matter of the transfer.

On the following day, December 13, the contract of sale was duly executed at Yerba Buena. It was signed by the contracting parties, Kostromitinoff and Sutter, and witnessed by Francisco Guerrero, J. J. Vioget and Jacob Leese. Under the terms Sutter bound himself to pay the sum of $30,000 "within four years counting from the year 1842," payments to be made in produce during the first and second years in the amount of

$5,000 each; in the third year, $10,000, and in the fourth year $10,000 in coin. It is expressly stated in Article 1 that the purchase did not include the land.

On December 19 Kostromitinoff officially advised Governor Alvarado of the transfer to Sutter and mentioned that Alvarado had personally assured him on the occasion of his call at Monterey that he would not interfere with any sale that might be made. In the body of the letter he included a copy of Article 9 of the contract in which the mortgage of all Sutter's properties was accepted as security for payments by himself or, in the event of his prior death, by his heirs. In closing, he announced the departure of the Russian "employees and inhabitants." . . .

So ended the thirty years of Russian occupation of a section of California. Henceforth until 1867 the standards of the Tsar waved northward of 54° and 40′ and thereafter nowhere in the western hemisphere.

*During the first part of the twentieth century, Frank A. Golder
(1877–1929) was one of the few professional historians
working on Alaskan history. He concentrated his scholarly
attention on early exploration, the Russian period, and the sale
of Alaska. Professor Golder taught at Stanford University,
and was director of the Hoover War Library. His article
on Russian mining appeared in the* Washington Historical
Quarterly, VII (July, 1916), 233–38.

Mining in Alaska Before 1867

FRANK A. GOLDER

It has generally been assumed that the Russians in Alaska were either indifferent or ignorant of the mineral resources of that territory. That they were not indifferent may be proved from the fact that the desire to find precious metals was one of the reasons why Peter the Great sent out voyages of discovery. The men who followed Bering to America made careful inquiries of the natives as to the existence of metals and minerals on their islands. When the Russian American Company was organized in 1799 it demanded the exclusive right to all the underground riches of Alaska. One may with equal ease refute the charge of ignorance. At the time of the transfer of the territory to the United States gold had been discovered, native copper found, and coal mines opened. Graphite was known to exist on Atka Island, red ochre on Krenitizin, black obsidian and porphyry on Umnak, naptha and amber on the Alaska Peninsula. Copper had been located on Unalaska, Copper Island, Cook Inlet, and the Copper River. Each year the natives came down that stream and sold quantities of that metal to the Russians, but would not show them the place it came from. In the same manner the natives of Cook Inlet offered mica to the traders but refused to disclose the source of the supply. The knowledge of the mineral resources was not wholly derived from the natives. Reliable information was obtained from the writings of Father Veniaminov, from the accounts of the more intelligent of the naval officers, from the bulletins of the agents of the Imperial Academy of Sciences, especially that of Vosnosenski, who stayed five years (1840–1845) in the Northwest making a natural history collection, and from the special reports of the scientists and mining engineers, such as H. J. Holmberg, who made a mineral survey of Kodiak, Peter Doroshin who spent five years in prospecting for gold and coal, and Ialmar Furuhelm who came out to Alaska in 1850 or 1851 and remained ten years in the employ of the company prospecting and superintending the mine on Kenai. The question one naturally asks: if the company knew so much about the mining possibilities of Alaska why was so little done in developing the industry? The answer is that it was too much occupied with the fur trade.

The gradual extermination of the sea-otter and the discovery of gold in California were two factors that greatly influenced the company to give serious attention to mining. In 1848 (1849) it sent out to Alaska Peter Doroshin, a mining engineer, or geognost as he was then called. He reached Cook Inlet late that year but not too late to wash out a few pans of sand and find a few colors. He took up the work in 1850 and commenced prospecting in earnest on the Kenai Peninsula, near the mouth of the Kaknu River.* He had, all told, twelve men to assist him, and the number of working days for that season were not more than forty-nine; so that under the circumstances he could not have been expected to accomplish a great deal. He reported that everywhere he dug he found colors. He returned in 1851 with the intention of going up the Kaknu and two other streams for the purpose of tracing the deposits to their source. Although he put in sixty-six days, in his investigations he could not reach the

*Kenai River.—Ed. Note.

mountains where he hoped to locate the mineral veins. In his report he states that the farther up he went the larger were the grains of gold but nowhere was it in paying quantities. He should have liked to continue his researches for another year or two had the company been willing.

The following year, 1852, Doroshin was set to work to look for coal. During that summer he explored a large part of the territory and located many of the mines known today. He shipped the specimens which he dug out to the Mining Department of St. Petersburg where they were analyzed. The first coal vein examined was at Port Graham, Kenai. It was an eight foot vein and the samples analyzed:

Volatile matter	45.87
Fixed Carbon	42.91
Ash	12.22
Coke	45.13
Heat units[1]	4,294.

On the way from Port Graham to Kachemak he inspected several beds of lignite and passed them by as of little value. But on the northwestern part of Kachemak Bay he found coal which seemed promising. It analyzed:

Volatile matter	48.53
Fixed Carbon	38.91
Ash	12.55
Coke	51.47
Heat Units	4,131.

From Kachemak he sailed north along the eastern shore of the Inlet to its head, crossing the mouths of the streams but not entering them, thence down the western shore as far as Kamishak Bay. Here he left the boat and struck out over the mountains to Lake Iliamina, making notes on the geologic formation of the country as he went along. On the lake there was a boat to take him down the Kvichak River and some distance into the bay of that name and from there up the Naknek River and lakes and the Mishket[2] River to the rapids. At this point he left his boatmen and crossed over the mountains and came to Katmai. In

[1] Probably calories.

taking the route he did Doroshin was prevented from examining the coal in Kanikagluk[2] Bay. (Kukak?), east of Katmai. He, therefore, sent men thither for samples which, when analyzed, gave this result:

Volatile matter	34.45
Fixed carbon	52.44
Ash	13.11
Coke	65.55

Heat Units   5,774.

He was quite enthusiastic about this coal which he regarded as the best in the territory.

Continuing his investigations along the peninsula, Doroshin observed many veins of coal and lignite of minor importance. In one place, probably in the region of Chignak, he discovered naphtha and, what he believed to be natural gas, but he was not certain. He spent some little time at Unga inspecting the coal deposits on that island and concluded that they were not worthy of development because of the poor quality, the high cost of mining, and danger in transportation owing to the large amount of pyrites in the coal. He had planned to go to Port Moller but was prevented because of lack of time. He did the next best thing and sent for specimens. Doroshin himself sailed down to Pavlof Bay and from there returned to Unga. Here he took ship going for Sitka and landed at this place about the middle of October, 1852. The samples from Port Moller, taken from two different veins, analyzed as follows:

Volatile matter	61.57
Fixed Carbon	37.18
Ash	1.25

Heat Units   4,472

and

Volatile matter	50.73
Fixed carbon	39.74
Ash	9.53

Heat Units   4,443.

[2] The names of places have changed considerably since Doroshin's day and it is rather difficult to identify them.

On making inquiries he was told that there was coal on Tigalda Island and on Norton Sound but he was unable to obtain samples from either of these places. From one of the ships in search of Franklin he secured a few chunks of coal which were taken from a vein in the neighborhood of Cape Lisburne. He also had sent to him specimens from Korovin Bay, Atka, which showed on analysis that it contained:

Volatile matter	52.41
Fixed carbon	45.28
Ash	2.53
Heat units 4,893.	

In the region of Sitka Doroshin also made investigations and located several small veins of coal. He had analyzed the coal from Kotznahoo Inlet, Chatham Strait, and got encouraging results.

Volatile matter	38.08
Fixed carbon	50.73
Ash	11.19
Heat units 4,800.	

He was of the opinion that a better grade and thicker veins of coal were to be found in southeastern Alaska, judging by the Canadian product. He made a special trip to inspect the mine in Winterhausen Bay (Winter Harbor?), Vancouver and the samples which he brought back analyzed:

Volatile matter	38.67
Fixed carbon	44.00
Ash	17.03
Heat units 5,009.	

Doroshin returned to Russia towards the end of 1854 or early in 1853.[3] He at once submitted his report to the company and urged upon it to develop the coal beds at Port Graham. On the strength of this recommendation, coupled with the demand for coal in San Francisco, the company decided to venture into the coal mining industry. Work was begun in 1855, a pump was

[3] Doroshin laid his specimens before Professor Heppert of Breslau, who said that the coal from Cook Inlet belonged to the miocene formation of the tertiary period.

put in in 1857, the buildings were completed in 1858, and by 1859 there was a tunnel seventy feet long. In 1860 a fire wiped out the whole plant and ruined the machinery.

After five years of trial the company found that it had lost money. There were many reasons for the failure. The company was working with the view of obtaining immediate returns and not of developing a mining property. By 1860 it had not yet touched the principal vein of coal. Then again the company did not employ skilled miners nor make use of the best machinery. The men who worked in the mines were Siberian soldiers on garrison duty in Alaska. They were independent, worked or idled as they pleased. They knew nothing about mining when they came to Alaska and by the time they had learned something their term of military service, five or seven years, had expired and they departed. They were paid by the day and not by the ton and as a consequence they wasted much time. It was figured out that at one time the mine had on its pay roll 131 men and the daily output was from 30 to 35 tons. When the coal had been mined it was not sorted but all dumped together in the open.

The officers of the company on the spot were in doubt as to the real value of the coal. Some thought it was worthless and others, like the engineer, Fraser, on the steamer Alexander II, were of the opinion that for steaming purposes 10 tons of Kenai was equal to 7 tons of English coal; and if the Alaska coal were sorted 10 tons would equal 8 tons of English. The only markets available at that time were San Francisco and Hong Kong. Five hundred tons were shipped to California and were there sold for six kopeks the prood, or about $1.75 a ton. At this selling price the company was losing heavily, for it cost much more than that just to mine the coal. During the years 1857–1860, the annual output of the mine was about 920 tons, at an actual cost in wages, not counting the outlay on the investment, buildings, ships, office expenses, etc., of 38,480 rubles, or a little more than 41 rubles (assignats) per ton, equivalent to about $15 (?) of American money. At that time, 1860–63, at Hong Kong Japanese coal was selling for $5, Sidney coal for $8 and English coal for $15 the ton. Kenai coal could not compete on such terms.

After the buildings had burned down the company was in doubt as to how to proceed in the future. Ialmar Furuhelm came out from Alaska in 1862 to report on the situation. After several conferences with the directors of the company Furuhelm offered to lease the mine, provided he were allowed a free hand in every way. An agreement was soon reached, according to which Furuhelm was given exclusive control for seven years, from the day of signing the contract, over all the underground resources of Alaska, the right to sell his metals and to buy his machinery and goods where he pleased without paying duty of any kind, to cut whatever timber he needed, to make use of the streams, to carry the flag of the company on his ships, to hire his workmen wherever he liked. In short neither the company nor the government could interfere with him in any way. In return he bound himself to pay the company, beginning with the second year, five per cent of the exported product, and this sum to be increased each year by one per cent. At the end of seven years the mines and all underground improvements were to revert to the company without compensation, and the buildings, machinery, ships, etc., if Furuhelm should decide to sell them, the company promised to buy at a price to be mutually agreed. This arrangement was concluded early in 1863 but it was not put into force because at that time it was uncertain whether the company would have its charter renewed.

The discovery of gold in Oregon and British Columbia raised the question whether this metal might not also be found in Alaska. In 1863 the Russian minister in Washington called his government's attention to that fact. That same year there was a rumor that gold had been found on the Stikine River, and the company's officers became excited and, fearing a stampede of American miners, appealed to the government for a man-of-war. In 1865 the Russian minister wrote again to St. Petersburg reporting a conversation with Professor Whitney, geologist of California, who assured him that there must certainly be gold in Alaska because the geologic coast formation of that territory is the same as that of other parts of the Northwest where gold had been discovered. Whitney was willing to go to Alaska to investigate and the minister urged that he be commissioned to do so. The following year, 1866, it was reported in the Russian papers that some men in Sitka while digging a hole for a telegraph post accidentally found gold. The Russian government, however, had decided long before this to get rid of Alaska, partly because it had become an economic burden and partly for fear should gold be discovered in large quantities the American miners would rush in faster than they could be kept out and this situation might bring about bad feeling between the United States and Russia. These were some of the reasons why Alaska was sold and why all the mining propositions died an untimely death.

If the plans of Furuhelm had been allowed to work out and if Whitney had been sent to investigate, perhaps the mineral resources of Alaska would have been heard of long before they actually were.

PART II

THE TRANSITION

Anatole Mazour was born in Kiev, Russia, and received his Ph.D. from the University of California in 1934. He has taught at the University of Nevada, and is now an emeritus professor of history at Stanford University. Here he considers some of the reasons why Russia decided to sell Alaska. As Professor Mazour indicates, this facet of the topic has not been the subject of definitive scholarly investigation. The article appeared originally in the Pacific Historical Review, X *(September, 1941), 311–19.*

The Prelude to Russia's Departure from America

ANATOLE G. MAZOUR

ecent publications on Russian eastward expansion, including colonization in the New World, confirm a point of view long held by the present writer, namely, that until the papers of the Russian-American Company in the USSR are brought to light, an exhaustive history of Russian activity in America will not be possible. Frequent references in Soviet historical literature indicate that there are still rich and unexplored materials in the Central Archives of Leningrad and in those of the Foreign Office.[1] Until the papers in the Library of Congress,

[1] Upravlenie tsentralnykh gosudarstvennykh arkhivov Leningrada; fond glavnogo pravleniia Rossiisko-Amerikanskoi kompanii. Arkhiv venshnei politiki; fond ministerstva inostrannykh diel; Aziatskii department. These are the chief depositories which contain most of the materials pertaining to the Russian-American Company and to Alaska. Recent publications in Russia, documentary and secondary, pertinent to the subject are as follows: "K istorii russko-amerikanskikh otnoshenii vo vremia grazhdanskoi voiny v Soedinennykh Shtatakh Ameriki [Concerning the history of Russian-American relations during the Civil

159

those in the Bancroft Library, and possibly additional material in Alaska, together with scattered material in the states of Washington and Oregon are brought together with the collections buried in the archives of the USSR, all efforts to give a complete synthetic account of Russia's colonial activities in America will prove futile. This article is a summary based mainly upon recent material published in the Soviet Union.

The climax of Russian colonial ambitions in America was reached on September 4, 1821, when the Imperial Government by an *ukaz* proclaimed its ownership of the Pacific Coast as far south as 51° north latitude and the barring of all foreigners from trading and fishing rights within one hundred Italian miles of the coast. Shortly after that act both Great Britain and the United States, alarmed by the grandiose designs of Alexander I, took up the issue with the aim of curbing the claims of Russia in the Northwest. This was accomplished in 1824 when Russia and the United States signed a Convention, according to which the former's territorial claims in the Northwest were limited to the southern boundary of Alaska at 54° 40'. A year later Great Britain came to a similar agreement with Russia, which recognized the same line of demarcation in the south but continued it north to the Arctic Ocean, thus checking future Russian colonial expansion in America.

Such a retreat can hardly be condemned since it is questionable whether the government could have hoped ever to hold those territories to which the two Conventions entitled Russia. From a strategic point of view Alaska, including the Aleutian and Kuril Islands, constituted a potential liability which would

War in the United States of America]," *Krasny Arkhiv*, III (94), 1939, pp. 97–153; S. B. Okun, "K istorii prodazhi russkikh kolonii v Amerike [Concerning the sale of the Russian colonies in America]," *Istoricheskie zapiski*, II, 1938, pp. 209–39; *idem, Russkie poseleniia v severnoi Amerike* [Russian settlements in North America] (Moscow, 1938); *idem*, "Polozhenie promyslovykh rabochikh v russkikh poseleniiakh v Amerike [Conditions of the trade workers in the Russian settlements in America]," *Uchenye zapiski. Seriia istoricheskikh nauk*, No. 48 (1939), issue 5, pp. 157–70; *idem, Rossiisko-Amerikanskaia kompaniia* [The Russian-America Company] (Moscow, 1939); M. Malkin, *Grazhdanskaia voina v Soedinennykh Shtatakh i tsarskaia Rossiia, 1861–1865 gg.* [The Civil War in the United States and tsarist Russia, 1861–1865] (Moscow, 1939).

have required great sacrifices in case of war, as has been ably discussed by the late Professor Frank A. Golder.[2] The looming conflict between Great Britain and Russia in the early fifties therefore placed the Russian-American Company in a precarious situation and forced it to seek means to avert total annihilation. Faced with such a problem, P. S. Kostromitinov, Russian Vice-Consul and agent of the Company at San Francisco, elaborated a plan whereby the colonies would be sold fictitiously to an America-Russian Company of San Francisco, organized in 1853, presumably for the purchase of ice in the Northwest, but in reality to supply Alaska with food in case of blockade. The matter was broached by Baron Stoeckl, Russian Minister to Washington, to Secretary of State William L. Marcy, but he was given little encouragement since the deal was too obviously fictitious and Great Britain would not have respected the transfer. Simultaneously, the resourceful Consul began to scheme for the organization of an adequate force of privateers to be directed from San Francisco and to operate in Pacific waters against British and French ships, but his plan never materialized. The coolness of the United States government toward such schemes was not due to enmity between the two countries. On the contrary, Washington sympathized with Russia rather than with Great Britain; its desire was merely to let the Russian-American Company linger until it died a natural death, and in the meantime to watch vigilantly lest Britain should decide to take over the coveted territory.

Having failed thus far, some members of the Company thought of turning to diplomatic means, but there was strong opinion among others that any such attempt would serve only as an indication to London of the weakness of Alaska, and therefore they urged that the colony be sold outright to a neutral power, presumably the United States. Still others recommended that the Company appeal to the Russian government to assist in the erection of necessary fortifications and to prepare to defend the colony in case of attack. In spite of the opposition en-

[2] Frank A. Golder, "The Purchase of Alaska," *American Historical Review*, XXV (1920), 411–25.

countered, the view prevailed that diplomacy should be resorted to, and an effort was made to assure neutrality for Alaska during the expected war. Recognition of such status would have involved a guarantee by the Hudson's Bay Company of the inviolability of territorial and property rights of the Russian-American Company. The former company would have been rewarded by a renewal of the lease by which it had held the mainland of southeastern Alaska since February 6, 1839. Accordingly, on January 25, 1854, the Russian-American Company appealed to St. Petersburg for official permission to open diplomatic negotiations, to which the government's reply was that the Emperor would consider the plan favorably, provided the proposed agreement were ratified by both British and Russian governments. On March 31, 1854, such an agreement was reached and approved by London and St. Petersburg, providing that Alaska be respected as a neutral territory with the exception that its ports might be blockaded and ships under the Russian flag in the Pacific might be seized. One accomplishment was evident — Alaska was spared from being drawn into the theater of war.

That Great Britain was none too eager to conduct a war to aid the United States in gaining Alaska is quite clear. It was because of this feeling that London was willing to respect any agreement granting neutrality to Alaska and allowing citizens of an enemy state to continue unmolested activity. During the entire period of the Crimean War, Britain adhered loyally to the terms of the agreement, Alaska thus escaping blockade and — what it feared most — seizure and incorporation within Canada. Stoeckl was convinced that Britain did this because of her desire to prevent the possible sale of Alaska to the United States. "This act of condescension," he wrote to Gorchakov, Russian Minister for Foreign Affairs, "so little in agreement with English selfishness, had an underlying motive: at that time a rumor spread that we intended to sell our colony to the United States, and in order to prevent such sale the British Government ratified the agreement between the two Companies."[3] That Great

[3] *Istoricheskie zapiski*, II, 1938, 215.

Britain could easily have seized Alaska goes without saying, but the British government was well aware that the act would later have involved a conflict with the United States, which it then sought to avoid at any cost: the Crimean War and the Taiping Rebellion which had broken out in 1853 had kept Britain busy enough without additional trouble in America.

Russia's liquidation of her colonial interests in America began, therefore, with the Crimean War, and the attempt, though fictitious, to transfer the Company to another organization was in fact the prelude to an actual legal deal. London and Washington watched developments carefully, each suspecting the other, each anxious not to be outwitted, each endeavoring to get first chance. On the eve of the Crimean War Secretary of State Marcy and Senator William M. Gwin of California carefully inquired of Stoeckl if Russia would consider selling Alaska, but the reply was negative, chiefly because it was considered a premature issue, since neutrality for the territory had been obtained. But with the end of the war, the problem of the future of Alaska came up again. This time the question was raised in St. Petersburg by Grand Duke Constantine, brother of the Emperor, at that time head of the Admiralty. Taught by the severe lessons of the past war, he sought a radical solution for Russia's foreign policy, including the question of Alaska. Accordingly, in a note dated December 19, 1856, he urged the Foreign Office to take up the issue at once.

After analyzing the status of the Empire, Constantine concluded that Russia would never be able to provide adequate defense for her American colonies, were she to come into conflict with a naval power. Therefore, Alaska should be sold or handed over to a totally private concern, and the state should wash its hands of the entire matter. Since the United States was bound to look toward territorial consolidation as its manifest destiny, Constantine further argued, she would naturally make an attempt sooner or later to annex Alaska. In such a case, Constantine concluded, what chance would Russia have? The United States government, he maintained, was able to purchase the colony, and the natural solution would be to sell it in an amicable fashion before it was seized by force.

The Foreign Office agreed with Constantine's views, but it feared that it would antagonize Britain by such an act, and it therefore insisted upon postponing such action until a more propitious moment. Meanwhile Stoeckl was instructed to learn what was the opinion of Washington concerning the matter, being cautioned, however, not to press the issue, since undue anxiety might result in lowering the value of Alaska. But Constantine was impatient and continued to insist to the Foreign Office that since the war was over there was no sense in delaying a deal that was unavoidable; he argued that delay of the sale might only cool Russian-American relations and undermine their commercial intercourse. Constantine was supported by Stoeckl, the latter's argument being that seventeenth and eighteenth century companies with monopoly privileges were doomed and that the Russian-American Company was no exception; that if the historical process prescribed the relinquishment of territory held by an empire, it would be better to comply with all good grace.

There was a great deal of truth in the arguments of those who urged the government to sell the Russian colonies to the United States. For some six decades [4] the government had observed a chartered company enjoying monopoly privileges, still supported by subsidies from the state. By the middle of the nineteenth century, the Company had proved neither a commercial nor a political success, neither a private nor a strictly state concern, but one which in time of peace contributed little materially and in time of war constituted a source of great anxiety. Although during the Crimean War it had miraculously escaped disaster, there was no guarantee that in the future it would enjoy similar good fortune. Beside the aid it received from the government, the Russian-American Company derived profits from the tea trade with China and the fur trade through ruthless exploitation of Alaskan natives; the latter particularly armed

[4] The Russian-American Company was founded in 1799 and given complete monopoly over the Alaska fur trade extending as far south as 55°.

advocates of colonial liquidation with powerful arguments in favor of their theories.

Mineral resources the Company had exploited insufficiently, and what little was done in this respect had been accomplished through concessions to foreigners, mainly to the Hudson's Bay Company as a reward for maintaining neutrality. Yet the question of concessions had frequently marred the cordial relations between Russia and Britain on one hand and the United States on the other. Citizens of both countries had sought concessions and had used diplomatic agents for the exertion of pressure to obtain them. To appease the greed of both sides all the Russian-American Company could do was to find enough concessions to satisfy all claimants, a task not always easy.

In 1866 the total income of the Company amounted to 706,188 rubles, of which 200,000 came as a government subsidy; the cost of administering the organization in the national capital alone absorbed ten per cent of the entire income (71,500 rubles); there remained at best a sum of 10,828 rubles for the payment of dividends to shareholders, or one ruble and forty-five kopecks to every member who held a 150-ruble share. With such small dividends it is little wonder that the Company's 500-ruble shares fell as low as seventy-five in the stock market of 1866. Briefly, this was the situation: if the Company were to continue its existence, it must depend upon annual state subsidies of at least 200,000 rubles; moreover, it would be compelled to shift the responsibility for accumulated arrears to the government, which would have precluded the payment of dividends for a considerable period in the future.[5] It was quite evident that to instill some life into the weak organization and to place it on a sound financial basis required not subsidies but a long-term loan. Incidentally, the London stock market was willing to grant such a loan and for good reason, since it preferred to retain an impotent organization under British financial dominance rather than allow it to fall into the hands of the rapidly encroaching Yankees. Although the London banks were willing

[5] *Istoricheskie zapiski*, II, 1938, 223–24.

to offer a loan, they sought in return a guarantee that the Company be assured its existence, that is, that it not be liquidated through a sale to the United States, and that the loan be approved by the Tsar and the Russian Minister of Finance, Reutern. Such a pledge with all its political implications the Russian Foreign Office seriously opposed, since it was virtually determined in favor of a deal with the United States at the earliest opportune moment.

The liquidation of Russia's possessions in America was further hastened by the fact that not only was Russia unable to defend Alaska, but she was unwilling to do so. By the middle of the nineteenth century the government had decided upon a policy of consolidating its interests in the Far East on the mainland along the Amur River, a policy approved by men like Muraviev-Amursky, Grand Duke Constantine, Baron Stoeckl, and Baron Wrangell, all of whom maintained that only such a course would make Russia a power on the Pacific.

An even more weighty cause that drove Russia toward the abandonment of Alaska was the fear of peaceful economic penetration which would be followed by the loss of the colony from within. Nineteenth century history had more than one illustration of this form of imperialism,[6] and there was no reason to assume that Alaska could escape this fate. In 1857 rumors reached Stoeckl's ears that the Mormons, led by Brigham Young, planned to move northward to Alaska. He immediately reported to St. Petersburg a conversation with President Buchanan during which he had asked point blank whether the Mormons intended to come to Alaska as peaceful settlers or as conquerors. Buchanan's reply was that it mattered very little as long as the government got rid of them. Although Stoeckl added that fear of a Mormon exodus constituted no danger at the moment, he noted, however, that in such an eventuality Russia would be forced either to defend or to surrender Alaska altogether. The sale of the colony seemed, therefore, the wisest course. Alexander II, reading Stoeckl's report, made a marginal

[6] F. A. Golder, "Mining in Alaska before 1867," *Washington Historical Quarterly*, VIII (1916), 233–38.

note: "This confirms the idea of an immediate regulation of the question of our American possessions." At the end of 1857, Gorchakov instructed Stoeckl to approach Washington officials in such a way as subtly to make them understand that Russia would be willing to discuss the matter.

Rumors that gold had been discovered in various parts of Alaska further intensified apprehension. That the presence of gold, coal, and copper in Alaska had been known to the Russians for some time before the sale is now a well-established fact, but the confirmation was carefully guarded, even from the government, partly through fear that the Company would be deprived of the right of exploiting the resources, and partly because if it leaked out, the news would bring a flood of gold seekers and cause serious political complications. Such information could not long be kept from the world. In 1860 Captain Golovin, after an inspection tour through Alaska, reported that gold and valuable minerals were present along the Copper River. This further convinced the government of the advisability of ridding itself of the territory. Paradoxical as this might seem, it was true and for good reason. California had served as an excellent illustration of what could happen when such news leaked out to the world. The same thing would occur in Alaska: a gold rush would commence, and Russia would not have a chance to maintain sovereignty over her claimed territories. Demands for concessions from either the Hudson's Bay Company or United States citizens, or most likely from both, would be inevitable, and the government would face the alternative of either granting or refusing them — in either case gaining very little.

As time went on and the press began to refer more frequently to the discovery of gold in Alaska, further concealment of the fact was entirely out of the question, and the Russian-American Company was at a total loss as to how to avert a serious crisis. At first it continued to deny all rumors. Later it admitted that they contained some truth, but stated that the amount of gold had been grossly exaggerated by greedy prospectors. Finally, when it realized that the presence of gold had become widely known, it appealed in alarm to St. Petersburg for a warship to guard the colony against possible invasion. Meanwhile, two factors prevented the Russian government from taking any energetic measures. Engaged in the consolidation of the recently acquired Maritime Province and somewhat disturbed by the Taiping Rebellion, Russia was compelled to concentrate all forces on the mainland, and the outbreak of the Civil War in the United States further postponed the issue.

The old notion, therefore, that the Tsarist government was stupid to sell such a valuable gold mine as Alaska for a mere song must be dismissed as sheer nonsense. The government knew well what it had on its hands. It realized the difficulty of holding Alaska after a gold rush, and it did not wish to lose its possessions altogether with no remuneration whatever. Various government officials as well as laymen protested through the press against the sale of Alaska, buttressing their arguments with the assertion that within a short time Russia could obtain more gold from Alaska than the United States could ever have offered for it. In short, the Russian government was not blind to what it was offering to sell; nor were many Russians enlightened on the subject unaware of the potentialities offered for the future by maintaining sovereignty over Alaska. Zavalishin's bitter complaints against the sale of Fort Ross portentously indicated the sentiments of this opposition as early as 1849.[7] What the government feared, and quite naturally, was that if it continued to maintain its weak hold upon the North American possessions, the territories, would be swarmed over by an army of Canadian and United States prospectors. This would probably have resulted in annexation either by Great Britain or the United States.

There were three possible courses of action before the Russian government: either to maintain the status quo, which for reasons explained above had become extremely difficult; or to transfer all territories into crown lands and thereby place the responsibility for their management entirely upon the govern-

---

[7] Anatole G. Mazour, "Dimitry Zavalishin: Dreamer of a Russian-American Empire," *Pacific Historical Review*, V (March, 1936), 26–37.

ment; or finally, to get rid of them altogether at the earliest favorable opportunity. The government decided upon the last-named course, and for obvious reasons, it did so quite logically. On July 1, 1862, the charter of the Russian-American Company was to lapse unless renewed, and in 1860 the Company had already commenced to appeal for its extension. As far as the government was concerned, it had practically settled the question of liquidation, but for a number of reasons, both political and economic, it had to disguise that decision; it continued negotiations with the Company until 1867, when the fate of the American possessions had been legally sealed, then transferred them to the United States. Meanwhile, the Company functioned according to the terms of a royal decree issued on May 29, 1861, which allowed it to operate on the basis of the old charter.

One more aspect must be mentioned, namely, the sale of Alaska as motivated by *Weltpolitik*. What further convinced the Russian government of the advisability of selling Alaska was the expectation that the United States, taught by earlier experiences during the Civil War and the enmity of Great Britain toward the North, would assume a friendly attitude in international affairs toward Russia. Russia at that time sought friends in world affairs, since its government nurtured the idea of reopening the Near Eastern question regardless of British opposition, and hoped to have the perplexing problem of the Straits solved once and for all. On the other hand, by holding off the deal with the United States, Russia might have been able to denounce the clauses of the Treaty of Paris pertaining to the demilitarization of the Black Sea with less opposition from London. This second scheme was soon achieved under different circumstances with the aid of Bismarck, who repaid St. Petersburg for Russia's benevolent neutrality during the Franco-Prussian War. There remained the eternal Near Eastern problem, where the attitude of Bismarck was neither clear nor reliable, and therefore whatever diplomatic support might come from Washington would be helpful. Altogether, holding out further was futile. Russia therefore sold Alaska at a price that aroused much criticism as being too low, but the low price was motivated by the desire for friendship against a traditional diplomatic foe, Great Britain. London would probably have offered a higher price, but the Foreign Office was not interested in such a deal, even if financially more attractive. It had greater stakes. St. Petersburg was well aware that after California and Oregon, the transfer of Alaska to the United States would constitute a serious blow to British influence on the Pacific. With these motives negotiations assumed a more practical tone early in 1865, culminating in the sealing of the deal in 1867. The rest of the story is too well known to be repeated here.[8]

[8] The reader is referred to an admirable study on this subject by Victor J. Farrar, *The Annexation of Russian America to the United States* (Washington, 1937). A penetrating chapter is to be found in Thomas A. Bailey's recent work, *A Diplomatic History of the American People* (New York, 1940), 395–405. See also the *New York Times*, December 24, 1939, where a revealing letter describes the thrilling story of the attempt to establish telegraphic communications with Europe across Siberia as a factor in the purchase of Alaska.

Born and educated in the state of Washington, Edward
Keithahn *taught school in Alaska for the Bureau of Education
and Indian Service. From 1941 to 1965, he was curator of
the Territorial (State) Museum and Library in Juneau. He has
published numerous Alaskan articles in popular periodicals,
including the* Alaska Sportsman, Outdoor America, *and*
Sunset. Mr. Keithahn *now lives in Eugene, Oregon.* "Alaska
Ice, Inc." *appeared in the* Pacific Northwest Quarterly, XXXVI
(April, 1945), 121–131.

Alaska Ice, Inc.

E. L. KEITHAHN

One of the most elusive chapters in Alaska's colorful history concerns the operations of the American Russian Commercial Company of San Francisco. Overlooked and often confused with the Russian-American Company because of the similarity of names, this corporation was founded by San Francisco capitalists apparently for the main purpose of exploiting Alaska's ice. And strange as it may seem, it had the distinction of importing the first horses to Alaska, planting its first oats, building its first road, laying its first iron rails, and operating a sawmill, the principal product of which was sawdust.

Back in 1850, ice was an expensive luxury in San Francisco, but California was in the midst of its gold boom and could afford luxuries. Ice was being sent from Boston via Cape Horn at terrific expense but not in sufficient quantity to meet the ever-increasing demand. It was then that enterprising Californians thought of Alaska, for if there was one thing that Alaska had and California needed, it was ice.

The initial contract for Alaska ice was made in 1851 between a party of San Francisco businessmen and Chief Director Rosenberg of the Russian-American Colonies. According to Bancroft[1] it provided for the purchase of 250 tons of ice at $75 per ton. This shipment was made in February, 1852. Dall states that the "Company" — meaning the American Russian Commercial Company — "received about $18,000 at $75 per ton" for the ice in San Francisco. He does not say what it cost in Sitka.[2]

The sale of the first shipment having met with success, in October of the same year a new contract was made wherein the Russian-American Company agreed to furnish the American Russian Commercial Company with 1000 tons annually at $35 per ton, the contract to be binding for three years.

The Ice Company, as it is generally known, did not get around to incorporating until May, 1853. According to the certificate of trustees, the corporation was formed "for the purpose of importing Ice from the Port of New Archangel and other Ports in the Russian Settlements in North America, into the State of California, and trading in the same, and for the purpose of engaging in Foreign and Domestic Trade and Commerce generally." Those signing were Chas. Minturn, C. J. Brenham, Edmund Randolph, Sam'l Moss, Jr., Wm. H. White, Charles Baum, Lucien Herman, Arch'd C. Peachy, and Beverly C. Sanders. All except Brenham and Peachy were listed as trustees.[3]

According to Farrar, the secret and principal object of the company was not to deal in ice, but to supply Alaska with provisions during the Crimean War (1854–1856).[4] At that time there was danger of Alaska falling into the hands of the British. To forestall such an eventuality a fictitious sale of Alaska to the American Russian Commercial Company of San Francisco was arranged. The proposed bill of sale was made out with blank

[1] Bancroft, *History of Alaska* (San Francisco, 1890), 587.

[2] Dall, *Alaska and Its Resources* (Boston, 1870), 346.

[3] By-Laws of the American Russian Commercial Co. (San Francisco: O'Meara & Painter, Printers, 132 Clay Street, 1855). Document in possession of the Alaska Historical Library and Museum, Juneau, Alaska.

[4] Victor J. Farrar, *Annexation of Russian America to the United States* (Washington, D. C., 1937), 1–2.

spaces for dates and similar details, and was sent to the Russian minister at Washington, D. C., Baron Edouard de Stoeckl, for his approval. Stoeckl went to Secretary of State William L. Marcy and Senator William M. Gwin of California for counsel as to the wisdom of making the transfer public as a genuine transfer of ownership. Both men told him that England could see through the scheme and would not respect the sale.

However, Russia had already leased to the Hudson's Bay Company the mainland of Alaska from Dixon's Entrance to Cape Spencer. Since the two companies enjoyed a community of interests, the officers of the companies persuaded their respective governments to place Alaska outside the theatre of war, whereupon the idea of the fictitious sale was dropped.

Whether or not the "ice" business was originally a blind is a question, but it is beside the point. Selling Alaska ice proved to be a very profitable business enterprise and continued long after the emergency had passed.

Bancroft states that three icehouses were constructed at Novo Arkhangelsk (Sitka) and two at Kodiak in 1852–1853. The original plan was to cut the ice at Sitka, but the mild climate experienced there made ice-forming unpredictable. In fact, in the winter of 1853–1854 one of the California ice ships was forced to load glacier ice from Baird glacier at the head of Thomas Bay, north of Petersburg, presumably because no satisfactory ice formed at Sitka that winter.

Lieutenant Doroshin, writing to General Helmerson of the Russian Imperial Academy in 1855, gives us our first brief mention of the Company's establishment on Woody Island: "On Wood Island, Kadiak harbor, during a number of years past, horses have been kept to perform certain labor in connection with a mysterious ice company, and for the use of these horses a field of 12 acres of oats is regularly sown. . . ."[5]

Nothing further is heard of the company until 1859. In that year, according to Dall, the concern encountered serious difficulties.

[5] *Seal and Salmon Fisheries and General Resources of Alaska*, IV (Washington, D. C., 1898), 286.

The President of the Ice Company in San Francisco proved to be a man of no capital. He could not build the necessary houses to receive the ice in San Francisco, and the fish and ice arriving from Sitka were spoiled for want of storage. Misunderstandings arose. The bank failed in which the Ice Company kept their funds, and the President absconded with the money. At last Captain Furuhelm was sent from Russia to California to annul the contract and make a new one. He succeeded in doing this without resort to legal process, but the proceedings were not consummated for several years.[6]

The new ice contract was finally arranged by Captain Furuhelm in 1863. The Russian authorities were to furnish 3000 tons of ice annually at $7 per ton, delivered at Sitka or Kodiak, but not to any other than the San Francisco company, on the coast of Oregon, California, or Mexico, at less than $25 per ton. Sitka having too mild a climate to form good ice, or in sufficient quantities, the depot of the Ice Company was fixed on Woody Island, near Kodiak.

It is just possible someone has wondered why the price paid for Alaska was not in round numbers, say $7,000,000, instead of $7,200,000. Since the latter figure is the fact, what then, did the $200,000 above the "round number" stand for?

During the course of the Seward-Stoeckl negotiations for the sale and purchase of Alaska the earliest draft on the price to be paid read: "Mr. Seward proposes United States pay 7 million dollars at Washington."[7] The minimum that Stoeckl was instructed to accept was $5,000,000, which Seward offered at the second interview, but which he said he might be able to raise to $5,500,000. Stoeckl held out for $7,000,000, and Seward went up to $6,500,000 stating that the entire Cabinet was against him and that he could not exceed that figure. However, when Stoeckl yielded several points in the matter of property and franchise of the Russian-American Company, Seward agreed to pay $7,000,000 — the price he had secretly decided on at the beginning.

[6] Dall, *op. cit.*, 348.

[7] Farrar, *op. cit.*, 47.

But there were complications that involved the Russian-American Company's lease of the mainland of southeastern Alaska to the Hudson's Bay Company and its contract with the American Russian Commercial Company. Stoeckl was advised by his government that the United States must assume these obligations. Seward, however, would not listen to such a proposal, for he had memories of earlier entanglements with the Hudson's Bay Company, and he intended to free Alaska from like experiences.[8]

At Seward's insistence, Article VI of the treaty provided that "The cession of territory and dominion herein made is hereby declared to be free and unincumbered by any reservations, privileges, franchises, grants, or possessions, by any associated companies, whether corporate or incorporate, Russian or any other, or by any parties, except merely private individual property holders. . . ."

On March 23, 1867, Seward sent Stoeckl the following note:

'With reference to the proposed convention — I have the honor to acquaint you that I must insist upon that clause in the sixth article of the draught which declares the cession to be free and unincumbered by any reservations — and must regard it as an ultimatum; with the President's approval, however, I will add two hundred thousand dollars to the consideration money on that account.'[9]

Stoeckl accepted this stipulation in a note of reply dated March 25; and at Seward's insistence he cabled a summary of the treaty to the Russian Foreign Office with a request for the Emperor's full powers to sign. In a telegram dated March 28 (new style), which reached Washington on the 29th, Stoeckl was informed that the Emperor approved the sale of Alaska for seven million dollars and authorized him to sign the treaty, but as the ice contract with the California company would not expire until January 1, 1868, he was to try to induce the United States either to assume the obligation or to grant the company the exclusive right to export ice. In any case, however, he was

[8] Farrar, *op. cit.*, 49–50.
[9] *Ibid.*, 51–52.

to conclude the treaty without further reference to the Foreign Office.

Since Seward had already added $200,000 to the basic price of $7,000,000, and since the ice contract would probably expire anyway before the actual transfer took place, Stoeckl ignored the item and informed Seward the Emperor had given his assent to the treaty. Seward thereupon decided to engross and sign the treaty that very night so as to have it ready for submission to the Senate on the following day; the historic document was signed at four o'clock on the morning of March 30, 1867.

Perhaps it was for its "nuisance value" only, but at any rate the American Russian Commercial Company figured prominently in the purchase of Alaska and accounted for approximately 3 per cent of the entire price paid. Seward had bought his "ice box."

On November 21, 1867, a special correspondent of the *Alta California* of San Francisco, writing from Sitka, gave a sketch of the "Ice Business" as follows:

The American-Russian Company was organized 14 years ago. Their leading purpose was to procure ice from some available point on the North Pacific Coast. By flowage they converted a low swamp, a mile back of Sitka, into a pond of sixty acres, and built an ice-house of a capacity to hold 10,000 tons. But the ice is too porous and brash for exportation, and for several years past no ice has been stored here. The company at this time procure their ice from artificial ponds on a small island adjacent to Kodiak. The winters there afford solid ice from 18 to 25 inches thick. The company, having recently become exclusively Californian, is enlarging operations. The agent, General Dana, is making preparations at Redutsky Lake, fifteen miles east of here, for procuring a part of the annual supply. A dam has been built giving a flowage of ten feet, and affording at its fall an excellent chance for catching salmon. As the prevailing winter wind sweeps the lake longitudinally, the ice will be obtained from an artificial lake of eight to ten acres at the head of the dam, the waters of which cannot be disturbed by the winds. The company hereafter expects to transport 20,000 tons of ice annually, and have now in store, a stock sufficient for two years.

In the same year, George Davidson, of the U.S. Coast Survey, offered the following report describing the ice industry at Woody Island:

The ice lake is about 500 yards from the shore and nearly surrounded by wood, so that the spray from the ocean beach does not reach it. It is partly artificial, having been increased in area and depth by the formation of a dam sixteen feet high, which gives the lake an extent of 2200 feet by 700, and a depth of 22 feet. The surplus water drives an over-shot wheel giving motion to a sawmill. The ice crop comes to maturity by December; the cutting commencing when there is 12 inches thick of clear, solid ice, and ending in February when it has generally increased to 18 inches. The cold is uniform and the ice has not been known to make more than one and a half inch per night, although the temperature has been once recorded as low as 18 degrees below zero during the last five or six years. During these unusual cold epochs the air is quite calm and labor practicable.[10]

Frederick Whymper, an Englishman traveling in Alaska shortly after its purchase by the United States, regarded the ice industry important enough to justify the purchase. He wrote:

A San Francisco Company leased from the Russians the privilege of obtaining ice from St. Paul's, Kodiak Island. The Americans, as it is unnecessary perhaps to remark, use ice at table to a far greater extent than we do, and in the Atlantic States it is sold at an almost nominal price. California, about the warmest state in the Union, naturally consumes a large quantity of ice. It is cut from an artificial lake, which has an area of forty acres. The laborers are all Aleuts (Aleutian Islanders), and are principally engaged for three or four months of winter, while the ice is firm, in cutting it up and storing it for summer consumption. The larger part of this luxury is consumed in San Francisco, but it finds its way to Mexican, Central, and even South American ports. Kodiak, which is included in the purchase, is therefore by no means an unimportant acquisition.[11]

[10] Report of George Davidson, U. S. Coast Survey, November, 1867, pp. 246–47.

[11] Frederick Whymper, *Travel and Adventure in the Territory of Alaska* (London, 1868), 104–05.

Probably the best known Alaskan name associated with the Ice Company was that of J. S. Kostrometinoff, who in 1849 came to Sitka from St. Petersburg, Russia, as general agent for the Russian-American Company, and also acted as agent for the San Francisco ice concern. It was in the winter of 1859 that a ship came from San Francisco to Wood Island for a cargo of ice. Shortly after it was moored to the wharf, Kostrometinoff attempted to go on board but slipped on the gangplank, which was covered with ice, and fell between the wharf and the ship. Since the tide was low, he fell quite a distance, suffering injuries from which he died a few hours later. He was buried at St. Paul (Kodiak), Kodiak Island.[12]

Peter S. Kostrometinoff, an elder brother, had come to Alaska even earlier and was commandant of the Russian possessions in California at Fort Ross. It was he who made the sale to John A. Sutter on December 13, 1841. Later he was a Russian consul in San Francisco. His connection with the ice industry is verified by a letter he wrote on stationery which indicated he was "Agent in California" for the Russian-American Company. The letter addressed to Messrs. Augustine Heard & Co., Hongkong, China, reads:

> Gentlemen, I take the liberty to beg you to inform me by opportunity if it would be profitable and possible to send cargoes of Ice to your Port or any other in China. You are perhaps already aware that California is supplied with Ice from the Russian American Colonies and therefore it would be desirable to know, if not some thing could be done in this branch of trade in China.
>
> Hoping you will favor me with your kind information and opinion, I remain, Gentlemen, your most obedient servant,
>
> P. S. Kostrometinoff,
> 9th, August, 1858.[13]

An item in the *Alaska Herald* of July 1, 1868, indicates that in addition to fish and ice, the Company was by that time in the

---

[12] *The Alaskan,* March 30, 1907.

[13] Letter in possession of the Alaska Historical Library and Museum, Juneau, Alaska.

fur business. Headed "How to Preserve Furs from Moths," the item states:

> Of all the discoveries which have been made in this important matter, the latest and best is that of the Ice Company, which packs its furs in ice and transports them from our Northern Possessions to this city. In a late shipment 132 Silver Fox; 21 Red Fox; 57 Cross Fox; 4 Sea Otter; 38 Land Otter; 8 Beaver; 104 Sable; 1 mink; all valuable furs, we believe intended for the European market, were packed in this way, and arrived here in good condition.

Further evidence of activity in the fur trade is indicated in the following letter, which is quite revealing of trading methods in those times. The Company's activities apparently were under observation by the U. S. Customs, for the letter was among the evidence collected by the investigator.

Office of the American Russian Comm. Co.
Belkofsky, June 15th, 1869

Instructions for Charles Gondorius.

Sir: I find it necessary to keep an old trader, Trachar Duschkin in his place and to let him have charge of shop and goods. He will have charge of all the goods and be responsible for them. For the goods in his charge he will give me a receipt.

The lumber, powder, guns, brandy and rum will be in your charge, about. From the three first articles you will let him have whatever he wants. From rum or brandy you will give him and Toyon [native chief] each one bottle a week. When the hunting party goes away you may give to them according to the number 3–6 bottles. If the hunting party comes back you can give them a glass or two each.

When a customer brings a good sea-otter to the shop you may give him a glass. To Peter Dushkin, Alex. Dushkin, Kinaserrow, some of the old fellows which I shall point out to you and to some of our good customers give now and again a glass. On big holidays you may treat them and altogether use your own discretion about it.

Our object in having you here is to find out how things is going on and to look out that a account is kept of things going out and coming in.

Do this however in a quiet way without appearing to watch them.

The invoices on shore you will translate for our trader. The trader has order to lower or raise the price if necessary or advisable. See in a quiet way that we get the benefit of it. If the trader desires it I wish you would help him in the store. See that the houses are in good order; that goods are kept dry and in good order and make yourself otherwise for us usefull.

Look out against any danger from fire. Be friendly and on good terms with the trader, Toyon, and all the people. The trader has order to let you have out the store what you want, keeping an account of it. The furs collected, see that they are kept in a dry and safe place.

Otter killing is prohibited but we buy those of the natives which they have killed for their subsistence.

The Chief gets from us too Rubs [two Rubles] in month in goods. Watch him quietly and see if sells furs to Ossman but don't say anything till my return.

Before my return you and the trader make out a list of our standing property such as houses, both [boat] oars, poles, furniture in house or shop with the cost price. Also a list of goods most in demand and the quantities.

If the inhabitants of the surrounding villages come here treat them a little and try to get their trade. Get as many furs as possible, prevent as much as possible other people from trading here. Represent our company in case a American war or revenue vessel should come here. Your full salary goes on from June 1st, 1869. Hoping you will do all in your power to further the interests of our company.

I remain yours

(*Seal of Co.*)   (*signed*) John G. Landman[14]

On September 15, 1868, the *Alaska Herald* protested the Russian-American Company's interests being sold to Hutchinson, Kohl, and Company in preference to the San Francisco company as follows:

The Ice Company five years ago paid a bonus to the Russian Government of $500,000 for certain restricted rights. Their influence

[14] United States Customs Records, Juneau, Alaska, "All Correspondence, 1869–1874," vol. 16.

for good among the natives has been infinitely superior to that of the Company. They have furnished more profitable employment to the natives and have rendered their condition better, purer and happier, and being an old established firm, extending its benefi- cence over a large section of the country it is strange that Maxutoff should not have offered these immense interests to them, instead of to a penniless Baltimore adventurer.

The following year, February 1, 1869, the *Herald* carried a story which indicated that San Franciscans were beginning to rebel at the high price of ice and were seeking to interest some other concern in the ice business, with the hopes that compe- tition would tend to reduce the price. The item headed "New Ice Company" was as follows:

The present Ice Company has its establishment in Lesnoy an island near Kadiak. They furnish ice to our citizens at 5¢ per pound, a price so high, as to place it beyond the reach of common use. On the Island of Kadiak, are splendid lakes of pure and healthy water with magnificent neighboring forests. A new ice company started at Kadiak could afford to furnish ice in this market at 3¢. Will no one step in?

Apparently no one was interested in challenging a company so well established and on its own ground; yet an entirely new competitor suddenly entered the picture — one which was in the end to spell the doom of the Ice Company. This was arti- ficial ice, which at that time was making its first appearance in San Francisco. A notice in the *Alaska Herald* of January 20, 1871, reads as follows:

Beware! . . . The difference between good and pure water, and bad and unwholesome water often amounts to the difference be- tween good and bad health. Pure ice is as essential as pure water. The best is that supplied by the Kadiak Ice Company, which is made by nature from pure spring water. Its price is two cents a pound. Buy it in preference to that, which is made artificially.

In the same issue of the *Alaska Herald* appeared the following advertisement:

ICE!   ICE!   ICE!
No. 718 Battery Street, Corner of Broadway

———————

The price of Ice for one hundred pounds and over, taken at Ice House, will be in future one and a half cents per pound.

Parties supplied by wagons as usual at two cents per pound. Orders sent to depot or given to drivers will be promptly attended to.

American Russian Commercial Company
D. E. Martin, Superintendent.

W. T. Wythe, writing in the *Overland Monthly* of June, 1872, gives the most complete and interesting description of the Wood Island establishment and its native personnel, revealing for the first time the "Russian" aspects of the bi-national ice company. His description follows verbatim:

Wood Island, the depot of the Sitka Ice Company at Kodiak is low and covered with a dense growth of fir. From the centre of the island a small stream runs toward the coast, which has been dammed in several places, forming large ponds of pure, clear water. The ice is cut in the usual manner, and stored for the San Francisco market. The ice-houses are large and well built, and are said to have capacity for ten thousand tons. The company owns a number of vessels, and employs during the winter from one hundred and fifty to two hundred men, who receive about twenty cents per diem, their food, and a drink of black rum. During the summer, the men are employed in hunting furs and fishing, and the women assist in cleaning and packing codfish. A large village of Aleuts, of the same tribe as those on Kodiak, is located near the company's headquarters. Their houses are not so well built as those of their neighbors, being merely large holes in the ground, covered with a roof of timber. The church, recently erected by the company, has a bell, and is crowded with natives every Sunday. At noon, when the bell strikes, the workmen, all warmly clad in European costume, flock from all quarters for their ration of vodka, or black rum. A large iron kettle, with a shallow saucer chained to the edge, is brought out of the house and placed in front of the door. As each name is called, the owner steps forward, and, taking off his cap, makes a low bow, fills the saucer to the brim, and literally throws the rum down his throat, and so quickly that not a drop falls to the ground. Replacing his cap, after making a second bow, he walks off, bearing on his countenance a smile expressive of full satisfaction. In a few moments, the kettle, which holds about five gallons, is empty, and a second kettle is brought to complete the ceremony. These men are small of stature, strongly built, and bow-legged from their cramped position while occupying the bydarkas.

Although the Ice Company was fading from the Alaska scene in 1879, an item appearing in the *Alaska Appeal* on March 6 of that year stated that the American Russian Commercial Company "still continues to put up a quantity of ice every winter at Wood Island."

The final picture we have of the Ice Company's Wood Island establishment is that of Ivan Petroff in the *10th Census Report* of 1880. On page 28 under the heading "Population and Resources of Alaska" he says:

From Kadiak we are next led to review the settlement of Wood Island opposite, where 156 people are living in 13 frame and log houses and 8 barrabaras. They are engaged in sea-otter hunting during the summer, and cutting up and storing ice during the winter. Here are kept the only equines of the Territory — as many as 20 or 30 head; and they also have the only road in the Western Territory worthy of mention, one running around the island 12 or 13 miles in length, made principally with a view of exercising the horses aforesaid in the summer time when they have no ice to haul. They also have a small ship-yard here, where little vessels of 25 or 30 tons are built for fishing and trade.

In the same article, Petroff indicates operations were about over, soon to stop forever:

In all Western Alaska but one small saw-mill is known to exist, which is on Wood Island, Saint Paul, Kadiak. This mill was first set up to supply saw-dust for packing ice, but since the collapse of that industry its operations have been spasmodic and not worth mentioning.

Petroff does not say how the industry collapsed, but Mr. W. J. Erskine, pioneer Kodiak merchant, has memories of the company, of the "Ice King," a man named Morris, who died insolvent, and of the last days of that historic enterprise. First, the Southern Pacific was built through to the Coast, making it feasible to ship natural ice from the Sierras into San Francisco. Then artificial ice was invented, with the result that the price was forced so low as not to justify the huge investment and shipping risk required to bring ice from Kodiak. Contributing also were the adverse conditions of the times — those seventeen dreary years of such flagrant misrule, abuse, and neglect (1867–1884) that practically nothing, spiritual or material, of the Old Alaska was able to survive. The ice venture failed, it is true, but not until it had demonstrated the fact that even the ice in Seward's "ice box" could be turned to a pretty profit.

Yankee sea captains had traded along the Northwest Coast around the turn of the century. They returned in the 1830's, this time as whalers. Soon the hardy New Englanders were charting courses into Bering Sea and the Arctic Ocean, searching for the relatives of Moby Dick. Whaling was still a major industry in the North Pacific when the Confederate warship Shenandoah *steamed into Alaskan waters during the Civil War.*

Professor Gilbert received his doctorate in history from the University of California, and now teaches at San Jose State College. He is the author of many scholarly articles on California history, the American West, the Civil War, and maritime history. This contribution is from the Journal of the West, *IV (April, 1965), 169–82.*

The Confederate Raider
Shenandoah

BENJAMIN FRANKLIN GILBERT

Second only to the C. S. S. *Alabama*, the Confederate raider, the C. S. S. *Shenandoah* carried the Stars and Bars around the world on an epic 58,000-mile cruise. Immortal in name for firing the last Confederate shot upon the seas, she committed the most destructive phase of her mission in icy northern waters shortly after the Civil War had ended. She was launched as the *Sea King* in Glasgow at Stevens and Sons shipyard in 1863. On her maiden voyage the vessel transported British troops to New Zealand; her log recorded that she could sail more than three hundred twenty miles a day. Such speed caught the watchful eyes of Confederate Agent James D. Bulloch, who clandestinely purchased the ship and proposed using her to operate against the American whaling fleet in the Pacific. In the Confederate Navy Department at Richmond Commander John M. Brooke, who was familiar regarding movements of whalers from his service with the North Pacific

Exploring Expedition, devised a comprehensive plan for the cruise.[1]

The *Sea King's* dimensions were two hundred twenty feet in length and thirty-two feet in beam. Her tonnage was seven hundred ninety and she had two decks and a poop. She was a combination sailing vessel and steamer. A full-rigged ship with three iron masts and lower yards, her sails were royal studding with Cunningham's patented reefing topsails. At first her battery comprised two Whitworth muzzle-loading rifled 32-pounders, four seven-inch guns, and two smaller guns. Later the seven-inch guns were replaced by eight-inch smooth bore guns.[2]

The outfitting of the *Sea King* and her conversion into a Confederate cruiser was veiled in secrecy. She stood out of London as a typical Indiaman flying the British flag and under the command of Captain Peter Corbett with clearance papers for Bombay. A few hours earlier a Confederate supply ship, the *Laurel*, sailed from Liverpool. On October 18, 1864, the two ships rendezvoused at Las Desertas, an uninhabited island of the Madeiras. The *Sea King's* log for that day recorded that the vessel was sold to James Waddell, but her actual transfer to this Confederate naval officer and her renaming as the *Shenandoah* had been prearranged. Twenty-three officers and about a dozen enlisted men had sailed in the *Laurel* with armaments and cargo. The enlisted men constituted a select group of veteran seamen from the recently sunk *C. S. S. Alabama*.[3]

[1] THE WAR OF THE REBELLION: *A Compilation of the Official Records of the Union and Confederate Navies in the War of the Rebellion* (Washington, D. C., 1894–1922), Ser. II, Vol. II, pp. 64–65, Mallory to Bulloch, May 9, 1861; pp. 707–709, Bulloch to Mallory, August 19, 1864; hereinafter cited as *O. R. N.*; Cornelius E. Hunt, THE SHENANDOAH: *or The Last Confederate Cruiser* (New York, 1866), pp. 9–10. James R. Soley, THE NAVY IN THE CIVIL WAR: *The Blockade and the Cruisers* (New York, 1898), pp. 219–220.

[2] *O. R. N.*, Ser. II, Vol. I, pp. 266–67; *Geneva Arbitration, Log Books*, Vol. 6, *Shenandoah*, et. al., *Copy Register for Transmission to Chief Register of Shipping* (Microfilm, Public Record Office, London).

[3] John T. Mason, "The Last of the Confederate Cruisers," *The Century Illustrated Monthly Magazine*, Vol. LVI (August, 1898), p. 600; James D. Bulloch, THE SECRET SERVICE OF THE CONFEDERATE STATES IN EUROPE, *or How the Confederate Cruisers Were Equipped* (London, 1883), Vol. II,

Lieutenant James Waddell, an Annapolis graduate and experienced seafarer, assumed command of the *Shenandoah*. From the combined crews of the *Laurel* and *Sea King* he hoped to enlist some sixty or seventy men for duty; however, only twenty-three men volunteered and Waddell had only one-half his needed complement. Among the officers three had served previously aboard the *Alabama*.[4]

On October 19, the *Shenandoah* set sail from the Madeiras, heading southward. Eleven days out she captured and burned her first prize, the whaler *Alina*, in a position fifteen degrees above the equator. From the crew of this victim Captain Waddell gained six new recruits. After capturing five more prizes, the raider entered the South Atlantic whaling grounds in December. She captured a bark, and then stopped at the forsaken island of Tristan de Cunha to put prisoners ashore. The raider next set her course to round the Cape of Good Hope. En route to Australia the *Shenandoah* captured only one vessel in the Indian Ocean, and she made one stop at St. Paul Island where fresh water and fish were procured for her stores.[5]

During her stay at Melbourne from January 25 to February 18, 1865, Captain Waddell utilized the port as a base of operations for the *Shenandoah's* projected cruise into the Pacific. Here food, coal and supplies were obtained. Repairs were made, prisoners put ashore, and new men recruited. United States Consul William Blanchard adamantly protested the assistance rendered, demanding that Sir Charles Darling, Governor of Victoria, seize the vessel for "piratical acts." Instead, Darling decided to treat the *Shenandoah* as a belligerent warship; Blan-

---

p. 142; *Official Log Book, Sea King*, October 18, 1865 (Microfilm, Public Record Office, London).

[4] Bulloch, *op. cit.*, Vol. II, p. 145; *Norfolk Pilot*, January 19, 1920.

[5] Mason, *op. cit.*, p. 603; Hunt, *passim*; Jan Brander, TRISTAN DA CUNHA, 1506–1902 (London, 1940), p. 186; Margaret Mackay, ANGRY ISLAND: *The Story of Tristan da Cunha*, 1506–1963 (Chicago, 1964), p. 88; the latter study erroneously describes the *Shenandoah* as hovering off Tristan da Cunha in 1862 and mistakenly refers to the vessel as a prize captured from the United States Navy.

chard answered that the United States would claim indemnity for both past and future damages committed by the raider.[6]

In vain Consul Blanchard attempted to stop Captain Waddell from enlisting men to augment his crew. Although Waddell denied all charges of recruiting, his ship's log for the afternoon watch on the day of departure read as follows: [7]

> At 1 discharged Pilot. Forty-two men found on board. Thirty-six shipped as sailors and six enlisted as marines. Several sails in sight.

After sailing from Melbourne, the *Shenandoah* headed for the New Zealand coast where it was expected that American whalers would be found. However, since no shipping was located, the raider turned northeastward to cruise in the vicinity of Fiji, Gilbert, and other island groups of the Southwestern and Western Pacific. On March 23, Drummond's Island was sighted. Here Waddell hoped to capture several whalers, but he learned from natives, who approached the ship in canoes, that there were no sails in the area.[8]

Entering equatorial waters, the cruiser overhauled the Hawaiian schooner *Pfiel* on March 30, but again heard no news of potential prizes. The *Shenandoah* passed Strong's Island without seeing a sail. On April 1, the warship sighted Ascension Island (Ponape) of the Caroline group, a rendezvous for United States whalers. Sails were furled and the vessel entered Lod Harbor under steam, terrifying the natives who had never observed a steamer. Thomas Harrock, the resident English pilot and an escaped convict from Botany Bay, guided the ship inside the reef to an anchorage about a mile from four whalers. Once inside the harbor the whalers were taken as prizes as the raider's log entry revealed: [9]

[6] Edward E. Morris, A MEMOIR OF GEORGE HIGINBOTHAM: *An Australian Politician and Chief Justice of Victoria* (London, 1895), pp. 84–85; Ernest Scott, "The Shenandoah Incident, 1865," *Victorian Historical Magazine*, Vol. XI (September, 1926), pp. 55–75; *Melbourne Argus*, February 27, 1865.

[7] *Log of the Shenandoah*, (Microfilm), February 18, 1865.

[8] *Confederate Documents*, Vol. LI, *Waddell Papers*, No. 80 (Microfilm, The National Archives), p. 77; William C. Whittle, "The Cruise of the Shenandoah," *Southern Historical Society Papers*, Vol. XXXV (1907), p. 251.

[9] *Log of the Shenandoah*, April 1, 1865. The *Pearl* was owned by parties in

Fitted out 4 boats and boarded each vessel. They proved to be the American whalers "Edward Cary" of San Francisco, the "Hector" of New Bedford, the "Pearl" of New London and the "Harvest" of Honolulu, nominally, but really an American under false colors having no bill of sale on board bearing her American name & in the same trade as before, consequently condemned her as a prize in connection with the other three.

As the Dixie tars from the four boats effected their captures the *Shenandoah* fired a blank and ran up the Stars and Bars. After the sailors removed all precious cargo from the whalers, they permitted the natives to ransack whatever remained, and then the Confederates applied the torch to their prizes.[10]

While in port Captain Waddell extended an invitation to the "King" of the local tribe to visit the *Shenandoah*. The ship's log for April 2 stated:[11]

1000 sent an officer on shore with the Pilot to invite the Chief to visit the ship. 10:30 he came on accompanied by 4 attendants and large number of boats. Sent ashore 22 prize muskets and 2 boxes of tobacco as presents to the Chief.

The officer dispatched ashore on this delicate diplomatic mission was Cornelius Hunt, who took the Captain's gig with six armed men and the English pilot to serve as interpreter. When they landed, the natives at first stoned them, but eventually Hunt persuaded the natives of his peaceful intentions. He obtained an audience with the Chief who accepted the invitation. The Captain's gig was escorted by seventy decorated war canoes. The Chief and his attendants each wore a wreath of flowers on his head and an apron of sea weed around his waist. The tattooed islanders, whose bodies were covered with coconut oil, were piped aboard the Confederate warship. After a tour of inspection, Captain Waddell took the Chief into his cabin where they conversed and smoked the pipe of peace.

Honolulu. The *Harvest* was owned by Messrs. Pfluger, Dowseth, and Molteno of Honolulu, none of whom were United States citizens. See *Pacific Commercial Advertiser* (Honolulu), August 12, 1865.

[10] Hunt, *op. cit.*, pp. 128–29.

[11] *Log of the Shenandoah*, April 2, 1865.

Upon conclusion of the visit the delighted Chief returned ashore with his gifts. On April 12, Captain Waddell informed the Chief that he was sailing the next day. According to Waddell the chief said: "Tell Jeff. Davis he is my brother and a big warrior. . . ," and he gave the Captain a present of two chickens to send to the President of the Confederate States.[12]

On the day of departure, one hundred thirty prisoners from the whalers were paroled, given provisions, and put ashore with the Chief's permission. Eight other sailors volunteered to ship aboard the *Shenandoah*. Whaling charts obtained from the captured prizes later enabled the Confederates to locate more easily the cruising grounds of the whaling fleet.[13]

The *Shenandoah* weighed anchor and stood out to sea, sailing in a northerly direction. For five weeks little excitement occurred aboard the ship. In hope of capturing prizes the raider cruised briefly in the track of ships plying between San Francisco and Hong Kong, but only mustering of hands, reading the Articles of War, and gun practice were recorded in the ship's log. On May 20, Onnekotan Island was sighted; the next day the vessel steamed for Amphrite Strait, entrance to the Okhotsk Sea whaling grounds. As the *Shenandoah* plowed slowly through the ice floes in search of prey the lofty mountain peaks of the Kamchatka Peninsula became plainly visible.[14]

Upon sighting a sail on the afternoon of May 27, the raider gave chase, but it took several hours to navigate through the ice to the prospective prize. The *Shenandoah* deceitfully hoisted a Russian flag and her victim matter-of-factly answered with the Stars and Stripes. Immediately the false colors were lowered and the Stars and Bars were run up. A blank was fired at the bark *Abigail* of New Bedford. This whaler and its outfit were valued at fifteen thousand dollars and twenty barrels of whale oil aboard were valued at $1,705. Stores, including tobacco, ham, rice, and potatoes, were transferred to the raider. The Southern officers expropriated many Japanese curios found

[12] *Waddell Papers*, p. 93.
[13] *Ibid.*, pp. 83–84; *Shenandoah Log*, April 13, 1865; Whittle, *op. cit.*, p. 252.
[14] *Shenandoah Log*, April 13 to May 20, 1865; Hunt, *op. cit.*, pp. 141–150.

aboard the prize. Both officers and men also requisitioned some liquor, and several became intoxicated while on watch, fomenting much bedlam. Before the *Abigail* was burned, thirty-five prisoners were transferred to the *Shenandoah*. Eleven prisoners shipped on the cruiser, and Thomas S. Manning, second mate of the *Abigail* and an experienced Arctic navigator, agreed to assist in locating the whaling fleet.[15]

The *Shenandoah* cruised for twenty-two days in the Okhotsk Sea, but heavy ice floes prevented her from reaching her intended destination, the right whalers' rendezvous at Jonas Island, about midway inside the sea. On June 14, the warship sailed out the Amphrite Strait and set her course for the Bering Strait. The ship ran between the most eastern of the Komandorskie Islands and Attu Island, entering the Bering Sea within two days.[16]

On June 22, the *Shenandoah* stood off Cape Thaddeus. At 0900 hours a lookout sighted two sails off the port quarter. Sails were furled and the chase under steam began. Two hours later the whaler *William Thompson* was captured. The second sail, the ship *Euphrates*, was captured at noon.[17]

After burning these two prizes, the *Shenandoah* proceeded northward towards the main part of the whaling fleet in the Bering Strait. On the afternoon of June 23, several whalers were sighted. The *Milo* of New Bedford was boarded and bonded for $46,000. The logbook of the *Milo* delineated the capture in the following curt words: [18]

1865 — Ship Milo of New Bedford in June — Kamshatka Sea Friday 23 — This day wind N at 2 p.m. The Steamer Shenandore spoke to us, paroled us, put four ships crews on board us. Consequently we have to make port. Men employed at ships duty. So ends this day.

---

[15] *Shenandoah Log*, May 27, 1865; Hunt, *op. cit.*, pp. 162–63.

[16] Hunt, *op. cit.*, pp. 157–67; Whittle, *op. cit.*, p. 252.

[17] *Shenandoah Log*, June 22, 1865; Bulloch, *op. cit.*, Vol. II, p. 154; *New Bedford Evening Standard*, August 25, 1865, p. 2.

[18] *Log of Milo* (transcript), June 23, 1865, from letter dated December 17, 1946, to author from William H. Tripp, possessor of the original logbook.

Despite the truthful pleas by several whaling captains that the war was over, Captain Waddell unsparingly pillaged the Arctic whaling fleet. He set the torch to twenty craft, and ransomed four others to transport prisoners to Honolulu and San Francisco. The raider's course could be plotted across a chart by burning hulks of her victims. Fortunately, several whalers managed to elude the *Shenandoah* because Captain Ebenezer F. Nye of the *Susan Abigail* escaped in a boat to forewarn them. On June 29, the *Shenandoah* passed through the Bering Strait into the Arctic Ocean, but soon was forced to return because of heavy ice floes. An excerpt from the log of the *Congress*, which was whaling in the Arctic on July 2, indicated the alarm caused by the Dixie raider's appearance as follows: [19]

> First part light breeze from S.E. with fine weather cruising along the ice gaming with the STEPHANIE at 8 P.M. Capt. Sinclair. Returned thick fog. Latter part at 1 A.M. fog lit up. 1:30 A.M. saw the bark JOHN HOWLAND with his colors up. Run down and spoke to him. Capt. Fraisure reports a rebel privateer in the straits, having burnt about forty ships. Hoisted all colors to git the ships down to inform them of it. Spoke the CORAL Capt. Crandell came on board to get the news. Ships all get colors set. A great exsightment among us all. Fresh breeze from S.S.E. Lat. 67:40N.

By this time, however, the *Shenandoah* was considerably south of the remaining whalers. On July 5, she passed through the Amukta Pass of the Aleutian Islands and left the Bering Sea. Waddell set his course for the California Coast, hoping to capture Panama ships. Aboard some of the captured whalers he had found California newspapers which told of Lee's surrender, but also of the Danville Proclamation by Jefferson Davis, urging a continuation of the war. Waddell planned to enter the Golden Gate and lay San Francisco under retribution. From newspapers he gained intelligence concerning inadequate harbor defenses of that port. Waddell confidently believed that he could ram and capture the ironclad warship guarding the Golden Gate. However, before attempting such a daring proj-

[19] *Log of Congress* (transcript), July 2, 1865, from letter dated December 17, 1946, to author from William H. Tripp, possessor of the original logbook.

ect, he first intended to communicate with a ship recently out from San Francisco.[20]

On July 18, headlines of a San Francisco newspaper blared: [21] "THE PIRATE SHENANDOAH! SHE STEERS IN THE TRACK OF WHALERS! TERRIBLE HAVOC EXPECTED!" This news was based upon a story from the *Honolulu Advertiser* on June 24, relating that a suspicious warship, believed to be the *Shenandoah*, had stopped the Hawaiian schooner *Pfiel* on March 30, near Ascension Island, and had inquired about whalers. Two days after the appearance of the news, frenzied excitement marked the arrival in San Francisco of the ransomed whaleship *Milo* with prisoners aboard. Her log of July 20, 1865, merely recorded the following prosaic entry: [22]

> This day at 4 P.M. passed Point Rezs. Middle part calm and head tide. At 10 A.M. come two of San Francisco. Paid out 45 fathoms of chain, firled sails, maid all snug. Men employed at ship's duty. So ends this day.

On the same day, Captain David McDougal, commandant of Mare Island Navy Yard, wired Secretary of the Navy Gideon Welles: [23]

> Ship "Milo" arrived to-day from the Artic [sic] with crews of ten whalers destroyed by the "Shenandoah" — Admiral Pearson has been notified by Steamer "America" which sails to-day for Panama.

Three days later McDougal sent Welles a second telegram relating: [24]

[20] Whittle, *op. cit.*, p. 253; *Waddell Papers*, p. 17; Waddell served aboard the U. S. S. *Saginaw* in San Francisco Harbor for several months in 1859. See *San Francisco Chronicle*, December 2, 1875, p. 3. For data on the defenses of San Francisco see B. F. Gilbert, "San Francisco Harbor Defenses During the Civil War," *California Historical Society Quarterly*, Vol. XXXIII (September, 1954), pp. 229–240.

[21] As quoted in Murray Morgan, DIXIE RAIDER, *The Saga of the C. S. S. Shenandoah* (New York, 1948), p. 255.

[22] *Log of Milo* (transcript), July 20, 1865, from letter dated January 8, 1947, to author from William H. Tripp, possessor of the original logbook.

[23] *Letters to the Secretary of the Navy*, Vol. II (August 18, 1863, to December 4, 1865), p. 250, McDougal to Welles, July 20, 1865 (The National Archives).

[24] *Ibid.*, July 23, 1865.

Great apprehensions felt by mercantile community of San Francisco in consequence of depredations of "Shenandoah." Merchants, shipowners and Underwriters have addressed a memorial requesting me to telegraph Department for authority to charter, arm and man Steamer "Colorado" of Pacific Mail Company to pursue that vessel.

Charles T. Hopkins, secretary of the California Insurance Company, had hastened to Mare Island to deliver the memorial. Both of McDougal's telegrams went astray, and he heard no word from Washington. Since McDougal had no suitable warship ready to send after the *Shenandoah*, he was willing to outfit the *Colorado* which was already armed with two 32-pounder and two 20-pounder Parrott guns. A civilian scheme to install an additional gun, to enlist a volunteer crew, and to search for the "pirate" was seriously considered, but did not materialize.[25]

Meanwhile, the *Daily Alta California*, in an editorial entitled, "The Piracies of the Shenandoah," asked: [26]

> And why is it that we have no national vessels on this coast, fit and ready to go and chase down this pirate? What has become of the great American Navy, of which we have heard so much? Are the shores of the Pacific unworthy of protection? Does the Secretary of Navy know that San Francisco is the third, if not the second seaport in the United States?

Since sailing from Melbourne, the *Shenandoah* had destroyed a total of twenty-nine whalers in the Pacific Ocean and Bering Sea. Three of these were owned by San Francisco interests, one had owners in Honolulu, and the remainder were out of the New England seaports of Fairhaven, New Bedford and Warren. New Bedford suffered most with nineteen losses. Although San Francisco did not suffer as much as New England, her mercantile and shipping interests expected additional dep-

[25] *Daily Alta California*, July 23, 1865, p. 1; Lloyd C. M. Hare, SALTED TORIES: *The Story of the Whaling Fleets of San Francisco* (Mystic, Connecticut, 1960), pp. 38–39; Arnold S. Lott, A LONG LINE OF SHIPS: *Mare Island's Century of Naval Activity in California* (Annapolis, 1954), p. 87.

[26] *Daily Alta California*, July 21, 1865, p. 1.

redations. Underwriters placed war-risk insurance between San Francisco and Hawaii at one percent, and to ports in the north at three percent for the round-trip voyage. Vessels in ports south of San Francisco and bound to that city were charged one percent.[27]

Commandant McDougal's message to Admiral George Pearson, commanding the Pacific Squadron, reached him at Acapulco on July 29. Pearson immediately ordered Captain Gustavus H. Scott of the *U. S. S. Saranac* to search for the *Shenandoah*. The next day the *Saranac* stood out of Acapulco as the *U. S. S. Swanee* arrived in port. Pearson also ordered Commander Paul Shirley of the *Swanee* to join the search. At the same time Pearson ordered the not-too-seaworthy *U. S. S. Saginaw* to leave San Francisco at once so that a warship could be at Acapulco to protect properties of the Pacific Mail Steamship Company and other American interests as French re-occupation of that Mexican port was momentarily expected. With the search for the *Shenandoah* at last under way Pearson prepared his flagship, the *U. S. S. Lancaster*, to sail for Panama.[28]

After her departure from the Bering Sea, the *Shenandoah* had sailed southward along the meridian of 129° West. On August 2, 1865, when several hundred miles off the Mexican Coast, she sighted a bark and began the chase under steam. As the *Shenandoah* overhauled the bark, Waddell ordered his engine stopped, and a boat was lowered to board the prize. She proved to be British, the *Barracouta* of Liverpool, thirteen days out of San Francisco. The log of the *Shenandoah* described the meeting in these words: [29]

> Having received by the Br. Barque "Barracouta" the sad intelligence of the overthrow of the Confederate Government, all attempts to destroy shipping or property of the United States will cease from this date.

[27] *Mercantile Gazette and Prices Current* (San Francisco), August 2, 1865, p. 2, September 1, 1865, p. 2 and October 2, 1865, p. 2.
[28] *Letters Received from the Pacific Squadron*, Acting Rear Admiral George F. Pearson (Microfilm, The National Archives), hereinafter cited as *Pac. Sqdr. Ltrs.* (Pearson), Pearson to Welles, August 4, 1865.
[29] *Shenandoah Log*, August 2, 1865.

The bewildered Captain Waddell at first set sail for Sydney, but then changed his course and headed for Cape Horn, deciding to return to Liverpool. All war-like appearances were removed from the *Shenandoah*. Her crew busily dismounted guns, fired all pistols, closed port holes, and whitewashed the smoke stack. The former marauder became a non-entity, with neither armament nor nationality.[30]

On the same day the *Shenandoah* spoke to the *Barracouta*, a second paroled whaler, the *General Pike*, stood into San Francisco with additional prisoners. The *Mercantile Gazette and Prices Current*, a San Francisco financial journal, repeated a now familiar lament, when it complained: [31]

> Unfortunately our Government had no war vessels in port to send after the freebooter, who is thus left sole monarch of the Northern Seas, with power to annihilate for the time our commerce in those regions.

As the *Shenandoah* sailed southward a considerable distance at sea, the *Saranac* and *Swanee* out of Acapulco plied in the opposite direction nearer to the coast on their search. Fighting strong head winds and rough seas, the *Saranac* stopped each ship she sighted for possible news of the *Shenandoah*. Many of these were whalers which had not heard of the raider's havoc. Eleven days after her departure from Acapulco, the *Saranac* entered the Golden Gate and proceeded to Mare Island in order to coal and refit for a long reconnaissance cruise. She put into drydock to be calked and coppered. Day and night workmen stowed coal aboard the warship. After three days at the shipyard the *Saranac* sailed down to San Francisco. A thick fog at the Golden Gate compelled her to anchor off Fort Point during the night. By morning when the fog began to lift, she slowly steamed out to sea bound for Hawaii. Two days out she altered her course as a result of certain information received from a passing ship, and headed for Vancouver Island. Eventually the

---

[30] Mason, *op. cit.*, p. 609; Douglas S. Freeman, ed., *Journal of Charles E. Lining, C. S. S. Shenandoah* in *A Calendar of Confederate Papers* (Richmond, 1908), p. 152.

[31] *Mercantile Gazette and Prices Current*, August 2, 1865, p. 2.

Saranac sailed through the Strait of Juan de Fuca and came to anchor in Esquimalt Harbor on August 20.[32]

Meanwhile, when Captain McDougal's telegrams finally came to the attention of the Navy Department in Washington, the Mare Island commandant received the following telegram on August 18: [33]

> Dispatches 20th and 23rd July received today. Delay embarrasses Department in advising relative "Shenandoah." If Pearson left before receipt of news, charter and arm "Colorado" for pursuit, if advisable at this late day. If Pearson is at San Francisco he will act at discretion, sending him this dispatch.

Captain McDougal informed the Navy Department that the *Saranac* had moved north in pursuit of the *Shenandoah*. After obtaining repairs, coal, and provisions at Mare Island, the *Swanee* joined in the search to the north. She sailed from San Francisco on August 22, for the Puget Sound area.[34]

The search in the northern waters offered no clues as to the raider's location. The *Saranac* next sailed alone to Hawaii, leaving Esquimalt on August 22.[35] Two weeks later she obtained repairs and coal at Honolulu. An enlisted man, W. P. Marshall, serving aboard the *Saranac*, later wrote in his reminiscences: [36]

> Our news here from the Shenandoah was meager and indefinite. Our prospects of a conflict with the pirate, and subsequent prize

[32] W. P. Marshall, AFLOAT ON THE PACIFIC (Zanesville, Ohio, 1876), pp. 86–89; *Pac. Sqdr. Ltrs.* (Pearson), McDougal to Pearson, August 29, 1865; the *Victoria Colonist*, August 21, 1865, described the armament of the *Saranac* as heavy. There were thirteen guns consisting of eight broadside 8-inch Dahlgren guns, one 11-inch pivot gun, two 80-pound Parrott guns and two 24-pound howitzers. A side-wheel steamer of 1,484 tons register, she carried a complement of 270 officers and men. The newspaper also stated that the British warship, *H. M. S. Devastation*, according to officers of the *Saranac*, had left Acapulco in pursuit of the *Shenandoah*. However, the *Victoria Colonist* of September 11 stated that the report was incorrect. Although the *Devastation* had sailed from Acapulco on the same day as the American warships, she did not participate in the search and arrived at Esquimalt on September 10.

[33] As quoted in Morgan, *op. cit.*, p. 259.

[34] *Daily Alta California*, August 21, 1865, p. 1; *Pac. Sqdr. Ltrs.* (Pearson), McDougal to Pearson, August 29, 1865.

[35] *Daily Alta California*, November 20, 1865, p. 9.

[36] Marshall, *op. cit.*, p. 95.

money, did not grow brighter; yet we did not give up all hopes of getting along side of her. On the contrary, the laurels of Winslow and the Kearsarge, though they did not keep us from sleeping, yet acted powerfully on our imaginations. We pictured, in fancy, the glory we should win in a bloody conflict with the marauder.

On September 17, the *Saranac* stood out of Honolulu bound for Nuku Hiva in the Marquesas Islands to investigate a rumor that a large shipment of coal had been landed there for the *Shenandoah.* The rumor proved false, and the warship then visited Tahiti. Upon her return to Honolulu, she met whalers from the Okhotsk Sea, but heard no news about the "pirate." On November 8, the *Saranac* sailed for San Francisco, entering the Golden Gate eleven days later. Since her departure from British Columbia, the *Saranac* had completed a tour of 13,165 miles.[37] Meanwhile on October 1, Admiral Pearson had reported to Secretary Welles as follows: [38]

> . . . I have done all in my power to effect the capture or destruction of the pirate "Shenandoah." I shall continue to use all vigilance to defeat the object of the pirate.

As early as July 21, the *Daily Evening Bulletin* of San Francisco had proposed that a British gunboat from Esquimalt be sent in pursuit of the *Shenandoah,* for it would be three weeks in advance of any American warship sailing from Acapulco.[39] Three days later, Allen Francis, United States Consul at Vancouver, and Judge Edward Lander of Washington Territory, called upon Governor Arthur E. Kennedy of Vancouver Island. They requested that a British warship be dispatched to notify the *Shenandoah* of the collapse of the Confederacy. However, the Governor replied that he could not act in the matter without official sanction.[40]

On September 7, the British Foreign Office notified Governor Kennedy that the *Shenandoah* should be detained in any British

[37] *Daily Alta California,* November 20, 1865, p. 9.
[38] *Pac. Sqdr. Ltrs.* (Pearson), Pearson to Welles, October 1, 1865.
[39] *Daily Evening Bulletin,* July 21, 1865, p. 2.
[40] *Victoria Colonist,* July 26, 1865.

port she might enter, and that force could be used if necessary.[41] On October 1, the Admiralty instructed British naval forces in the Pacific to detain the *Shenandoah* provided she put into a port, or to seize her, in the event she were equipped as a warship upon the high seas. Admiral Joseph Denman, commanding the British warships, was directed to treat the *Shenandoah* as a "pirate."[42] His instructions read:[43]

> You are at liberty to communicate these Instructions to the Commander of any cruizer [sic] of the United States' Navy; and, without actually detaching any of the vessels under your command in pursuit of the "Shenandoah," you may render any assistance in your power in putting an end to the mischievous career of this vessel.

On October 11, the Foreign Office sent Governor Kennedy a confidential circular dispatch, stating that if the *Shenandoah* were either detained or captured, she should be delivered to the United States, but that her crew could be set free.[44]

While the search by the United States Pacific Squadron continued, the *Shenandoah* finally came to anchor in the Mersey at Liverpool, on November 6, 1865.[45] On December 12, Admiral Pearson informed the Navy Department of the return of the *Saranac* and *Swanee* from their unsuccessful search. He stated that inasmuch as he had "reliable information" of the surrender of the *Shenandoah* in England, he would discontinue his search.[46]

With the Confederate threat to American whalers and Panama steamers ended, Admiral Pearson turned his attention again to French and Spanish encroachments. He sent the *Saranac* to Acapulco to relieve the *Saginaw*. He ordered the *Swanee*

[41] *Circular Despatches*, 1865–66 (Provincial Archives, Victoria, British Columbia), Cardwell to Kennedy, September 7, 1865.
[42] *Ibid.*, confidential circular, Cardwell to Kennedy, October 11, 1865, enclosures: W. G. Romaine of the Admiralty to Rear Admiral J. Denman, October 1, 1865, and the Law Officers of the Crown to Earl Russell, September 21, 1865.
[43] *Ibid.*, Romaine to Denman, October 1, 1865.
[44] *Ibid.*, Cardwell to Kennedy, October 11, 1865.
[45] Mason, *op. cit.*, pp. 609–610; *London Times*, November 7, 1865, p. 9.
[46] *Pac. Sqdr. Ltrs.* (Pearson), Pearson to Welles, December 12, 1865.

to Callao and the Chincha Islands, for the United States was gravely concerned over Spain's war in the Pacific. The fruitless pursuit of the *Shenandoah* by the Pacific Squadron had prevented a closer observation of developments in the troubled waters of South America where Spain flagrantly violated the Monroe Doctrine.[47]

The pursuit of the raider pointed out the need for a coaling station in the South Pacific, paving the way for the acquisition of a naval base in Samoa during the next decade.[48] Moreover, the depredations of the *C. S. S. Shenandoah* and the weakness of American sea power in the North Pacific indirectly figured in the Alaska purchase issue.[49] Secretary of State William H. Seward favored securing naval outposts, and during the debate in the House of Representatives over the purchase of Alaska Congressman William Higby of California hyperbolized:[50]

> We want no skulking place on that coast for piratical craft, such as we had a few years ago, when the Shenandoah sought harbor off Victoria.

The *Shenandoah* incident was the first international affair in Australian history. The hospitality afforded the Confederates at Melbourne was a major reason for the heavy damages later assessed Great Britain in the Geneva Arbitration.[51] Although the

[47] *Ibid.*, Pearson to Welles, February 16, 1866; for data on French encroachments in the Pacific see B. F. Gilbert, "French Warships on the Mexican West Coast, 1861–1866," *Pacific Historical Review*, Vol. XXIX (February, 1955), pp. 25–37, for data on Spanish encroachments see William C. Davis, THE LAST CONQUISTADORES: *The Spanish Intervention in Peru and Chile*, 1863–1866 (Athens, 1950), and Carlos E. Grez Perez, *Los Intentos de Unión Hispano-Americana y La Guerra de España en El Pacifico* (Santiago, Chile, 1928).

[48] Thomas A. Bailey, A DIPLOMATIC HISTORY OF THE AMERICAN PEOPLE (New York, 7th ed., 1964), p. 422.

[49] B. F. Gilbert, "The Alaska Purchase," *Journal of the West*, Vol. III, No. 2, (April, 1964), pp. 163–174.

[50] As quoted in James R. Robertson, A KENTUCKIAN AT THE COURT OF THE TSARS, *The Ministry of Cassius Marcellus Clay to Russia, 1861–1862 and 1863–1869* (Berea College, Kentucky, 1935), p. 23.

[51] Scott, *op. cit.*, pp. 55–57; *The Case of the United States to be Laid Before the Tribunal of Arbitration to be Convened at Geneva*, Senate Ex. Doc. No. 31 (Washington, D.C., 1872), pp. 165–180; J. Holland Rose, *et. al.*, eds., THE

search for the *Shenandoah* demonstrated the inadequate strength of the Pacific Squadron as well as the necessity for improved communications between Washington and the Pacific Station, the post-Civil War years did not see any increase in the American sea power in that area.[52]

During her cruise the *Shenandoah* carried the Confederate flag around the world. Of the thirty-eight United States vessels she captured, most were destroyed in the Pacific and Arctic Oceans. Four were ransomed and used to transport prisoners while the others were burned. The value of ships, according to the sum of all depositions given by the master of each ship at the time of capture, totaled $1,361,983. From all prizes 1,053 prisoners were taken.[53]

Although the Confederate raider struck a heavy blow at the United States whaling fleet in the Pacific, the discovery of petroleum in Pennsylvania in 1859 had already caused a decline in the consumption of whale and sperm oil. The remainder of the Pacific whaling fleet was crushed by Arctic ice in 1871 and 1876.[54] Throughout the course of the Civil War the commanders of the United States Pacific Squadron expected attacks upon the Pacific whaling fleet and California gold shipments. The United States Navy prevented the attempt by Asbury Harpending and Ridgeley Greathouse, two Confederate sympathizers, to outfit the *J. M. Chapman* as a privateer at San Francisco on March 16, 1863. After the failure of that Confederate venture, warships were dispatched to British Pacific waters to investigate alleged plots by Southerners to outfit privateers at Victoria. Finally, the Navy frustrated the effort of Thomas E. Hogg and six of his accomplices to capture the steamer *Salvador* for the

---

CAMBRIDGE HISTORY OF THE BRITISH EMPIRE (New York, 1929–36), Vol. VIII, Pt. I, p. 528.

[52] For data about the Pacific Station after the Civil War see Robert E. Johnson, THENCE AROUND THE HORN: *The Story of United States Naval Forces on Pacific Station, 1818–1923* (Annapolis, 1963), pp. 124–42.

[53] Bulloch, *op. cit.*, Vol. II, pp. 152–53.

[54] George W. Dalzell, THE FLIGHT OF THE FLAG: *The Continuing Effect of the Civil War Upon the American Carrying Trade* (Chapel Hill, 1940), pp. 229–230.

Confederate Navy at Panama on November 11, 1864. Hogg, a master's mate in the Confederate service, had specific orders to strike a blow at the California trade and whalers in the Pacific. All Confederate forays to plunder American commerce in the Pacific failed during the Civil War; paradoxically, the only actual success came after the war had ended.[55]

Captain James Waddell remained in Liverpool and Paris until the war feelings subsided. Then he returned to the United States and later became captain of the Pacific Mail Line steamer, *City of San Francisco,* engaged in trade between San Francisco and Yokohama. On one of his trips the steamer was wrecked on an uncharted rock. The captain saved all his passengers and crew and was exonerated from any blame. In 1884 he was appointed commander of the Maryland oyster fleet and held this position until his death on March 15, 1886.[56]

As to his ship, she was surrendered to the United States Consul at Liverpool. On March 22, 1866, Nathanial I. Wilson, a Liverpool merchant and shipowner, bought it at public auction. Wilson resold the ship to the Sultan of Zanzibar and it was renamed *El Majidi.* On April 15, 1872, the vessel was wrecked in a hurricane at Zanzibar. Details concerning the fate of the vessel are a matter of dispute.[57] At least it is known that her last days

[55] For details about privateers and the *Salvador* pirates see B. F. Gilbert, "Kentucky Privateers in California," *Register of the Kentucky Historical Society,* Vol. XXXVIII (July 1940), pp. 256–66; "Rumours of Confederate Privateers Operating in Victoria, Vancouver Island," *British Columbia Historical Quarterly,* Vol. XVIII (July–October, 1954), pp. 239–55, and "The Salvador Pirates," *Civil War History,* Vol. V (September, 1959), pp. 294–307. Also see William M. Robinson, Jr., THE CONFEDERATE PRIVATEERS (New Haven, 1928), pp. 257–89.

[56] *Baltimore Sun,* March 16, 1886.

[57] According to Dalzell, *op. cit.,* p. 229, Wilson sold the ship immediately to an agent of the Sultan of Zanzibar. However, a letter to the author of this article from F. L. Lawrence, Office of Shipping Editor, Lloyd's of London, dated January 1, 1947, stated that a search of Lloyd's records indicated that the vessel was sold to the Sultan of Zanzibar apparently in 1871. The vessel arrived at Zanzibar on June 11, 1871, and was wrecked in the harbor during a hurricane on April 15, 1872. The wrecking of *El Majidi* is recorded also in *Lloyd's List* of May 21, 1872. A letter to the author from Sir J. Gray, Chief Justice of the High Court of Zanzibar, dated December 11, 1946, stated that the vessel does not appear to have been at Zanzibar during the hurricane, which destroyed all shipping in the harbor

were spent in the service of the Sultan of Zanzibar. Such was the end of the famed raider, *Shenandoah*.

---

except one vessel. The Chief Justice stated that her loss apparently occurred toward the end of 1872. The two most recent books about the vessel give divergent accounts of the loss. Stanley F. Horn, GALLANT REBEL, *The Fabulous Cruise of the C. S. S. Shenandoah* (New Brunswick, 1947), p. 291, states that the vessel was wrecked in the hurricane and then salvaged. In July, 1872, she sailed for Bombay, but disappeared. Survivors indicated that the ship might have been purposely scuttled by her captain. Morgan, *op. cit.*, p. 332, states that the vessel was destroyed in 1879 on a coral reef in the Indian Ocean. The executive officer of the *Shenandoah*, Whittle, *op. cit.*, p. 258, also states that the vessel was lost in 1879 on a coral reef as did Philip A. Bruce in a biographical article about William C. Whittle that appeared in the *Norfolk Landmark* of January 29, 1911. Bulloch, *op. cit.*, Vol. II, p. 187, also adhered to the 1879 date. Bulloch stated that the *Shenandoah* ". . . carried many a cargo of 'ivory, gum, coral, and coal' for his sable majesty, and weathered the blasts of many monsoons, until at last, in 1879, fourteen years after she struck the Confederate flag, the teak planks were torn from her bottom by a rough scrape on a coral reef, and her iron ribs were left to rust and crumble on a melancholy island in the Indian Ocean."

Charles Vevier, who received his Ph.D. from the University of Wisconsin in 1953, has taught at Rutgers and the University of Rochester. He is a professor of history and vice chancellor of the University of Wisconsin at Milwaukee. In this excellent article, Vevier explores the relationship between the intercontinental telegraph and American westward expansion. The essay first appeared in the Pacific Historical Review, *XXVII (August, 1959), 237–53.*

The Collins Overland Line
and American Continentalism

CHARLES VEVIER

The idea of locking together Eurasia and the Western Hemisphere with a telegraph line sixteen thousand miles long was an ambitious enterprise even for a company as successful as Western Union. In 1864 it created a subsidiary company, the Collins Overland Line, and attempted to snake a line from California to the mouth of the Amur River in eastern Asia via British Columbia, Alaska, and Bering Strait. The product of technology in an age of national expansion, the Collins Overland Line smacked much of the America that went into it — the entrepreneur intent on exploiting a communications system and government aid to private enterprise that was held to be vital in the national interest. More important, the project illustrated the influential presence of a geopolitical outlook — American continentalism — that was derived from two principal sources: the expansionist experience of the nation across the North American continent in the nineteenth century and an estimate of the place of the United States as a leading force in the extension of Western civilization throughout the world. Usually regarded as separate lines of historical development, these concepts were united by the blend of economic expectation with the high moral purpose of an American mission in the form of a project that was intended to place "in the hands of American enterprise the control of the commerce of the world." It was certain to "bind the old world with the new, and unite the inhabitants of the globe in one great civilized and Christian brotherhood."[1] Although the venture was not completed, it did not end in total failure. It helped to maintain American interest in the purchase of Alaska from Russia in 1867, an event which was interpreted as another demonstration that the United States would not only control North America but achieve a lasting economic and political position in Asia along the great circle route of the North Pacific Ocean.

If the times provided a figure who identified with this strand of American ideology, Perry McDonough Collins might easily have been the man. Collins, the original driving force behind the Russo-American telegraph project said:

> The earth will persist in being eight thousand miles in diameter and some twenty-four thousand miles in circumference . . . everybody does not live on Manhattan Island, we very confidently conform to circumstances, and take the world and whatever there is in it, or upon it and do the best we can.[2]

In keeping with a prevailing American social trend, Collins went to the big city, to New York, to seek the fortune that apparently was not available to him in Hyde Park, the place of his birth. Although he lacked a formal education, he did read law in New York. He possessed sufficient initiative and drive to spark his optimism and self-confidence, qualities that he needed in New York since nothing of note happened to him there.

[1] Excerpts from letter by Ezra Cornell, May 8, 1864. Collection of Regional History, University Archives, Cornell University.

[2] P. McD. Collins, "Overland Telegraph Communication via Behring Strait and Across Asiatic Russia to Europe." Western Union, *Statement of the Origin, Organization and Progress of the Russian-American Telegraph Western Union Extension, Collins Overland Line* (Rochester, 1866), 153.

In 1846 to 1849, Collins was a clerk in the office of a shipping firm in New Orleans in the days when the steamboat had revolutionized transportation and communication. Here he met William McKendree Gwin and Robert J. Walker, men whose careers were to be linked closely to American expansionism. From New Orleans he went to California at the time of the gold rush, confirming the feeling about him that he floated on the tides of material development that swept over America in the middle period of its history. When Collins went west, however, he did not carry a spade and pan. Together with J. W. Dent, the father-in-law of Ulysses S. Grant, he was moderately successful as a dealer in gold dust and a banker in what passed for finance in the helter-skelter boom of the gold fields.[3]

The Oregon Treaty in 1846 and the cession of California from Mexico in 1848 that gave the United States a solid front on the Pacific facing Asia also revealed two related reasons for linking the new territory with the rest of the country. In 1844, the nation had acquired the first of its open door trading privileges from China and by 1855 the American Navy had opened Japan to the commerce of the Western world. At home, beginning in 1845 and continuing throughout the 1850's, the national debate over the route of a transcontinental railroad, occasioned by the need for communication with the Pacific Coast, emphasized not only the internal development of the continental mass but also the great commercial future that the United States might have if a railroad were available for goods going across the country to and from Asia. The two units of this argument acquired more significance as Americans watched Russia's eastward march across Siberia under the leadership of Nikolai Muravieff

[3] Biographical data on Collins is scanty, but useful information can be found in an investigation carried out by Philip E. McDonald, "Perry McDonough Collins, A Generous Benefactor of New York University," in Philip McDonald to Donald McNicol, June 10, 1928, McNicol Collection (microfilm copy through the courtesy of the Douglas Library, Queens University); *New York Herald*, October 24, 1860, stating that Collins lived in Tuolumne County, California; Eldon Griffin, *Clippers and Consuls* (Ann Arbor, 1938), 335–346, calling attention to Collins' role in American diplomatic history. The latest source is in a valuable study written by Vilhjalmur Stefansson, *Northwest to Fortune* (New York, 1958), 245–253.

in the 1850's.[4] Stimulated by the course of current events and enlightened by his reading of Russian explorations in the North Pacific in the 1820's, Collins looked westward to Siberia and "fixed upon the river Amoor as the destined channel by which American commercial enterprise was to penetrate the obscure depths of Northern Asia."[5]

In 1856, Collins went to Washington and outlined a plan to navigate the Amur River, discover the resources of the area around it, and formulate some kind of developmental plan for the benefit of American commerce, particularly that of California which he claimed was "seeking a market in exchange for such commodities as she does not produce."[6] Collins freely admitted later that he had his own private interest in the area[7] but it was clear to him that he would succeed only if the foreign policy of the United States recognized the trade of the Amur as an issue in the national interest. President Franklin Pierce, Secretary of State William Marcy, and Baron Edward de Stoeckl, the Russian minister to the United States, listened to him. Stoeckl made inquiries on his behalf to St. Petersburg while Pierce, impressed by the representations made to him by the California delegation to Congress, appointed him American commercial agent for the Amur River.[8]

On April 12, 1856, Collins left for St. Petersburg and points east. The trip lasted almost two years and took him across eastern Siberia to the Pacific coast of Asiatic Russia. He had the distinction of being the second American to cross the Ural Moun-

[4] Robert R. Russel, *Improvement of Communication with the Pacific Coast as an Issue in American Politics, 1783–1864* (Cedar Rapids, Iowa, 1948), 14, 19, 23–24, 274; Ernest G. Ravenstein, *The Russians on the Amur* (London, 1861), 113ff.

[5] Perry McDonough Collins, *A Voyage Down the Amoor* (New York, 1860), 1.

[6] Collins to President Pierce, February 29, 1856, 35th Cong., 1st sess., *House Ex. Doc. 98*, pp. 2–3.

[7] Collins to Frederick W. Seward, September 18, 1861, in National Archives, Consular Dispatches Amoor River, January 14, 1861–June 30, 1874 (Hereafter referred to as NA, Amoor River).

[8] Collins to Pierce, February 29, 1856, 35th Cong., 1st sess., *House Ex. Doc. 98*, p. 4; Frank A. Golder, *Guide to Materials for American History in Russian Archives*, II (Washington, 1937), 13; Cass to James B. Clay, January 15, 1859, 35th Cong., 2nd sess., *House Ex. Doc. 53*, p. 2.

tains and was the first foreigner to descend the Amur to its mouth. A salesman, public relations man, and diplomatic agent, Collins' published account of the journey would make an excellent manual for the fledgling drummer in a foreign land. He collected political information, noted trade possibilities, made climatological observations, and became an amateur archeologist and anthropologist of northern Asia. He enjoyed the hospitality and friendship of influential merchants and government officials residing at the Russian capital and along the route of his travels. Muravieff, the governor and developer of eastern Siberia, allowed him to navigate the Amur and spoke with him about the commercial opportunities in the region.[9] Exhilarated by the life he led as a "pioneer in these wilds in the shape of a live Yankee," he encountered many of the "difficulties [that] all western men who have blazed the first trail in a new country know by experience." [10]

This reference with its flavor of the westward movement and the opening of a new frontier in which he had participated in the United States long before Frederick Jackson Turner formalized it as an explanation of American history, revealed the drift of Collins' understanding of Russia's eastward expansion through Siberia to the Pacific. In order to secure her conquests from China in the Amur region, he felt that the Russians would have "to follow our example in the acquisition of Louisiana." Manchuria was "as necessary to the undisturbed commerce of the Amoor as Louisiana was to our use of the Mississippi." Only the Great Wall of China might contain Russian expansion, an eventuality "not so remote to Russia here at this day as the Rocky mountains in Jefferson's day were to us, much less, the mouth of the Columbia River, which we acquired then." Alert to the pressure on the Chinese empire exerted by the weight of internal strife and the renewed demands of the foreign powers for trade and diplomatic privileges, Collins forecast a loosen-

---

[9] New York *Herald*, April 8, 1859; New York *Times*, April 9, 1867; Collins to Marcy, September 10, 1856, 35th Cong., 1st sess., *House Ex. Doc. 98*, p. 6; Ravenstein, *Russians on the Amur*, 139.

[10] Collins, Extract from Notes, February 28, 1857, 35th Cong., 1st sess., *House Ex. Doc. 98*, p. 50.

ing of China's control over Manchuria and Mongolia. From its newly acquired bastion on the Amur, Russia could march on the Great Wall of China where "twenty thousand Cossacks would overrun and hold the country as easily as our little army moved on to Santa Fe and conquered New Mexico."[11] With this eventuality in mind and precisely because the United States had acquired California, the geopolitical and commercial relationships between the United States and northern Asia had changed dramatically. Now, in Collins' view, the Amur could be penetrated from the American west coast on a line from Kamchatka via Japan or from Hawaii via the same route.[12] "It must be recollected," he wrote to the State Department, "that in Siberia, the United States is no longer to the West of Russia or of Europe, but to the East, by way of the Amur River. . . ." Thus, the Pacific coast, incorporated within the continental limits of the United States, and the major port cities of the East and South — New York, New Orleans, Boston, Philadelphia, and Baltimore — "all these names [were] burning household words in Siberia and [Russia was] now looking to the rising Sun for steamboats, railroads, and telegraphs."[13] Even in the schools of Irkutsk, the capital of Siberia, students were learning the "American language."[14]

A rough-hewn geopolitician who drew upon his own experience and understanding of American territorial expansion, Collins also nationalized an old European dream with a geopolitical perspective that fixed upon the North American continent as the vital link between Europe and Asia. The sight of the Amur River and the lands adjacent to it as a natural funnel, directing trade to the United States, was established in his vision by a conviction that the first step, the settlement and development of the American continent under the auspices of the

[11] Collins to Marcy, January 31, 1857, 35th Cong., 1st sess., *House Ex. Doc.* 98, pp. 16–17, 19–20.

[12] Collins, Extract from Notes, February 28, 1857, *ibid.*, 63.

[13] Collins to Department of State, November 21, 1858, NA, Amoor River, February 29, 1856–December 21, 1861.

[14] *Ibid.*

United States, had already been accomplished. He later wrote that:

> The problem of a North-western passage to India . . . which has occupied the great minds of Europe for some centuries, has been solved by the continuous and onward march of American civilization to the West. . . . the commerce of the world will find its path across this continent. . . .[15]

By appropriating the traditional European image of a westward course of traffic moving to Asia under the auspices of the old world and changing it to a flow going eastward, Collins claimed for the United States the role of the central agency and the position of the potential area of international economic activity. Together with the assumption of hegemony over the North American continent by the United States, it meshed well with the anticipation of commercial wealth from Asia and converted the westward movement of the United States into an international event as well as a domestic development. In this way, Collins framed both the ideology of a manifest destiny and the exaltation of the American frontier within a system of informal thought which more properly should be called American Continentalism. The compass points of its world view arched the Pacific, one end piercing the Mississippi Valley and the other resting in the Amur River basin.[16]

Inspired by this vista, Collins came to the Russians with plans and projects that were influenced further by what he had learned in his travels in Siberia and the promise of American economic activity both at home and in Asia. Out of this peculiarly intuitive faith in the forces that had shaped American

[15] "Lecture by Collins," Western Union, *Statement of Collins Overland Line*, 164.

[16] The term, American Continentalism, should not be confused with Charles Beard's use of Continental Americanism. Charles A. Beard, *A Foreign Policy For America* (New York, 1940), 12ff. The idea has largely been unexplored by writers although there have been many suggestive commentaries touching it. See Frederick Jackson Turner, "The Significance of the Section in American History," in *The Significance of Sections in American History* (New York, 1952), 74; Bernard DeVoto, *The Course of Empire* (Boston, 1952), page xiii; Henry Nash Smith, *Virgin Land* (Cambridge, 1950), 29.

history as well as his own expectations, Collins created a telegraphic communications project that symbolized his whole outlook.

One of his early schemes was the creation of a railroad to connect Lake Baikal in Siberia with the Amur River. As a complement to this line, he proposed the use of steamships on the Amur, the Yenisei, the Lena, and the Oby Rivers that would form a transportation network that would "realize more to commerce and civilization than the discovery of the 'Northwest passage in India.' This route . . . would realize, in fact, a northeastern passage to India. . . ."[17] He also proposed to the Russians that they construct a railroad line to link the Amur River with the important trading city of Kyachta and Irkutsk, the capital of Siberia.[18] These projects fell through but on his return to Washington in 1858 he suggested the construction of an overland telegraph system that would link Asia and Europe with the United States via Russia. "In transversing the whole extent of Northern Europe and Asia . . . ," he informed Secretary of State Lewis Cass, "the idea was strongly forced upon my mind that . . . telegraphic communication could be constructed . . . uniting Europe with America."[19] Collins did not lack an attentive audience. He was given the credit for bringing to public attention the value of the Amur River to American trade, his reports were published in the press, and they were used in preparing data for the Congressional debates then going on over the proper route for a transcontinental railroad line.[20] His proposal took the form of an overland telegraph route running north from a point on the American transcontinental system then projected by Western Union, through British Colum-

[17] Collins to Marcy, November 30, 1856, 35th Cong., 1st sess., *House Ex. Doc. 98*, p. 10.

[18] Collins, *Voyage Down the Amoor*, 383ff.

[19] Collins to Cass, September 20, 1859, NA, Amoor River, February 29, 1856–December 21, 1860.

[20] H. C. M. Laughlins to G. J. Abbott, January 17, 1861, NA, Amoor River, January 14, 1861–June 30, 1874; Boston *Daily Advertiser*, January 27, 1859; Griffin, *Clippers and Consuls*, 349, note 11; Senator William M. Gwin and Representative Charles Scott to Cass, June 4, 1858, 35th Cong., 2nd sess., *House Ex. Doc. 53*, p. 4; 35th Cong., 2nd sess., *Congressional Globe*, 1858–1859, Part I, 471.

bia, across Alaska, beneath the Bering Strait via a submarine cable and southwestward along the coast of northeastern Asia to some point on the Russian telegraph system then building eastward. Although the Russians had been approached as far back as 1854 by foreign interests who wished to build a telegraph system that would keep pace with Russia's expanding empire, the offers were rejected. Collins, however, adapted the ideas of the chief of the Russian telegraph system for eastern Siberia and returned to Russia in 1859 ostensibly to resume his post at Nicolaevsk on the Amur. In reality, he went to further the telegraph project,[21] particularly since he had attracted the attention of Hiram Sibley, the president of the Western Union Telegraph Company.

Sibley was well acquainted with Russia's telegraph program. He had entertained visiting Russians who had observed American telegraph construction operations in the western prairies. Under his direction, Western Union had become one of the two most powerful corporations in American telegraphy and Sibley pressed for the construction of a transcontinental telegraph line to California. In 1860, the federal government provided the necessary legislation and subsidies and the work went ahead. Simultaneously, Cyrus Field, associated with the American Telegraph Company, Sibley's principal rival, had failed in his attempts to lay an intercontinental cable on the floor of the Atlantic Ocean. Telegraphers were now convinced that a long submarine cable was ineffective and would never work. Sharing in this judgment, Sibley welcomed Collins' telegraph project. Although he was aware of the potentials of the Asian business, he also hoped that Collins' overland line would draw European telegraph messages eastward through Russia and on to the United States as well.[22]

[21] New York *Times*, September 2, 1865; Ravenstein, *Russians on the Amur*, 146–147; Collins to Department of State, October 8, 1859, and May 1, 1860, NA, Amoor River, February 29, 1856–December 21, 1861; *Scientific American*, 1 (October 15, 1859), 251, announcing that Collins had made arrangements for setting up a Canadian company to carry the line through British Columbia.

[22] Hiram W. Sibley, "Memories of Hiram Sibley," Rochester Historical Society *Publication Fund Series*, II (1923), 126; Edward R. Foreman (comp. and ed.),

He was a fit colleague for Collins. An aggressive business-man, unafraid of risk, Sibley had "large, quick, broad ideas . . . [and] when he set out on an endeavor, it became a crusade . . . like the Israelites of old, he blew his horn lustily until the walls fell."[23] In this case, he directed a loud blast at Secretary of State William Henry Seward, who, through a political confusion at home, had appointed another man to the Amur agency in Collins' place.[24] Senator Milton Latham of California accompanied Collins to a conference with Seward in September, 1861, in which it was made clear that the secretary had made a mistake. Seward was well aware of the publicity about commerce in the Amur region that Collins had created and reappointed him. As added insurance, however, Sibley and his associates on the board of directors of Western Union petitioned the Secretary of State to retain Collins, asserting that he would be of great future importance not only to the government but in commercial affairs affecting the United States. It was made clear to Seward, that Minister Stoeckl and the visiting Russian official in charge of communications in Siberia, Colonel Romanoff, would render their assistance in bringing the Russians to assent to the construction of the line through their territory.[25] Sibley kept in touch with Collins' project and pushed through the completion of the Western Union transcontinental line in October, 1861, while Collins went to Russia to apply for American construction rights for an overland telegraph line from the Asiatic side of Bering Strait to Nicolaevsk, Russia's administrative outpost near the mouth of the Amur. Despite an earlier

Centennial History of Rochester (Rochester, 1931), I, 160; Collins Amoor River Report, "Commercial Relations of the United States with Foreign Nations for Year Ending September 30, 1861," 37th Cong., 2nd sess., *House Ex. Doc. 45*, p. 215; Robert L. Thompson, *Wiring a Continent* (Princeton, 1947), 371–372.

[23] James D. Reid, *The Telegraph in America* (New York, 1879), 518.

[24] Griffin, *Clippers and Consuls*, 342.

[25] Process Verbal of an Interview with the Honorable William H. Seward, Secretary of State of the United States of America at Washington [n.d. but after September 9, 1861, and before September 18, 1861], Seward to Collins, September 18, 1861, NA, Amoor River, January 14, 1861–June 30, 1874; Sibley to Seward, December 31, 1861, NA, Appointment Papers 1861–1869, Tray 258, Perry McDonough Collins 1861–1862.

overture by Collins to the Czar [26] and the intercession of the American minister in St. Petersburg, Cassius Clay, the Russians refused, asserting that they intended to build the line themselves.[27] Sibley, however, remained undiscouraged. When his construction crews had finished the line to California, he reported that they were "pressing me hard to let them go on to Bering's Strait next summer. . . ."[28] In the summer of 1862, Collins, Senator Latham, and Seward worked together to bring the Russians around.

At a meeting in Washington, they worked out a memorandum for the guidance of Simon Cameron who was sent to Russia to replace Cassius Clay who had returned home. Cameron was specifically charged with the mission of informing the Russians that the United States government would subsidize the projected line just as it had done for the Pacific telegraph built by Western Union. The State Department would give it all diplomatic aid and encouragement and felt strongly that the line would be of great commercial benefit for all concerned.[29] Collins set out again for St. Petersburg to follow up this overture from Washington,[30] while Cameron presented the project to the Czar and to the Russian Foreign Minister, Prince Gorchacov.[31] In December, 1862, Collins submitted his plans to the Russians in St. Petersburg only to meet delay, but in May, 1863, the idea was revived. Two months later, Clay, now back on the job in St. Petersburg, informed Seward that Collins had been granted

[26] Collins to F. W. Seward, September 18, 1861, NA, Amoor River, January 14, 1861–June 30, 1874.

[27] Clay to Seward, May 19, 1863, 38th Cong., 1st sess., *House Ex. Doc. 1,* p. 86.

[28] Sibley to Collins, October 16, 1861, *Statement of Collins Overland Line,* 37.

[29] Collins to Seward, June 9, 1862, and Memorandum, Seward to Cameron, same date, NA, Amoor River, January 14, 1861–June 30, 1874, Frederick Seward, *Seward at Washington* (New York, 1891), III, 49–50; Seward to Cameron, June 9, 1862, 37th Cong., 3rd sess., *Sen. Ex. Doc. 10,* pp. 1–2.

[30] Collins to Abbott, July 28, 1862, NA, Amoor River, January 14, 1861–June 30, 1874.

[31] Cameron to Seward, July 23, 1862, 37th Cong., 3rd sess., *House Ex. Doc. 1,* p. 449; Cameron submitted the project to the Russian Imperial Ministry of Foreign Affairs on September 17, 1862, 38th Cong., 1st sess., *House Ex. Doc. 1,* p. 850.

a charter.[32] With Russia's permission in hand, Collins then travelled to London with the support of Secretary Seward who requested the American minister to Great Britain, Charles Francis Adams, to help Collins in his negotiations for the right-of-way through British Columbia. By February, 1864, Collins had discussed the matter with Lord Palmerston, the Duke of Newcastle, and the Governor of the Hudson's Bay Company and received their approval to run the line through the territory.[33]

Once the news had reached Sibley, he prodded the board of directors of Western Union, and the company purchased Collins' rights to the project for one hundred thousand dollars, the right to one-tenth of the shares of new stock issued for a special company created to build the line, and the additional right to subscribe for another one-tenth of the stock on an equal basis with others. Collins, moreover, was appointed to the board of directors of Western Union and made manager of the Russian-American Telegraph, Western Union Extension which was popularly known as the Collins Overland Line.[34] In its circular to

[32] *Statement of Collins Overland Line*, 54; Clay to Seward, May 19, 1863, and June 17, 1863, 38th Cong., 1st sess., *House Ex. Doc. 1*, pp. 868, 872. Details of the grants from Russia and Great Britain are in "Copies of Grants by Russia and Great Britain of the Right of Way to Perry McD. Collins," 38th Cong., 1 sess., *Sen. Misc. Doc. 126*, pp. 1–5.

[33] Seward to Charles Francis Adams, July 13, 1863, 38th Cong. 1st sess., *House Ex. Doc. 1*, p. 358; Collins to F. W. Seward, August 18, 1863, Collins to F. W. Seward, December 31, 1863, and February 8, 1864, NA, Amoor River, January 14, 1861–June 30, 1874.

[34] Western Union, *Statement of Collins Overland Line*, 7ff. For his leadership in securing the concession, Sibley received special stock privileges from the board of directors of Western Union. The board also set aside 6,500 shares in the Collins Overland Line for distribution among railroad and telegraph men and "others whose influence it may be deemed necessary to secure. . . ." One hundred and twenty shares were granted by the board to a William B. Swift at the request of the Russian Minister Baron Stoeckl. Moreover, Stoeckl was awarded 300 shares by the board for his "distinguished aid and good offices not only with his own Government but before the Government of the United States; and which greatly contributed to the advancement of the enterprise." Later the board offered to refund $6,000 in calls paid by Stoeckl for the stock and reissue him 100 shares free of calls and assessments. Finally, the board resolved to set apart 1,000 shares of stock to be awarded to those Russians designated by Minister Clay. These shares were to be subject to all conditions set on American holders of the stock. Clay was to deliver the stock and make any collections of

prospective purchasers of the stock of the new line, moreover, the company revealed that the over-all project had scope greater than that of connecting Russia with the United States. Pointing out that the Russian telegraph system was already linked with India through Persia as well as with the European telegraph system, the company announced that it was projecting extensions of the line from the Russian system to China and Japan. "Consequently, when the Extension line of this Company shall be completed the commerce of the whole of Europe, Asia and North America, radiating from their great commercial centers will be tributary to it." And, to cap the whole enterprise, plans were under way to unite future overland lines in Mexico and Central and South America with the Western Union Extension.[35] The scheme that originally involved an intercontinental line between North America and Eurasia now anticipated a linkage with all of Latin America, "thus concentrating the globe upon our overland lines." [36]

At this point, Secretary Seward drew attention to the fact that Collins' coup had been effected "under the instruction and with the approbation" of the State Department, and supported the entire venture with all the expansionist vision and eloquence that he commanded. He saw the continental experi-

---

calls and assessments levied by the company. All this information is found in Office of the Secretary of the Company, "History of the Organization, Construction and Progress of the Collins Overland Telegraph Line via Behring's Strait to the Mouth of the Amoor River in Asia," courtesy of the Western Union Telegraph Company. Board of Directors Meeting March 19, 1864, June 8, 1864, Executive Committee Meeting of the Board of Directors on November 23, 1864, November 17, and November 27, 1864. Stoeckl thanked the board for its gesture on January 8, 1866, in a note mentioned in its minutes. The suggestion to refund Stoeckl's money and grant him stock free of calls and assessments was noted by the executive committee of the board on July 5, 1866. The recommendation to make Collins manager of the Overland Line and to the board of directors was noted on July 14, 1864.

[35] Western Union, *Statement of Collins Overland Line*, 15.

[36] Collins to Seward, July 30, 1864, NA, Amoor River, January 14, 1861–June 30, 1874. Collins asked the board of Western Union for special stock privileges for a Mr. M. A. Zabriskie who, as he informed the State Department, was the man with whom he negotiated for the Latin-American extensions; Collins requested the sale of 100 shares to Zabriskie at $5 a share, Office of the Secretary, "History of Collins Overland Telegraph Line," n.d.

ence of the United States as the basis upon which this aspect of the economic and cultural foreign policy of the United States should rest. "Commerce on the American continent defies political restraint and centralizes itself within our own country," he said. "For practical purposes we may regard the whole telegraph system of the American continent as our own." The plan for the Collins Overland Line and its related projects demonstrated that there were no limits "to the increase of the national influence of the United States. . . ," for it would extend "throughout the world American ideas and principles of public and private economy, politics, morals, philosophy, and religion." [37]

Having made arrangements for the purchase of materials and the organization of a construction expedition to work on the line in British Columbia, Alaska, and Siberia, Collins and Sibley, with the strong backing of the State Department, set out to complete final arrangements. Collins opened negotiations through an intermediary with the governments in Central and South America for links with telegraph lines planned in those countries that would complete a circuit throughout the Western Hemisphere. [38] In the winter of 1864-1865, he and Sibley journeyed to St. Petersburg in order to negotiate a final agreement with the Russians that would clarify all the details of the complex enterprise. With the help of Cassius Clay, who was an enthusiast of Russian-American cooperation in the Far East, they met the Czar and Prince Gorchacov. They dined at Clay's home with influential Russians and gained an entree to other important Russians through the aid of Serge Abasa, a young Russian nobleman who was later employed by Western Union to lead its exploring party in Siberia. [39]

[37] Seward to Chandler, May 14, 1864, Western Union, *Statement of Collins Overland Line*, 51.

[38] O. H. Palmer to Tolstoy, July 31, 1864, McNicol Collection; Seward to Diplomatic Officers in South America, August 18, 1864, Allen Burton to Antonio Del Real, October 25, 1864, and Del Real to Burton, November 5, 1864, Western Union, *Statement of Collins Overland Line*, 134ff.

[39] Seward to Clay, September 24, 1864, 38th Cong., 2nd sess., *House Ex. Doc. 1*; Joseph Schafer (ed.), *Memoirs of Jeremiah Curtin* (Madison, 1940),

Two problems gained the center of attention for the American negotiators. The question of a China extension touching the Russian lines was deemed of great importance by Collins. He urged the Russians to notice the great value of a branch line from their own system that would tap the trade-rich China coast. Unless this was done, he warned, rival British interests building from India would reach the area first and divert European telegraph and commercial traffic from Russia.[40] Since any increase in the China telegraph business would enhance the profit potential of the American-built section of the Russian system, Collins projected his own analysis of the importance of the American continental position to that of Russia. He wrote Clay:

> When the continuation of the Siberian telegraph shall have come in contact with the prolongation of the American system the span will have become complete, and the whole telegraphic system of Russia will teem with the commerce of the whole world, and Russia will stand as the intermediary between Europe and America, uniting them with China and Japan through Northern Asia.

If St. Petersburg did not strive for the Chinese business, it would be a "great misfortune to all concerned, because the prosperity of the Russian lines will be so intimately connected with ours that both must be affected from like causes. . . ."[41] Although Clay followed this line of persuasion, he emphasized the anti-British aspect of the China project, hoping to exploit Anglo-Russian tension, while Seward ordered the American minister in China, Anson Burlingame, to make representations to the Chi-

---

176, remarking that Clay received $30,000 in paid-up stock for helping Sibley and Collins in St. Petersburg. He also charged that Clay received a large sum of stock for distribution and sale in Russia in order to gain further influence for the project. Curtin, however, was not on good terms with Clay and the report, except for data above in note 34, cannot be checked. Albert Parry, "Cassius Clay's Glimpse Into the Future," *The Russian Review*, II (Spring, 1953), *passim*; Palmer to Bulkeley, May 8, 1865, Executive Committee of the Board of Directors, April 5, 1865, Office of the Secretary, "History of the Collins Overland Telegraph Line."

[40] Clay to Seward, November 14, 1864, 39th Cong., 1st sess., *House Ex. Doc. 1*, p. 363; Western Union, *Statement of Collins Overland Line*, 130–131.

[41] Collins to Clay, November 16–28, 1864, 39th Cong., 1st sess., *House Ex. Doc. 1*, p. 371.

nese for permission to build a line to the Russian telegraph trunk.[42]

But it was in the realm of business at hand that gave the entrepreneurs of the Collins Overland Line the greatest difficulty. As they interpreted the original agreement made with Collins in 1863, the Russians had promised to give the American interests a 40 per cent rebate on messages transmitted to and received from the United States over the American-built portion of the line in eastern Siberia. Russian officials, however, proposed a method of accounting that determined the basis of the rebate in a manner that reduced the share to the Collins Overland Line because it included the expenses of Russian telegraph lines "not directly involved in transmissions to America." And when it became clear to Sibley that Russian law would decide the merits of any differences between the Collins Overland Line and the Russian government, he objected. The rebate, he complained, had "formed the leading inducement in the formation of the company and the subscription to and sale of its shares." The Russians, however, remained adamant and warned Sibley that the company's rights might be forfeited, an eventuality that would result in loss of capital and money already invested. "Pressed by the vast interests involved," Sibley reported, "we were compelled to submit. . . ."[43] On March 21, 1865, after months of arduous bargaining, an agreement was signed on the Russians' terms. Simultaneously, Sibley and Collins filed an official protest with the Russian government and informed Minister Clay of the dispute for the information of the State Department.[44] The dispute continued and Clay, aware of the issues, laid on a heavy hand just as Sibley returned to

[42] Clay to Gorchacov, November 20–December 2, 1864, Seward to Clay and to Burlingame, December 13, 1864, 39th Cong., 1st sess., *House Ex. Doc. 1*, pp. 365, 370, 424; Executive Committee of Board of Directors, January 25, 1865, Office of the Secretary, "History of the Collins Overland Telegraph Line."

[43] *Ibid.*

[44] Clay to Seward, March 24, 1865, Sibley and Collins to Gorchacov, March 9–21, 1865, 39th Cong., 1st sess., *House Ex. Doc. 1*, pp. 369, 375; Tolstoy to Collins, October 6, 1865, McNicol Collection.

the United States, a victim of illness that forced him to resign the presidency of Western Union.

The company insisted that the Russian method of calculation involved it unnecessarily in the expenses incurred by the entire Russian telegraph system, but its appeals to the Russian courts were rejected.[45] Clay followed a somewhat erratic course in taking up the cause of the Collins Overland Line. He wanted the company to hold fast to its interpretation of a 40 per cent rebate, urged it to appeal to Seward, and also suggested that it compromise.[46] Then, in other correspondence with the Secretary of State, he reported that he did not believe the Russians were trying to back out of the bargain though he felt they were trying to avoid paying the rebate. Having filed an official protest with the Russians, he confidentially informed Prince Gorchacov that the United States held the Russians responsible for "all loss to American citizens." He charged that the agreement with Sibley and Collins had been "wrested from them by moral compulsion." Building on this accusation, he expressed his conviction that Russia was morally wrong by stating that he hoped for an amicable settlement since it was the "axiom of his country to ask for nothing but what is right and to submit to nothing which is wrong. . . ." Personally satisfied with his roughshod diplomacy that antagonized the Russians, Clay, with Sibley's permission, suggested a compromise settlement of a 20 per cent rebate for a period of sixteen and a half years. After deliberation, this was accepted by the company only to learn that Clay had taken a new tack. "I think we have had enough of petitioning and compliment and must now stand upon our rights as the *equals* of Kings and Emperors,"[47] he informed Western Union.

[45] Palmer to Tolstoy, July 31, 1865, McNicol Collection; Palmer to Seward, August 1, 1865, Office of the Secretary, "History of the Collins Overland Telegraph Line."

[46] Clay to Directors of the Company, June 24, 1865, *ibid.*

[47] Clay to Seward, September 5, 1865, NA, Diplomatic Dispatches Russia, March 13, 1863–December 28, 1865; Clay to Gorchacov, March 21–April 2, 1865, Clay to Sibley, April 13, 1865, Clay to Board of Directors, April 24, 1865, Palmer to Clay, June 30, 1865, Clay to Palmer, June 22, 1865, Office of the Secretary, "History of the Collins Overland Telegraph Line."

By the late summer of 1865, the Russians would not be budged and Clay was reduced to weak and ineffective suggestions as to means of overcoming Russian resistance.[48] Construction and exploration operations of the Collins Overland Line, therefore, began in 1865 despite a severe dispute between the principals which was not resolved, and, in fact, was later to influence the decision of the company to withdraw from the project.

Abruptly in the winter of 1867, Western Union cancelled the building of the Collins Overland Line and recalled the construction expeditions.[49] The company that already had expended some three million dollars saw its project doomed because it had underestimated Cyrus Field's determination to lay an Atlantic cable. Five times, from 1857 onward, Field had tried unsuccessfully to lay a cable on the floor of the Atlantic and his inability to set an unbroken line was aggravated by the difficulty of maintaining a sufficiently powerful signal in the wire. Sibley had watched Field renew his preparations in 1865 at the time that the Collins project was getting underway. "I would give $50,000," he told Field, "to know if you are ever going to succeed. I hope you will; but I would like to know for certain before we spend any more in Russia."[50] The only guarantee that Field provided Sibley was the achievement itself. In the summer of 1866 he succeeded brilliantly.

A glum board of directors of Western Union reconsidered the many factors of its position. Clearly Field's cable was cheaper to operate now that it had been laid down and its technical defects mastered. A direct connection with Europe, it frustrated Western Union's aspiration to draw commercial communication from the Old World via Russia, Asia, and North America. Moreover, in spite of the intervention of the State Department, the plans for telegraph extension in China fell through. The unsettled dispute with the Russians over the 40 per cent rebate added to the company's gloom since it mud-

[48] Clay to Palmer, August 6, 1865, *ibid.*, Tolstoy to Western Union Company, August 24, 1865, McNicol Collection.
[49] Thompson, *Wiring A Continent*, 433–435.
[50] Quoted *ibid.*

died the expected stream of profits that were to flow into its coffers. Perhaps the most revealing factor was the coalition of the American Telegraph Company with Western Union. Since Field's undersea telegraph was linked with the lines of the American Telegraph group in North America, the merger provided Western Union with a share of the profits from the Atlantic cable.[51] It made the Collins Overland Line obsolete. The way was clear and the men of business began an ordered retreat.

They publicly arranged an exchange of stock of the Collins Overland Line for interest-bearing bonds of the parent corporation, the Western Union Company. The transaction, as Robert Luther Thompson, the historian of American telegraphy, has written, transferred the losses of the Collins Line to Western Union whose directors held a goodly share of the Collins stock. In effect, the directors seized an opportunity to become their own creditors. Then, early in the spring of 1867, they abandoned the Collins Overland Line. A chorus of criticism arose, and the enterprise that was to girdle the earth ended in recrimination, disappointment, and failure. "What now remains to be done?" the company asked the State Department.[52]

Seward had an answer. He regretted the cancellation of the project, but he did sympathize with the company's unwillingness to go ahead with a venture which it claimed entailed a financial loss. In any case, he felt that the arrangements between Western Union and the Russians might be modified because a new state of affairs had arisen between the United States and Russia.[53] On March 28, 1867, Seward bought Alaska from Russia for over seven million dollars. Although overtures for the purchase had been made since the Crimean War, Russian indecision and the outbreak of the American Civil War prevented a

[51] Burlingame to Seward, May 22, 1867, 40th Cong., 2nd sess., *House Ex. Doc. 1*, pp. 483ff.; Thompson, *Wiring A Continent*, 424, 434.

[52] *Ibid.*, 436; William Orton and O. H. Palmer to Seward, March 25, 1867, 40th Cong., 2nd sess., *House Ex. Doc. 1*, p. 386.

[53] Seward to Clay, March 28, 1867, 40th Cong., 2nd sess., *House Ex. Doc. 1*, p. 385, Seward to Palmer, April 30, 1867, McNicol Collection.

concrete negotiation. By 1860, the issue had bogged down.[54] With the advent of the Collins Overland Line, two developments occurred that contributed to the ultimate purchase of the territory and its acceptance by the Senate.

In the winter of 1864-1865, when Collins and Sibley went to St. Petersburg to deal with the Russians for a detailed agreement for the Collins Line, Sibley discussed Alaska with Gorchacov. The foreign minister had been plagued by demands at home to sell Alaska but had delayed accepting the idea. Speaking with Sibley, he questioned Western Union's ability to obtain a right-of-way through British Columbia since the Hudson's Bay Company might object. Sibley replied that he might have to buy a controlling interest in the company and was prepared to do so for a large amount of money. When Gorchacov learned the sum, he remarked that Russia would sell Alaska for a figure not much larger.[55]

Quick to sense an opening, Sibley received permission from the Prince to inform the United States government of his attitude. At the time, Cassius Clay, busy squiring Collins and Sibley around St. Petersburg, did not overlook the usefulness of Sibley's suggestion, particularly since it coincided with his own views. While Sibley was still in Russia, in November, 1864, Clay informed Seward that it would be in the interest of Russia to sell its holdings in North America. It "would not only make more secure our telegraph lines," he informed Seward, but also enhance the commercial welfare of American traders, fishing interests, and whalers.[56] The issue, brought to Seward's attention in 1864, was revived two years later. Other American interests pressed the Secretary of State to purchase the territory from Russia. Simultaneously the Russians decided to sell. The occasion of the Collins Overland Line became an important transitional step between the blocked negotiations for the pur-

[54] Frank A. Golder, "The Purchase of Alaska," *American Historical Review*, XXV (1920).

[55] "Hiram Sibley," *Telegraph and Telephone Age* (March 16, 1925), 142–144; Hiram Sibley, "Memories of Hiram Sibley," *Publication Fund Series*, 129.

[56] Clay to Seward, November 14, 1864, NA, Diplomatic Dispatches Russia, March 13, 1863–December 28, 1865, Volume II, 1–98.

chase of Alaska before 1860 and the resumption of negotiations in 1866.

The purchase, however, met with considerable opposition in the United States and supporters of the measure were hard put to muster arguments that would convince the Senate. Here, the support of scientific endeavor in the field by the Collins Overland expedition demonstrated its value. Faced with public ignorance of the potential value of Alaska, Seward and Senator Charles Sumner, Chairman of the Senate Committee on Foreign Relations, relied on the data that came in from the scientific corps of the expedition. The explorations of the Yukon River, the extent of mineral resources, the existence of large forest preserves, furs and fisheries, climate and agriculture — these facts were made available in an organized and coherent form by the exploring party that had travelled through Alaska. Just as the purchase treaty was submitted to the Senate in the spring of 1867, Lieutenant Henry M. Bannister returned to Washington after a long stay at Norton Sound in Alaska where he had served in the expedition. Immediately, he went to work organizing and interpreting the materials and information that had been gathered by the expedition and earlier exploring parties. Other members of the expedition bolstered Sumner's argument that Seward had bought wisely. "The project of the Western Union Telegraph Company of an overland telegraph across Bering Straits to Europe was a failure," Bannister wrote, "but its greatest result was the annexation of Alaska." [57] *

The purchase of Alaska had come as a redemption, evidence that the great continental power in the Western Hemisphere was yet determined to become a world force. "The prime gain," said the New York *Times* of the Alaska purchase, "would have

[57] James Alton James, *The First Scientific Exploration of Russian America and the Purchase of Alaska* (Evanston, 1942), 35–45.

* The view expressed here and in the source cited in note number 57 is modified in M. B. Sherwood, *Exploration of Alaska, 1865–1900* (New Haven and London: Yale University Press, 1965), 31–33, though the purchase of Alaska and the promotion of the telegraph were both evidence of an attitude which Vevier, in this important article, calls "American Continentalism." — ED. NOTE.

to be sought in the increased influence which our government would acquire in all that affects individual states on this continent and the relations of the whole, alike with Asiatic and European powers." [58] In the long run, the "main importance" of Alaska lay in its promise for increased economic relations with eastern Asia. "It seems inevitable that all that commerce should be American." The acquisition of the vast territory provided an American halfway house between two continents, a means of capitalizing on the American continental position in North America and extending it westward. The overland telegraph had failed, but the "northwestern limb of our continent" would allow the United States to take a stride to Asia. [59]

[58] New York *Times*, March 31, 1867.

[59] *Ibid.*, April 1, 8, and 9, 1867; Collins to Seward, January 4, 1869, NA, Amoor River, January 14, 1861–June 30, 1874; Collins to Seward, April 4, 1867, reprinted in the New York *Times*, April 9, 1867.

Reinhard Luthin, a biographer of Lincoln, died in 1963. He taught at Columbia and the University of Pittsburgh. According to his obituary in the American Historical Review *(April, 1963):"He was a cosmopolitan figure, an independent scholar, and a writer of Johnsonian dimensions, as well known to some of the best chefs of New York City as to figures in the publishing world." Luthin's essay is from the* Slavonic and East European Review, *XVI (July, 1937), 168–82.*

The Sale of Alaska[1]

REINHARD H. LUTHIN

he resumption of American diplomatic relations with the Soviet Union inspires an interest in the intercourse of the United States with the Russia of the Romanovs, of which comparatively little has been written, except of a "popular" variety.

Historically, the subject that has occupied the centre of the stage in Russian-American diplomacy seems to have been the negotiation by which Alaska was ceded to the United States[2] — an incident in which William H. Seward, then Secretary of State, played the central part. Indeed, so closely has Seward's name been interwoven with the purchase of the territory, that the parts of the other players in this significant event in Ameri-

[1] For aid in research in the preparation of this paper, the present writer wishes to acknowledge his indebtedness to Professor Harry J. Carman, of Columbia University. The suggestions of Professor J. Fred Rippy, of Duke University, and of Professor Charles C. Tansill, of the American University, Washington, D.C., are deeply appreciated.

[2] A Soviet historian has referred to the sale of Alaska to the United States as "an unpardonable blunder." Serebrovsky, A., "Aliaska," *Krasnaya Nov*, March, 1929, p. 169.

233

can diplomacy have remained obscured. Highly enlightening phases of the Alaska cession could be framed around various personalities of post-Civil-War Washington. Undoubtedly the most absorbing of these stories would be that detailing the part in the affair of Robert J. Walker, of Mississippi.[3]

The agitation for the acquisition of the Tsar's American possessions has been mentioned as originating with Walker, who, as early as 1845, is said to have urged President Polk to secure them.[4] Having deserted Martin Van Buren in his fight for a presidential nomination in the Democratic Convention of 1844, primarily because he was not "right" on the Texas annexation question, Walker, then a United States Senator from Mississippi, steered his large personal support to Polk. For this service he was tendered the post of Secretary of the Treasury in the new administration.[5] In accepting the cabinet portfolio in March, 1845, he maintained in later years, he wrote Polk that the expulsion of the English from the Oregon country was vital, for it "would leave no European power upon our Pacific coast except Russia, whose well-known friendship for us would, it is hoped, induce her then to cede to us her North American territory."[6]

Before accepting the claim of Walker to agitation for Alaska at such an early date, it is well to consider that no evidence has been uncovered thus far to warrant this contention, beyond the word of Walker himself; and he wrote this in 1868, under circumstances which will be recounted in the following pages.

[3] For scholarly accounts of Walker, *see* Dodd, W. E., *Robert J. Walker, Imperialist* (Lynchberg, Va., 1915); Jordan, H. Donaldon, "A Politician of Expansion: Robert J. Walker," *Mississippi Valley Historical Review*, XIX, 362–381.

[4] Callahan, James M., *The Alaska Purchase and Americo-Canadian Relations* (Morgantown, West Va., 1908), pp. 3–4; Thomas, B. P., *Russo-American Relations*, 1815–1867 (Baltimore, 1930), p. 145.

[5] Dodd, *op. cit.*, pp. 12–13; Learned, H. B., "The Sequence of Appointments to Polk's Original Cabinet . . . ," *American Historical Review* (October, 1924), XXX, 78–79; Claiborne, J. F. H., *Mississippi as a Province, Territory and State* (Jackson, Miss., 1880), I, 420–421, 451–452.

[6] *Letter of Robert J. Walker on the Acquisition of Alaska, St. Thomas, and St. John* (Washington, 1869); Washington *Daily Morning Chronicle*, 28, 29, 30 January, 1868.

Although Walker's old crony in Mississippi politics, Senator William M. Gwin,[7] of California, was the first to engage in activities to bring Alaska into the American domain, the Mississippi politician was close on his heels. There is adequate evidence that Walker was agitating for the purchase of the territory in 1863.[8] But it was Walker's work after Secretary of State Seward's treaty with Russia was ratified by the United States Senate in 1867, that is of major significance.

According to the traditions of American diplomacy, approval of the Alaska purchase treaty by the Senate[9] should have closed the issue. The necessary legislation in the House of Representatives to appropriate the sum of $7,200,000, with which to pay Russia, was supposedly a foregone conclusion. But it became apparent long before the close of the year 1867 that the payment was to be strenuously resisted.[10]

Undoubtedly the two most troublesome snags set up against the Appropriation Bill in Congress were the tactics of ardent anti-expansionists, and the intrigues of certain members who were pressing a shady litigation against the Russian government known as the Perkins Claim. In November the House of Representatives had approved a resolution sponsored by Cadwalader C. Washburn, of Wisconsin, which emphasized the inexpediency of territorial acquisitions and placed the House on record as being "under no obligation to vote money to pay for

[7] Matrosov, E., "Sudby Byvschikh Russko-Amerikaniskikh Vladenii Pod Vladichestvom Respubliki Soedinennikh Shtatov," *Istoricheskii Vestnik* (St. Petersburg, 1902), vol. 90, p. 712; McPherson, Hallie M., "The Interest of William McKendree Gwin in the Purchase of Alaska, 1854–1861," *Pacific Historical Review*, III, 34 ff.

[8] William S. Hodge to Sumner, 30 March, 1867, Charles Sumner Papers. Widener Library, Harvard University, Cambridge, Mass.; Clay to Seward, 10 May, 1867, MSS., Department of State, Russia, Despatches; Statement of Robert J. Walker in *House Report*, no. 35, 40th Congress, 3rd Session, serial no. 1388, p. 19.

[9] *Executive Journal, U. S. Senate*, 1867, XV, 675.

[10] The first two American scholars to reveal the interesting aspects connected with the Alaska payment were the late Professors Dunning and Golder. *See* Dunning, William A., "Paying for Alaska," *Political Science Quarterly*, XXVII, 385 ff.; Golder, Frank A., "The Purchase of Alaska," *American Historical Review*, XXV, 411 ff.

any such purchase unless there is greater present necessity for the same than now exists."[11] To the advocates of the Alaska Treaty the sympathisers with Perkins in Congress were also most distressing. Led by General Benjamin F. Butler, Member for Massachusetts and best known for his notorious military administration of New Orleans during the War, the Congressional satellites of this fraudulent claim were insisting that the House refuse to vote money to pay for the territory unless the Russian government would agree to "settle" with the widowed Mrs. Perkins for fire-arms alleged to have been furnished to the Russian Army by her late husband. In introducing a resolution, which would withhold no less than $500,000 from the Alaska payment for "the widow," Butler, in an eloquent appeal, had informed his colleagues in Congress that Mrs. Perkins was pleading with them: "If you are going to send $7,200,000 out of the country, hold enough of it back for me and my orphan children, that I may get justice done me against this autocrat (the Tsar)."[12]

Seward was naturally alarmed. He feared, and with good cause, that this renaissance of anti-expansionism, as expressed in the passage of Washburn's resolution, would wreck his programme of territorial aggrandisement. Butler and other calculating Congressmen, suddenly concerned for widows and orphans, by no means made the situation simpler. The predicament was doubly embarrassing to Seward, inasmuch as ratifications of the treaty had been exchanged with the Russian Government and the territory had been formally handed over to the authorised American commissioner in October.[13] At this time the Secretary of State was reported by an observing newspaper correspondent to be "wonderfully troubled."[14]

The Russian Minister at Washington, Baron Stoeckl, was likewise becoming decidedly uneasy. The matter of payment for

[11] *Congressional Globe*, 40th Congress, 1st Session, p. 792.
[12] *Ibid.*, 40th Congress, 2nd Session, pp. 4052–53; also *Appendix*, p. 403.
[13] Ludecke, Edward, "Our First Troops in Alaska," *Alaska-Yukon Magazine*, IV, 146; Bloodgood, E., "Eight Months at Sitka," *Overland Monthly*, II, 175 ff.
[14] Cincinnati *Daily Gazette*, 23 December, 1867.

Alaska was intensely personal to him, for he anticipated a reward from his government should he succeed in foisting the unwanted territory on the United States.[15] In September, Stoeckl, in an official despatch, had confided his anxiety to Seward regarding the tactics of the advocates of Perkins in Congress.[16]

The outcome of a conference between Seward and the Russian Minister was a decision to enlist the aid of outside influences. And the principal ally drafted for service was Robert J. Walker. Seward had the utmost respect for the Mississippian, whose hunger for land was as insatiable as his own. "If his bold and enlightened statesmanship could have ruled in his time," so the Secretary of State eulogised Walker, "the republic would now be the continent of North America."[17]

At the time when he was approached with the proposal to carry on the fight for the Alaska Appropriation Bill, Walker was embarrassed financially and threatened with the loss of his Washington estate, "Woodley."[18] As if to add to his despair, his daughter had been stricken with an ailment which necessitated costly treatment. He had even appealed to the noted Washington banker, W. W. Corcoran, to aid him in his economic distress.[19] This unhappy personal situation, added to his jingo ideals that called for a greater portion of the western hemisphere over which the American eagle could spread its wings, had recently induced him to accept the offer of the Danish representative to influence public sentiment in favour of Seward's Treaty with Denmark for the purchase of the West Indian islands of St. Thomas and St. John; a document that lay collect-

---

[15] Golder, *op. cit.*, p. 421.

[16] Stoeckl to Seward, September [no date], 1867, MSS., Department of State, Notes from Russian Legation.

[17] Savidge, Eugene C., *Life of Benjamin Harris Brewster* (Philadelphia, 1891), p. 16.

[18] Walker to Corcoran, 16 April, 1867, W. W. Corcoran Papers, Library of Congress.

[19] Walker to Corcoran, 30 April, 1867, *Ibid.*

ing dust in the Senate Committee on Foreign Relations.[20] Accordingly, Walker was in a receptive mood when he was approached by Stoeckl, working on Seward's suggestion. The former Secretary of the Treasury readily agreed to draw the sword in the parliamentary struggle for Alaska.

Walker set to work immediately. By the close of January, 1868, he had completed his first effort to stimulate sentiment. He prepared a lengthy brief in which were condensed the arguments for the Russian and Danish Treaties. It was printed in the Washington *Daily Morning Chronicle* in three installments.[21] For the use of his newspaper, John W. Forney, Editor of the *Chronicle*, received no less than $30,000, according to both President Andrew Johnson,[22] and his private secretary, Colonel Moore.[23] John Bigelow, intimate friend of Seward, recorded in his diary at the time that the Secretary of State confided to him that Forney's price was $20,000.[24]

In addition to appearing in the *Chronicle*, Walker's brief was published in pamphlet form, under the title *Letter of Hon. R. J. Walker on the Acquisition of Alaska, St. Thomas and St. John.* In this piece of work, Walker saw fit to devote most of his space to the Danish Treaty, for he had ascertained that the chances in Congress for Denmark's West Indian islands were less promising than those for Alaska. In his arguments in favour of the appropriation of $7,200,000, with which to settle with Russia, Walker dwelt on the pleasant climate and the richness of the natural products of Alaska. "It must be the great fur country of the world; it abounds in gold and copper." The ultimate struggle for command of the world, argued Walker, would be decided on the Pacific. The acquisition of Alaska, with the Aleutian Islands, carried America half-way to China and Japan. The

[20] Tansill, Charles C., *The Purchase of the Danish West Indies* (Baltimore, 1932), pp. 126–127.

[21] Washington *Daily Morning Chronicle*, 28, 29, 30 January, 1868.

[22] Memorandum, undated, in President Johnson's handwriting, Andrew Johnson Papers, Library of Congress, cited in Dunning, *op. cit.*, p. 386, and in Thomas, *op. cit.*, pp. 159–160.

[23] William G. Moore Diary MS., undated, Library of Congress.

[24] John Bigelow Diary MS., 22 September, 1868, New York Public Library.

cession could be opposed only by those narrow-minded individuals and cranks who would have liked to see the Ohio River
the western boundary of the United States.[25]

Other articles that appeared in the *Chronicle*, mostly from
Walker's pen judging by the style and composition, made
Alaska particularly alluring. There were in the territory count-
less valuable mines and an overabundance of fisheries.[26] White
men were there collecting gold "by the handful," and the
weather at Sitka was "charming." [27] By July many intrepid
American pioneers were forsaking California and rushing to the
Alaskan gold "diggings." [28] Then there was to be considered the
extension of Christianity to China and Japan — traditionally a
favourite argument for the expansionists. "Commerce," the
Chronicle emphasised, "like St. John in the Wilderness, will be
the precursor, but the Bible and Christianity will soon follow." [29]

Walker did not confine his activity to the newspaper columns. Through long experience in political life at Washington,
he had a clear conception of the depths to which he might be
forced to submerge if he were to achieve his objective; well he
knew that the ethical standards and criteria of private life were
often ruled out of politics. The pen was a mighty weapon, but
tactics of a less academic nature than coining elegant phrases
would have to be employed. And since his freedom from scruple
was on the same titanic level as the rest of his intellectual com-
plexion, his conscience did not intrude on his plans. He in-
vaded the hall of the House of Representatives where, in his
capacity as former Senator, he was permitted access to the floor
— as was the rule in those days.[30] He was particularly active on
the floor of the House during the days when the Alaska legis-

[25] *Letter of Hon. R. J. Walker on the Acquisition of Alaska, St. Thomas and
St. John* (Washington, 1869).

[26] Washington *Daily Morning Chronicle*, 25 June, 1868.

[27] *Loc. cit.*

[28] Washington *Daily Morning Chronicle*, 1 July, 1868.

[29] *Ibid.*, 13 July, 1868.

[30] For a denunciation by one Congressman of allowing Walker and other
former members on the floors of Congress, *see* Providence *Daily Journal*, 27
February, 1869.

lation was debated and voted.[31] The Appropriation Bill was finally passed on 14 July, 1868.[32]

While the parliamentary duel on the legislation was being fought bitterly — with the Alaska advocates pitted against a coalition of Washburn's anti-expansionists and Butler's Perkins brigade — another player entered the arena, Uriah H. Painter.

Painter was the Washington Correspondent of the New York *Sun* and the Philadelphia *Enquirer*. His deep interest was awakened when he heard rumours that Baron Stoeckl was to distribute an attractive lobby fund and had retained Walker as "counsel" to assist in steering the Alaska Bill over the dangerous legislative reefs and shoals that imperilled its course in Congress. Of Painter's motives in rudely intruding on the understanding between Walker and Stoeckl, two accounts are available — that of Walker and that of Painter.

According to Walker, his law partner, the former Representative, Frederick P. Stanton, of Tennessee, came to him one day while the Alaska debates were raging and declared that he had received a message from Painter who had heard that the Russian Minister had engaged him, Walker, as counsel; that Painter demanded of Stanton that he be "employed" to use his influence with the newspapers and Congress on behalf of the Bill. Walker's story, given under oath, is as follows: [33]

> Mr. Stanton told me that he was requested by this Mr. Painter to inform me that he could influence the Press to a great extent for or against the Bill; that he could control the votes of a good many members for or against it (which I did not believe) and that he understood that the Russian Government had placed in my hands any amount of money to aid the passage of this Bill. I told Mr. Stanton to tell him that I had no money for any such purpose. . . .
> Mr. Stanton called upon me again and told me that he had delivered my answer, and that Mr. Painter seemed to be quite angry about it, and had said that if I did not employ him he would defeat

[31] Baltimore *Sun*, 15 July, 1868; Providence *Daily Journal*, 15 July, 1868; New York *Sun*, 15 July, 1868.

[32] *Congressional Globe*, 40th Congress, 2nd Session, p. 4055.

[33] *House Report*, no. 35, 40th Congress, 3rd Session, serial No. 1388, p. 18.

the Bill. . . . I became a little excited — perhaps more so than I ought — and I told Mr. Stanton to tell him that I had no money for any such purpose; . . . that if any money were used in that way to carry the Bill, I should retire from the case altogether, and that if he, Painter, called at my office and made such a proposition to me, I should kick him out of it.

Painter, for his part, gave a decidedly different version of the incident. Portraying himself as a public-spirited champion of reform and relentless foe of corruption in political life, Painter made the following statement: [34]

> I heard that Mr. Walker was interested in it at the time; some one told me that he was writing articles that were published daily in the *Chronicle*, and that he was engaged in advocating the matter; and I knew that he was a man that would not do a thing of that kind without money. . . . I asked him [Stanton] . . . if Walker was not in it. He said he did not know. I said I guessed he was and told him the first time he met Walker to put it right to him and see if he would acknowledge it. I thought it was a big swindle, and that they were running it through with a bold hand. . . . I had attacked it [the Alaska Treaty] from the day the Treaty came to the Senate, as one of Seward's jobs. . . . I told several members of Congress that all this money was not going to Russia, and I thought if I could get at those who were at the bottom of the affair it would do some good.

Of the two accounts, there is little from which to draw a confident conclusion, or to decide whether Walker or Painter was the more careless purveyor of the facts. Walker's version seems the more authentic, although some of his allegations must be accepted with reservations — particularly that in which he declared: "If any money were used in that way to carry the Bill, I should retire from the case altogether." One of the more reliable Washington Correspondents of the period, in writing his memoirs, was also inclined to discredit Painter's story. He quoted Painter as saying: "I have some friends in Congress — not to mention my two newspapers, both daily — who are op-

[34] *House Report*, no. 35, *op. cit.*, pp. 34, 38–9.

posed to this appropriation. But if Mr. Walker will retain me I will be able to influence them to vote for it." [35]

And valiantly did Painter endeavour to defeat the Alaska Bill on the eve of its passage through Congress. He wrote a despatch to one of his newspapers, the New York *Sun*, in which he reported that Seward, in his programme of expansion, was completing negotiations with Denmark for the purchase of Greenland and Iceland.[36] Painter made sure of sending this absurd news to his journal while the temper of the House of Representatives was at white heat over the issue whether it shared the treaty-making power equally with the President and the Senate: in fact, on the very day when Representative Delano, of Ohio, proposed a resolution which expressly denied to the President and the Senate the right to acquire territory, "except by the will of the nation, given by express grant or implied acquiescence." [37] Painter likewise furnished to Washburn, who still led the anti-expansionist offensive in the Lower House of Congress, this fictitious story that Seward was about to announce the purchase of Denmark's two polar colonies.[38] The *Sun* Correspondent also attacked Walker personally in his columns shortly before the approval of the legislation. One of his despatches to his newspaper read: "Robert J. Walker is in charge of the lobby at work to secure the Alaska appropriation. He appears boldly upon the floor of both Houses plying his vocation." [39]

The controversy between Walker and Painter subsided with the passage of the Alaska Bill. But it was not the end of the Correspondent's warfare against the former Secretary of the Treasury: merely an armistice adopted by Painter until further developments.

On 1 August Baron Stoeckl was presented by the Treasury Department with a warrant for $7,200,000 in payment for

[35] Townsend, George A., *Washington, Outside and Inside* (Hartford, Conn., 1874), p. 516.

[36] New York *Sun*, 1 July, 1868.

[37] *Congressional Globe*, 40th Congress, 2nd Session, p. 3616.

[38] *House Report*, no. 35, *op. cit.*, p. 39; New York *Sun*, 2 July, 1868.

[39] New York *Sun*, 20 July, 1868.

Alaska. On the same day the Russian Minister endorsed the warrant in favour of his financial agent, George W. Riggs.[40] A noted Washington banker and partner of Corcoran, Riggs had been on terms of friendship and intimacy with Walker ever since the old days of the Polk administration.[41] In return for the warrant, Riggs drew from the Treasury in Washington transfer checks on the New York sub-treasury. On 1 August he drew out two checks for $7,000,000 and $100,000; on the 3rd, one for $25,000; on the 4th, another for $35,000; the rest of the money was drawn from the Treasury by Riggs during the following month.[42]

Estimates vary as to the amount that Walker received for his lobbying labours in support of Alaska. On receiving the money from Riggs, Walker merely wrote to Corcoran on 7 August: "When the money was handed me by Riggs, I requested him to write and inform you of my good fortune."[43] Secretary Seward confided to both President Johnson[44] and John Bigelow[45] that Walker's price was $20,000. Later Walker himself admitted:

[40] Treasury Warrant no. 927, MSS., General Accounting Office, U. S. Treasury Department, Washington, D. C. The present writer was permitted to examine this original warrant for the Alaska payment, with Baron Stoeckl's endorsement in favour of Riggs, underneath which is Riggs's endorsement, under date of 1 August, 1868. The fact that there is a single warrant for $7,200,000 would seem to contradict the statement made in 1912 to Franklin K. Lane by Charles Glover, president of the Riggs National Bank and once office employee in the banking firm of Corcoran & Riggs, to the effect that two warrants for the Alaska purchase passed through his hands: one for $5,800,000 and the other for $1,400,000. If Lane understood Glover correctly, two explanations suggest themselves: 1. That the two supposed warrants which Glover handled in his duties as a subordinate in the Corcoran & Riggs office were some other form of financial transfers used in the firm's system of book-keeping. 2. That the book-keeping in the Treasury Department was conducted in such a way as to cover up some unusual method of effecting the payment to Russia. See *Letters of Franklin K. Lane* (New York and Boston, 1922), p. 260.

[41] The late Professor Justin H. Smith, in his classical work, *The War with Mexico* (New York, 1919), II, 488, emphasises Walker's "too intimate" relations with the firm of Corcoran & Riggs.

[42] *House Report*, No. 35, *op. cit.*, p. 7.

[43] Walker to Corcoran, 7 August, 1868, W. W. Corcoran Papers.

[44] William G. Moore Diary MS., undated; Dunning, *op. cit.*, p. 386; Thomas, *op. cit.*, p. 160.

[45] John Bigelow Diary MS., *op. cit.*, 22 September, 1868.

"After paying . . . \$5,000 in greenbacks to Mr. Stanton I had remaining \$21,000 in gold, and about \$2,300 in greenbacks which I retained on the request of Baron Stoeckl as an additional fee." [46]

As soon as the "fee" was paid to him, Walker, with gold and greenbacks in his pockets, proceeded to New York. There a sad fate overtook him. In some mysterious manner his pocket was "picked" — and \$16,000 worth of gold Treasury certificates were stolen from him. [47]

In all New York that night no one must have slept worse than Walker. The police set to work immediately, and within a few days the thieves were detected in Buffalo and brought back to New York. [48] Naturally Walker was in an ecstasy of relief at recovering the certificates. But, determined that the episode must end right there if publicity were to be avoided, he declined to prosecute the criminals. [49] The imagination may well conceive how the pickpockets were startled at this paternal kindness. So confused and bewildered was a leading New York daily at Walker's refusal to press any charge against the thieves, that it printed the story under the headline: "A Police Case With A Mystery." [50]

Meanwhile, Painter had not been idle in Washington. From the time when Walker departed on his ill-fated trip to New York, the Correspondent devoted time and energy to peering into the more informal details of the manner in which the Alaska payment had been made. When word came from New York of the robbery of Walker's Treasury certificates, Painter redoubled his efforts. He testified later: [51]

> I met Mr. Stanton and asked him if he knew of Mr. Walker's pocket being picked in New York. He said he did not. I then related to him the circumstances, that I had seen it in one of the New York papers. He said it was all news to him. I asked him what he sup-

[46] *House Report*, no. 35, *op. cit.*, p. 14.
[47] New York *Herald*, 27 August, 1868.
[48] Buffalo *Commercial Advertiser*, 25 August, 1868.
[49] New York *Herald*, 27 August, 1868.
[50] *Ibid.*
[51] *House Report*, no. 35, *op. cit.*, p. 40.

posed Mr. Walker was using these $5,000 gold checks about, and if he did not think it was some of the Alaska money held by him. He said he did not know.

His suspicions aroused more than ever by the strange ignorance of Walker's law associate, Painter hastened to the Treasury Department and sought Treasurer Francis E. Spinner. Painter's story, which corresponds in major detail with the sequence of events, may be quoted in part: [52]

I went in there [to the Treasury Department] one day and asked him [Spinner] if he could inform me in regard to the time that the money was drawn from the Treasury for the payment of the Alaska matter, stating that I had noticed in a cable dispatch that about five million only of it had gone through London to Russia; that I had never believed the thing was an honest legitimate transaction; and that I would like to know when the money was drawn from us; and, as it was about six weeks or two months before its reception in London, I thought it had taken a long time after the money was appropriated for it to get there. He replied, "I have been expecting for some time that that thing would be stirred up." I said, "Why?" He replied, "The day that the papers were signed, after the money was appropriated, Mr. Riggs went to Mr. McCulloch [the Secretary of the Treasury] and told him that he must have $200,000 that day in currency, and wanted Mr. McCulloch to let him have it in gold. Mr. McCulloch said that he would have to see me. I at first declined to have anything to do with it, but subsequently, on their agreeing to leave the gold and to draw out currency instead of gold, I thought there was no risk in that, as it was an accommodation to them and to the Russian Government. I had not thought so much about it at the time as I have since, and so I concluded to let them have the currency." And he continued: "Mr. McCulloch has been very anxious since to know what became of this $200,000, and where it was distributed." I asked him, "Why did they not sell their gold and get the currency in that way?" He replied, "They were in too big a hurry. Congress had just adjourned and they wanted it right off that day." I then asked him when the rest was drawn, and he sent for one of the clerks and referred me to him — a Mr. Tuttle. I went in with Mr. Tuttle, and we got out

[52] *House Report*, no. 35, *op. cit.*, p. 33.

the checks showing that it was drawn out in various sums, from the 1st of August to the 16th of September.

After completing this diligent inquiry into the disposition of the money, the indefatigable Painter proceeded to enlist the aid of General Butler. The latter, it will be recalled, had led the Perkins forces in Congress in the attempt to withhold a portion of the Alaska funds; Baron Stoeckl had named the Massachusetts soldier-politician as the holder of $30,000 worth of shares in that unsavoury claim.[53] Therefore, Painter believed, he would lend an eager ear to the sensational news. Accordingly, the Correspondent dispatched a confidential letter to Butler, who was at his home in Massachusetts. The letter read thus: [54]

> I have in my possession some facts in connection with the corruption by which the Treasury was robbed of the $7,200,000 to pay for Alaska and if you desire will show you how to uncover the biggest lobby swindle ever "put up" in Washington. The men who got the huge slices are in great trepidation at the leaking out of the fact that only $5,000,000 went to Russia. *Secy. McCulloch* is somewhat disgusted because, after loaning Riggs $200,000 in currency to make some of his payments for the Baron, he did not get a "thank you, sir." "Little Bobby Walker" who wrote against and worked against impeachment and ran the Chase movement got $20,000 gold. When will you be here?

In emphasising Walker's part in opposing the impeachment of President Johnson and his sponsorship of Chief Justice Chase's fight for the Democratic presidential nomination, Painter was appealing to deeply rooted prejudices of the extreme Republican, Butler, who had led the fight for impeachment and had violently assailed Chase's ambitions to occupy the White House. From his Massachusetts home Butler answered: "My dear Painter: Will be there on Monday. Yours, B.F.B." [55]

To narrate what occurred when Painter and Butler met in

[53] Golder, *op. cit.*, p. 422 n.
[54] Painter to Butler, 27 November, 1868, Benjamin F. Butler Papers, Library of Congress.
[55] Copy of Butler's reply, in his handwriting, on reverse side of, *ibid.*

Washington, would be only to conjecture. But it soon became evident that the adroit New Englander, despite his hostility to Walker, had no intention of pressing for an investigation by Congress, as was obviously desired by Painter. An associate in the Perkins Claim revealed that Butler, for a financial consideration, had deserted his colleagues in the Perkins camp; that in the last days of debate on the Alaska Appropriation Bill he had been giving mere lip service in a sham battle on behalf of the Claim.[56] If this be true, it is scant wonder that Butler was loth to listen to Painter.

Eluded by Butler, Painter was not yet vanquished. Determined to give his findings the widest publicity, he sent to the New York *Sun* a lengthy and detailed account of his suspicions. He related that on the day when the major portion of the Alaska money was drawn from the Treasury by Riggs, over $200,000 had been divided among certain "patriots" who had been most eloquent in declaring that the national honour would be degraded if Russia remained unpaid. Painter did not mention Walker by name, but in the despatch to his paper he alluded to the Mississippian in the following words: [57]

> An old gentleman of some distinction, who sat upon the platform of Tammany Hall when Seymour was nominated, was put in to the extent of $20,000 in gold, yet it is doubtful if he really influenced the vote of a single member of the House. When Congress meets, the whole question will doubtless be investigated.

Painter was seeking to call down on Walker the wrath of civic reformers and Republicans alike in linking him with the Tammany element of the Democratic party, merely because the former Secretary of the Treasury had finally supported Governor Horatio Seymour, of New York, for the Democratic presidential nomination.

Other newspaper correspondents took up Painter's cry of "corruption." One in particular, Richard J. Hinton, who conducted a column in the Worcester *Daily Spy* under the ap-

[56] Washington *Evening Star*, 28 January, 1869; New York *Herald*, 27 January, 1869.
[57] New York *Sun*, 30 November, 1868.

propriate *nom de plume* "Observer," wrote a particularly lengthy account on 7 December, shortly after the convening of Congress. Walker had received a *douceur* of $25,000 in gold and "some of the Riggs $300,000 appears to have passed into his hands";[58] so Hinton alleged, in giving the substance of "rumours" that had been heard from the lips of a certain newspaper correspondent in Washington.

Although Painter's revelations in the New York *Sun* of 30 November had preceded the appearance of those of Hinton by a full week, it was the latter's Worcester *Daily Spy* article that directly inspired an investigation by Congress. Ironically enough, it was the saintly dignitary, Representative Fernando Wood, whose political virtue had been deeply stained by a term as Mayor of New York city, who sponsored the motion for the inquiry.[59]

The investigation into the Alaska payment was conducted by the Committee on Public Expenditures of the House of Representatives.[60] Walker was summoned to appear on 17 December. Painter, fearing the worst, now assured his readers: "He (Walker) says he will charge the attacks upon him for his part in the case to envy of those members and newspapers that failed to get a slice."[61]

When Walker gave his evidence, he suspected the whole "misunderstanding" to be the work of certain individuals who desired to share in his "counsel fee." As for his services on behalf of the legislation, Walker testified:[62]

> Well, I told him [Baron Stoeckl] I had never lobbied Congress in my life, and that I never meant to, and that if he wished me to lobby Congress generally I must decline. He said . . . his object was to get me to argue and discuss the question as I had done successfully many others, to print pamphlets, and write articles for the newspapers, presenting all the arguments in favour of the ap-

[58] Worcester *Daily Spy*, 7 December, 1868.
[59] *Congressional Globe*, 40th Congress, 3rd Session, p. 75.
[60] The proceedings of this investigation have been drawn on by the present writer only in so far as they relate to Walker.
[61] New York *Sun*, 14 December, 1868.
[62] *House Report*, no. 35, *op. cit.*, pp. 12, 14.

propriation. He said he wished me also to confer with Mr. Sumner (Senator from Massachusetts) and General Banks (Member of Congress from Massachusetts), who were warmly supporting the measure. I told him if that was all that was required of me, I could consider it entirely professional, and that I would do it. After some other conversation he proposed to pay me for such services, as I have stated, $20,000 in gold, to which I assented. He was good enough afterwards voluntarily to increase that sum. . . . He paid me in the first place through Mr. Riggs, on a gold check which Mr. Riggs gave me on his house in New York for $26,000. . . . After paying the $5,000 in greenbacks to Mr. Stanton I had remaining $21,000 in gold, and about $2,300 in greenbacks, which I retained on the request of Baron Stoeckl as an additional fee.

On 2 February of the new year, Stanton was called to give evidence. Naturally, he corroborated Walker's statements in the main, adding that Painter had desired to be engaged to assist in securing favourable action on the Alaska appropriation; that he and Walker would have nothing to do with the correspondent.[63]

When Painter gave evidence, his story was an emphatic denial that he had sought to be associated in the lobby. He avowed:[64]

I never dreamed of such a thing; I couldn't take such employment because, when the matter first came into the Senate, I put myself fairly and squarely against it; and several despatches I sent to Philadelphia and New York, assailing it as a job, were cut down by the editors as too severe. I never could have gone into the matter without destroying my honour and reputation.

After which testimony, the *Sun*, voicing its confidence in its Washington correspondent, adorned its first page with the headline: "The Conspiracy Against Mr. Painter,"[65] while Painter himself assured his readers: "Your correspondent will be completely vindicated."[66]

It cannot be said that the members of the Alaska investigating

[63] *Ibid.*, pp. 22–5.
[64] *Ibid.*, p. 39.
[65] New York *Sun*, 8 February, 1869.
[66] *Ibid.*, 9 February, 1869.

committee were particularly enthusiastic in their conduct of the hearings and in the summoning of key witnesses. Their printed report is truly a unique document and is remarkable chiefly for what it does not show. With the exception of Walker and Stanton, it did not tar with a broad stripe any of those obviously involved in the bounty of the generous Tsar. As one reads the entire report, numbering forty-one pages of contradictory charges, denials, and counter-charges, one is quite apt to agree with the leading Washington daily that summed up the results of the investigation in the flippant words: [67]

> What Mr. Stanton says Mr. Painter said — What Mr. Walker said about what Mr. Stanton said Mr. Painter said — What Mr. Painter said when Mr. Stanton said what Mr. Walker said about what Mr. Stanton said Mr. Painter said.

Certainly no other episode in Walker's crowded political career summarises better than the Alaska affair the pith and marrow of some of his principles and characteristics; the union of love for gold and country, intellectual gifts, recklessness and carelessness in money matters — all combining to result in a dramatic scandal in the last year of his life. Engaged in other work during his crowded public and professional career, Walker emerged in a happier position. His manipulation of the Alaska affair, his political swan-song before passing to the other side, was the final application of careless genius in the service of its profession. Within a year following his humiliation in the witness box, death overtook him — but not before he managed to grind out a pamphlet advising the Canadians to crawl from beneath the claw of the treacherous British lion and come under the more desirable wing of the American eagle.[68]

The role of Walker in the Alaska purchase suggests certain historical conjectures. If the Appropriation Bill had failed of enactment, if Painter had succeeded in his efforts to defeat the legislation, and Alaska had remained a Russian colony to this

[67] Washington *Evening Star*, 27 February, 1869.
[68] *Letter of Hon. Robert J. Walker on the Annexation of Nova Scotia and British America* (Washington, 1869).

day, what would have been the consequences arising from a Soviet base on the mainland of North America? The complications resulting from its close proximity to the Pacific coast territory of the United States would undoubtedly have placed Russian-American relations in an utterly different diplomatic setting than hitherto, particularly from the fall of the Romanovs to the present day.

The editor was born and raised in Alaska, and received his doctorate in history from the University of California at Berkeley. He taught at the University of Cincinnati, and is now assistant professor at the University of California, Davis. The article is from the Pacific Historical Review, *XXVIII (May, 1959), 141–54.*

George Davidson
and the Acquisition of Alaska

MORGAN B. SHERWOOD

O n March 30, 1867, a treaty was submitted to the United States Senate for approval. Secretary of State William Seward and Baron Stoeckl, the Russian minister, had quietly negotiated the transfer of Alaska for $7,200,000. With the aid of Senator Charles Sumner, the document was ratified on April 9. Almost overnight, by Washington time schedules, the United States had obtained option on a giant strategic outpost, a land that dominated the entire North Pacific. The causes and events surrounding the purchase have been the subject of much research, but one important phase has been almost totally overlooked: the story of the first official scientific expedition to Alaska and the role of its leader, George Davidson, in subsequent congressional deliberations.

Despite the relative ease with which the first stages of the transfer were accomplished, it soon became evident that the treaty would be challenged in the House of Representatives. In the Alaska purchase, opponents of the administration found new fuel to feed the bonfire of abuse they had lit earlier under President Johnson. First, the treaty had been prepared clandestinely. Second, the question of jurisdictional competency arose. The treaty required an appropriation and therefore needed House approval. Ignoring this, Seward had exchanged ratification and arranged for formal transfer. Seward had, in the eyes of some congressmen, subverted the constitutional right of the lower house. Third, Alaska was a vast *terra incognita*. An accurate estimate of its size was not even available. The opposition branded the territory utterly valueless, and a small but vocal segment of the press launched a vigorous campaign to denounce Alaska as a worthless acquisition.

The administration addressed itself to the task of controverting the unfavorable publicity with an "educational" campaign of its own. Said the New York *Herald*: "the illustrious Premier [Seward] is working the telegraphs and the Associated Press in the manufacture of public opinion night and day. . . ." [1] At the end of the year, Seward was still on the prowl for data about Alaska, but most of the available material in Washington had been examined previously by Sumner in preparation for his speech in the Senate.[2] The administration's campaign, combined with the dubious activities of Stoeckl, resulted in an investigation later. Seward denied that he had spent vast sums to subsidize the press, and very little evidence was presented to support the allegation that Stoeckl had used some of the purchase money for the same purpose,[*] and to suborn congressmen.[3]

The need for more information about Alaska had been recognized before opposition to the purchase solidified. Sumner men-

[1] Quoted in T. A. Bailey, "Why the United States Purchased Alaska," *Pacific Historical Review*, III (1934), 44.

[2] Henry to Seward, December 23, 1867. 40th Cong., 2nd sess., *House Doc. 177*, p. 86.

[*] R. H. Luthin, in the preceding article, details the shady activities that surrounded passage of the Alaskan appropriation bill. — ED. NOTE.

[3] "Alaska Investigation," Committee on Public Expenditures, 40th Cong., 3rd sess., *House Report 35*, pp. 21, 22.

tioned the desirability of a scientific expedition in his Senate speech in favor of the purchase, a speech that was both a classical example of the period's florid political rhetoric and a masterpiece of direct research. On April 29, 1867, the New York *Herald* also publicized the need for an exploring expedition:

> Our government should, without delay, despatch a steam revenue cutter from San Francisco for special service this summer in exploring that portion of the coast, which half a century of experience has taught the Russians is available for general commercial purposes. . . . Such a flying expedition, of course, could not be expected to . . . effect any detailed exploration of the interior; but with an active and wide-awake little corps of proper men, untrammeled by red-tape restrictions, the expedition would bring back more live information on all important points than could be obtained by years of fumbling among the accounts of ancient navigators and musty books of travel.[4]

The administration, probably in line with its "educational" campaign, decided to launch such a flying scientific reconnaissance.

Organization of the expedition proceeded at a pace equal in swiftness to that followed by Seward in his negotiation with Stoeckl. Instructions were prepared by the Smithsonian Institution and by the Treasury Department, which supervised the activities of both the Coast Survey and the Revenue Service. Benjamin Peirce, who succeeded Alexander Dallas Bache as Superintendent of the Coast Survey, conferred with Seward and Hugh McCulloch, Secretary of the Treasury. Peirce decided that George Davidson should lead the "wide-awake little corps" of scientists.

Davidson was born on May 9, 1825, in England. With his parents, he immigrated to America in 1832. While a student at Central High School in Philadelphia, he met Alexander Bache, the distinguished mathematician, who taught at the school. Bache became head of the Coast Survey, and in 1845, he hired his former pupil. In 1850, Davidson was assigned to the Pacific Coast. Like so many of his scientific contemporaries, Davidson

[4] Quoted in *House Doc. 177*, p. 189.

had a wide variety of intellectual interests. He was a civil engineer, hydrographer, geographer, irrigation engineer, astronomer, and geodesist. As a result of his geodetic duties, he developed a collateral interest in the history of marine exploration on the West Coast. By 1900, he was a recognized authority on early voyages of exploration along the Pacific littoral of North America. His biographer calls him, "the pioneer West Coast scientist." [5]

Though Davidson was chosen to lead the scientific group, the general direction of the expedition was given to Captain W. A. Howard of the Revenue Service. The duties of the Coast Survey party were to be subordinate to the special duties of the revenue cutter. [6]

Howard was ordered to proceed directly from San Francisco to Sitka. After presenting his credentials to the Russian authorities at Sitka, he was to employ the vessel according to his "best judgment to effect the purposes of the expedition, between the southern limits of the country and the westerly extremity of the Aleutian islands." McCulloch did not expect him to pass north of the Aleutians, though Howard was at liberty to do so if he deemed it necessary. Howard was also instructed to ascertain the "most available channels of commerce, the probable haunts of smugglers, and the most suitable points for custom house and revenue stations." Further, he was to make a general reconnaissance of the coast, select appropriate locations for navigational aids and coaling stations, determine the location of fishing banks, and follow the suggestions of the Smithsonian Institution regarding the collection of information about geographical characteristics, resources, productions, and climate. McCulloch directed that a comprehensive report on the results of the exploration be transmitted without delay, to be received in Washington, "if possible," not later than December 1, 1867. [7] It was a big order to fill in so short a time. Little wonder that the final

[5] Oscar Lewis, *George Davidson, Pioneer West Coast Scientist* (Berkeley and Los Angeles, 1954).

[6] George Davidson, *Coast Pilot of Alaska. . . , From Southern Boundary to Cook's Inlet* (Washington, 1869), 3.

[7] Instructions dated June 4, 1867. *House Doc.* 177, p. 191.

report contained many extracts from "the accounts of ancient navigators and musty books of travel."

The Smithsonian instructions, of special interest to Davidson's party, were hardly less demanding. They were divided into three main categories: meteorology, ethnology, and natural history. Detailed climatic observations were requested, from the usual temperature, rainfall and pressure readings, to "the color of the water," and "the direction of the motion of the highest fleecy clouds." The scientists were asked to obtain the vocabularies of "all the Eskimo tribes, including the Namollos of the Asiatic side of Behring [*sic*] strait, of the Aleutians, the Kenaiens, and the Koloshians [Tlingit], in their various languages and dialects." Also, "a collection of skulls representing each tribe should be made as far as possible, particularly of the Eskimo nations. . . ." There is an obvious discrepancy between what the scientists were supposed to collect and where the revenue cutter was expected to cruise. The Smithsonian instructions put the expedition far north of the Aleutians, in the Eskimo regions of Alaska, even on the coast of Asia, while McCulloch's instructions more or less restricted the exploration to areas south of the Aleutian chain. In the field of natural history, the Institution desired skins of the sea otter, black fox, seal, walrus, goat, bear, whale, porpoise, salmon, cod, halibut, and other animals of "economic value." Specimens of timber trees and "any other plants of known economical value" were also requested. "An allowance, too, will probably have to be made to meet [the] expense of purchasing such furs as cannot otherwise be obtained, as sea otters, &c., as it is of great importance to be able to exhibit them to Congress." [8]

At this point, an assumption is unavoidable. Apparently, the expedition was to concern itself mainly with the acquisition of favorable evidence, evidence that could be used to convince the American public in general, and congressmen in particular, that Alaska was worth the purchase price. "Under the circumstances," said the *Alta California*, "the expedition that leaves

[8] *Ibid.*, 192–195.

. . . for Alaska will be considered an epoch in the history of the spread of American empire over American soil." [9]

By June 3, preparations were complete, and Seward was notified of Howard's impending departure. "Captain W. A. Howard, of the revenue service," wrote McCulloch, "will proceed to San Francisco, by the next steamer, and take charge of the steam cutter Lincoln, which is preparing for a voyage to Sitka. . . ." [10] The *Lincoln*, built in Baltimore, was brought to the West Coast by Captain J. W. White in 1866. She was a screw steamer rigged for sail, of about six hundred and forty tons, and carried a crew of fifty-seven men. Her armament included seven-inch guns. [11]

Before the *Lincoln* got under way, a small deck cabin was constructed forward. The additional space enabled Davidson to take along more assistants than he had originally planned. His staff included A. T. Mossman, astronomical assistant, and Mossman's aide, Stehman Forney; George Farquhar, draughtsman and hydrographer; William Hamel, draughtsman, interpreter, and surveyor; John Leeds, tidal observer for Sitka; Theodore A. Blake, geologist and mining engineer; W. G. H. Harford, conchologist and naturalist; and Dr. Albert Kellogg, botanist and ship's surgeon. Davidson, Kellogg, and two assistants shared the deck house, four of the party were accommodated in the ward room, and the tidal observer slept on the berth deck. [12]

During the morning hours of July 21, 1867, the *Lincoln* cleared San Francisco harbor and steamed north. Six days later, she stopped to coal at Victoria, British Columbia. Her departure from that port was delayed a few hours when she ran aground on one side of the Victoria channel. From Victoria, the *Lincoln* sailed by the Inside Passage to Port Simpson, in the vicinity of

[9] (San Francisco), July 21, 1867.
[10] McCulloch to Seward, June 3, 1867. *House Doc. 177*, pp. 53, 54.
[11] *Alta California*, April 12, 1869.
[12] *Report of the Superintendent for 1867*, Appendix 18, *United States Coast Survey* (Washington, 1869), p. 88; *House Doc. 177*, p. 78; Davidson, "Sketch of the Life and Work of Dr. Kellogg," in Albert Kellogg and E. L. Greene, *Illustrations of West American Oaks* (San Francisco, 1889), page v.

54° 40'. At Port Simpson, the propellor was repaired, and members of the Coast Survey party engaged in their respective scientific pursuits. From there, the ship proceeded "outside" to Sitka, in order to verify the headlands of Prince of Wales and other islands which comprise the southern boundary of Alaska.[13]

Nasty weather attended the journey from Simpson to Sitka: "there was actually nothing to be seen, felt, touched or tasted but fog, fog, fog."[14] On August 12, the vessel moored off Sitka. "The first view of the town is far from inviting," wrote an *Alta California* correspondent aboard the *Lincoln*. ". . . Having landed, however, one is agreeably surprised to find hidden behind the ugly yellow line several neat looking log houses; . . . a line of workshops; a neat country house. . . ."[15] The next day, the ship's officers and the officers of the Coast Survey paid a formal call on the manager of the Russian-American Company, Prince Dmitri Maksoutoff. Howard's credentials were unnecessary, for Maksoutoff considered the territory United States property from the day of ratification, and looked upon the formal transfer as a mere matter of ceremony.[16]

After a ten day layover, the expedition departed from Sitka. Howard intended to make Fort Constantine, Port Etches, at the entrance to Prince William Sound, but thick weather altered his plans. On August 26, the *Lincoln* anchored off St. Paul, Kodiak Island, where she remained for five days. Only one and one-half days of the five were clear. Davidson's operations were consequently hampered.[17]

Officers of the Russian-American Company attempted to dissuade Howard from going to Unalaska so late in the season. He ignored their advice and sailed southwest by west on August 31. A few days later, the expedition almost came to an unceremonious end in the icy waters of the North Pacific:[18]

[13] *House Doc. 177*, pp. 195, 197. See also, *Coast Survey* (1869), 190.
[14] *House Doc. 177*, p. 77.
[15] *Alta California*, July 14, 1868.
[16] *House Doc. 177*, p. 197.
[17] *Coast Survey* (1869), 192, 193.
[18] *House Doc. 177*, p. 200.

On Wednesday the 4th September, steering southwest by west, heavy sea and very foggy, we sounded at intervals for fishing banks. At 12:45 breakers were suddenly discovered directly ahead; put the helm down, took in all sail, and with great difficulty cleared the breakers, head off; sounded in seven fathoms of water. Had the ship run twice her length further all hands must have perished; the sea was tremendous.

Two days after the close call at Sanak Reef, the *Lincoln* arrived at Unalaska Island, where she took on coal while her scientific passengers pursued their separate duties in dreary weather. During the party's brief stay at the remote station, Kellogg, Blake, and four members of the expedition made an ascent of Makushin Volcano, and Davidson trained the Russian-American Company surgeon, an Aleut, as tidal observer. On September 13, the expedition began the return journey. After a boisterous passage of eight and one-half days, made mostly under canvas, the vessel anchored once more in Sitka harbor.[19] So far, the members of the expedition had not set foot on the mainland of Alaska.

The expedition tarried in the vicinity of the old capital while Howard searched for a harbor more suitable than Sitka. At the time, Sitka was preparing for the formal transfer ceremonies. Howard apparently wanted to participate in the festivities, so for several days the ship was of little use in the furtherance of the expedition's goals. Finally, the *Lincoln* weighed anchor for Chilkat country.

On the side trip to Chilkat, after almost three months had passed since the departure from San Francisco, the "explorers" made their first contact with Alaskan Indians in their native environment, and paused for the first time near the Alaska mainland. The natives were saucy and quarrelsome. They seemed more interested in the acquisition of gifts, especially whiskey, than in idle chatter. As one chief observed: "Talk without whiskey was nothing; s'pose plenty whiskey and presents, then talk

---

[19] *House Doc. 177*, pp. 202–206, and *Coast Survey* (1869), 195. See also, Davidson, "The First Ascent of the Volcano Makushin," *Appalachia*, December, 1884, pp. 1–11.

good." [20] One thing must have been painfully obvious to the revenue officers: to police the liquor traffic in Alaska would be a difficult task indeed.

The expedition returned to Sitka on October 19, one day too late for the transfer ceremony. From Sitka, the *Lincoln* began her return voyage via the Inside Passage to the Stikine River, Kake Island, and south through Clarence Strait. At Kake, the Indians were something less than hospitable. When no whiskey was forthcoming, the chief doubled the price of potatoes. Howard thereupon refused to give the Indian a document or "paper" which conferred quasi-official recognition on him as "head chief." The custom of presenting such "papers" was an old technique in these parts.

> A very good custom prevails on this coast, in giving Indians what they term "paper," stating the character of the bearer; these "papers," particularly by Hudson Bay Company Officers, state fairly the character of the Indian, his influence, if any, with his tribe, his power and willingness for harm and good. One of the minor chiefs handed me a paper warning everyone to place no confidence in him. These papers are highly valued and kept for years unsoiled.[21]

The expedition arrived at Victoria on November 11, and a few days later, it departed for San Francisco.

The *Alta California* had predicted that the information gathered by the scientific party, "will be eagerly sought for," [22] as it undoubtedly was. But had the expedition accomplished its goals? Did it return with enough significant material for a conclusive opinion on the value of Alaska? A correspondent for the paper, who was aboard the vessel, qualified his praise of the new territory. "The expedition may be considered as a success, scientifically considered. As for the value and resources of the country — well, seven millions is a good deal of money." [23]

George Davidson was more or less satisfied with the results of the expedition. He was especially enthused about the vast

[20] *House Doc. 177*, p. 208.
[21] *Ibid.*, 210.
[22] *Alta California*, July 10, 1867.
[23] *Ibid.*, November 20, 1867.

supplies of sea food available in Alaskan waters. In some of Alaska's bays, he reported, the progress of a boat may be impeded by thousands of salmon. "But the most valuable fish on the coast is the cod." Halibut, herring, and whale were other sources of potential wealth.[24] As for shell fish, the expedition's conchologist had listed sixty-three specimens. "I regret exceedingly," he apologized, "that the collections are so meagre."[25]

Davidson was less enthusiastic about the agricultural potential. In southeastern Alaska,

> potatoes yield well, but are of small size and watery. Turnips, beets, carrots, parsnips, and other root crops, with cabbages and the like, are cultivated in a few gardens. . . . None of the cereals are cultivated, and it is very doubtful that they would succeed.[26]

He reported, however, that potatoes grown at Unalaska were huge. Kellogg spoke favorably of the pasturage at Kodiak, where the cattle were fat, though butter had a disagreeable taste. Timber was considered the most important vegetable resource. Sitka spruce grew in abundance, and the soil nurtured valuable yellow cedar trees, some of which achieved considerable size. Altogether, about two hundred and seventy plant specimens were listed.[27] According to the Davidson report, climatic factors were the chief hindrance to successful agricultural pursuits.

Weather charts, combined with the casual observations of the scientists, did not present a very pleasant picture of Alaska's climate. The heavy rainfall produced a thick mat of moss, which, in the eyes of the explorers, was Alaska's characteristic vegetable cover. "The whole extent of country subject to these rains is covered with sphagnum from one to two feet in depth; even on the steepest hillsides this carpet is saturated with water. . . ."[28]

Davidson's report also evaluated the fur, ice, and ivory in-

[24] Davidson, *Coast Pilot*, 40–49. Unless otherwise stated, information in the *Pilot* also appeared in Davidson's official report of the reconnaissance.

[25] *Coast Survey* (1869), Report of W. G. W. Harford.

[26] Davidson, *Coast Pilot*, 29, 30.

[27] *House Doc. 177*, pp. 214–218. Kellogg's Report.

[28] Davidson, *Coast Pilot*, 24.

dustries, outlined the strategic importance of the country, and contributed ethnological information of interest. Population statistics and the characteristics of the indigenes were noted. Two charts, one prepared by Lisiansky about 1806, which listed the languages at Unalaska, Kodiak, Kenai, and Sitka, and another containing two hundred and thirty words and twenty-seven phrases of the Tsimshian, prepared by Davidson, were appended to the report.

There was disagreement on the mineralogical value of Alaska. The party searched in vain for reported silver, iron, and gold deposits in southeastern Alaska, but made no attempt to investigate the alleged petroleum, copper, and gold resources elsewhere. Fifteen miles from Sitka, the scientists located large quantities of fine marble. Not much farther away, pieces of coal were found intermixed with rock along the bed of a rapid stream. An important coal seam was also reported on the shore of Cook Inlet, but the expedition did not touch the mainland in that area.[29] No member of the party actually saw a coal bed during the visit, a fact that would be noted with cynical delight by certain congressmen several months later. In October, the *Alta California* published an article based on information received, "from a private letter to a friend," which stated: "The coal deposits in Russian-America are pronounced worthless; being very thin seams, much impaired by earthy matter, and by actual trial have been found unfit for steamers. . . ." It would have been more correct to say "the *known* coal deposits." Geologist Blake made the distinction in his report: "Exaggerated ideas have been formed of the *known* mineral wealth of Alaska."[30]

Davidson's observation of the ocean currents led to an examination of old exploration narratives, and resulted in the addition of valuable information on the Alaska Current. More

[29] *Ibid.*, 19, 35–37; *House Doc. 177*, p. 79; and Davidson, "Scientific Expedition to Alaska," *Lippincott's Magazine*, II (1868), 473.

[30] *House Doc. 177*, p. 324. The *Alta* article appeared October 1, 1867. See also, *Proceedings of the California Academy of Sciences*, San Francisco, January 20, 1868.

important, precise latitude and longitude determinations were obtained for a half-dozen places and the first accurate magnetic observations were attempted.[31]

George Davidson acknowledged his debt to the early explorers, to what the New York *Herald* had called "musty books of travel." "Details of the coast line, harbors, bays, headlands, &c.," he wrote, "are given, in part from personal observation, but principally from descriptions of Vancouver, Mearer [*sic*], Portlock, Dixon, Lisiansky, &c." [32] Davidson also relied heavily on library research for information about resources, meteorology, and ethnology. He could do no less and still submit a reasonably well-rounded report. After all, the expedition spent most of its time at the civilized island stations of Sitka, Kodiak, and Unalaska. Even Port Etches, which was not visited by Howard because of thick weather, is on an island. In all, the party probably stepped ashore on the mainland of Alaska in only two places, Chilkat and the Stikine, both of which are within a few miles of the Canadian border and in the same climatic area as Sitka. Davidson knew that Cook Inlet and the Kenai Peninsula possessed a milder climate than the limited areas explored, but Howard made no attempt to investigate the region. Under the circumstances, the scientists had done about all they could do. Howard begged leave, "to bear testimony to the untiring exertions of Mr. Davidson and the Coast Survey party to accomplish an almost impossibility." [33] The members of the party were forced to apologize for their scant accomplishments. They blamed the climate and the press of time. Their chief, Davidson, found it necessary to resort to bookish research and reports of reports in order to fill out his own report. It is not surprising that the results were of mixed value to debaters in the House of Representatives.

When Davidson returned to Washington, he conferred with Seward, McCulloch, and Sumner, appeared before House and

[31] Davidson, "Biographical Sketch and Essay on Irrigation," MS, Bancroft Library, Univ. of Calif., Berkeley.

[32] *Coast Survey* (1869), 187.

[33] *House Doc. 177*, p. 211.

Senate committees, and read a paper on Alaska before the National Academy of Sciences. There is a common belief that his activities and report influenced the passage of the purchase appropriation bill in the House. Davidson himself did not exactly discourage the belief. In a manuscript autobiography submitted to Alonzo Phelps, in 1879, a section to this effect is crossed out.[34] But later in the century, Davidson wrote:

> the report found defenders on the floor of the House, as it certainly had done in the committees. Its statements were never traversed, but used on every occasion, and I was assured that this report and my conferences had large weight in the passage of the bill appropriating the money.[35]

His biographers credit him to a greater or lesser degree with the consummation of the purchase. Yale states that Davidson's work "influenced the passage."[36] Holway says the report had "great influence," and Lewis cites an "authority" who employs the same terms.[37] Christy, Dickie, and Harrison claim that the report "largely influenced Congress to act favorably on the purchase of Alaska."[38] The most extravagant claim is advanced by Hunt. According to him, Davidson's work, "undoubtedly influenced Seward in proceeding with the purchase of Alaska by the United States."[39] Hunt would have us believe that Davidson completed his exploration before Seward even signed the treaty.

If there is doubt about the extent of Davidson's positive influence on the passage of the appropriation bill, there is no doubt that frequent reference was made to his testimony. The Coast Survey report was available to every congressman. When-

[34] Whether by Davidson or Phelps is unknown to the writer. Davidson, "Biographical Sketch," MS, Bancroft Library.

[35] 55th Cong., 2nd sess., *Cong. Record*, 2473.

[36] C. G. Yale, "Professor George Davidson," *Mining and Scientific Press* (San Francisco), August 15, 1885.

[37] R. S. Holway, "Professor George Davidson," *Science*, XXXV (1912), 259; Lewis, *Davidson*, 44.

[38] S. B. Christy, G. W. Dickie, and Ralph Harrison, "George Davidson," *Proc. Calif. Acad. Sciences*, April 9, 1914, p. 12.

[39] R. D. Hunt, *California's Stately Hall of Fame* (Stockton, 1950), 407.

ever the question of Alaska's value was raised, reference was made to the report, directly or indirectly.

Representative Johnson of California made cautious use of Davidson's material. "Imperfect as it may be, our Coast Survey shows that this whole extent of water front is indented by capacious bays and commodious harbors without number. . . ." Johnson expected to see the day when Alaskan salmon competed with Welsh salmon on London's markets. "It is admitted by all," he continued, "that every animal wearing a fur coat may be found in that country."[40]

Representative Myers recommended the Coast Survey report to an opponent of the bill, "as evidence in regard to the riches of the country."[41] That particular opponent, Ferris of New York, *had* read the report, and had noted passages referring to the limited agricultural possibilities and to the inclement weather.[42] Congressman Munger had anticipated Ferris' argument. In 1852, the Coast Survey had been hampered by bad weather in California. The incident, Munger explained, was used as evidence that California was barren and sterile, used in the same way that Davidson's report was now used to belittle Alaska.[43]

Opposition arguments about Alaska's value were not easily dispatched. Congressman Peters, "would not deny that her cod fisheries, if she has them, would be somewhat valuable, but it seems doubtful if fish can find sun enough to be cured on her shores."[44] Representative Williams of Pennsylvania was especially thorough in his abuse of Alaska's wealth as recorded by the Coast Survey party. He quoted Kellogg's description of the miry "morass," and referred sarcastically to the simple "reports" and "opinions" of Davidson and Blake.[45]

[40] 40th Cong., 2nd sess., *Cong. Globe*, 3625, 3626. Johnson was an accurate prognosticator. Davidson later reported that 105,902 cases of Alaska salmon had been shipped from San Francisco to Great Britain in 1887. See *Resources and Developments in Alaska*, Bull. No. 4, U. S. Coast and Geodetic Survey (Washington, 1888[?]).

[41] 40th Cong., 2nd sess., *Cong. Globe*, 3662.

[42] *Ibid.*, 3667.

[43] *Ibid.*, 3659.

[44] *Ibid.*, 3668.

[45] *Ibid.*, Appendix, 489–490.

The loudest controversy raged between Nathaniel P. Banks of Massachusetts and Congressman Washburn of Wisconsin. Banks, as chairman of the House Foreign Relations Committee, was the bill's chief sponsor. Washburn was its most bitter enemy.

Banks, using the testimony of Davidson and others, presented a golden picture of Alaska. His enthusiasm about her fisheries prompted Price of Iowa to say:

> As I stood there, Mr. Chairman, listening to the gentleman from Massachusetts with fish to the right of me, fish to the left of me, fish all in front of me, rolling and tumbling, I had to acknowledge that the picture, as painted, made Alaska a good country for fish.[46]

Banks continued:

> We have received within a few days, a carefully prepared and elaborate statement of Professor Davidson, whose opinions cannot be discredited, who says that in this territory is to be found the purest and the best coal upon the Pacific Coast.

Washburn asked: "Will the gentleman be kind enough to refer to the page of Professor Davidson's testimony?"

"I will give the statement hereafter in Professor Davidson's own words," Banks replied:

> Pure copper is found in large cubic masses. Copper plates, hammered out by the natives, and with hieroglyphics engraved upon them, the history of their tribes and families, have been found. Silver is also found in many places. Also quartz, with sulphate of iron and lead. Gold has been reported at Cook's inlet, on the Stikine river.

"Reported," said Washburn curtly.[47]

Washburn soon had his hour on the floor. He cited the Survey report extensively:

> Professor Davidson is forced to say that — "While the vast forests of wood exist upon the waters of Puget Sound, Admiralty inlet, and Straits of Fuca, it may be commercially unprofitable to cut

[46] *Ibid.*, 380.
[47] *Ibid.*, 390.

and ship even this yellow cedar to the California market, unless native labor can be obtained at low rates to get it out."

Referring to Howard, Washburn commented: "He afterward found one fishing bank, and its position was ascertained by Mr. Davidson, but I assert here that that fishing bank is not within the limits of the jurisdiction of Russian America."[48] A gloomy description of the Prince William Sound area that Davidson had unwisely extracted from Tebenkof (1848), was also offered in evidence, as was Blake's quotation on the mineral resources of the country.

At one point, Banks submitted a document. "As the gentleman from Wisconsin refers to the testimony of Professor Davidson, I will ask to have an extract of a letter from him read."

"Give me the page," snapped Washburn, "and I will find it."

"I will send it to the clerk's desk to read," said Banks.

But Washburn protested:

I object to that letter being read. Anything Professor Davidson has reported officially I do not object to having read. But I am opposed to the reading of any of this manufactured testimony recently got up for the purpose of getting through the treaty.

"The gentleman asked for testimony as to coal in Alaska, and I have given it." Banks did not let the matter drop. He repeated his offer later. "I hope the gentleman will allow Mr. Davidson's letter to be read."

Washburn submitted. "Well, as my friend from Massachusetts has shown anxiety to have the extract of the letter of Professor Davidson read, I will yield for that purpose. It is so seldom he produces any authority I like to oblige him. . . ."

The clerk read the document. In it, Davidson mentioned the seam of coal reported on Kachemak Bay, Cook Inlet. To mine the bed, he explained, would require more engineering talent than the Russian-American Company possessed. He stressed the need for a coal source nearer the west coast market, and indicated that coal shipped 14,500 miles presently sold for twenty dollars per ton.

[48] *Ibid.,* 399.

When the clerk finished, Washburn addressed the chair.

I have listened to the reading of that letter, and I hesitate not to assert that there is no proof contained therein that there is a vein of coal anywhere in Alaska. Mr. Davidson does not pretend that he ever saw a vein there. He says in his letter, just read, that coal is worth twenty dollars a ton in gold. Is it possible that a seven-foot vein of coal exists on Cook's inlet, and not opened while coal is worth twenty dollars a ton? The statement is preposterous.

Washburn referred to Howard as, "This modern Jason, who was sent to Alaska in pursuit of the golden fleece."

"And came back shorn," interrupted James Blaine of Maine.[49]

The Congressman from Wisconsin was also interested in precedent.

But are we to stop with the purchase of Alaska and St. Thomas? No sir, I believe a treaty is now being negotiated with Denmark for the purchase of Greenland and Iceland. [There was laughter in the House.] . . . This is not mere loose talk. I have had placed upon my table since I began to speak today some pages of a document now printing at the Government Printing Office for the State Department which shows that the purchase of Greenland is in contemplation.

Higby inquired: "Was it written by Professor Davidson?"[50]

This rather curious question was asked by a firm supporter of the appropriation bill, of Davidson's character, and of the Survey report. With reference to Washburn, Higby said: "The gentleman was careful to read only those portions that made against the country."[51] Higby did not bother to indicate that Banks had quoted only those parts of the report that made *for* the territory.

The report had serious defects as progaganda favorable to passage of the bill. There was too much talk of sphagnum, inclement weather, and the like. The descriptions of mineral and timber wealth were often vague or qualified. There were too many reservations about the economic potential of Alaska.

Perhaps these defects were unavoidable. First, the expedition

[49] *Ibid.*, 398.
[50] *Ibid.*, 399.
[51] *Ibid.*, (not Appendix), 3806.

was supposed to be a scientific enterprise. Cautious phrasing was therefore in character. Second, a very brief time had been allotted for the exploration of a land one-fifth the size of the United States. Over a hundred years of Russian hegemony had failed to reveal any definitive information about Alaska's interior regions. How then could Davidson's little party be expected to return with a comprehensive estimate of the country's value? Third, the revenue officer in charge elected to limit his cruise to a few inhabited island areas. The expedition never even landed on the mainland of central Alaska.

The report was quoted by opponents of the bill, as well as by its advocates. Consequently, to assert that Davidson's activities "greatly influenced" the consummation of the purchase is to assume a great deal. That they had some influence is indicated by the frequent references made to Davidson and the Coast Survey report in the House debates. The appropriation measure was finally passed in July, 1868, by a vote of 113 to 43, with 44 abstentions. Consideration of the Alaska bill had been delayed by the President's impeachment trial. Critics of Davidson's report were probably less interested in determining the value of Alaska than they were in discrediting the administration. And there was the question of the Senate's right to conclude a treaty that required the appropriation of money. It may be that concern about the value of Alaska was little more than a tactical diversion.

Withal, the expedition was an important enterprise. It confirmed, for at least some congressmen, the view that Alaska was worth the purchase price; it illustrated the need for systematic surveys of the territory; and it stimulated Davidson's abiding interest in our new acquisition.

Richard Welch's essay should lay to rest, once and for all,
the old view that American press opinion howled "in united
chorus, 'Seward's Folly!'" He suggests, rather, that a majority
of American newspapers did not oppose the Cession Treaty,
a viewpoint advanced earlier by Thomas A. Bailey in the
Pacific Historical Review *(March, 1934).*

 The author graduated from Dartmouth College and received
his Ph.D. from Harvard. He taught at Colgate University
and the Virginia Military Institute, and is an associate professor
of history at Lafayette College in Easton, Pennsylvania. The
article appeared in the American Slavic and East European
Review, *XVII (1958), 481–94.*

American Public Opinion and the Purchase of Russian America

RICHARD E. WELCH, JR.

The American purchase of Alaska from Russia in 1867 is often cited today as an example of providential intervention in behalf of America's national security. Commentators shudder at the thought of Soviet air bases in what was once Russian America and praise the near miraculous foresight of Secretary of State William Seward.

Comprising as it does the only real estate transaction ever completed by Russia and America, Seward's annexation of Alaska properly holds a rather unique place in the diplomatic annals of both countries. The tendency of textbook writers to over-dramatize the role of Providence and to imply that Seward alone saw the value of Russian America is, however, both mistaken and unfortunate.[1] It tends to make the Alaskan Treaty of

[1] One receives from many secondary accounts the impression that virtually the only American who did not think the acquisition a complete folly was Mr. Seward. That gentleman by lobbying and legerdemain somehow forced the

1867 the mysterious property of a single individual, a thing foisted on the American people and accepted by them, reluctantly, only from a sense of obligation to Russia for her supposed aid to the Union government during the Civil War. It is possibly congenial to our current self-esteem to believe that only in our generation have Americans appreciated the value of American ownership of Alaska. Such a view, if gratifying, is incorrect. Contemporary public opinion — as reflected in the newspapers of the day — was far from universally opposed to our purchase of Alaska.[2]

The initial response of certain newspapers, upon hearing of the unexpected transaction, was one of some bewilderment. But the editorial mind of many was soon affected by the March 30th dispatch of the Associated Press, by the quantities of information eagerly supplied by the State Department, or by a reasoned weighing of the increasingly available evidence. Each of these influences requires perhaps a brief explanation.

The March 30th dispatch of the Associated Press was a lengthy account, relating the existence of the treaty, its chief

---

United States to accept his treaty despite a solid hoot of derision from the American public. See, for example: Hubert Howe Bancroft, *History of Alaska* (San Francisco, 1890), vi; Henry Wadsworth Clark, *History of Alaska* (New York, 1930), pp. 78–81; Asa E. Martin, *History of the United States* (Boston, 1931), II, 334; Foster Rhea Dulles, *America in the Pacific: A Century of Expansion*, 2d ed. (Boston, 1938), pp. 83–88; R. E. Riegel; D. F. Long, *The American Story* (New York, 1955), I, 423; Oscar Handlin, *Chance or Destiny* (Boston, 1955), p. 119; H. U. Faulkner, *American Political and Social History*, 7th ed. (New York, 1957), p. 626.

The last four works cited testify to the persistence of this view despite the provocative article by Professor Thomas A. Bailey, "Why the United States Purchased Alaska," in the *Pacific Historical Review*, III (1934), 39–49. Bailey sampled contemporary editorial opinion in six Pacific Coast newspapers and reached the conclusion that these newspapers were definitely favorable to the Alaskan Treaty. He admits, however, that geographic proximity and special commercial interests could have made press opinion in the Far West a rather special case.

[2] The measure to which newspaper opinion reflects public opinion must always be a point of dispute. It is surely a component part of the public opinion of a period, and, to a degree, usually both influences and mirrors general contemporary opinion.

provisions, and its supposed origin.[3] It was not dictated by Secretary Seward, but he was certainly its anonymous, responsible source. The dispatch implied that the Johnson Administration, inspired by a concern for the economic welfare of our citizens in the Washington Territory, was solely responsible for initiating the treaty. The implication was clear. If this treaty was rejected, the innocent and obliging Russian Emperor would consider himself insulted and betrayed, and let all remember that Alexander II was the one European monarch who had "befriended" the United States during the Civil War.

The influence of the State Department on the American Press, in general, though apparent, was not conclusive. Surely Secretary Seward "planted" some information, and made available to the press certain letters he had received,[4] various official scientific reports, and copies of Charles Sumner's eloquent speech in the Senate; surely all the information so distributed was favorable to the purchase. This need neither surprise the historian, however, nor give rise to the assumption that the press was bribed or controlled by Secretary Seward. Charges current at the time, and later, that vast sums of government money were expended by Seward to subsidize large portions of the press, seem definitely unfounded. What Seward termed his "education campaign" was neither extravagant nor illegal; indeed, it has perhaps been rather over-emphasized by certain writers. Indirectly, this educational campaign influenced both congressional approval and the acquiescence of a large part of the articulate public. It did not alone create this approval and acquiescence. Any belief in Seward's omnipotence is perhaps disproved by the fate of the Secretary's West Indian project.

For the purpose of this paper the *extent* of Seward's influence on the press is somewhat irrelevant. It is with the opinions and given reasons of American journalists that we are concerned;

---

[3] See in this connection Victor J. Farrar's excellent monograph, *The Annexation of Russian America* (Washington, 1937), pp. 56–57.

[4] *House Exec. Doc.* #177, 6–109.

whether they obtained these opinions and reasons from prepared releases or original research is relatively unimportant.

The press was not dependent for information on Alaska solely
from Secretary Seward, in any case. It is quite erroneous to
believe that Alaska was *terra incognita* for all Americans in
March, 1867. Not only had New England whalers brought back
news of seal furs and walrus ivory, as well as sperm oil and
ambergris, but the mishaps of the Perry Collins-Western Union
Telegraph project, and the exploits of the "Rebel pirate," *Shenandoah* had acquainted various Americans with Alaska's existence. Moreover, after March, 1867, information on Alaska increased considerably, thanks to the reports of the combined
coast survey-scientific expedition sent out by the Government
in 1867; the research efforts of Professors Baird, Bannister, and
Henry of the Smithsonian Institute; the literary labors of Frederick Whymper, artist of the ill-fated "Telegraph Expedition";
and the "Alaskan lectures" of the indefatigable William H. Dall.

Editors would also, of course, consult local leaders whose
views would reflect local economic interests. New England papers, for example, mentioned the whalers of New Bedford; West
Coast papers, the needs and desires of Louis Goldstone and
the California fur traders.[5]

As the initial bewilderment of many papers was overcome
by second thoughts and growing information, one must not accept the first editorial comment as the considered judgment
of a paper; neither must one confuse a touch of good-natured
raillery with confirmed antagonism. The walrus and the polar
bear lent themselves to jest and remarks of supposed wit, and
even many pro-Alaska editors could not resist a facetious comment or two. James Gordon Bennett of the New York *Herald*
favored the treaty, but could not forbear to print certain edi-

---

[5] A group of California fur traders headed by Louis Goldstone had for some
years envied the favored position which the Hudson's Bay Company enjoyed
under charter in Russian America. Using Senator-elect Cornelius Cole of California as intermediary, they began in 1866 to negotiate with Russian Minister
Stoeckl for the expiring rights of the British company. Baron Stoeckl led them
on, and, after they had made a formal request, made his refusal the opening
wedge in his March, 1867, talks with Seward.

tor-manufactured advertisements to the effect that any impoverished European monarch who wanted to sell worthless territory "should apply to W. H. Seward, State Department, Washington, D.C."[6]

The forty-eight newspapers consulted (for the months of April, 1867, and July, 1868) constitute, it is believed, a reasonably representative sample, geographically and politically. Most of the quotations will be found to carry an April, 1867, dateline. Very few editors seem to have taken the trouble to express any real interest in the House proceedings of July, 1868, when the appropriation bill was debated. This can perhaps be accounted for on the grounds that the physical transfer of the territory was then an accomplished fact, and the presidential campaign of 1868 well under way.

The papers consulted will be divided geographically. Chief concentration will be placed on the Eastern newspaper capitals of Boston, New York, and Philadelphia, and for all sections only those papers will be mentioned which offered opinionated editorial comment concerning the Alaskan Purchase.

The Boston press was almost uniformly favorable to the purchase, evincing no trace of fear that the Alaskan fishing grounds would affect adversely New England interests in the North Atlantic fisheries.

The Boston *Herald* (moderate Republican) of April 11, 1867, declared, regarding Alaska, that:

> . . . those who know most about it, estimate it most highly. The climate on the Pacific side [at that latitude] is not to be compared to that on the Atlantic side of the continent. . . . The country is reported to abound in furs, forest, and minerals, while its rivers and bays on its coast swarm with as fine fish as ever were caught. [Alaskan timber] will be particularly valuable in the development of our domain on the Pacific coast and the commerce of the Pacific which has just been entered upon. As to the price, there can be but one opinion — it is dog cheap.

The Boston *Daily Evening Transcript* (April 3, 1867) emphasized "the great value and growing importance of our fisheries,

---

[6] New York *Herald*, April 12, 1867.

both for whale and cod, in the waters of the North Pacific. . . ." Though by no means ardent in its favor of the purchase, the *Transcript* seemed to think Alaska a reasonably good buy at $7,200,000. It had not changed its mind fifteen months later, though it expressed shock at the rumors that only four of the seven millions would reach Russian soil.[7]

The Boston *Advertiser* (Democratic) warned that the "treaty is not a matter to be dismissed lightly in ignorance." There was involved "the great whale fishery of the Northern Pacific and of Behring Straits, in which Massachusetts is so deeply interested." The western tip of Alaska, moreover, would provide a commanding naval station. (April 6).

A letter to the editor (April 9) declared that the Aleutian Islands would make fine coaling stations between our country and China, and that the products of India would soon be flowing across the Pacific to America, in ever-mounting quantities.

The Republican *Daily Evening Traveller* gloated over the supposed excitement the purchase had caused among the British, and editorialized to the effect that Alaska's "chief value is now its fur trade and its fisheries; but . . . of vastly more importance than all other things, will be the command it will give us of the western and the northwestern territory of this continent."

This paper could not resist mocking (April 12) the "great change [that] has come over the American mind with respect to Russian America. Everybody is looking at Russian America, and it is discovered that that country, which *once* was scarcely supposed fit for the presence of civilized men, is one of the

[7] This is a reference to the old "mass bribery charge" that was well disposed of by Professor William A. Dunning in 1912, but which still crops up on occasion. For the origins of this charge see the New York *Sun* of November 30, 1868, the Worcester *Spy* of December 4, 1868 (Worcester, Massachusetts), and Reports of the Committee on Public Expenditures, *House Reports* (40th Cong., 3d Sess.), #35; #1388.

Professor Dunning's article, "Paying for Alaska" is to be found in the *Political Science Quarterly*, XXVII (1912), 385–98. See, also, Ellis P. Oberholtzer, *A History of the United States Since the Civil War* (New York, 1917), I, 556; Reinhard L. Luthin, "The Sale of Alaska," *The Slavonic and East European Review*, XVI (1937), 168–182.

finest parts of the globe." The *Traveller*, however, by no means condemned the turn the public mind had taken. "It deserves praise rather than censure." Whether the bargain would be a good or bad one would depend in the final analysis on the use that should be made by America of the acquisition. ". . . the change in Russian America, there is reason to hope and expect, will prove as great as that which within living memory has taken place in the country purchased from Napoleon. . . ."

The Boston *Journal* (Republican) made little editorial comment on the purchase, but its Washington correspondent proclaimed that Sitka would follow the example of San Francisco, and in ten years would be a city of 50,000 persons.

The leading northern New England papers of the period were the Bangor (Maine) *Daily Times* and the Manchester (New Hampshire) *Daily Union*. Though for a time rather neutral, both finally concluded that the purchase was a good thing. In the opinion of the editor of the *Daily Union* (Democratic), it was well worth seven millions "to get good boundaries like the Pacific and Arctic Oceans." (April 10).

Of the seven New England papers consulted not one may be classified as an opponent of Alaskan annexation.

Among New York papers was the great journalistic opponent of the treaty, Horace Greeley's New York *Tribune* (then radical Republican). It opened fire on April 1 with a charge that the Administration was trying to divert attention from its domestic difficulties by plunging the country into foreign complications We had no use for this territory and were putting "ourselves in the attitude of seeking ostentatiously the friendship of a power not friendly to England, and of contracting what is tantamount to an alliance for the sake of an affront."

By April 8 the *Tribune* was complaining that "national good will does not usually extend so far that one nation will sacrifice its interest merely to oblige another," and warning that Alaska was "territory on which Great Britain holds a virtual mortgage, and in which her fishermen and hunters will have equal rights with ours." On the following day the *Tribune* printed a story to the effect that Admiral Fox had once been told by Prince

Gortchakoff that Russia would gladly *give* Alaska to the United States, just to be rid of it. The lobbying activities of Seward and his "Esquimaux ring" were steadily criticized by Greeley, and the Senate, when it ratified the treaty, was accused of land mania — "if it is at the North Pole, no matter." (April 10).

The *Tribune* initially expressed the hope that the House would refuse to appropriate the money to effect this hideously expensive and tax-burdensome folly, this acquisition of impossible "deserts of snow" (April 11); but by July 16, 1868, was grandly conceding: "We have not felt justified in urging the House to refuse the acquisition appropriation. We believe it was advisable to pay the money. Having received it, we wish Russia would consent to receive back the territory as a free gift from this Republic."

Of the other New York papers only the *Independent* (April 18, 1867) and the *Sun* (July 1, 20, 1868) joined the *Tribune* in real opposition to the acquisition of Alaska. The *World, Commercial Advertiser, Times,* and *Herald* were all on the other side of the fence.

The New York *World* (Democratic) was increasingly favorable to the acquisition as the first week of April, 1867, wore on. In its first editorial (April 1), it asked: "But have we done wisely in buying it? If estimated by what it is now, certainly no; if by what the purchase may hereafter lead to, perhaps yes." As an advocate of expansion the *World* was inclined to favor the treaty because, "It is an advancing step in that manifest destiny which is yet to give us British North America."

Twenty-four hours were sufficient to evoke other arguments in the treaty's favor. "The whaling merchants of New England and settlers in Oregon and California will no doubt find some way of profiting by the annexation. . . . Our commerce . . . ought pretty certainly to be benefited by the opening of ports along this extreme verge of the continent, and by the attendant expansion of the fur trade and the fisheries." [8]

[8] Though the *World* favored this extension of our boundaries, it was sufficiently anti-Seward to mock the arguments and methods used by the Secretary to help effect the purchase, and to mock the self-conflicting extravagances of the

The New York *Commercial Advertiser* (Democratic) was both pro-Seward and pro-treaty, and in the New York *Times* the purchase had one of its most influential advocates.

While narrow minded political bigots have been exhausting all their resources in branding him [Seward] as a traitor to his party, he has been quietly pursuing great objects of permanent and paramount interest for his country. The main importance of this acquisition grows out of its bearing upon our future trade with Japan, China, and the other countries of Eastern Asia. . . . Reluctant as that body [the Senate] may be to accept even so great a boon as this from the hands of the President and Mr. Seward, its sense of public duty will constrain its ratification. (*Times*, April 1).

With its next issue the *Times* was ready boldly to declare that the purchase was "a natural though perhaps unexpected consummation of negotiations dating back to the time of Monroe, and its tendency is to lessen the likelihood of 'further entanglements' by removing Russia from the diplomatic area so far as the future policy of this continent is concerned."[9]

In later editorials it mentioned the undeveloped coal seams of the new territory, spoke of the possibilities of the Aleutian Islands as a naval station, and declared that seven millions "was a mere bagatelle compared with the magnitude and importance of the acquisition." (April 8, 10).[10]

---

treaty advocates. "Tropical Disadvantages Offset by the Value of the Ice Trade — Secretary Seward's New Ice-othermal Line — A Great Opening for Soda-Water Fountains and Skating Ponds" ran the headline of April 9.

[9] Like many Eastern papers, the *Times* printed large sections from Charles Sumner's famous and scholarly address in the Senate. Sumner's speech, incidentally, was most influential in producing the large pro-ratification majority in the Senate, and had probable influence as well on American press opinion.

[10] The *Times* still strongly favored the purchase fifteen months later, but on abstract constitutional grounds agreed with the pretensions of the "House Constitutionalists." (July 15).

A group of "House Constitutionalists" or "House Rights Men" succeeded initially in attaching to the Alaskan Appropriation Bill the Loughridge Amendment. By this amendment the House of Representatives asserted its right to be "previously consulted" respecting any future purchase of territory. It was but an exhibition of jealousy by the House over senatorial prerogative in treaty-making, similar to that demonstrated in connection with the Jay Treaty. In both cases, the House had finally to give way.

The New York *Herald* (Republican) favored the treaty mainly on grounds of international policy:

> Politically considered, however, this cession of Russian Alaska becomes a matter of great importance. It indicates the extent to which Russia is ready to carry out her "entente cordiale" with the United States. . . . it places British possessions on the Pacific coast in the uncomfortable position of a hostile cockney with a watchful Yankee on each side of him. . . . [It is a] flank movement for this greater object [Canada]. . . . we are satisfied that the proposed purchase from its political bearings will be at once approved by the public sentiment of the country and will, perhaps, be considered a bargain at seven millions, simply as a speculation in fish oil and the fur business. (April 1).

The *Herald* was a sharp critic of the "pushing" tactics of Mr. Seward, however, and with reference to Seward's "promotional" dinner parties declared: "But with his Pennsylvania roast beef, his Virginia oysters, his smoked walrus from Behring Strait, his Esquimaux stews and ice, his California wines and Kentucky Bourbon, his seven millions and the lobby, the undaunted Seward, perhaps, will best them yet" (April 9).

Despite such exercises in literary irony, the *Herald* was a treaty advocate. The leading paper in extracting names and quotes from the executive sessions of the Senate, and the first paper to publish the treaty text, the *Herald* was sure that this new empire, "in area more than twice the size of France" would prove valuable as a factor in the international scene and valuable, too, for its fisheries, whales, fur trade, and coal. (April 12).

The New York Evening *Post* demonstrated an inexplicable example of editorial indecision. In its first edition of April 1, it declared that the territory was a "frozen, sterile, desert region . . . of no value present or prospective. . . ." In its second edition of the same date, it asserted: "The purchase of the Russian Territory is a step towards the retrieval of this blunder [the Oregon 'Compromise' of 1846] not only by giving us the undis-

---

For the views of the "House Constitutionalists" see *Congressional Globe*, 40th Cong., 2d Sess., IV, 3621–25; 4052–55; V, 4392–94.

puted prominence on the American coast of the Pacific, but by pushing it out of the power of England to extend her territory in that quarter." The forests there were immensely valuable, its agricultural capabilities had never been developed, and, as for its fisheries, "the advantage of our whaling and fishing interest in these northern seas, in having always ports of their own country to run into, will develop its value with the advance of our population in the Pacific."

On April 8, however, the *Post* declared, "We hope the Senate will reject the proposed purchase." The next day it spoke in resigned tones of the acquisition, and on April 19, went so far as to make plans for the future of the various areas of Alaska when "the increase of population and of trade requires a division of the territory."

The only thing that seems certain about the attitude of the *Post* is that it was neither decisively for or against the treaty. Of the seven New York papers which took a definite stand, four were, on balance, favorable to Alaskan annexation.

In Philadelphia the editor of the *Inquirer* (Republican) was a most ardent advocate of the purchase:

> [Alaska] might become very useful to any power having naval interests in the Pacific. . . . A time may come, when the possession of this territory will give us the command over the Pacific, which our extensive possessions there require. (April 1).
>
> . . . If there is any value in the timber, furs, and fisheries of that region, and it must be great, the consideration of the cost of the territorial government is not worthy of a moment's thought. (April 8).

The *Inquirer's* Washington correspondent was equally enthusiastic over the territory's possibilities and spoke of the Pacific Coast's desire for Alaska, and of the treaty's value in preserving the Union Party in the Far West. Numerous letters to the editor were published, all of them favorable to the purchase.

The Philadelphia *Ledger* (Democratic) was less decided in its support of the treaty, but despite some merriment over the possibilities of political elections among the polar bears (April

11), offered no real objection to the treaty. The expansionist-minded *North American Gazette* (Republican) also favored the results of Seward's latest project. Philadelphia, indeed, produced little or no journalistic opposition to Seward's treaty.

Moving South, the press of Washington, D. C. was generally favorable. The Washington *Evening Star* scouted the opposition to the treaty, jibing that it paralleled the foolish reluctance of some in 1803 to accept the Louisiana Purchase. It viewed the treaty as a proper piece of expansionism and dogmatically pronounced: "There are few full-blooded Americans who do not devoutly believe in the doctrine that this country is to absorb not only Russian America, but all the British possessions in North America." (December 21).

The *National Intelligencer* was equally convinced:

> The Russian possessions will secure us furs, fish and lumber in the greatest abundance to say nothing of the undisputed route of an overland telegraph. The fisheries, in the hands of our hardy seamen, would be of priceless value, and, as we are soon to have the Pacific railway, which will give an extraordinary impetus, we wonder that American statesmen should hesitate. (April 5).

The *National Republican* voiced its support in turn. In an editorial entitled, "Now is the Day and Hour for the Confirmation of the Treaty with Russia" (April 6), it lectured to the following effect: "American civilization has pushed itself through to the Pacific sea, where a commerce is growing up . . . which demands that the United States have absolute sovereignty over the entire coast from California to Bhering [*sic*] Straits." In listing various reasons for desiring the territory, the *National Republican* mentioned the protection it would afford our fisheries and fishermen there, the splendid nature of the rivers and harbors of Russian America, the territory's use as a broad base of trade with Japan and China, and the chance it gave us to fill out and protect our Continental Republic. The friendship of Russia was noted by way of further justification, and the warning given that "if we shall ever need the aid of any foreign power . . . it will be the immense and almost immaculate power of Russia." (April 8).

Whatever might have been the case when the purchase was before the House, it is most likely that John Forney's *Daily Morning Chronicle* was a free and unbribed agent in April, 1867, quite uninfluenced by the labors of former Senator Robert Walker or the purse of Minister Stoeckl. In this early and "amateur" phase, the *Chronicle* heartily applauded the treaty, if not with the violence it was to exhibit later: "Our people have faith in the manifest destiny of the nation. They look to the eventual absorption of the whole North American continent, and the Senate has undoubtedly gratified a national instinct in ratifying the treaty. . . ." (April 11).

The favor with which the *Chronicle* received this treaty is indicated by its quoting in full — and with marked approval — an editorial in the Rochester (New York) *Democrat*, which virtually eulogized the possibilities of the Alaskan territory.

The Wilmington (Delaware) *Daily Commercial* favored the acquisition of the territory, but opposed its purchase: "It seems to us the worst of policies, for it . . . is certainly to become ultimately the property of our Yankee nation, and we consider it fair to presume at a price next to nothing at all. If this were our last chance, and the lowest offer likely to be made, we might urge its acceptance. . . ." (April 4).

The Baltimore *Sun* (Democratic) and *American and Commercial Advertiser* (Republican) were not so economy-minded. The latter printed the highly favorable and nationally quoted Associated Press dispatch of March 31 as its first news of the treaty, and followed this up with a pair of editorials in which the value of the area's fisheries and fur trade was discussed at great length.

The *Daily Journal* of Wilmington, North Carolina approved the purchase only "in view of ulterior events." The expansion of the fur trade and whale fisheries on the Pacific Coast and the increased likelihood of garnering the British possessions in North America furnished such "events." (April 4).

The Louisville (Kentucky) *Daily Journal* favored the treaty, observing: "The great commercial advantages secured by it are universally admitted." (April 3).

The Memphis *Daily Post* (moderate Republican) urged the purchase in these terms:

> In view of our growing commerce in the Pacific, the establishment of lines of steamers to run regularly between China, Japan, and Australia, the increase of the coastwise trade, the completion of the Pacific Railroad and the Russo-American telegraph . . . the acquisition of this vast possession is desirable, and seven millions of dollars is a small consideration to pay for it. (April 5).

The Memphis paper, however, reviled the manner in which Seward had "unscrupulously urged" the treaty, and insisted that the actions of the Secretary and the President in this connection would further damn them in the eyes of the public. (April 15).

The Washington dispatches of both the Savannah *Daily Republican* and the Augusta *Daily Press* included press releases, telegrams and Seward-inspired "reports from Washington" highly favorable to the purchase.

Of the New Orleans papers the *Commercial Bulletin* seems to have been the most enthusiastic, virtually urging an alliance between the now-enlarged Northwest and the South:

> The demands for cotton goods in the new region of the Northwest will be enormous, and there is no reason why these goods should not be manufactured in the South, thereby employing our poor and industrious population, and adding greatly to our resources. . . . it will be seen that the South will be greatly advanced by the acquisition and settlement of the Russian American possessions. (April 15).

The New Orleans *Times* and the newborn New Orleans *Republican* contained a large number of dispatches and letters favorable to the purchase, but *La Tribune de la Nouvelle-Orleans* had mild doubts about the value of the territory. It suspected that if the Russians were willing to shed the territory it must be of little value. (". . . évidemment inutile aux Russes, elle ne peut pas être d'un bien grand profit pour les Americains.") (April 3).

The Galveston *Republican*, though making no editorial comment, printed at considerable length the panegyric on Alaska delivered by Representative Banks during the debate in the House. (July 13).

Of the sixteen Southern newspapers consulted, only two may be labelled outright opponents of the Alaskan Purchase.

In the Middle West, the city of Chicago saw its two leading papers somewhat divided on the desirability of Alaska. The *Evening Journal* cheered the purchase without qualification of any kind, but the reaction of the *Republican* was less clear. The Washington correspondent of that paper was vehemently anti-treaty; its editor, tepidly favorable. The same issue of the *Republican* that found the correspondent calling the treaty a "huge farce," found the editor pontificating that it was "very natural that Russia and the United States should form an alliance. . . . Russia has demonstrated her good faith in this matter by ceding to our Government all her possessions on the American continent." (April 1). Even though the editor jocosely declared some four days later that the real reason for the purchase was to give the Fenians a base of operations, and even later (April 13) spoke of the danger of soon seeing in the House a representative from Sitka "dressed in a grizzly bear-skin overcoat and seal-skin unmentionables," the attitude of the paper seems to have been, on the whole, one of hesitant favor. "As evidence of the good will of the Russian Government toward the United States, this treaty has its chief significance. Future explorations may prove it to be rich in mines, while it will undoubtedly prove of increasing value to the Pacific states for its fisheries." (April 10).

The Cincinnati *Daily Gazette* rather opposed the purchase, but its sister paper, the *Commercial*, favored it. Other affirmative voices were those of the Detroit *Free Press* and the St. Louis *Times* and *Daily Missouri Democrat*. The latter stressed the wonderful effect of the Japanese current on the climate of Alaska, and asserted that the acquisition "affords another perspective of Uncle Samuel's 'manifest destiny' to absorb the continent." (April 11).

The Alaskan Treaty does not seem to have interested Mid-Western editors to the extent it did those on the East and West coasts, but even the few examples given show that the press of this section was in no sense solidly opposed to the purchase.

What then can be said of the reaction of the press as a whole?[11] First, that all statements to the effect that the newspapers were uniformly unfavorable to the treaty are erroneous. Secondly, that though the sample of newspapers consulted is perhaps too small to support any sweeping generalizations, it can be suggested that a majority of the American press seems either to have favored the treaty or at least not to have been opposed to it.[12] Thirdly, that neither the political allegiance nor the geographic location of a newspaper was usually decisive in determining its stand. Finally, that the main arguments advanced by the press in support of the purchase, listed perhaps in order of increasing importance, were: the propriety of maintaining the friendship of Russia; the possibility that the purchase would facilitate the acquisition of British Columbia and generally promote our predestined expansion and power; and the probability that we should derive great economic benefits from the purchase.[13]

[11] The writer has not made a sufficient study of contemporary periodical literature to warrant any over-all conclusions in that area. Of the fifteen "national" periodicals consulted, however, only three expressed an editorial opinion adverse to the Alaskan Purchase: *Leslie's Weekly*; the New York *Nation*; and *Harper's Weekly*.

[12] Though there was much initial hesitation on the part of many editors to express a definite opinion, the statement of Theodore Clark Smith that "the bewildered comments of the newspaper press during the week when the treaty was pending indicate clearly the absence of any popular feeling for or against annexation" is a statement of doubtful validity. T. C. Smith, "Expansion After the Civil War, 1865–1871," *Political Science Quarterly*, XVI (1901), 415.

[13] These arguments were interestingly enough almost identical to those made in Congress during the ratification and appropriation debates. All can be found in Senator Sumner's speech (*House Exec. Doc.* #177, 124–188). In the House of Representatives see the speeches of Representatives Schenck and Banks on "Russian Friendship"; Representatives Orth, Donnelly, Maynard, Myers, Spalding, and Munger on "Expansion and British Columbia"; and Representatives Munger, Higby, Johnson, and Banks on "Economic Value." *Congressional Globe*, 40th Cong., 2d Sess., IV, 3625–27; 3659–60; 4054 and V, Appendix, 386–432.

These arguments and motives also appear prominently in the private letters received by Senator Sumner in 1867 from such correspondents as Professor Spencer Baird, G. V. Fox, Commander John Rodgers, Major General Meigs, W. Beach

"Russian friendship" and the "assistance" Russia gave the Federal Government during the Civil War was often mentioned by the American press, though usually as an auxiliary argument.[14]

Contemporary press opinion indicates that there was a good deal of latent expansionism in the United States in 1867. The Civil War had caused certain Americans to think for the first time of the desirability of such objects as naval and commercial bases, and that quasi-mystical doctrine, "Manifest Destiny," had still its supporters. Belief in the inevitable and benevolent assimilation of North America by the politically and morally superior United States was nurtured in many an editorial heart and column. In so far as Manifest Destiny was basically an agrarian movement, the desire of certain Americans for Alaska was not an offshoot of Manifest Destiny. But Manifest Destiny also had its "commercial" side, and in this sense, the Purchase was the vestigial remain of that nation-shaping doctrine. Certain papers emphasized the importance of Alaska's harbors for our Oriental trade, and more spoke of the necessity of checking British expansion and securing a favorable balance of power for the United States in the Pacific West. Various editors on the Pacific Coast went so far as to express hope that the purchase of Alaska, by putting British Columbia in "an American vice," would mean the ultimate acquisition of that choice and strategic area by the United States.[15]

Lawrence, John M. Forbes, and Louis Agassiz. Sumner Correspondence for the year 1867 *Sumner Papers*, Widener Library, Harvard University.

[14] It was an argument and "motive," however. The statement of John G. Latané to the effect that the research of Professor Frank A. Golder in the Moscow archives "leaves one with the impression that Russian friendship can no longer be considered an important factor in the purchase of Alaska" is erroneous. Golder's concern was the motives of Seward and the Johnson Administration, not public opinion and its inspiration. Myths have as much influence on public opinion as facts. Latané, *A History of American Foreign Policy* (New York, 1927), pp. 424–25. Golder, "The Purchase of Alaska," *American Historical Review*, XXV (1920), 411 ff, "The Russian Fleet and the Civil War," XX (1915), 801 ff.

[15] Bailey, "Why the United States Purchased Alaska," *loc. cit.* See, especially, Sacramento *Daily Union*, April 1, 1867; Seattle *Puget Sound Gazette*, April–May, 1867. See, too, Chicago *Evening Journal*, April 1, 1867.

The chief argument of those members of the press who supported the purchase, however, was that, in economic terms, Alaska was worth the purchase price. Because of its supposed resources in fish, whales, furs, timber, and minerals, because of its very real commercial value, Alaska was thought a good bargain.

These were arguments and motives that could have clear appeal for the average educated American. Surely they were such as to deter press or public from howling in united chorus, "Seward's Folly!"

PART III

THE AMERICAN PERIOD

*Of the younger professional historians engaged in researching
and writing the American period of Alaskan history, none
is more prolific or writes with more verve than Ted Hinckley.
He received his Ph.D. from Indiana University in 1961
and teaches at San Jose State College in California. Contrary
to the stereotype of the missionary as a disruptive frontier
element, Hinckley believes that Sheldon Jackson protected the
natives from undesirable influences and was a positive force
in the development of early American Alaska. The selection
is from the* Pacific Northwest Quarterly, *LIV (April, 1963), 66–
74.*

Sheldon Jackson and
Benjamin Harrison

TED C. HINCKLEY

To declare that laws are made by men is but a commonplace. Behind any statute or ordinance stand the individual senators, congressmen, or legislators who sponsored it, defended it, and steered it through extended debates until at length it was enacted into law. But to determine the influences and pressures which produce the laws is not so simple. Legislators speak not for themselves alone, but for other individuals or groups whose interests in a bill or a policy are more intense and specific. Often they express the demands of some persistent lobbyist or voice the wishes of some special group of constituents. Pressures affect no less the implementing and enforcement of a law, since provisions ill suited to meet a local situation are inevitably weakened and may have little force.

Such was the case with Benjamin Harrison, United States Senator and later President, as he attempted to deal with the problems of policy and legislation for Alaska. For the earlier

293

years the story is one which reveals the persistent pressure and influence of the zealous Presbyterian missionary and lobbyist Dr. Sheldon Jackson. The sequel, drawn from the years of the Presidency, illustrates the futility of legislating prohibition for a far northern territorial outpost where local opinion was adverse and where the conditions of administration were such as to make enforcement quite impossible.

In 1880 Indiana elected Benjamin Harrison, Republican, to the United States Senate. Questions posed by the still undeveloped West soon attracted the Hoosier's attention.[1] He became a member of the Committee on Territories and inspected the western lands; as the committee chairman, he sought statehood for North and South Dakota, Montana, Washington, and Idaho. The former lawyer also took an active part in the Committee on Indian Affairs. His usual assiduousness found him an on-the-spot investigator of Indian reservations. Harrison's most recent biographer, Father Harry Sievers, notes that, although the Hoosier officially sponsored only "three bills . . . in behalf of the Indians, there is more than ample testimony that he worked hard in the committee room to protect their interest."[2] It was a decade when the humanitarians were demanding a reform of federal Indian policy, and Harrison reflected this prevailing trend.

The Senator's sympathy for the red man was in part a reflection of his Christian conscience. William Allen White described him as "a devout Presbyterian without being sanctimonious . . . a serious, old-fashioned, deeply religious man." Harrison

---

[1] Charles Latham, Jr., "Benjamin Harrison in the Senate, 1881–1887" (unpublished MS, senior thesis, Dept. of History, Princeton University, April 12, 1939), offers insight into Harrison's senatorial career. His fascination for matters western remained with him throughout his life. Mary Lard Harrison, comp., *Views of an Ex-President by Benjamin Harrison: Being His Addresses and Writings on Subjects of Public Interest Since the Close of His Administration* (Indianapolis, 1901), 16.

[2] Harry Joseph Sievers, *Benjamin Harrison, Hoosier Statesman: From the Civil War to the White House, 1865–1888* (New York, 1959), 245. See also: William Hagan, *American Indians* (Chicago, 1961), 123; Robert Riegel, *America Moves West* (New York, 1930), 500–501; Loring Benson Priest, *Uncle Sam's Stepchildren* (New Brunswick, 1942), 66.

had joined the Church early in life, and by the time he had risen to a partnership in Indianapolis' most prominent law firm, he was a Bible teacher and elder in the city's First Presbyterian Church. This was the connection which brought him in touch with Sheldon Jackson.[3]

For more than a century, Presbyterians had struggled to alleviate the suffering of the Indians. Their missionaries had labored in nearly every section of the Trans-Mississippi West. Thanks to Jackson, Presbyterians had discovered Alaska as well and were aroused to help the native population there. "Should we not attempt to do something for them now," the General Assembly declared, "that a 'remnant may be saved' before they are overwhelmed and debauched and put aside by . . . more stalwart and enterprising people?"[4]

Dr. Sheldon Jackson, already famous as the Presbyterian Rocky Mountain Superintendent, had founded at Fort Wrangell in 1877 the first formal United States Protestant mission in Alaska. In 1880 the Presbyterians were active also in the boom town of Harrisburg (Juneau). During the next several years a number of embryonic mission schools were brought into existence, six of which were under Presbyterian auspices. Not content with such efforts in Alaska itself, Jackson undertook a campaign of lecturing, publishing, and lobbying in the United States. He made himself popular as a speaker, established contact with federal officialdom in Washington, D.C., and carried on a voluminous correspondence with key leaders in Congress. By such means he endeavored to galvanize public opinion and to achieve more adequate legislation for Uncle Sam's northern province.[5]

[3] William Allen White, *Masks in a Pageant* (New York, 1930), 70, 85; Sievers, *Benjamin Harrison*, 8.

[4] *Minutes of the General Assembly of the Presbyterian Church in the United States of America* (New York, 1879), 10, 594–95.

[5] Sheldon Jackson, *Presbyterian Church in Alaska* (Washington, D.C., 1886), 2; Priest, *Uncle Sam's Stepchildren*, 31; Sheldon Jackson, *Alaska and Missions on the Pacific Coast* (New York, 1880), 140 ff.; Sheldon Jackson, *Neglect of Education in Alaska*, U.S. Bureau of Education, Circular of Information No. 2, Proceedings of the Department of Superintendence of the National Education Asso-

In his efforts he won the backing of Benjamin Harrison, whose support unquestionably contributed to his successes. Just when he met the Senator, we cannot be sure. Quite possibly they discovered each other's talents when they attended the 1874 General Assembly at St. Louis, Missouri. Harrison was present as one of fourteen Presbyterians who represented the Synod of Indiana, South.[6] The peripatetic Jackson found the St. Louis meeting a convenient starting point for one of his Rocky Mountain guided tours. Whether the two Christians first crossed paths in St. Louis or some other church conclave is not too important. What is relevant is that the combined efforts of these two men had a direct and important impact on Alaska's history.

Jackson's efforts to secure federal funds for Alaska focused first in demands for the support of education. On February 2, 1880, he and the Methodist minister, Dr. John Lanahan, introduced a memorial to the House and Senate which declared that the people of Alaska were "self-supporting . . . needing no annuities, clothing or rations from the government, but do need teachers." The Commissioner of Education was asked to expend $50,000 for this purpose. James A. Garfield presented the memorial in the House, and Henry L. Dawes did so in the Senate. It died in the Committee on Education and Labor.[7] Seemingly, Jackson's 1880 plea was to no avail. It suggested, however, the course he was to follow during the next four years.

---

ciation at Its Meeting at Washington, March 21–23, 1882 (Washington, D.C., 1882), 70 ff.; Sheldon Jackson, "Reason Why Schools Should Be Commenced in Alaska," February, 1880, Sheldon Jackson Manuscript Collection, Presbyterian Historical Society, Philadelphia, Correspondence, Vol. 10, p. 33; Ted C. Hinckley, "Sheldon Jackson, Presbyterian Lobbyist for the Great Land," *Journal of the Presbyterian Historical Society*, XL (1962), 3–23.

No definitive study of Sheldon Jackson has yet been published. By far the most authoritative and comprehensive of the various writings about him is that done by his close personal friend, Robert Laird Stewart, *Sheldon Jackson: Pathfinder and Prospector of the Missionary Vanguard in the Rocky Mountains and Alaska* (New York, 1908). The Sheldon Jackson Manuscript Collection at the Presbyterian Historical Society in Philadelphia contains the bulk of his huge correspondence and scrapbook files. References to this Collection will be to Correspondence and to Scrapbooks by volume and page number.

[6] *Minutes of the General Assembly* (New York, 1874), 6, 11, 13, 45.

[7] Sheldon Jackson, *Education in Alaska*, 47th Cong., 1st Sess., *Senate Execu-*

Jackson reflected the widespread dissatisfaction with the annuity and reservation system. Instead of reducing the Alaska natives to a state of public peonage, his aim was to educate them. This partially explains why he wanted to have the funds controlled by the Bureau of Education instead of the Bureau of Indian Affairs. By a fortunate coincidence, General John Eaton, the Commissioner of Education from 1870 to 1886, was also an active Presbyterian and Jackson's loyal personal friend. When again in 1881 Jackson's prodding proved futile, Commissioner Eaton printed Jackson's special report on Alaska education. The lobbyist unabashedly included in the document a proposed educational aid bill which declared "that the sum of one hundred thousand dollars or so much as may be necessary . . . [should be] appropriated from the revenues of Alaska in the Treasury." This demand, like the previous one, aroused no response.[8]

In 1882 Alaska bills were presented to both houses of Congress, but with no better results than before. Jackson appeared before the House Committee on Education and was greatly encouraged when Representative J. T. Updegraff put in a bill to provide schools for Alaska. There followed a flurried drive to energize the Protestant churches in support of the measure. Jackson's Home Board chiefs reminded Harrison how much they depended upon him, and they received in reply a courteous assurance that he would "take pleasure in looking after the appropriation." But once again the legislation was defeated. "It is . . . slow and discouraging work attempting to get the ear of Congressmen," Jackson admitted. "Anyone that has not tried it, would not believe the amount of work that I have given

---

tive Document No. 30 (Washington, D.C., 1881), 20–21; 46th Cong., 2nd Sess., *Congressional Record* (Feb. 2, 1880), 644, 666.

[8] Priest, *Uncle Sam's Stepchildren,* 12; John Eaton to Secretary of the Interior Henry M. Teller, Feb. 4, 1882, Correspondence, Vol. 12, p. 88; Alice Fletcher to Jackson, March 20, 1884, Correspondence, Vol. 13, p. 323; First Annual Message of Benjamin Harrison, Dec. 3, 1889, in James D. Richardson, *Compilation of the Messages and Papers of the Presidents* (New York, 1911), Vol. 12, p. 5483; Jackson, *Education in Alaska,* 28. In later years Eaton asserted that much of Jackson's success was due to his relationship with Benjamin Harrison. John Eaton, "Sheldon Jackson, Alaska's Apostle and Pioneer," *Review of Reviews,* XIII (June, 1896), 695.

it, and so far only created some public sentiment, nothing tangible secured." The only windfall that year was the publication of Jackson's speech on "The Neglect of Education in Alaska." Sixty thousand copies of this pamphlet were printed by the United States Bureau of Education as an official circular of information.[9]

Meanwhile, the problem of governmental organization and administration engaged Harrison's attention. As a member of the Committee on Territories, he was struck by Alaska's legal and governmental deficiencies. Perhaps he was familiar with Jackson's lurid accounts of lawlessness on the northern frontier. At all events Jackson recognized the Senator's interest and linked his own proposals to it. As a result the bills which would provide federal support for education in Alaska came to be more closely related to those which called for a more adequate civil government for the Territory.[10]

During the next two years (1883–84), popular interest was drawn to Alaska to an unusual degree, and Jackson labored energetically to take advantage of it. He approached all the leading Protestant denominations and solicited the support of the National Education Association and of other teachers' organizations. One hundred thousand circulars went out to the "friends of education" importuning them to "rally and flood their Congressmen with petitions asking special attention to the claims of Alaska." More specifically, they asked appropriations for an industrial school at Sitka and for common schools at the

[9] H. R. 3754, Jan. 30, 1882, S. 1153, Feb. 9, 1882, H. R. 5492, March 27, 1882, Scrapbooks, Vol. 9, pp. 93, 95; printed letter to Presbyterian Board of Home Missions, April, 1882, printed letter from John M. Reid, Secretary, Missionary Society, Methodist Episcopal Church, Scrapbooks, Vol. 7, pp. 65, 66; printed letter of Henry Kendall to Presbyterian Ministers, April, 1882, printed letter of Rev. Henry L. Morehouse to Baptist Ministers, April, 1882, Scrapbooks, Vol. 8, pp. 118, 51; J. T. Updegraff to Jackson, Jan. 25, 1882, Benjamin Harrison to Henry Kendall, June 26, 1882, Correspondence, Vol. 12, pp. 103, 222; Jackson to J. G. Brady, March 6, 1882, John G. Brady Papers, Yale University (hereafter cited as Brady Papers); Jackson, *Neglect of Education in Alaska*, 61–75.

[10] Benjamin Harrison to Jackson, March 22, 1881, Correspondence, Vol. 11, p. 97; Albert T. Volwiler, "Correspondence Between Benjamin Harrison and James G. Blaine, 1882–1893," *Memoirs of the American Philosophical Society*, XIV (1940), 3–4.

chief centers of population. Hiram Price, Commissioner of Indian Affairs, favored the support of the Presbyterian Industrial School at Sitka. Distinguished leaders, including William Graham Sumner, Cyrus Northrop, and Wendell Phillips, the old warhorse of humanitarian causes, offered their backing. The 48th Congress, which convened in December, 1883, was deluged with petitions from more than twenty-five states. New York alone forwarded some twenty memorials.[11]

Civil government bills had aroused little interest in previous Congresses; some two dozen of them had been stillborn in the sixteen years from 1867 to 1883. Now, however, the prospects were brighter. Senator John F. Miller introduced a measure of his own but declined to incorporate Jackson's education plan with it. Connecticut's Orville H. Platt was more coöperative, and it was his bill, including educational features, which Harrison steered into the Committee on Territories of which he was now the chairman. By December 11 four bills to provide civil government for Alaska had been introduced in the lower house.[12]

Harrison introduced his own bill (Senate Bill 153) on December 4, 1883, and took a close personal interest in it during the course of committee consideration. During the ensuing months he reconciled the provisions of this measure with re-

[11] Jackson to Henry M. Teller, Secretary of the Interior, Oct. 13, 1883, Bureau of Indian Affairs, Record Group 75, National Archives; Circular Issued to Teachers of the United States, 1883, Jackson to Price, July 7, 1883, "Request for an Indian Industrial School," H. Price to Jackson, Aug. 11, 1883, Wendell Phillips to Jackson, Dec. 29, 1883, Thomas W. Bicknell to Secretary of the Interior Henry M. Teller, July 11, 1883, Correspondence, Vol. 13, pp. 268, 165, 267, 193, 266, 170; Memorials to the Congress of the United States for Education in Alaska, December, 1883, Endorsement of Churches, Alaska Education, Correspondence, Vol. 23, pp. 199–205, 245, 246; Resolutions of a Special Committee of Presbyterian General Assembly, May 1883 (these were later entered in the 48th Cong., 1st Sess., *Congressional Record* [Jan. 23, 1884], 597–98), Scrapbooks, Vol. 8, p. 142; Second National Education Assembly, Scrapbooks, Vol. 11, p. 21; Report of the National Education Association, Scrapbooks, Vol. 5, p. 71.

[12] John F. Miller to Jackson, Dec. 3, 1883, Correspondence, Vol. 13, p. 247; S. 148, 48th Cong., 1st Sess., Dec. 4, 1883, S. 72, 48th Cong., 1st Sess., Dec. 4, 1883, Scrapbooks, Vol. 9, pp. 101, 102; 48th Cong., 1st Sess., *Congressional Record* (Dec. 4, 1883), 14.

lated but divergent bills. Meanwhile, Jackson emphasized the importance of education for Alaska before the Senate Committee on Labor and Education. He also urged Harrison to add an educational provision to his Senate Bill 153, but the time was not favorable, and Harrison calmed his fellow Presbyterian with a terse note: "Not till after the holidays." On January 22, Harrison introduced an amendment to provide "free public schools for the instruction of children . . . without regard to race." Furthermore, he recommended a "superintendent of education" to administer these schools. Existing mission schools were to be recognized. "Where free schools have already been established," proposed Harrison, "by private benevolence or by any religious society the commissioner of education may with the consent of such persons or society adopt said schools as a part of the school system of said district."[13]

Senators John G. Ingalls and Preston B. Plumb voiced strong protests to the pending Senate Bill 153, but Harrison countered these attacks. He used one of Jackson's old arguments that the Alaska Commercial Company had by itself returned one-half of the original purchase price to the United States Treasury; the pending expenditures were long overdue.[14] On January 24, Senate Bill 153 passed the Senate and was ordered to be printed as amended and sent to the House. Senators Henry Dawes and George Hoar of Massachusetts complained that the measure was insufficient, and Senator Harrison admitted that this was indeed true:

[13] Jackson before Committee on Education and Labor, Scrapbooks, Vol. 8, p. 45; 48th Cong., 1st Sess., Dec. 4, 1883, Scrapbooks, Vol. 9, pp. 99, 113; Benjamin Harrison to Jackson, Dec. 1883, Correspondence, Vol. 13, p. 257; 48th Cong., 1st Sess., *Congressional Record* (Dec. 18, 1883), 152; 48th Cong., 1st Sess., *Congressional Record* (Jan. 22, 1884), 565.

[14] 48th Cong., 1st Sess., *Congressional Record* (Jan. 24, 1884), 565, 566; printed copies of these amendments, Scrapbooks, Vol. 9, pp. 110, 111, 114, 154. Exactly why the solons permitted the Alaska Commercial Company to be labeled the "Alaska Fur Seal Company" has always been an enigma. As the final bill was not to become law until May, it seems inescapable that Harrison and Jackson were cognizant of the error. For some reason they allowed the misnomer to remain. For the entire debate on S. 153 in the Senate, see 48th Cong., 1st Sess., *Congressional Record* (Jan. 24, 1884), 527–31, 564–67, 593–602, 627–37, 656–61; for the debate in the House, see *ibid.*, 4118–27.

I agree that the appropriation is inadequate: indeed, I am willing to confess upon the challenge of almost any Senator here that all the provisions of the bill are inadequate. It is a mere shift; it is a mere expedient; it is a mere beginning in what we believe to be the right direction toward giving a civil government and education to Alaska. . . . The committee . . . adjudged what they believed to be the payable limit of the generosity of the Senate. . . . For myself I would rather have seen $40,000 [for education] in the bill than $25,000.[15]

He defended the measure, however, as being the best that could be had.

Throughout February, March, and April, 1884, Jackson urged the adoption of Harrison's bill. On May 13 Representative John H. Evins of South Carolina introduced the bill into the House where, after several hours of floor discussion, it was accepted exactly as presented. On May 17, 1884, President Chester Arthur signed the bill, and it became law. Though the House had not amended it, Harrison had been forced to accept a considerable revision of his original proposals, and later commentators complained that the legislation had been somewhat mangled. But Jackson was highly gratified with the educational provisions.[16]

Section 13 of the law required the Secretary of the Interior to make "needful and proper provision for the education of children of school age in the Territory of Alaska, without ref-

[15] S. 153, Scrapbooks, Vol. 9, p. 113; 48th Cong., 1st Sess., *Congressional Record* (Jan. 22, 1884), 567; *ibid.* (Jan. 23, 1884), 587.

[16] 48th Cong., 1st Sess., *Congressional Record* (Jan. 24, 1884), 4118. Alaska's first Organic Act is printed in full in Fred F. Barker, comp., *Compilation of the Acts of Congress* (Washington, D.C., 1906), 25–30. John Eaton's tribute to Jackson's perseverance is found in *Report of the Commissioner of Education, 1882–1883* (Washington, D.C., 1884), xlv–xlvi. Particularly worthy analyses of the 1884 Organic Act are to be found in Jeannette P. Nichols, *Alaska: A History of Its Administration, Exploitation, and Industrial Development During Its First Half Century Under the Rule of the United States* (Cleveland, 1924), 71–82; George Washington Spicer, *Constitutional Status and Government of Alaska*, Johns Hopkins University Studies in History and Political Science, XLV (Baltimore, 1927), 25–30; Ernest H. Gruening, *The State of Alaska* (New York, 1954), 49–53; Hubert Howe Bancroft, *History of Alaska, 1730–1887*, in *Works*, XXXIII (San Francisco, 1887), 718–24.

erence to race, until such time as permanent provision shall be made for the same." To finance this action, the legislators appropriated the sum of $25,000. Further, the mission schools were each assured 640 acres, provided, moreover, "that the Indians . . . shall not be disturbed in the possession of any lands . . . now claimed by them."

Harrison had earned the distinction of presenting Alaska with her long-sought organic act. Under it a governor, four commissioners, and lesser officials were to be appointed by the President. The Harrison-Jackson struggle was but a preview of what lay ahead in Alaska's political future. Many more years and a vast amount of legislative maneuvering would be necessary before the Great Land would obtain either a delegate in Congress or a territorial legislature. Still, the first step had been taken.

The problems of Alaska continued to occupy Jackson's attention and, more occasionally, Harrison's too after the passage of this first legislation. One of Jackson's most trusted supporters, John G. Brady of Sitka, a missionary turned merchant, was appointed a district commissioner. Jackson himself became Alaska's first General Agent for Education. When Harrison became the Republican candidate for President in 1888, Jackson was much pleased. "Alaska hastens to send congratulations. . . . Will most earnestly pray for your election believing that you would end the rule of godless, drinking and gambling officials." [17] Perhaps his enthusiasm derived in part from the fact that President Arthur's appointees in Alaska had once confined

---

[17] Benjamin Harrison to Jackson, Dec. 5, 1884, Correspondence, Vol. 13, p. 436; Carrie L. Harrison to Jackson, Feb. 24, 1886, Correspondence, Vol. 14, p. 168; Benjamin Harrison to Jackson, July 27, 1888, Correspondence, Vol. 15, p. 82; Benjamin Harrison to Jackson, Nov. 15, 1884, H. McCulloch to Benjamin Harrison, Jan. 15, 1885, Peter French to Benjamin Harrison, Feb. 10, 1885, Correspondence, Vol. 23, pp. 433, 229, 231; Benjamin Harrison to Jackson, Jan. 14, 1885, Benjamin Harrison to Jackson, Feb. 26, 1887, Correspondence, Vol. 24, pp. 1, 237; Jackson to Benjamin Harrison, July 11, 1888, Correspondence, Vol. 26, p. 237; Jackson to Benjamin Harrison, Feb. 24, 1887, Sheldon Jackson Papers, Speer Library, Princeton University Theological Seminary, Alaska Schools, Vol. 4, p. 392 (hereafter referred to as PUTS with letter book volume and page cited).

Jackson in a Sitka jail, while Grover Cleveland's gubernatorial appointment had been hardly less troublesome.

Harrison's election produced yet greater elation. Upon receipt of this good news, Jackson wrote: "When the steamer this noon announced your election tears of joy filled my eyes. I wanted to get away from the noisy shouting crowd to my own room, where I could thank God that he had given us one who would give us good officials." The Presbyterian Board of Home Missions was similarly hopeful and optimistic. The Presbytery of Alaska petitioned the President-elect: "Our great need here is Christian men in office, who will both enforce the laws and also use their personal influence in favor of sobriety and chastity." Subsequently, Jackson urged Harrison to consider John G. Brady for the governorship. "Alaska has suffered so much from Godless, drinking officials that we are looking to you for a different kind." [18]

Clearly, the problem of government for Alaska called for more than educational appropriations and a suitable organic law. It required this appointment of worthy and competent officials. Beyond this, as Jackson saw it, Alaska needed prohibition.

In the opinion of the missionaries, Alaska's grief was rooted in the "drinking officials" and their drinking supporters. Ever since their first arrival in Alaska, the Presbyterians had been appalled at the baleful influence of liquor, and Jackson, who knew the problem from his years in the Rocky Mountain ministry, fought valiantly to find a solution to it in the Far North. Some federal officials also recognized the necessity of action, and the United States policy was shaped to prevent the distribution of liquor among the Indians and natives.[19]

[18] Benjamin Harrison Papers, Library of Congress, Vol. 47, pp. 10334–35; Benjamin Harrison to Jackson, Dec. 4, 1888, Correspondence, Vol. 15, p. 112; Alaska Presbytery Meeting at Sitka, Dec. 8, 1888, S.J., Stated Clerk of Alaska Presbytery, to Benjamin Harrison, Correspondence, Vol. 25, pp. 176, 180; Jackson to Benjamin Harrison, Jan. 22, 1889, Brady Papers.

[19] For official statements by the Presbyterian Church on prohibition, see the *Minutes and Reports of the General Assembly of the Presbyterian Church* for 1876 (p. 85) and 1877 (p. 558). The *Report of the Centenary Conference*

It was a difficult matter, however, to control the liquor traffic. Indians easily mastered the art of transforming potato mash, berries, flour, ginger, cayenne, pepper, and anything else that was hot and would rot, into Hoochinoo. (Our word "hootch" is derived from this. The Hoochinoo tribe proved unusually adept at the white man's craft. Their home brew was purchased by United States soldiers, and thus the beverage was honored with their name.) [20]

---

on the Protestant Missions of the World (London, 1888), 535–36, reveals Christian temperance enthusiasm on an international scale. The following are merely samples of the published material in which both the missionary and the public servants made numerous references to the liquor imponderable: H. A. Cody, *Apostle of the North: Memoirs of the Right Reverend William Carpenter Bompas, D.D.* (New York, 1908); Thomas Crosby, *Up and Down the North Pacific Coast by Canoe and Mission Ship* (Toronto, 1914); Hudson Stuck, *Ten Thousand Miles with a Dogsled* (New York, 1915); Eugene S. Willard, *Life in Alaska* (Philadelphia, 1884); Julia McNair Wright, *Among the Alaskans* (Philadelphia, 1883); Capt. George W. Bailey, *Report upon Alaska and Its People, 1879* (Washington, D.C., 1880); Capt. Charles Bryant, *Report of Treasury Agent in Charge of St. Paul and St. George* (Washington, D.C., 1872); Capt. L. A. Beardslee, *Relative to Affairs in Alaska*, 47th Cong., 1st Sess., *Senate Executive Document* No. 71; Henry Wood Elliott, *Report on the Pribilof Group or Seal Islands of Alaska* (Washington, D.C., 1875); William G. Morris, *Report upon the Customs District, Public Service and Resources of Alaska Territory*, 45th Cong., 3rd Sess., *Senate Executive Document* No. 59; Laurence F. Schmeckebier, *The Office of Indian Affairs: Its History, Activities and Organization* (Baltimore, 1927), 25–42. The Alaska Act of July 27, 1868, gave the President power to prohibit the importation of liquor. Thereafter repeated presidential directives and congressional legislation sought to enforce Alaskan prohibition by official enactments and not much else. It was the good fortune of Alaska's indigenous peoples never to fall under the legal designation "Indian Country." A signal major exception to this was in regard to liquor control. In March, 1873, two sections of the old 1834 act "to regulate trade and intercourse with the Indian tribes" were applied to Alaska. These sections forbade the selling or disposing of any spirituous liquor to any Indian (note that under this specific provision all of Alaska was designated as Indian country) or the setting up of any distillery for manufacturing ardent spirits. An informative letter which explains this legal point is that written by Charles Devens, Attorney General, to John Sherman, Secretary of the Treasury, Sept. 24, 1878, Alaska Custom House Records, Alaska State Historical Library, July, 1877–December, 1881 (hereafter cited as ACHR).

[20] For excellent descriptions of their stills, see S. Hall Young, *Alaska Days with John Muir* (New York, 1915), 77; *Presbyterian Monthly Record*, August, 1878; J. G. Brady to Dr. Lindsley, March 17, 1878, Correspondence, Vol. 7, p. 287.

Understandably, Alaska's few customs officers felt the seizures of liquor to be futile in the face of a corresponding increase in the importation of molasses, which was a popular liquor base and which was sold quite openly. Furthermore, the
checking of a clandestine whisky trade along a littoral so broken
with inlets and screened with hundreds of islands would have
taxed the resources of a fleet command. According to Hubert
Howe Bancroft, one steamer landed nine hundred gallons of
pure alcohol marked "coal oil." John Muir and the Presbyterian
minister S. Hall Young found entire villages hilariously drunk,
"mothers lying helpless on the ground with hungry babies rolling over them . . . and unspeakable scenes of debauchery and
sin." [21]

By the 1880's the military and the missionaries together had
brought the worst of the liquor trade under some degree of restraint. Distilleries were raided and destroyed. Native police
went on patrol, and temperate forces campaigned to secure
pledges of abstinence. The Protestant churches lobbied for the
passage of a law (1886) which made the study of temperance
mandatory in all schools under federal control. Alaska's capital
city organized a chapter of the Woman's Christian Temperance
Union, and the citizens of Sitka were host to Miss Jessie Ackerman, national lecturer for that organization, who was noted for
her famous discourse, "San Francisco by Gaslight; or the Vices
of a Great City." Over the years Frances Willard sent other
lecturers with ammunition for the battles on the northern frontier. Meanwhile, the missionary lobby forced the inclusion of a
provision in the Organic Law of 1884 which prohibited "the
importation, manufacture, and sale of intoxicating liquors . . .
except for medicinal purposes." [22]

[21] See advertisements in the Sitka *Post*, Nov. 20, 1876; Morris, *Report*, 151;
Bancroft, *History of Alaska*, 622; S. Hall Young, *Hall Young of Alaska: An Autobiography* (New York, 1927), 165–66; Young, *Alaska Days with John Muir*, 77;
John Muir, *Travels in Alaska* (Boston, 1915), 131–33.
[22] Charles A. Anderson, ed., "Letters of Amanda R. McFarland," *Journal of
the Presbyterian Historical Society*, XXXIV (June, 1956), 98; Young, *Autobiography*, 166–67; Morris, *Report*, 158; *Alaska Appeal*, July 30, 1879; Fanny Kellogg
to Jackson, Oct. 22, 1878, Correspondence, Vol. 8, p. 274; *Rocky Mountain*

But enforcing prohibition in Alaska was like blocking the movement of the Muir Glacier. Within a few years after the law was passed, some of the veteran missionaries agreed to a *modus vivendi* with their thirsty parishioners. Perhaps Jackson would have been wise to have done the same. Or he might have refrained from including whites in his efforts to enforce prohibition. The first annual report of Alaska's second governor, Alfred Swineford, came to the crux of the problem. "We have here simply a repetition of the workings of prohibition in communities adverse to it. . . . A stringent licensing law would be much more efficatious and restraining in its operation. . . ." Swineford made an effort, though vainly, to license the manufacture and sale of liquor. Henry W. Clark later summarized the situation: "The people of Alaska took the position that Congress passed the prohibition law for the Indians and not for the whites, and consequently felt justified in opposing it." [23]

In Swineford's view prohibition served only "to flood the Territory with liquors most vile and poisonous to the enrichment of a few who have been engaged in their illegal importation." Repeatedly he urged that a strict license law would be

---

Presbyterian, November, 1879; *Report of the Commissioner of Education for the Year 1887–1888*, 185; J. Armenia Ackerman to Jackson, May, 1881, Correspondence, Vol. 11, p. 175; M. B. Reese to Jackson, Feb. 7, 1887, Correspondence, Vol. 14, p. 269; *Home Mission Monthly*, December, 1888. A major factor in the destruction of the Tlingit village of Angoon was liquor pandemonium. Ted C. Hinckley, "Punitive Action at Angoon," *Alaska Sportsman*, XXIX (January–February, 1963); Mary Earhart, *Frances Willard: From Prayers to Politics* (Chicago, 1944), 191–92; Alaska Governors Papers, GSA, Sand Point, NAS, Seattle, Washington (hereafter cited as Gov. Papers); William Van DeVenter, Asst. Attorney General to Secretary of the Interior (n.d.); Jackson to Alaska Teachers, July 10, 1886, Weinland Papers, Huntington Library, San Marino, California; *The Alaskan* (Sitka), June 23, 30, 1888, May 11, 1889; Alice E. Briggs to Jackson, Nov. 12, 1886, Correspondence, Vol. 14, p. 244; Frances E. Willard to Jackson, Oct. 27, 1891, Correspondence, Vol. 16, p. 24; Barker, *Compilation of the Acts of Congress*, 30.

[23] *Report of the Governor of Alaska, 1885* (Washington, D.C., 1885), 15; Nichols, *Alaska*, 107; Henry W. Clark, *History of Alaska* (New York, 1930), 196–97; see same appraisal in the *Report of the Governor, 1896*, quoted in Spicer, *Constitutional Status*, 53. The fact that the Governor unfailingly enjoyed liquor with his dinner and only rarely attended church hardly improved his standing with Alaska's "drys." Interview by the author with Mrs. Agnes Shattuck (Swineford's daughter), Juneau, July 30, 1962.

far preferable to prohibition poorly enforced and hypocritical. Jackson, however, refused to agree and fought such recommendations stubbornly and successfully. Swineford concentrated his energies upon bootleggers who sold liquor to the Indians. Beyond this, little improvement was possible.[24]

Presbyterians saw in Harrison a "dry," even a prohibitionist. He had fought against Sunday saloon openings and in 1883 had signed a petition which urged a constitutional amendment "to prohibit the manufacture and sale of all alcoholic beverages throughout the national domain." During the floor debate over Senate Bill 153, he had advocated prohibition for Alaska. The Catholic bishop of Indianapolis recalled that Harrison was for "temperance without fanaticism."[25]

Harrison's appointment of Lyman Knapp of Vermont as Governor of Alaska seemed at first to augur well for the future. Knapp recognized Jackson (though unofficially) as lobbyist for Alaska in Washington, D.C., and accepted for himself an assignment as Sunday school teacher in Sitka. However, he reinstated the license system which Swineford had introduced tentatively, and this, in the eyes of the temperance enthusiasts, meant nothing less than opening Pandora's box. Knapp fully appreciated the difficulties of dealing with the commerce in liquor. He proposed to bring action against those who sold intoxicants to the native population. On the other hand, he was a realist who accepted the fact that the people generally opposed the enforcement of prohibition.[26]

[24] *Report of the Governor of Alaska, 1886* (Washington, D.C., 1886), 47. Alaska's early governors were bereft not only of power but of sufficient public funds. Swineford's shortlived licensing scheme aimed not only at liquor regulation, but actually did provide some income. L. Dawson to H. E. Haydon, Dec. 10, 1887, Correspondence, Vol. 24, p. 271.

[25] Earhard, *Frances Willard,* 212 ff.; C. Vann Woodward, *Origins of the New South* (New Orleans, 1951), 171; Leland L. Sage, *William Boyd Allison: A Study in Practical Politics* (Iowa City, 1956), 184; Volwiler, "Correspondence," 90; 47th Cong., 2nd Sess., *Congressional Record* (Jan. 8, 1883), 944; 48th Cong., 1st Sess., *Congressional Record* (Jan. 24, 1884), 632; Sievers, *Benjamin Harrison,* 362.

[26] Volwiler, "Correspondence," 51; C. A. S. Swineford (Governor A. P. Swineford's brother) to President-elect, Feb. 1, 1889 (copy sent to John G. Brady,

Max Pracht, United States Collector of Customs for Alaska, sought to assist the governor in his licensing scheme, but was attacked both by the missionaries and by the liquor interests as well. Meanwhile, John Brady wrote to Harrison, lashing out at the judicial officers for their failure to support prohibition. To Jackson, Brady declared,

> I feel sadly disappointed in Governor Knapp. I assure you that the saloon men themselves are greatly surprised at the course of the Gov. and Collector. Of course they will stock up to the extent of their money and credit for they know well that it is all against the laws and cannot last long.[27]

The prophecy was essentially correct, for the pressures upon Harrison produced results. On April 7, 1891, Secretary of the Interior, John W. Noble, notified Governor Knapp, "By direction of the President, I have to request that no license for the sale of intoxicating liquor be issued in the Territory of Alaska, and that any action favoring such issue you will please explain to this department without delay."[28]

President Harrison refused to sanction a licensing procedure, since it would have had the effect of legalizing the liquor trade in a manner forbidden by the law of 1884. Beyond this, however, he showed some reluctance to act. In fact, he showed plainly enough that he was not disposed to be goaded by Presbyterians or others of prohibitionist leanings. When indignant temperance ladies protested to him about the state of affairs in

---

Feb. 2, 1889), Brady Papers; Jackson to Kendall and Irwin, July 23, 1889, PUTS, Vol. 1, p. 90; Irwin to Jackson, n.d., Six Sitka Officials to Hon. W. T. Harris, Dec. 20, 1889, Correspondence, Vol. 15, pp. 212, 240; *Report of the Governor of Alaska, 1890* (Washington, D.C., 1890), 6; Governor Knapp to John C. Heid *et al.* Committee, March 4, 1890, Governor Knapp to J. Healy, July 26, 1890, Gov. Papers, Box 1.

[27] J. M. Healy to Governor Knapp, Oct. 25, 1891, Gov. Papers, Box 1; John G. Heid to Jackson, Dec. 15, 1890, J. G. Brady to Benjamin Harrison, Nov. 29, 1890 (given to Jackson to hand to the President), J. G. Brady to Jackson, Dec. 16, 1890, Correspondence, Vol. 15, pp. 299, 292, 295.

[28] Secretary of the Interior J. W. Noble to Governor Lyman Knapp, April 7, 1891, PUTS, Vol. 3, p. 352; Governor Knapp to C. S. Johnson, Nov. 2, 1891, Gov. Papers, Box 1.

Alaska, he treated them courteously, but insisted that vague assertions concerning his appointed officials would not do; he must have specific charges, "with names of drinking men who had been appointed." [29]

Jackson himself received a somewhat similar treatment and was embarrassed by it. Impelled by his friends in Alaska, he addressed himself to the President in strong language:

> If you could make me an appointment of fifteen minutes some time, I could give you considerable insight into the wretched state of Government now existing in Alaska. It is much worse than during Mr. Cleveland's administration. . . . There has been no time since you secured us a civil government and a prohibitory liquor law, that liquor has been so . . . disastrous to the people as now.
>
> The captain of the mail steamer reports recently landing six tons of liquor at Fort Wrangell for two licensed saloons . . . your administration in Alaska will be remembered as the "Whiskey one." Now I have not lost faith in your earnest desire to give Alaska good officials, but you have been woefully deceived by politicians urging these men upon you.
>
> In God's good providence, you and a portion of your excellent cabinet are Presbyterians. This has given rise to the term "Presbyterian Administration" and it is the constant taunt the Alaska missionaries are called to bear, as the Godless point to the Collector, the Judge and some other officials and say, "see your good Presbyterian officials." [30]

Harrison's response was to refer the communication to the United States Attorney General, who began an investigation on the basis of it. This was not at all what Jackson wanted. "This letter is personal (for you only) and not to be shown to others," he explained. He asked to have it back, and he reminded the President that an earlier indiscretion had resulted in complaints and persecution. Jackson's correspondence with the White House dropped off noticeably thereafter, and he turned to other

[29] Sarah D. L. Fetra to Jackson, Feb. 7, 1890, Representatives of W.C.T.U. to the President of the United States, Jan. 30, 1890, Correspondence, Vol. 15, pp. 247, 248.

[30] Jackson to President Harrison, Jan. 8, 1891, Correspondence, Vol. 25, p. 255.

problems, particularly to the importation of Siberian reindeer to meet the Eskimos' food shortage.[31]

The licensing proposal was aired again early in 1892, this time in the chambers of Congress. Oregon's Senator Joseph N. Dolph, who had been in Alaska during the preceding summer, was much distressed by what he found. Illegal breweries and saloons were even more numerous than they had been when he had visited the same towns five years earlier. Dolph too was persuaded that strict licensing was the only possible alternative, and he proposed a bill to that effect.[32]

This time Jackson let it be known he would not object, provided that the new regulations were applied only to the Alaska panhandle. But the opposition of church groups and temperance societies was as vehement as ever, and even the Alaskans themselves gave little encouragemnt to the plan. The killing of a government schoolteacher who tried to arrest some smugglers, an incident that was reported during the debates, further contributed to the defeat of the licensing bill.[33]

Quite possibly Harrison would have preferred to see Dolph's proposals given a trial. Since the opposition was determined not to allow it, the President had little choice but to tighten up the enforcement of the 1884 law as best he could. To accomplish this purpose, and perhaps to ease the pressure of temperance forces, he published an executive order "prohibiting the sale of intoxicating liquors in Alaska."

It was a vain effort. "The President . . . seems to think this is going to do all the work," Jackson commented wryly. Later that same year a special investigator for the Attorney General reported on the effectiveness (or lack of it) of the recent effort. "In a population of 42,000 of which only 4,303 were white, there are in operation and openly engaged in the liquor traffic, five breweries. . . . I found also . . . sixty places in Alaska where

[31] Jackson to Harrison, Jan. 15, 1890, PUTS, Vol. 2, p. 35; E. W. Halford to Jackson, Jan. 23, 1891, Correspondence, Vol. 15, p. 374; Jackson to President Harrison, Jan. 8, 1891, Correspondence, Vol. 25, p. 255.

[32] Nichols, *Alaska*, 118.

[33] Jackson to Senator Dolph, Jan. 19, 1892, Amendments to Senate Bill 1076, Jan. 19, 1892, PUTS, Vol. 2, pp. 206, 296; Nichols, *Alaska*, 118–19.

intoxicating liquors were either manufactured or sold." It is hard to resist the conclusion that the advocates of prohibition in the territory abetted the very conditions they sought to eradicate. Alaska's liquor control dilemma was an ominous portent of what lay ahead for the United States itself following World War I.[34]

In 1892 Harrison was defeated in his second campaign against Grover Cleveland. Jackson, however, remained Alaska's General Agent for Education. President Cleveland had no illusions about Jackson's abilities and his power. If he had any doubts about the crusty civil servant, they were dispelled by the President's brother Rev. William Cleveland, a Presbyterian minister who was one of Jackson's staunch admirers. Jackson knew that his close friend, John G. Brady, a Republican, would never gain approval from a Democratic administration. He therefore recommended another Alaskan, his Democratic coworker and steady churchman, James Sheakley, for the governor's post. President Cleveland acted favorably on this request.[35]

If the extant Jackson and Harrison papers are any criteria, neither of them sought to continue their working relationship

[34] Jackson to Samuel K. Johnson, March 23, 1892, PUTS, Vol. 2, p. 307. During the Alaskan gold rushes, high license finally came to Alaska. The 1899 law satisfied few — either dry or wet. Some of the worst aspects of the bootleg traffic appear to have diminished, although the aborigine was still able to find a bottle if he wanted it badly enough. George Perkins, U.S. Senate, to Governor John Brady, June 1, 1899, J. L. Parkhurst to Secretary of State, Nov. 8, 1905, Gov. Papers, Box 10; W. F. Rilgara, U.S.R.M., to John R. Beedle, Sept. 9, 1900, ACHR, July, 1899–November, 1901; *Stickeen River Journal*, June 4, 1898; *Report of the Governor of Alaska, 1898* (Washington, D.C., 1898), 35–36, 48.

David Starr Jordan could only lament the evil fruit picked from the tree of good intentions. "One of the least fortunate acts of the United States Congress in regard to Alaska has been the enactment of a most rigid prohibitory law as to alcoholic liquors. This is an iron-clad statute forbidding the importation, sale, or manufacture of intoxicants of any sort in Alaska. The primary reason for this act is the desire to protect the Indians, Aleuts, and Eskimos from a vice . . . which soon ruins them. But a virtuous statute may be the worst kind of law, as was noted long ago by Confucius. This statute has not checked the flow of liquor in Alaska, while it has done more than any other influence to subvert the respect for law." David Starr Jordan, *Imperial Democracy: A Study of the Relation of . . . Democracy to the Demands of a Vigorous Foreign Policy and Other Demands of Imperial Dominion* (New York, 1899), 208.

[35] Jackson to the President of the United States, March 29, 1893, PUTS, Vol. 3, p. 206.

after Harrison left the White House. Jackson became so engrossed with his introduction of the Siberian reindeer that he spent long weeks of every year at sea far from the capital. In 1897 the Presbyterian Church bestowed upon him its highest post, the moderator of the General Assembly. Undoubtedly the General Agent was touched when former President Harrison stepped forward and publicly praised his labors. But perhaps he enjoyed a greater satisfaction when President McKinley in 1897 appointed his protégé, John G. Brady, Governor of the Territory.[36]

In retrospect it appears that Benjamin Harrison's association with his Alaska gadfly, Sheldon Jackson, was one of considerable mutual trust. Both men possessed austere personalities and preferred a rather formal working relationship. Their most signal legislative success had been obtaining the Territory's first organic act; their most dismal failure lay in perpetuating the prohibition fiasco.

In terms of money or votes, grappling with Alaska's pioneer perplexities was a thankless task. The two Presbyterians would never have been so steadfast in their Alaskan labors without a Christian sense of social justice. Most Gilded Age Americans would have preferred to forget about their Great Land responsibilities. Granted that the Jackson-Harrison partnership suffered from periods of visionary myopia, their humanitarian insight envisioned a far greater future for Alaska than that discerned by a majority of their countrymen.

[36] Stewart, *Sheldon Jackson*, 436.

Charles Campbell received his Ph.D. from Yale University in 1938 and teaches at Claremont Graduate School. He worked for the State Department and taught at The Johns Hopkins University. His article examines a crucial juncture in the Bering Sea Controversy. The essay is from the Mississippi Valley Historical Review *(now the* Journal of American History) *XLVIII (December, 1961), 393–414. A follow-up article on the Controversy is "The Bering Sea Settlements of 1892,"* Pacific Historical Review XXXII *(November, 1963), 347–67.*

The Anglo-American Crisis
in the Bering Sea, 1890-1891

CHARLES S. CAMPBELL, JR.

ccounts of the Anglo-Canadian—American dispute over the fur seals of the Bering Sea have usually stressed the legal points debated by Secretary of State James G. Blaine and the British Prime Minister and Foreign Secretary, Lord Salisbury.[1] But during its most critical phase, in 1890 and 1891, the controversy was shaped far less by legal considerations than by three less obvious influences: pressure exerted in Washington by the powerful North American Commercial Company; a decision by Great Britain to use force if the United States attempted to arrest British sealers in the Bering Sea; and the ef-

[1] The fullest accounts of the controversy are in Alice F. Tyler, *The Foreign Policy of James G. Blaine* (Minneapolis, 1927), chap. xiii; James M. Callahan, *American Foreign Policy in Canadian Relations* (New York, 1937), chap. xviii; Charles C. Tansill, *The Foreign Policy of Thomas F. Bayard, 1885–1897* (New York, 1940), chaps. xiv and xv; and Tansill, *Canadian-American Relations, 1875–1911* (New Haven, 1943).

forts of an American naturalist, Henry W. Elliott, to save the seals from their human foes on land and at sea. The first of these influences served to hamper the reaching of an agreement between London and Washington, while the second and the third, in contrast, encouraged the finding of a solution to the fur-seal problem. The net result was that by the end of 1891 the Bering Sea controversy had turned the corner to an eventual settlement.

When the Republican administration of President Benjamin Harrison and Secretary Blaine assumed office on March 4, 1889, it inherited a dangerous controversy from the Democrats. In 1886 and 1887, President Grover Cleveland had permitted arrests of British sealers in the Bering Sea, much more than three miles from land. Angry protests had followed from London and Ottawa. Secretary of State Thomas F. Bayard, who did not believe the arrests legally justifiable, had succeeded in stopping them in 1888, but he had failed to reach agreement for a closed season with Great Britain or with Russia, the only other country with important sealing interests in the Bering Sea. In the closing days of Cleveland's administration Bayard's hope for agreement suffered a setback. On March 2, 1889, Cleveland signed an act directing the President to issue annually a warning that persons entering "all the dominion of the United States in the waters of Behring's Sea" would be arrested if they engaged in pelagic sealing (sealing, that is, at sea; a form of sealing considered by the United States to be criminally wasteful, in contrast to the regulated land sealing it espoused). As directed, incoming President Harrison issued such a warning on March 22, 1889; moreover, during that year (acting in this case beyond the requirements of the new law, which did not specify the extent of the American "dominion") he authorized the arrest of several British sealers on the open waters of the Bering Sea. This evidence that the Republicans planned to abandon Bayard's conciliatory policy of 1888 evoked a storm of anger in Canada. Great Britain, which still managed its Dominion's foreign policy, took a firm stand, and negotiations ensued among

Great Britain, the United States, and Russia.[2] It was these negotiations that set the stage for the British preparations to resort to
force in the Bering Sea.

The negotiations commenced hopefully enough on February 22, 1890, with a preliminary meeting in Washington at which
Blaine and the Russian Minister, M. de Struve, "hand and
glove" together, jointly proposed to the British Minister, Sir
Julian Pauncefote, an area within which a closed season for
pelagic sealing would operate.[3] The same men, together with
Charles H. Tupper, Canadian Minister of Marine and Fisheries
(and son of Sir Charles Tupper, Canadian High Commissioner
in London), who attended as Pauncefote's adviser, had their
first formal meeting on March 3. It proved to be their last meeting as well. Blaine, de Struve, and Pauncefote took it for granted
that some closed season would be set and that the conference
had been convened merely to define it. But the discussion ter-
minated abruptly when Tupper, on being asked his view, denied the need for any such season at all.[4] Secretary Blaine's
patience was never great, especially with Canadians. Summoning Pauncefote and de Struve, but not Tupper, to his office on
March 12, he avowed despair of his own ability to satisfy the
Dominion and asked Sir Julian to submit a British counter-proposal. The foresighted Englishman already had one in mind,
which he outlined then and there and which he agreed to refer
to his government.[5]

London approved the counter-proposal in principle but felt
constrained to make a show of deference to Ottawa.[6] "I do not

[2] Blaine had already negotiated, unsuccessfully, with Russia alone. See Baron
Rosen, *Forty Years of Diplomacy* (2 vols., London, 1922), I, 78–80; Tyler, *Foreign Policy of Blaine*, 380–82.

[3] Charles H. Tupper to Sir John A. Macdonald, March 3, 1890, Sir John A.
Macdonald Papers (Public Archives of Canada, Ottawa), Vol. 30; Sir Julian
Pauncefote to Lord Salisbury, February 22, 1890, Great Britain, Foreign Office,
*Blue Book, United States, No. 2 (1890): Correspondence Respecting the Behring
Sea Seal Fisheries, 1886–1890* (London, 1890), 412.

[4] Tupper to Macdonald, April 10, 1890, Macdonald Papers, Vol. 31.

[5] Pauncefote to Salisbury, March 21, 1890, *Blue Book, United States, No. 2
(1890)*, 419–20.

[6] Salisbury to Pauncefote, April 3, 1890, *ibid.*, 421.

think myself that there is here [in the Dominion] any growth of opinion either in favour of annexation to the States or of Independence for Canada," a person, almost certainly Governor-General Lord Stanley, had just written, "but if we are forced to believe that our interests here are not considered of any importance to the Home Government, we furnish to those who desire separation from England a very dangerous weapon & one which will be surely used against us at no distant date." [7] This familiar refrain rang ominously in London. However strongly Salisbury may have been convinced of the deleterious effects of pelagic sealing, he had to tread warily between Washington and Ottawa. "Telegraph whether, as I hope, your Government has agreed to Minister at Washington's proposed Behring's Sea Convention," the Colonial Secretary cautiously instructed the Governor-General. [8] Under these circumstances, it was difficult for Canada to persist in Tupper's stand against any closed season at all, but she did succeed in modifying Pauncefote's draft.

The British counter-proposal, presented to Blaine on April 29, 1890, provided for a joint commission of experts to report within two years on regulations needed to preserve the seals. Meanwhile a closed season on land and at sea was to operate during May and June and during October, November, and December. It was further proposed that sealing vessels should not be permitted to approach within ten miles of the large rookeries on the American-owned Pribilof Islands in July, August, and September. [9]

The United States now had the proposal it had requested; but it delayed action for three weeks. Pauncefote naturally assumed that he would be asked to reconvene with Blaine and de Struve to discuss his offer. To his great surprise, however, he read in the newspapers that on May 20 the Harrison cabinet

[7] Unsigned "very confidential" letter to Pauncefote, March 12, 1890, Macdonald Papers, Vol. 32.

[8] Lord Knutsford to Lord Stanley, April 11, 1890, *Blue Book, United States, No. 2 (1890)*, 422.

[9] Pauncefote to Blaine, April 29, 1890, *ibid.*, 455–57, and the draft convention, *ibid.*, 457–59.

not only had rejected the British proposal but had ordered American revenue cutters to dismantle all sealing vessels apprehended in the Bering Sea. In high dudgeon Sir Julian went straight to Secretary Blaine. Indignantly he remonstrated against release of the news prior to informing him, and against the issuing of provocative orders in the midst of negotiations. No less sternly, Blaine retorted that he could not control the press, that the Treasury Department was justified in carrying out an act of Congress, and that he had delayed answering the counter-proposal, which he termed "totally inadequate," until he could reply jointly with Russia. On being asked what he disliked about the proposal, the Secretary "inveighed" particularly against the contemplated regulation of land sealing.[10]

While this discourteous treatment of the British Minister cannot be defended, it can perhaps be explained. It was on March 12, 1890, that Blaine, having lost patience with Tupper, asked Pauncefote to submit a counter-proposal. On that same day another, more significant, event occurred: the award of a twenty-year lease of sealing rights on the Pribilof Islands to the North American Commercial Company, a California firm incorporated in 1889 with a capital stock of $2,000,000. Twenty years earlier, shortly after the United States acquired Alaska, these rights had been leased to another California concern, the Alaska Commercial Company. Since then this company had built up a seemingly impregnable position in Alaska and Washington, and it had bid for the new lease of 1890 with every hope of success. Superficially, it appeared that this powerful concern had lost out to the North American Commercial Company simply because the latter had made the government a better offer. But there was another reason — perhaps the crucial one — which was also to constitute a major factor in determining the course of the Bering Sea controversy.

In its early years the new lessee had only a small number of stockholders (apparently about five or six) and was dominated by two in particular. The first of these was Darius Ogden Mills,

---

[10] Pauncefote to Salisbury, May 22 and 23, 1890, *ibid.*, 465–66, 469–72. Blaine did not reject the counter-proposal in writing until May 29, 1890. *Ibid.*, 475–78.

who had amassed a huge fortune in California and was one of the wealthiest men in the country.[11] He was also the father-in-law of Whitelaw Reid, a powerful figure in the Republican party who in 1892 was to run with President Harrison as vice-presidential candidate. Reid was the editor and owner of the New York *Tribune*, a newspaper whose backing was indispensable to any candidate for the Republican presidential nomination. He was a long-standing friend and fervent supporter of James G. Blaine; "For twelve years," the latter wrote Reid in 1888, "you have given me the influence of the Tribune, superadded to the personal weight of your own name."[12] The second politically influential stockholder in the North American Commercial Company was Stephen B. Elkins. Blaine's financial adviser and intimate associate over the years, his campaign manager in 1884 and sponsor in 1888, and soon to be Harrison's Secretary of War, Elkins had close ties with the Republican party's two most eminent figures; ties that were the stronger because he seems to have been associated with the Secretary and his son, Emmons Blaine, in some West Virginia business ventures, and with Harrison's son, "Prince" Russell, in running a Montana ranch.[13] Thus through D. O. Mills and his son-in-law, Whitelaw Reid, and still more through Stephen B. Elkins, the North American Commercial Company had ready access to the State Department and even to the White House.

These intimate ties between the new lessees of the Pribilof Islands and the Harrison administration had a profound effect upon negotiations regarding the Bering Sea. Whether or not the

[11] See Mills's article, "Our Fur-Seal Fisheries," *North American Review* (New York), CLI (September, 1890), 300–306.

[12] Blaine to Whitelaw Reid, July 6, 1888, Whitelaw Reid Papers (Manuscript Division, Library of Congress), Box 104.

[13] Hearings before the House Committee on Expenditures in the Department of Commerce, 63 Cong., 2 Sess., *Investigation of the Fur-Seal Industry of Alaska* (Washington, 1914), 783; New York *World*, May 7, 1891; New York *Evening Post*, December 18, 1891; New York *Times*, December 21, 1891; Philadelphia *Record*, December 26, 1891. When Harrison appointed Elkins Secretary of War in 1891, the President's son wrote his father to express his appreciation. Russell Harrison to the President, December 17, 1891, Benjamin Harrison Papers (Manuscript Division, Library of Congress), Vol. 133.

company used its undoubted influence in Washington to secure the lease in the first place is not known, but there is good reason to look to Elkins and his associates for the major explanation of Blaine's termination of the negotiations with Britain and Russia and for the decision to send American revenue cutters to the Bering Sea on their provocative mission. On general principles it would be natural for the company to view with utmost alarm negotiations envisaging investigation of its privileged position in the seal islands and proposing further a closed season on land as well as at sea, and for it to protest to its prominent friends in Washington. According to two long articles in the New York *Herald* this is exactly what happened — with the consequent rejection of Pauncefote's counter-proposal and the orders to the cutters.[14]

The uncompromising attitude adopted by Washington in May, 1890, ushered in the most critical phase of the dispute. Two months before, Lord Salisbury had been worried by a remark of Blaine's that, though he would guarantee that no American revenue cutter would enter the Bering Sea before the middle of May, he would give no assurance for the remainder of the year.[15] The Prime Minister's concern had been apparent in a private communication to Pauncefote.

> We were a good deal disturbed [he said] by the letter that you received from Mr. Blaine. It is difficult to be certain what he means by it: whether it is simply written to spur on the Canadians to more rapid negotiations, or whether he really foreshadows the policy which in the absence of a treaty, the United States will pursue in the summer. In the latter case the news is very grave indeed, for

[14] New York *Herald*, June 26, July 24, 1890. According to the *Herald* and the New York *World*, July 24 and 25, 1890, Blaine favored accepting the British proposal but was overruled by Harrison and Secretary of the Treasury William Windom. This seems unlikely, though it is possible that Blaine favored negotiations to improve the proposal. The New York *Times*, July 24, 1890, saw no evidence of disagreement between Blaine and Harrison. See also the New York *Herald*, July 25, 1890.

[15] Pauncefote to Salisbury, March 25, 1890, Confidential Correspondence, America, Behring Sea Fisheries, 1890 (Foreign Office Library), 67. Blaine's letter was dated March 24, 1890. Pauncefote to Salisbury, May 23, 1890, *Blue Book, United States, No. 2 (1890)*, 472.

my Colleagues are all of opinion that we cannot tolerate a renewal of the captures. It is early to say what form our resistance will take; but I think I am justified in saying, from the judgment I can form of the state of opinion here, that we shall not be allowed, even if we were inclined, to permit United States cruisers to treat Behring Sea as if it were their private property.

I confess that the attitude, both at Washington & at Ottawa, makes me somewhat apprehensive of the result. . . . If both sides push their pretensions to an extreme, a collision is inevitable. We shall look with great anxiety to your reports of the progress of negotiations.[16]

Now Blaine's date, the middle of May, had come, and soon thereafter came Pauncefote's alarming report that American revenue cutters had been ordered to arrest British sealers. On receiving this grave news, Salisbury consulted the Queen and the cabinet. He then took two major steps. First, he telegraphed Pauncefote to warn the American Secretary of State that a formal protest would soon be delivered. Second, he gave secret orders for four warships to be held in readiness, two in Yokohama, two in Esquimalt (British Columbia), and for them to hasten to the Bering Sea if word came of American ships going there to arrest British sealers.[17] Salisbury further asked Sir Julian to consider the advisability of "slipping out" this information to Blaine. "Her Majesty's Government," he telegraphed, "must leave wholly to your discretion whether and in what manner Mr. Blaine should be made aware of this. The matter is one of great delicacy, and the announcement, if made, should

[16] Salisbury to Pauncefote, March 28, 1890, Lord Salisbury Papers (Christ Church Library, Oxford). Salisbury telegraphed Pauncefote to tell Blaine that if the captures were renewed the reaction in Britain would be "very serious." Salisbury to Pauncefote, March 28, 1890, Public Record Office (London), Foreign Office 5/2106. For Pauncefote's warning to Blaine, March 29, 1890, see Notes, Great Britain, State Department Records (National Archives).

[17] Salisbury to Pauncefote, May 29, 1890, *Blue Book, United States, No. 2 (1890),* 467; Salisbury to Pauncefote, May 23, 1890, *ibid.,* 466; Pauncefote to Blaine, May 23, 1890, *ibid.,* 473; Salisbury to Pauncefote, May 31, 1890, Foreign Office 5/2107. The warships were the *Severn* and the *Leander* of the China station and the *Amphion* and the *Champion* of the Pacific station. Evan MacGregor, Admiralty, to Under-Secretary of State, Foreign Office, September 11, 1890, Foreign Office 5/2111.

bear the appearance of an incidental remark rather than of a formal communication." [18]

Pauncefote, while keeping in close touch with the State Department, was waiting for more definite information about the sailing orders of the revenue cutters. News now began to come. From a "secret source" he learned that the *Richard Rush* and the *Corwin* would sail for Bering Sea about the middle of June.[19] It seemed best to act before the cutters were out of reach, and Sir Julian asked for and received permission to deliver Salisbury's official protest.[20] Though he may have hesitated when he heard, again from a secret source, that the *Rush* and *Corwin* had very probably (but not certainly) been ordered to remain at Seattle indefinitely,[21] he submitted the formal protest to Secretary Blaine on June 14.

> Her Britannic Majesty's Government [he said] have learnt with great concern . . . that the Government of the United States have issued instructions to their Revenue cruizers . . . under which the vessels of British subjects will again be exposed . . . to unlawful interference. . . . The Undersigned is in consequence instructed formally to protest against such interference, and to declare that her Britannic Majesty's Government must hold the Government of the United States responsible for the consequences which may ensue from acts which are contrary to the principles of international law.[22]

This solemn warning — an "ultimatum," the New York *World* erroneously called it [23] — could not be shrugged off by the American government. And about the same time that it received the protest, the State Department learned of the secret British

[18] Salisbury to Pauncefote, June 3, 1890, Confidential Correspondence, America, Behring Sea Fisheries, 1890 (Foreign Office Library), 125. In Foreign Office 5/2108 is a draft of this telegram in Salisbury's handwriting, with slightly different wording.

[19] Pauncefote to Salisbury, June 6, 1890, Foreign Office 5/2108.

[20] Pauncefote to Salisbury, June 10, 1890, *Blue Book, United States, No. 2 (1890)*, 478–79; Salisbury to Pauncefote, June 11, 1890, *ibid.*, 480.

[21] Pauncefote to Salisbury, June 13, 1890, Foreign Office 5/2108.

[22] *Blue Book, United States, No. 2 (1890)*, 507–508.

[23] New York *World*, July 24, 1890. The New York *Tribune*, July 24, 1890, called the protest a "bluff."

naval preparations. Pauncefote had not informed Blaine about the four warships for the excellent reason that the telegram instructing him to consider "slipping out" the news never reached him. But a day or two after delivering the protest, Sir Julian, to his great surprise, received a routine paraphrase of the telegram. He hastened to the Secretary of State's office and told Blaine that long-overdue instructions of the most serious nature had just arrived, instructions that made it vital to detain the American revenue cutters. In his report to Salisbury the Minister gave the following account of the interview:

> "I suppose," he [Blaine] said, "you refer to the 4 British ironclads ordered to Behring's Sea. We have known that for some time. We view it as a menace and shall not defer on that account for a single day the departure of our cutters. It is a violent assertion of a right to share in a fishery to which the United States can show an exclusive title for 80 years." I replied that on the contrary it was an act of self-defence against violent assertion by the United States of a right to interfere with the British flag on the high seas which could not be tolerated any longer and which would not have been tolerated so long from any other nation. He said we were crying out before we were hurt and that the presence of British ironclads in Behring's Sea would aggravate the difficulties of a friendly settlement.[24]

How Blaine had learned about the secret order is not known; but the possibilities were numerous. Agents of the United States may have deciphered the telegram that never reached Sir Julian; or Minister Robert T. Lincoln in London may have had a secret source of his own; or possibly the Secretary himself had made deductions from articles in British newspapers. He could have known, for example, that the London *Times* of June 4 had published what may have been an officially inspired statement that "British vessels of war must inevitably be ordered to follow the American cruizers to Alaskan waters."[25] In any case, the news of the British intentions, coming

[24] Pauncefote to Salisbury, June 16, 1890, Foreign Office 5/2108.
[25] London *Times*, June 4, 1890; see also London *Standard*, June 11, 1890. In his *Recollections of Sixty Years in Canada* (London, 1914), 209–11, Sir Charles

hard upon the formal protest, was sufficiently disturbing to command serious heed by the United States government; and the subsequent developments provide evidence that it was not ignored.

The sealing season of 1890 was now near, and British sealers, no doubt feeling safer because of the warning of June 14, began to move into the Bering Sea. Amidst considerable speculation as to the possibility that the warning and the menace of the British naval squadron would induce Washington to rescind the dismantling order, Blaine kept up a bold front. Though pressed by Pauncefote, he refused to give any assurance against captures of British vessels.[26] But Sir Julian's secret information that the cutters were being detained in Seattle proved to be correct. As the days passed and no American cutter departed for the Bering Sea, the British Minister became increasingly optimistic. Visiting Blaine in his home, he spoke of the danger of a collision in those northern waters. The Secretary responded: "Our revenue cutters have not left yet"—a remark that seemed significant to Pauncefote.[27] Then, too, further news from his secret informant strengthened his belief that the *Rush* and *Corwin* were being held subject to orders of the Secretary of State.[28] Calling again at Blaine's home, Sir Julian "pressed him [Blaine] as regards interference . . . with British sealers. Although he still refused to give any assurance, I am under a strong impression from his tone and certain expressions he used, as well as from secret information that the U. S. Govt. have within the last few days issued sealed orders to their revenue

Tupper said he told the Colonial Secretary, Lord Knutsford, on June 28, 1890, that if "prompt action is not taken, Canada can only come to the conclusion that the British flag is not strong enough to protect her"; and that as a result "Sir Julian Pauncefote was instructed to say to Mr. Blaine that if the British flag was interfered with the United States must be prepared for the consequences." Tupper did write to Knutsford in strong terms on June 27 (Foreign Office 5/2109), but the decision regarding the protest and the four warships had been made before that date.

[26] Pauncefote to Salisbury, July 3, 1890, Foreign Office 5/2109.
[27] Pauncefote to Salisbury, June 19, 1890, Foreign Office 5/2108.
[28] Pauncefote to Salisbury, June 26, 1890, *ibid.*

cruizers which will stop any action which might bring them into collision with our men-of-war." [29]

Sir Julian's impression was borne out by later press reports that First Comptroller of the Treasury A. C. Matthews had left Washington on June 23 and had sped across the continent on a secret mission, the object of which was to insure that there should be no captures of Canadian vessels in 1890.[30] It was further confirmed by the British Vice-Consul at Port Townsend, Washington, who reported that at a dinner party he had been told by the wife of Lieutenant Francis Tuttle of the *Richard Rush* that the *Rush* had received orders not to arrest British sealers, and by Captain Calvin L. Hooper of the *Corwin* that the *Corwin* was not going to the Bering Sea.[31]

But the best evidence of the accuracy of Pauncefote's impression was of course the fact that no seizures did occur in 1890. The President had issued a proclamation in March, as directed by the act of 1889, warning sealers not to encroach upon "all the dominion of the United States"; and Lieutenant Tuttle of the *Richard Rush* boarded the Canadian sealer *Ariel* and delivered copies of the proclamation with a verbal warning to the captain to "watch out" if he ventured into the Bering Sea. But when the *Rush* later came upon the *Annie Seymour* with her boats actually lowered and engaged in sealing, the American cutter, after steaming slowly around the nervous sealers for half an hour, sailed away, leaving them to their business.[32] The season ended without the seizure of a Canadian ship, and by October 14 the entire fleet had returned safely to port. Lord

---

[29] Pauncefote to Salisbury, July 3, 1890, Foreign Office 5/2109.

[30] New York *Herald*, July 24, 1890; New York *World*, July 24, 1890; New York *Times*, July 25, 1890.

[31] J. B. Alexander to British Consul in San Francisco, August 25, 1890, Foreign Office 5/2111. The dinner was on August 19. The Admiralty also received information at about the same time that Washington had ordered that British vessels not be molested. Foreign Office to Salisbury, August 22, 1890, Foreign Office 5/2110.

[32] Pauncefote to Salisbury, July 31, 1890, Foreign Office 5/2109; Rear Admiral Charles F. Hotham to Admiralty, September 10, 1890, Great Britain, Foreign Office, *White Paper, United States, No. 1 (1891): Further Correspondence Respecting the Behring Sea Seal Fisheries* (London, 1891), 17.

Salisbury had already sanctioned the release for service else-where of the warships set aside for an emergency in the Bering Sea.[33]

Thus were surmounted the dangers of 1890. In the face of Lord Salisbury's readiness to use force the United States had refrained from acting against the sealers. But a new sealing time would soon be at hand. When it came the President would again be obligated to order the arrest of pelagic sealers enter-ing "all the dominion of the United States," and presumably the Prime Minister would again detail warships to prevent such arrests. Foreboding rumors already were rife at the beginning of 1891. Fast American "coasting steamers" with considerable fire-power would shortly be stationed in the Bering Sea, it was said, and an American fleet would be mobilized in the Pacific comprising 23 ships, 118 guns, and 3,000 men, a force that would outclass the British Pacific fleet.[34] "As affairs will be next season in Behring Sea between Canada and the powerful company leasing our Pribyloff Islands," an editorial in the New York *Her-ald* warned, "an indiscreet or hot headed commander of a Brit-ish cruiser or an American revenue cutter may fire a hostile gun, letting loose popular passions now smouldering on the Pacific coast and elsewhere that neither the American Congress nor the British Parliament can control short of war."[35] So preva-lent were the rumors that Secretary Blaine thought it wise to reassure Pauncefote.[36] It was evident that the Anglo-Canadian-American disaccord continued to present explosive possibilities.

Washington's discomfiture in early 1891, already great be-cause of the revelation of the secret British naval orders, was increased by the embarrassing reports for 1890 (made public on February 10, 1891) from the Treasury Department agents

[33] Hotham to Admiralty (telegram), October 14, 1890, *White Paper, United States, No. 1 (1891)*, 18; MacGregor, Admiralty, to Under-Secretary of State, Foreign Office, September 11, 1890, Foreign Office 5/2111.

[34] London *Times*, January 6, 1891. For other reports see New York *Sun*, Janu-ary 7, 1891; New York *World*, January 18, 1891; Washington *Post*, January 21, 1891.

[35] New York *Herald*, January 23, 1891.

[36] Pauncefote to Salisbury, January 20, 1891, Foreign Office 5/2134.

stationed in the Pribilof Islands. All four agents attested to an alarming decrease in the number of seals; and three of them, more significantly, put the blame on land as well as pelagic sealing. The chief agent, Charles J. Goff, advised that the seals could be saved from extinction only by suspending killings on land and at sea "for an indefinite number of years." [37]

Even more significant was the report of Henry W. Elliott, which introduces a third underlying influence in the Bering Sea crisis. When the Alaska Commercial Company left the Pribilof Islands in 1890, Congress sent Elliott, the country's leading authority on fur seals, to the islands as a special agent of the Treasury Department, with the commission of investigating the state of affairs left by the old lessee. [38] Nearly twenty years earlier, in 1872, and again in 1874 and 1876, Elliott had visited these islands. While there he married a native girl, learned to speak the native language, and assiduously studied the fur seals. With considerable skill as a writer and artist to supplement his qualifications as a naturalist, Elliott depicted seal life vividly in numerous articles, books, and sketches. His early experiences on the islands made a profound and lasting impression upon him. The astonishing spectacle of millions of seals stretching out before him drove home to the young man an intense feeling for the inexhaustible abundance and prodigality of nature. From that time on, though he earned his livelihood in real estate, Elliott devoted his life to the welfare of the fur seals of the Bering Sea.

When Elliott arrived on the Pribilof Islands in 1890, for the first time since 1876, he was stunned to discover that the once

[37] Charles J. Goff to William Windom, July 31, 1890, *Senate Exec. Docs.*, 51 Cong., 2 Sess., No. 49 (Serial 2818), 6. See also Joseph Murray to Goff, July 31, 1890, *ibid.*, 8; Albert W. Lavender to Goff, July 26, 1890, *ibid.*, 9; and S. R. Nettleton to Goff, July 31, 1890, *ibid.*, 32. On reading these reports, John Anderson, a British Colonial Office expert on Canadian affairs, made the surprising comment: "It is evident . . . that the new Treasury Agents are deliberately cooking a case against the so called 'pirates.'" Minute by Anderson, March 10, 1891, Public Record Office, Colonial Office 42/808.

[38] *Cong. Record*, 51 Cong., 1 Sess., 2596–97 (March 25, 1890). The bill providing for an investigation was signed by the President on April 5, 1890. *Ibid.*, 3188 (April 9, 1890).

magnificent herd had shrunk to a mere fifth of its former size. It was no doubt largely in response to his pleading that Treasury Agent Charles J. Goff took the courageous step of ordering the North American Commercial Company, just embarking upon its first season, to discontinue killings after taking only 21,000 seals — barely one third the total of 60,000 permitted under the lease.[39] Elliott returned to Washington in September, 1890, and his report, completed in November, declared unequivocally that the seals had been injured by land sealing no less than by pelagic sealing. He recommended that commercial killing on the islands be prohibited for seven years, that an Anglo-American commission of experts be appointed to advise on desirable regulations, and that, meanwhile, pelagic sealing be banned.[40] Elliott and Secretary of the Treasury William Windom discussed these radical recommendations with Secretary Blaine on November 19, 1890, and again on January 6, 1891, at Blaine's residence in Lafayette Square.[41] Blaine must have heard with consternation the charge by the country's leading expert that land sealing was just as blameworthy as pelagic sealing for the decline in the herd. A more awkward statement at this juncture could not readily be imagined. If disclosed, Elliott's opinions would lend support to the British request for the regulation of sealing on land as expressed in their counterproposal of April, 1890. Furthermore, Blaine's influential friends in the North American Commercial Company would certainly repel any suggestion that they discontinue operations. Obviously, then, this explosive report must not be made public. Elliott agreed to suppress it, but only on Blaine's promise to pro-

[39] Elliott put the number of seals in 1874 at 4,700,000; in 1890 at 959,655. "In re Fur-Seal Investigation — Facts of Record Which Show the Decline of the Fur-Seal Herd of Alaska and the Cause of That Destruction of This Fine Public Property," Hearings before House Committee, 63 Cong., 2 Sess., *Investigation of the Fur-Seal Industry of Alaska*, Appendix, p. 53. See also Goff to George R. Tingle, July 8, 1890, *Senate Exec. Docs.*, 51 Cong., 2 Sess., No. 49, pp. 13–14.

[40] Elliott's report was not printed until 1896. See *House Exec. Docs.*, 54 Cong., 1 Sess., No. 175 (Serial 3421).

[41] Hearings before House Committee, 63 Cong., 2 Sess., *Investigation of the Fur-Seal Industry of Alaska*, 147.

hibit land sealing if Great Britain would prohibit pelagic sealing.[42]

About the beginning of 1891 a representative of the North American Commercial Company, reportedly Mills, called on Secretary Blaine. He told the Secretary that almost one hundred British and Canadian vessels were preparing to seal in 1891, with enormously enhanced destructive power; and he warned that unless the administration pursued a strong policy in the Bering Sea the Republicans would suffer in the elections of 1892 for "running away from Lord Salisbury last year."[43] Powerful indeed were such arguments to a man as intensely partisan in politics and nationalistic in foreign policy as Blaine. But there were also grave dangers in an uncompromising stand. Blaine well remembered Lord Salisbury's preparations a few months earlier to dispatch British warships to the Bering Sea. Equally compelling, perhaps, were the embarrassing reports of the Treasury agents. The Secretary was vulnerable to accusations of favoritism to big business; and openly to permit the North American Commercial Company to take seals, in the face of the unanimous expert testimony, could convict him and the administration of having sold out to a grasping business concern. This reaction would be certain if Elliott's authoritative report should leak out. Clearly the government was in a predicament. The only escape from it — since neither another capitulation nor a resort to force was politically feasible — lay through an agreement with Great Britain.

In this dilemma the administration moved awkwardly and in a manner indicative of disagreement within itself. It first offered the British a *modus vivendi* sponsored by Blaine, and then some three weeks later it offered another, quite different, plan, sponsored by Harrison. After consulting the President, Blaine proposed the first *modus* to Pauncefote on March 16,

---

[42] Elliott to the Editor, May 25, 1893, New York *Times*, May 29, 1893. Regarding the report's suppression, see Charles Foster to Secretary of State John W. Foster, February 23, 1893, *House Reports*, 63 Cong., 2 Sess., No. 500, Pt. 2 (Serial 6559), 15.

[43] Unsigned memorandum, March 4, 1891, Salisbury Papers.

1891: pending arbitration, the United States would not interfere with British vessels outside territorial waters in the Bering Sea if Great Britain would prevent them from approaching within twenty-five miles of the Pribilof Islands.[44] The prescription was ingenious. If Great Britain accepted it, the Secretary could claim to have closed a vital area to pelagic sealers; if, however, heedful of Canada, the British refused, he could with great plausibility attach the blame for any serious consequences squarely on their shoulders, and rally the country behind him. All this could be accomplished without sacrificing the North American Commercial Company, since it could kill up to the full quota and at the same time be assured of greater profits through a new limitation of pelagic sealing.

Sometime after March 16, however, President Harrison had second thoughts. On April 3, Sir Julian called on the Secretary at his home, and there, by order of the President (though he did not tell Pauncefote so), Blaine proposed an alternative *modus*: the cessation of all killing of seals, both at sea and on land, pending arbitration.[45] This offer, envisaging a complete prohibition of land sealing, was so contrary to the American government's unwavering stand up to that moment that Pauncefote was skeptical of its sincerity. He advised Salisbury that it probably was not meant to be a serious offer, but that Blaine hoped to use it to keep the Bering Sea question open for electioneering purposes during the coming political campaign — "his intention being to charge us with the extermination of the seals & of a valuable American interest, on a mere plea of strict & technical legal right, & to throw odium on the Democrats for their lack of patriotism in not backing him up in his struggle to defend American property from destruction."[46]

At some point during these discussions with Pauncefote, Sec-

[44] Pauncefote to Salisbury, March 16, 1891, Foreign Office 5/2135.

[45] Blaine to Harrison, April 29, 1891, Albert T. Volwiler (ed.), *The Correspondence between Benjamin Harrison and James G. Blaine, 1882–1893* (Philadelphia, 1940), 146; Pauncefote to Salisbury, May 4, 1891, *White Paper, United States, No. 2 (1891)*, 5. Tansill, *Canadian-American Relations*, 322, is incorrect in stating that the proposal originated with Pauncefote.

[46] Pauncefote to Salisbury, April 7, 1891, Salisbury Papers.

retary Blaine confided to Mills that the North American Commercial Company might be precluded from sealing.[47] Already sorely disappointed at having been restricted to approximately one third of their contract quota of skins in 1890, Mills and his colleagues were now dismayed at the prospect of no killings at all as their second season drew near. Believing that prompt action was necessary to avoid being pushed completely out of the Pribilof Islands, the company sent a long letter of protest to the new Secretary of the Treasury, Charles Foster. This letter sought first to discredit Elliott, whom the company suspected of intriguing against itself, by charging that he was secretly in the pay of the Alaska Commercial Company, which had boasted on losing the lease in 1890 that it would destroy the new lessee within two years. The letter also contended that although the government admittedly had the right to designate the number of seals to be killed it had no right to stop killings altogether.[48] This pressure on Secretary Foster was matched by the most effective pressure possible on Blaine. He was approached by his close friend, financial adviser, and political backer, Stephen B. Elkins, on behalf of the North American Commercial Company.[49] Elkins had already been in touch with Blaine for several months about sealing matters and, according to one of Pauncefote's informants, he had now succeeded in persuading the Secretary not to conclude Harrison's *modus* but

[47] Unsigned memorandum dated April 26, 1891, enclosed with Pauncefote to Salisbury, April 28, 1891, *ibid.*

[48] D. Ogden Mills to Charles Foster, April 2, 1891, Hearings before House Committee, 63 Cong., 2 Sess., *Investigation of the Fur-Seal Industry of Alaska*, 306–307. Elliott admitted that he had performed a few special assignments for the Alaska Commercial Company but denied several times under oath that he had ever been a regular employee; and there can be little doubt that he was telling the truth. For his connection with the company see especially *House Exec. Docs.*, 44 Cong., 1 Sess., No. 83 (Serial 1687), 169–70; *House Reports*, 44 Cong., 1 Sess., No. 623 (Serial 1712), 76–86; *House Exec. Docs.*, 62 Cong., 1 Sess., No. 93 (Serial 6113), 448–53, 988–89, 1153–62.

[49] Unsigned memorandum dated April 26, 1891, enclosed in Pauncefote to Salisbury, April 28, 1891, Salisbury Papers. See also Great Britain, Foreign Office, *Blue Book, United States, No. 3 (1892): Further Correspondence Respecting the Behring Sea Seal Fisheries* (London, 1892), 6, citing Boston *Herald* of about April 27, 1891.

to permit the company to kill as many seals as it wished, with any excess over 60,000 to be charged against the deficiency of 39,000 in 1890.[50]

Soon after Mills's letter appeared at the Treasury Department and Elkins himself at the State Department the administration changed to a policy which was more favorable to the North American Commercial Company. First, the Treasury removed Charles J. Goff about April 5, 1891, and replaced him as chief agent on the Pribilof Islands with an inexperienced man; but for the time being this step was kept secret. Then, on April 10, the President issued the usual warning to pelagic sealers not to enter "all the dominion of the United States" in the Bering Sea. Finally, on April 11, Secretary Foster secretly gave the company a permit to kill 60,000 seals in 1891. The last action was taken on Blaine's assurance that Great Britain was refusing to accept a closed season and that, consequently, penalizing land sealing would be unfair.[51] Since the second American proposal for a *modus* had been handed to Pauncefote only eight days previously, it was decidedly premature to charge the British with being unco-operative; and the New York *Times*, when it learned about the secret permit, called for an investigation of the "sealing scandal" it attributed to the Secretary of State.[52]

Having thus reassured Elkins and Mills, President Harrison and Secretary Blaine felt free to leave Washington; the former on a political trip to the West Coast, the latter for a rest at Virginia Beach. While they were away from the capital's tortu-

[50] New York *Times*, December 21, 1891. Unsigned memorandum dated April 26, 1891, enclosed in Pauncefote to Salisbury, April 28, 1891, Salisbury Papers.

[51] In his letter of April 28, 1891, to Salisbury, Pauncefote wrote: "The Coy have actually forced Mr. Blaine to dismiss . . . Goff." Goff himself said "I have long expected something of the kind. The North American Commercial Company was dissatisfied with me because I recommended complete cessation of the taking of seals for another year." Washington *Post*, May 3, 1891. For the dismissal of Goff and his assistants, Albert W. Lavender, see Hearings before House Committee, 63 Cong., 2 Sess., *Investigation of the Fur-Seal Industry of Alaska*, 142–45. Regarding the secret permit see Foster to Elliott, January 11, 1895, *ibid.*, 309, and Elliott to the Editor, May 25, 1893, New York *Times*, May 29, 1893.

[52] New York *Times*, December 21, 1891.

ous affairs, two telegrams arrived at the British Legation from Lord Salisbury. The first informed Pauncefote that Canada had done the unexpected and had agreed, as a temporary measure, to Blaine's original proposal for a *modus vivendi*, namely, that pelagic sealing be banned within a radius of twenty-five miles of the Pribilof Islands. The second dispatch stated that the Prime Minister himself preferred the alternative Harrison proposal — that sealing be discontinued on land and at sea. In accord with his chief's preference, Sir Julian informed Blaine about the second communication.[53]

This unexpected news placed the administration in an awkward predicament. It could not easily welcome Salisbury's compliance and proceed to ban sealing, if only from reluctance to outrage the North American Commercial Company, just assured it could kill 60,000 seals. Nor could it withdraw its proposal; for such a step would have been most damaging politically, as Blaine advised the President.[54] Caught off balance, Harrison and Blaine replied to London in a manner reflecting their discomfiture. The President, well started on his western trip, now imposed a condition on his acceptance of his own offer, namely, that Britain permit the lessee to kill sufficient seals to compensate it for the cost of supporting the natives. To this amendment Blaine added a condition of his own, that the *modus* should not become effective until agreement was reached on terms of arbitration.[55] Sir Julian's letter to Lord Salisbury concerning the addition of these conditions contains the following revealing account of his interview with Blaine:

> You will see . . . that Mr. Blaine is now trying to back out of his proposal for a "modus vivendi." I feel convinced that he made the proposal *under the belief that it would be refused* & with the

[53] Governor-General to Colonial Office, April 2, 1891, Foreign Office 5/2136; Salisbury to Pauncefote, April 17, 1891, *White Paper, United States, No. 2 (1891)*, 1; Pauncefote to Blaine, April 20, 1891, *Papers Relating to the Foreign Relations of the United States, 1891* (Washington, 1892), 552.

[54] Blaine to Harrison, April 29, 1891, Volwiler (ed.), *Correspondence between Harrison and Blaine*, 146.

[55] Harrison to Blaine, April 24, 1891, *ibid.*, 144; Pauncefote to Salisbury, April 27, 1891, *White Paper, United States, No. 2 (1891)*, 3.

intention of using such refusal as a weapon with which to attack us as being intractable in regard to any measure for the preservation of the Seals. For that reason I pressed him very hotly in my interview of yesterday . . . to agree to the modus vivendi being put in force at once to save the coming fishery season & in the meantime to send a Joint Commission to the spot to collect materials for the arbitration on the question of a close time. He clearly saw that I had guessed that his object was to hold us up to public indignation for refusing to cooperate in any measure for the preservation of the seals, & he was evidently disconcerted & angry, for he threw to the ground with much violence a Despatch which he held in his hand, when I remarked that if the modus vivendi were too late for this season it certainly would not be the fault of H.M. Govt. The fact is no doubt that the powerful Compy (with D. O. Mills & Elkins) exert an irresistible influence over him for electioneering purposes, & *they will not hear of the modus vivendi.*

Blaine never dreamed (I feel sure) that Your Lordship would listen to it. He finds himself therefore in a dilemma, & if Your Lordship approves of the language I held to him . . . I think it would be well that I should be authorized so to inform him, & thus place on record for publication the fact that H.M.G. have offered to accept the modus vivendi & to put it in force unconditionally & at once.[56]

Just prior to this interview the administration's distress had been vastly increased by a series of developments within its own circles. At a Washington party on April 11, 1891, a lady present overheard the attorney of the North American Commercial Company, N. L. Jeffries, boasting of the secret permit issued by Secretary Foster that very day. This lady had recently been told by Pauncefote, at another party, that an agreement to suspend sealing was near. Suspecting trickery, she consulted Henry W. Elliott. Elliott, furious at this indication that Blaine had broken his promise to halt land sealing, persuaded his fellow Ohioan, Congressman William McKinley, to demand an explanation from Foster. Reluctantly, Foster confessed that the permit did exist, but excused himself on the ground that Lon-

[56] Pauncefote to Salisbury, April 28, 1891, Salisbury Papers.

don was being "ugly" about a closed season.[57] Elliott now took an unusual step for one still employed by the Treasury Department. He called on Pauncefote on April 22 and inquired boldly whether Foster's characterization of the British position was warranted. On receiving Sir Julian's indignant denial, he immediately wrote a letter to the New York *Evening Post*, revealing the existence of the secret permit. The letter was published on April 24, and Elliott was dismissed from the Treasury the next day.[58] Unabashed, and with a minimum of delay, he proceeded to release additional confidential material, including the introduction to his suppressed report. Appearing in the Cleveland *Leader and Morning Herald* on May 4, 1891, this statement contained the startling recommendation that "no driving and killing of fur-seals . . . be permitted by the Government for a period of at least seven years."[59]

To Harrison on the West Coast these disclosures came with bewildering impact, and hard upon them came reproaches from Secretary Blaine. It was "embarrassing" to resist Sir Julian's pressure for a closed season, the Secretary telegraphed, "in view of the fact that abstaining from sealing this year was first suggested by yourself"; and "embarrassing," too, "not to have advantage of your presence for a decision."[60] Berated by his Secretary of State, disconcerted by the revelation of the secret permit, outmaneuvered by Britain's apparent readiness to accept his *modus*, the harried President had no option but to cancel the permit and to instruct Blaine to negotiate.[61] To this resolve he held fast despite three indignant letters from the North American Commer-

[57] Hearings before House Committee, 63 Cong., 2 Sess., *Investigation of the Fur-Seal Industry of Alaska*, 147–48.

[58] *Ibid.*, 148, 160–61, 309–10; *House Exec. Docs.*, 62 Cong., 1 Sess., No. 93, p. 1155.

[59] The introduction was reprinted in *White Paper, United States, No. 2 (1891)*, 53–61.

[60] Blaine to Harrison, April 29, 1891, Volwiler (ed.), *Correspondence between Harrison and Blaine*, 146–47. The New York *Times*, May 3, 1891, thought that Blaine was trying to excuse himself by blaming Harrison.

[61] Harrison to Blaine, April 30, 1891, Volwiler (ed.), *Correspondence between Harrison and Blaine*, 147; New York *Times*, December 21, 1891.

cial Company and an oral protest made to him, after he returned to Washington on May 15, by Attorney N. L. Jeffries.[62]

The administration was now in headlong flight. Just as in 1890 it had been routed by Britain's preparation to use force in the Bering Sea, so in 1891, after first being brought to a sudden halt by her unexpected acceptance of Harrison's *modus*, it was thrown into hopeless disarray by Elliott's disclosures. Secretary Blaine formally offered a new *modus vivendi* to Pauncefote on May 4, 1891. He proposed that until May 1, 1892, neither the United States nor Great Britain permit pelagic sealing and that the United States limit killings on the islands to 7,500, a number just sufficient, he contended, to compensate the North American Commercial Company for its expenses in caring for the natives. To this he added a curious insistence that an arbitral award be rendered before the terminal date of the *modus*, that is, May 1, 1892.[63]

It is unnecessary to describe the maneuvering that ensued. To Pauncefote must go the main credit for the eventual agreement. When Lord Salisbury wavered at one point, the Minister adjured him several times not to reject the *modus*; and it was doubtless because of these urgings that the Prime Minister reconsidered and twice cabled Ottawa to change its mind.[64] To say that the Canadians yielded would be misleading. They did agree "reluctantly" to accept the *modus* provided the sealers were compensated, the legality of the arrests was arbitrated, and interference with British sealers ceased pending an award.[65]

[62] Mills to Harrison, May 4, 1891; Jeffries to Foster, May 7 and 15, 1891; and Foster to Harrison, May 18, 1891, Harrison Papers, Vol. 122.

[63] Blaine to Pauncefote, May 4, 1891, *Foreign Relations, 1891,* p. 555.

[64] Lord Stanley to Pauncefote, May 12, 1891, Confidential Correspondence, America, Seal Fishing in Behring's Sea, 1891 (Foreign Office Library), 194; Pauncefote to Salisbury, May 13, 1891, *ibid.*; Pauncefote to Salisbury, May 17 and 20, 1891, *ibid.*, 204A, 214; Salisbury to Pauncefote, May 21, 1891, *ibid.*, 215; Pauncefote to Salisbury, May 22, 1891, *ibid.*, 216; Pauncefote to Salisbury, May 10, 1891, *ibid.*, 190; Cables of May 17 and 23, 1891, to the Governor-General, quoted in Charles H. Tupper to the Governor-General, June 15, 1891, Foreign Office 5/2141.

[65] Governor-General to Colonial Office, May 27, 1891, quoted in Tupper to Governor-General, June 15, 1891, Foreign Office 5/2141. Tupper referred to

But Salisbury seized hastily upon the essential point, that
Canada would agree, and blandly disregarded the qualifications. He ordered a bill to be submitted at once to Parliament
prohibiting Bering Sea sealing, and it became law in June,
1891.[66] Sir Julian was overjoyed. The news, he predicted, would
be "a crushing blow" to Blaine, who had done his utmost to prevent such a development in order to throw on Britain the odium
of refusing to save the fur seals.[67]

Once Washington could no longer evade an agreement to
suspend killing on land, and once Canada had consented, even
partially, to suspend killing at sea, the conclusion of a *modus
vivendi* was virtually assured. Certainly the consternation of the
pelagic sealers on learning what was afoot could not stave it off.
They protested to Charles H. Tupper, the Canadian Minister
of Marine and Fisheries, against any suspension of pelagic sealing; the premier of British Columbia supported their complaints; the president of the British Columbia Board of Trade
begged the Canadian High Commissioner in London to protest
in the "strongest possible manner."[68] But Great Britain replied
to Blaine's offer of May 4, 1891, by accepting the unequal proposition that 7,500 seals could be killed on land and none at sea.
The British did insist, however, that provision be made for a
joint commission of experts to determine what arrangements,
if any, were needed to safeguard the seals.[69] Washington hesitated. Exposing their company's intimate activities on the Pribilof Islands to British eyes would not be relished by Mills, Elkins, and their colleagues, already disgruntled.[70] The eventual

conditions named in Pauncefote to Blaine, June 27, 1890, *Blue Book, United States, No. 2 (1890)*, 511.

[66] Salisbury to Pauncefote, May 28, 1891, *White Paper, United States, No. 2 (1891)*, 11; *Parliamentary Debates*, 3rd Series, Vol. 353, 24 Parl., 6 Sess., 1631–34 (June 4, 1891), 1805–11 (June 8, 1891).

[67] Pauncefote to Salisbury, May 28, 1891, Salisbury Papers.

[68] Cox to Tupper, June 1, 1891, *Blue Book, United States, No. 3 (1892)*, 29; Marvin and Company to Tupper, June 5, 1891, *ibid.*, 61–63; Sir William S. Robson to Edgar Dewdney, June 2, 1891, *ibid.*, 28; J. G. Colmer to Colonial Office, June 3, 1891, *ibid.*, 12.

[69] Salisbury to Pauncefote, June 2 and 8, 1891; *ibid.*, 8, 13–14.

[70] Pauncefote to Salisbury, June 6 and 7, 1891, Foreign Office 5/2138.

compromise was that British observers, but not a joint commission, could visit the islands in anticipation of an arbitration, and that a full-scale joint commission would be appointed on conclusion of an arbitration treaty.[71]

Blaine became ill in May and left Washington for the summer, and the last stage of the negotiation was carried on between Pauncefote and Acting Secretary of State William F. Wharton, who signed the *modus vivendi* on June 15, 1891. The United States and Great Britain each agreed to prohibit pelagic sealing until May 1, 1892; and the United States agreed to prohibit killings in excess of 7,500 on the Pribilof Islands.[72] Nothing was said about Blaine's stipulation that an arbitral award must be returned by May 1, 1892.

The British and American governments may have been satisfied, but the North American Commercial Company most certainly was not. In a sarcastic letter to Secretary Foster it protested "against any order to cease sealing until the English law and proclamation have been executed and poaching has been discontinued; for what would it profit the United States, the lessee, or the fur-seal industry to direct the poachers to cease killing if they are beyond the reach of communication or if from any other cause the law and proclamation are not enforced"; and then, in a subsequent, more forceful letter, it gave notice of its intention to file a claim for any loss sustained because of the prohibition of land sealing.[73]

The Canadians were furious. Not a word did the *modus* say about their prime objective: payment of damages. The record does not show that Ottawa was consulted in the final stages of the negotiations. On the contrary, once Lord Salisbury had an excuse to go ahead, in the form of the Dominion's qualified consent, he hastened to get the agreement he wanted, while remaining completely silent about the qualifications the Canadi-

[71] Pauncefote to William F. Wharton, June 13, 1891, and Wharton to Pauncefote, June 13, 1891, *Foreign Relations, 1891*, pp. 569–70.

[72] *Ibid.*, 570.

[73] Jeffries to Foster, June 3, 1891, Harrison Papers, Vol. 123; Jeffries to Acting Secretary of the Treasury Oliver L. Spaulding, June 19, 1891, *Blue Book, United States, No. 3 (1892)*, 47.

ans wanted. In an acid memorandum, Tupper in effect accused Great Britain of dereliction of duty.[74] His indignation is comprehensible enough; but if the Canadians were not altogether in the wrong neither were they altogether beyond reproach. Pelagic sealing posed more of a threat to the fur-seal herd than they admitted, and it was fortunate not only for Anglo-Canadian-American friendship but for the seals as well that the *modus* was concluded.

The *modus* did not, of course, bring a final settlement. When it expired the next year, much difficult negotiation was required before an arbitration treaty could be arranged and an arbitration held in Paris in 1893. And for several years bitter words continued to pass between London, Ottawa, and Washington about the well-discussed fur seals. Nevertheless it is apparent that the controversy's turning point came in 1890 and 1891, when the combination of British readiness to protect Canadian sealers and Elliott's disclosure of the urgent need for restriction of sealing both on land and at sea forced the United States to accept an agreement unfavorable to the administration's influential friends in the North American Commercial Company. And once Canada had discontinued unregulated pelagic sealing, neither the United States nor Canada could conceivably have reverted to practices dangerous to the peace. After 1891 the Bering Sea held but few menaces for Anglo-American friendship.

[74] Tupper to Governor-General, June 15, 1891, Foreign Office 5/2141.

Jeannette Nichols received her doctorate from Columbia University and taught for many years at the University of Pennsylvania. Her classic Alaska . . . During Its First Half Century under the Rule of the United States, *published in 1924, is still one of the very few scholarly volumes available for the study of Alaskan history. The following essay is reprinted from the* Washington Historical Quarterly, *XIII (January, 1922), 20–26.*

Advertising and the Klondike[1]

JEANNETTE PADDOCK NICHOLS

With the advance of civilization come additional factors in the shaping of the courses of historical events. Along with the broadening of business activities has come the growth of a new science, advertising. We have had much written on the various economic phases of history, but, prior to the recent war propaganda, little or no attention has been paid to the possible effect of skillful advertising on history.

The American business man is continually in search of new fields of productivity. Although the breadth of his vision has never been exactly measured, it is known that he has played no small part in showing the Nation where to plant the flagstaff. His efforts have never been confined to small areas or to those close at hand. Sometimes the Orient, often the Caribbean,

[1] The basis for this study is a scrapbook collection of fourteen volumes entitled "Alaska and the Klondike" which was given the Library of Congress by Mr. Erastus Brainerd, who was Secretary of the Bureau of Information of the Seattle Chamber of Commerce during the period referred to. The collection includes manuscripts, telegrams, printed cards and circulars and the formal report of the Bureau to the Chamber dated March 1, 1898.

and occasionally even the Northwest have beckoned insist-
ently. The period of the Klondike craze in the last three years
of the nineteenth century is one of these occasions. It illustrates
an influential factor in the removal of the "last frontier" by
"westward expansion". This factor is advertisement.

During the autumn and early winter of 1897 the Klondike
rush promised growth and profit to the Pacific Coast cities.
Their thinking business men and boomers reasoned in this wise:

1. Outfitting of would-be Klondikers must mean money in the
   pockets of whoever sold the outfits.
2. Any given city would have all the trade which no other city
   seized.
3. Any means of diverting the flow of travel and trade from
   opposing cities was good business and permissible ethics
   from the point of view of the competing metropolis.
4. Incidentally a certain amount of service might be claimed as
   rendered to the public.

This reasoning brought on an inter-city rivalry which can be
understood by a discussion of Seattle's part in it.

On July 19, 1897, a certain Thomas J. Church wrote from
Chicago to General J. B. Metcalf of Seattle, describing the interest of midwesterners in Klondike possibilities, and the efforts
of the Southern Pacific to direct the route of travel toward San
Francisco. Similarly, the Canadian Pacific was advertising Vancouver and Victoria; the Oregon Washington Railway and Navigation Company, Portland; the Great Northern, Seattle; and
the Northern Pacific both Portland and Seattle. General Metcalf showed this letter to Mr. Cooper, a prominent business man,
with the result that a meeting of the Seattle Chamber of Commerce was called for August 30, following, to consider "measures for widely advertising the city of Seattle as the principal
outfitting point for Alaskan miners and also to counteract the
efforts of other cities in the same direction." At this meeting the
Chamber voted in favor of the appointment of special committees on advertising and finance, to make these measures effective.

Within four days the advertising committee had organized with Mr. E. F. Sweeney as chairman and Mr. Erastus Brainerd, be it noted, as Secretary. These gentlemen were able to prepare a Tentative Project of Work which was rewarded with the cordial approval of the committee. It carried the signatures and united opinion of all the committee members and declared their implicit faith, as business men and members of the Chamber of Commerce, in "elastic publicity". It advised a campaign of paid and unpaid advertising, strongly reinforced by propaganda, for the best results.

Mr. Brainerd at once presented this Project to the Board of Trustees and received their hearty approval and cooperation. He could have the use of the Chamber of Commerce rooms: the Republican State Committee would loan a desk and the cash would come from the business men, taxed according to the probable amount of benefit received by them. The special committee thus became permanent. The excellence of the choice of Mr. Brainerd as paid Secretary, student of psychology, and opportunist, was demonstrated by his energetic prosecution of the twelve points in the Project. Not the means he used, but the adjustment and correlation of them, made his work significant in the history of the Klondike and of advertising. The means employed, classify themselves in four groups: 1) Newspapers and Periodicals; 2) Civic Pride; 3) Circulars; 4) Interlocking Correspondence.

For the purposes of direct advertising, Seattle followed the lead of her competitors in choice of publication and type of advertisement. Because Portland and Victoria had been advertising in the *New York Journal*, Seattle paid $800 for three fourths of a page in a Sunday issue. Similarly, the *American Review of Reviews* had been carrying Canadian matter: *Munsey, McClure, Cosmopolitan, Harper, Century* and *Scribner's* enjoyed patronage with a like motive. The great ardor of each Chamber in correcting the misconceptions created by the others was exploited by the advertising mediums, whose business managers took much pains to follow up each tilt with suggestions that the aggrieved city set the world right by more advertising. Mr.

Brainerd felt these controversies were justifiable if cheap, and used clipping bureaus to inform him of inaccuracies about Seattle, as well as other cities. Taking clipping as an index, Seattle advertised five times as much as her competitors. Also the Secretary wrote feature articles, particularly a well-illustrated one for *Harper's* and one of two columns for the "Jubilee Edition" of the Tacoma *Ledger*. (It is not known why the Tacoma editor offered this courtesy.)

The Associated Press played no favorites. It used material from all sides as plate matter for editorials. At first, Mr. Brainerd felt it a real achievement when Seattle material went into plate editorials. But when his clippings showed him that his competitors were similarly blessed, he learned that most editors could blame the Association for errors on Klondike affairs. Thereafter, he tried to have his corrections placed in that part of a paper devoted to local matter. Thereby, his corrections were more widely read than the original error. Editorials were of course far less valuable than news items, of which an excellent example is the following paragraph widely published under the date line of Seattle, Sept. 3:

"As a result of the Klondike excitement, which has overwhelmed the city with inquiries from all parts of the world as to routes of transportation and cost of outfitting, there has been established, under the auspices of the Chamber of Commerce, a public Bureau of Information."

This confusion of cause and effect passed unnoticed by the general public.

Seattle's periodicals were used for purposes of distribution, to create a cumulative effect when the same correspondent had received a series of periodicals. Newspapers have a natural tendency to exploit themselves by special editions, so the "Klondike Edition" of the Seattle *Post-Intelligencer* served as capital in a gigantic scheme of distribution. It went to: every postmaster in the United States upwards of 70,000; every public library, 6,000; every mayor of a city, nearly 4,000; Great Northern Railway, 10,000; Northern Pacific, 5,000.

When the Secretary undertook to insert small advertisements in county seat newspapers only, he learned that the Western Newspaper Union and other publishing houses customarily mix county seat papers with village issues on the syndicate circulation lists. But he had studied the replies to circulars issued early in the game for hints as to the profitable advertising localities, and was able, by selecting three lists distributed over states in the middle west and southwest, to attain the large circulation of 9,990,400 papers. The most numerous responses to these advertisements came from regions in which an oversupply of labor caused industrial disaffection.

Mr. Brainerd understood the delight of rural townsfolk in published letters from former friends who have "moved away". The only thing necessary was to persuade the movers to send the letters. After experiment, he sent a confidential plea to employers and heads of organizations, explaining why it was not "desirable" to take this step publicly, drawing attention to the special value of personal letters in a neighborly community and asking them to urge their clients, congregations, subordinates, employees and friends, to at once correspond with their old home paper and friends in the East. For this, the Bureau offered to furnish the material all ready for the affixing of names and signatures, to pay the postage, and to post the letters. The "drive" was a psychological success.

The wastebaskets of our public officials mutely testify to the present commercial and political popularity of the circular idea. In 1897, the Seattle Bureau of Information carefully promulgated four circulars, varying with the intended recipient and his intended reaction: 1) To newspapers and publication; 2) To governors and mayors; 3) To important officials everywhere; 4) To Senators and Representatives.

Circular 1 informed every daily in the United States and every publication having over 5,000 circulation, that Seattle was *the* port of departures and outfitting station for the Alaskan gold-fields. It was generally printed by all classes of periodicals — without charge.

Circular 2 asked a number of questions, in order that the conservative business men of Seattle might avoid the pitfalls of stampedes and might inform inquirers as to the facts on the gold fields. Its attraction was enhanced by the Chamber stationery, typewriter type, and the word "dictated" prominently placed in an upper corner. It expressed solicitude for the good of the public. Finally, it inquired for prospective migrants and their place of outfitting. By most of the governors and mayors the circular was referred to their local dailies and printed. The personal response varied inversely with the size and importance of the locality and gave opportunity for a display of humor on the part of the officials of large places.

Mr. Brainerd analysed the replies to these circulars, consulted influential Seattleites, and achieved his masterpiece, Circular 4. This he was able to put forth as an official proclamation, because he persuaded the Secretary of State (of the State of Washington) to sign it. It was a combination of the paternal, advisory, and reassuring: it can have deferred few who had already made up their minds, and must have reassured the timid. For example, although shooting rapids was inadvisable, "Of those who have gone in . . . not more than half a dozen have lost their lives and these from carelessness in fording." (Conditions are still such that it is difficult to prove assertions about Alaska.) All were reminded of the willingness of the Seattle Chamber of Commerce to impart information. Because this message entered the channels of the press via public officials, it was considered seriously at home and abroad. The ministers of France, Belgium, Italy, Switzerland and the Baltic countries sent it as a communication to their governments, by whom it was gratefully printed. This foreign idea was pushed so far as to include Christmas gifts, sent to the crowned heads of Europe, of Alaskan and Klondike photographs and views. The Prince of Wales and President McKinley had a greater liking for their gifts, than did the German Emperor, who refused a package that "might contain dynamite."

The Canadian Pacific Railway and the Dominion cities, proclaimed the advantage of outfitting in Canada, as soon as their Government placed 30% tariff charges at Klondike ports of entry. United States railway officials sent Mr. Brainerd strong protests, and shortly thereafter, he sent Circular 4 to the "representative Americans" comprising the Senate and House of Representatives. As good protectionists, they were petitioned to nourish the "new field of American enterprise" in Alaska and at Seattle. The apparent cooperation of the British Government and the British Columbia Board of Trade, and the alleged activities of Lieutenant Governor McIntosh in diverting Americans from Alaska to the Northwest Territory made a strong case, on the strength of which the encouragement of Americans to outfit in American cities and to prospect on the American Yukon was urged. Quotation was made from a correspondent of *Harper's Weekly,* (Mr. Brainerd) as to the superiority of Seattle for Alaskan trade. Finally, the members of Congress were asked if they would favor an immediate settlement of boundary and tariff issues, the establishment of an army post on the Yukon, and the division of Alaska into two territories.

In spite of their preoccupation, a large number of replies to Circular 4 were received. These were in conformity with our legislative system and indicated an attitude of uninformed wariness. The legislators either refused to commit themselves for lack of knowledge, or reserved the right to change on more complete information. The more active promised to investigate the subject—which indicates the importance of a Chamber of Commerce. Party men remembered senatorial courtesy, as when J. D. Hicks and O. W. Underwood promised to be governed by the opinions of Senator Wilson and Congressman Lewis of Washington. Opposition to the present division of Alaska showed itself, although a better government and a delegate were advocated, in conformity with the national tradition of a colonial policy looking toward self government where possible.

Throughout this advertising campaign, the Seattle business men were bound together by an ingenious system of interlocking correspondence, which quietly gave merchants the names of possible customers and which made them prompt with the dues owing to the Bureau of Information. The nomadic character of western population, personal pique, editorial antipathies, and local pride, wove a network of espionage which was used to inform Seattle of her rival's plans that she might forestall them. All the Coast cities were contending with the railroad officials for the exclusive use of certain special privileges, such as cut rates, passenger running, and distribution of train circulars. Also they were trying to secure definite promises from Secretary of War Alger, for the outfitting of advertising.

Finally, what were the results? As to legislation, the March Report of the Bureau asserts that "No little of the energy and information of Congress shown in its dealing with Alaskan affairs at this session is due to the literature that they have received from this committee." The actual record of the 55th Congress shows an increase of at least 300% in the number of Alaskan bills passed, with a corresponding number which died in committee. Other factors in these increases are not hard to find. The question of the effect of the advertising upon the city of Seattle is equally debatable. Although the census shows an increase of population from 42,837 in 1890 to 80,671 in 1900, this increase was mostly in the laboring population, at the time when Alaska and Seattle both stood in greatest need of capital. It cannot be gainsaid that the Bureau of Information of the Seattle Chamber of Commerce gave momentum to the growth of both the Klondike and Seattle.

Leland Carlson received his Ph.D. from the University of Chicago in 1939, taught at Northwestern University, was president of Rockford College, and is now a professor at Claremont Graduate School and School of Theology. Dr. Carlson's main interest is in modern English history. His article on the discovery of gold at Nome appeared in the Pacific Historical Review, XV (September, 1946), 259–78.

The Discovery of Gold at Nome, Alaska

L. H. CARLSON

he average educated American associates the discovery of gold in Alaska with the days of '98, Dawson City, and the Klondike. He is surprised to learn that gold was discovered before 1898, that Dawson City is not in Alaska, and that the Klondike is not a river within the territory of the United States.

Gold was discovered in Alaska long before 1898. Even before the United States acquired Alaska in 1867, the Russians had found gold, but they discouraged any systematic search lest their fur trade suffer.[1] In Canadian territory adjoining Alaska, gold had been found on the Fraser River in 1858, and on the upper waters of the Stikine in 1861. During the next two decades miners prospected many of the numerous creeks of south-

[1] Peter Doroshin, a mining engineer of the Russian American Company, had discovered gold in the Kenai River basin in 1850 (Merle Colby, *A Guide to Alaska, Last American Frontier* [New York, 1939], p. 66).

ern Alaska. From this prospecting came two significant developments, which led directly to the stampedes up to Dawson City and Nome. In 1880 Joe Juneau and Dick Harris discovered rich deposits in Silver Bow Basin, and thereby initiated in 1881 the first gold rush in Alaska. The second event was the opening of the Dyea-Chilkoot Pass to American prospectors.[2] In 1879 a party of twenty prospectors had attempted to cross the Chilkoot Pass but had been prevented from ascending the trail by the Indians, who feared that their monopoly of the Yukon fur trade might be destroyed if the passes were opened to American gold hunters.

With the aid of Captain L. A. Beardslee, commander of the S. S. *Jamestown*, and with the cooperation of a naval lieutenant who dramatically explained the workings of a Gatling gun to the natives, the prospectors were successful. On May 29, 1880, the Dyea-Chilkoot gate was opened to white men for the first time. Thereafter a few hardy prospectors crossed the pass each year, explored the headwaters of the Yukon, and prospected the more accessible tributaries.[3] The lucky strike of Skookum Jim, Tagish Charley, and George Carmack, on Bonanza Creek, a tributary of the Klondike River, on August 17, 1896, caused a small stampede to the Dawson City area.[4] The arrival

[2] The first known white man to cross the Chilkoot Pass was George Holt, who made the ascent in 1878 (MS of William Douglas Johns, p. 62; Newberry Library, Chicago). Other men had been on the upper and the lower Yukon before 1878, but had proceeded up the river via St. Michael or had gone overland. Al Harper was the first man known to prospect for gold on the Yukon in 1872 (*ibid.*, p. 59).

[3] During the period 1880–1896 numerous small discoveries were made. In 1883 George Marks found gold on the bars of Stewart River, and in 1886 a man named Franklin discovered rich deposits near Fortymile River — in Franklin Gulch. The following year about 200 men hurried across the American side of the Yukon (C. L. Andrews, *The Story of Alaska* [Caldwell, Idaho, 1938]). A Russian-Indian half-breed found gold in 1893 on Little Minnook Creek near the lower ramparts of the Yukon, and in 1895 gold was found on Cook Inlet. This last discovery resulted in a rush of 1,500 men to "Sunrise City" in 1896 (W. P. Morrell, *The Gold Rushes* [New York, 1941], p. 401). For the part played by Captain Beardslee and the Gatling gun, see *Reports of Captain L. A. Beardslee, U. S. Navy, Relative to Affairs in Alaska*, 47th Cong., 1st sess. [ser. 1989], Senate Ex. Doc. No. 71 (1882).

[4] The claimants for the honor of being the discoverer of gold are George Carmack, Skookum Jim, and Bob Henderson. Skookum Jim, an Indian native, took

of the *Portland* in Seattle on July 17, 1897, with "a ton of gold," and the spread of wild stories about gold caused a feverish excitement[5] that culminated in the great stampedes of 1897 and 1898 to the Klondike and to the Seward Peninsula in 1898–1900.

The discovery of gold on the Seward Peninsula was bound up with the general prospecting which followed the Klondike rush. Nevertheless, the search for gold at Council City and Cape Nome has a history independent of the Klondike.

Gold had been discovered as early as 1866 in northwestern Alaska. In that year the Western Union Telegraph Company was constructing an overland line through British Columbia and Alaska to St. Michael, thence to the head of Norton Bay and Fish River, up the Niukluk River to Imuruk Basin, Grantley Harbor, Port Clarence, and Cape Prince of Wales, across the Bering Strait to Siberia and Europe. One of the members of this group, Daniel B. Libby,[6] who found colors on a tributary of the Niukluk River, made a few notes on the region and prepared a rough map for later use. Not until 1897, however, when the Klondike reports stirred the whole West Coast, did he decide to act. With the financial backing of some San Francisco capitalists,[7] D. B. Libby, A. P. Mordaunt, L. F. Melsing, and H. L.

---

a frying pan, panned in the creek, and found it "lousy with gold." His white brother-in-law, Carmack, took the credit and also Discovery Claim and No. 1 Below (MS of William Douglas Johns, pp. 110 f. See also *Report of the Director of the Mint . . . 1897*, 55th Cong., 3rd sess. [ser. 3784], House Doc. No. 47 [1898], pp. 76–86, for a different opinion favoring Carmack).

[5] John G. Brady, governor of Alaska, used the term "klondicitis" to describe the universal desire to go to the gold fields (see the "Report of the Governor of Alaska [for 1897]," *Annual Reports of the Department of the Interior — Miscellaneous Reports*, 55th Cong., 2nd sess. [ser. 3642], House Doc. No. 5, pp. 202–203).

[6] Libby Creek, a tributary of Niukluk River, is named for him. Libby had been shown rich samples of gold and silver ore by the natives, but was unable to prevail upon them to reveal the source. He did, however, find placer gold in Ophir Creek (E. S. Harrison, *Nome and Seward Peninsula* [Seattle, 1905], p. 202).

[7] These men were Charles Nelson, a lumber merchant and president of the board of trade, James Tyson, lumber man and shipowner, Corbell Brothers, and one other person whose name is not given (U.S. Circuit Court of Appeals, *P. H. Anderson, Appellant, vs. O. Jose Comptois, Appellee, In the Matter of the Alleged Contempt of Dudley Dubose in Having, It is Said, Advised O. Jose Comptois, the Appellee, to Disobey and Refuse to Comply with the Terms of the Writ of Supersedeas Duly Issued Herein* [3 vols.] II, 576–577).

Blake fitted out a vessel with tools and supplies to last four years, and sailed from San Francisco aboard the *North Fork* on August 18, 1897. From Norton Sound and Golovin Bay, which they reached on September 17, they went up the Fish River for approximately thirty miles, then up the Niukluk River about ten miles and established camp at Council City.[8]

During the fall of 1897 these men prospected the numerous tributary creeks of the Niukluk River. Blake found gold by Ophir Creek, Melsing discovered colors in Melsing Creek, and Mordaunt and Libby made further discoveries.[9] But it was not until April 24, 1898, that they staked claims on Melsing, Ophir, and other creeks; and on April 25 they organized the Discovery District and the Council City District. These were the first claims staked and the first mining districts organized in the Seward Peninsula.[10] The eight men who organized these districts were D. B. Libby, A. P. Mordaunt, L. F. Melsing, H. L. Blake, N. O. Hultberg, P. H. Anderson, J. S. Tornensis, and Dr. A. N. Kittilsen.[11]

[8] Council City was located at the junction of Melsing Creek and Niukluk River. Both the "city" and the creek were named by this party. Ophir Creek, four miles above Melsing Creek, also received its name from these men. Melsing and Ophir creeks were the richest streams in the entire Council City precinct.

[9] See H. L. Blake, "History of the Discovery of Gold at Cape Nome," in 56th Cong., 1st sess. [ser. 3878], Senate Doc. No. 441 (1900), p. 2. This version of Blake's own role must be used with care. It is biased and resentful, and it minimizes the role of others in the discovery of gold at Cape Nome.

[10] This is the first official staking of claims in the Seward Peninsula. It should be noted, however, that Libby had found gold in 1866, that natives had discovered rich gold ores, that a miner named George Johansen had prospected in the Council City region in 1895 (Harrison, *op. cit.*, pp. 216, 273) and that a mining party about 1881 had gone up Fish River sixty-four miles, then eastward up Omalik Creek, a tributary, about eleven miles to Omalik Mountain (see Walter Curran Mendenhall's article. "A Reconnaissance in the Norton Bay Region, Alaska, in 1900," in Alfred Hulse Brooks *et al., Reconnaissances in the Cape Nome and Norton Bay Regions, Alaska, in 1900* [Washington, 1901], 56th Cong., 2nd sess. [ser. 4198], House Doc. No. 547 [1901], p. 189).

[11] Hultberg and Anderson were missionaries at Cheenik; Tornensis was a Lapp reindeer herder, brought to the United States by the Bureau of Education to instruct the Eskimos on the care of reindeer. Hultberg had arrived in Alaska in 1893, Tornensis in 1894, and Anderson in 1897. Dr. Kittilsen arrived at Port Clarence, Alaska, in 1896 as the government's doctor for the reindeer herders. In December, 1897, he proceeded to Unalaklik with the reindeer herd, where he arrived in March, 1898 (Sheldon Jackson, *Report [for 1898] on Introduction*

The discovery of gold at Nome, Alaska, was not the result of a sudden chance strike, such as Skookum Jim and George Carmack made on Bonanza Creek, but it was the result of four separate prospecting trips. The first trip was made in December, 1897. The four men who had proceeded to Council City decided to spend Christmas at Golovin Bay. On their way down Fish River they stopped at a native village to drink tea. A native friend, Too rig Luck, invited Blake to his home and showed him some ore which he had found at Cape Nome while visiting natives there. Finding gold in the ore, Blake hired Too rig Luck to guide him to Cape Nome. On reaching Cheenik, Blake began making arrangements with John A. Dexter [12] for a dog team. Nels O. Hultberg,[13] missionary at Cheenik, having decided to accompany Blake, said: "You had better take reindeer; they will travel faster, and the whole of the government herd is at your disposal, if you want them."[14]

---

of Domestic Reindeer into Alaska, with Maps and Illustrations, 55th Cong., 3d sess. [ser. 3738], Senate Doc. No. 34 [1898], p. 11).

[12] John A. Dexter, a white man who had married an Eskimo, had established a trading station at Cheenik in the fall of 1893 (Supreme Court of Illinois, October Term, 1904; White Star Mining Company of Illinois *v.* Nels O. Hultberg, The Swedish Evangelical Mission Covenant of America, Claes W. Johnson, Peter H. Anderson, Merchants' Loan and Trust Co., *Abstract of Record,* pp. 226, 327; hereafter referred to as *Abstract of Record*). Cheenik is located on a peninsula on the east coast of Golovin Bay. The name is often spelled Chinik, Chinick, and sometimes Chenik. Throughout this paper I have followed the recommended spellings of Marcus Baker's "Geographic Dictionary of Alaska," United States Geological Survey *Bulletin* No. 187, Series F, Geography 27, 57th Cong., 1st sess. [ser. 4366], House Doc. No. 469 (1901).

[13] Nels O. Hultberg was sent in 1893 as a missionary to Alaska by the Swedish Evangelical Mission Covenant of America. He arrived at Golovin Bay on June 30, 1893 (Årsberättelse från Svenska Evangeliska Missions-Förbundets i Amerika, nionde verksamhetsår [1893], p. 20; *Abstract of Record,* p. 326).

[14] In 1891 the United States government, acting through Dr. Sheldon Jackson, introduced reindeer from Siberia into Alaska for the purpose of providing sustenance for the natives, whose food supply had been curtailed by the white man's depredations. One of the methods used by the government was that of lending herds to mission stations and selected persons and permitting them to keep part of the herd's increase.

The words spoken by Hultberg were quoted by H. L. Blake, who later developed an intense hatred of Hultberg because of the latter's success in outwitting Blake and staking claims without informing him (see Blake, *op. cit.,* p. 2). For information on reindeer, the best sources are found in Sheldon Jackson's

Taking six of the best sled deer, Blake and Hultberg set out for Cape Nome on December 28, 1897, with Too rig Luck and one other native guide.[15] Upon reaching the Cape Nome region, Too rig Luck felt uncertain of his exact whereabouts, pondered his directions, then led the party up a very steep mountain, stopped suddenly and said "Marney," meaning "Here." Blake cleared away the snow, dug out some quartz, and carried it to his tent. The next day [16] Blake and Hultberg came to a frozen creek,[17] panned at several open places, found gold each time, and on two occasions got excellent prospects. Concluding that it was a very rich creek, Hultberg suggested the plan of staking claims, but Blake replied that it would be better to return in the spring when the ice had gone, in order to prospect more thoroughly the creek.[18]

About January 13, 1898, Blake and Hultberg set out for Golovin Bay. They encountered a Russian *poorga*, one of those dreaded Arctic blizzards. The wind was so powerful, and the snow so blinding, that it was necessary for the men to crawl. They managed to reach the native village of Opiktillik on January 15 — with frozen cheeks and noses. There, to their great surprise, they encountered two white men, Lieutenant D. H. Jarvis and Surgeon S. J. Call, on their way to Point Barrow.[19]

In the latter part of January, 1898, Blake and Hultberg re-

---

sixteen annual reports, 1891–1906. All the reports except the first were published as Senate documents.

[15] *Abstract of Record*, p. 329.

[16] January 3 or 4, 1898. The party camped at the mouth of Nome River January 2 (*Abstract of Record*, p. 330).

[17] Blake claims that this was Anvil Creek — the richest and most famous creek of the Seward Peninsula. Hultberg testified that he and Blake crossed Snake River, prospected westward toward Penny River, but did not prospect on Anvil Creek, which is east of Snake River. Hultberg is probably more accurate than Blake (see *Abstract of Record*, p. 330).

[18] Blake, *op. cit.*, p. 3.

[19] These two men were part of one of the pluckiest and most dramatic rescue expeditions ever undertaken in Alaska. The story is graphically told in *Report of the Cruise of the U. S. Revenue Cutter Bear and the Overland Expedition for the Relief of the Whalers in the Arctic Ocean, from November 27, 1897, to September 13, 1898*, 56th Cong., 2d sess. [ser. 4167], House Doc. No. 511 (1899). For the encounter of Jarvis and Call with Blake and Hultberg, see *ibid.*, p. 49.

turned to Golovin Bay. Undaunted by his winter travels, Hultberg set out in February with Daniel B. Libby to prospect the Norton Bay region. Finding that travel was too difficult, the two men returned about a week later. Hultberg made a third trip in March to the headwaters of the Niukluk River and the Quinrock country. After prospecting for two weeks he returned to Golovin Bay.[20]

About April 21 Hultberg set out on a fourth trip, this time to Council City, accompanied by P. H. Anderson, Dr. Albert N. Kittilsen, and Johan S. Tornensis.[21] The party hauled up lumber for Blake, Libby, Melsing, and Mordaunt, who were at Council City. On April 23, 24 and 25 the visiting members staked claims on Melsing and Ophir creeks. Then the eight men organized the first mining districts in northwestern Alaska, Discovery District and Eldorado District.[22] After remaining at Council City for about four days, Hultberg, Libby, and Anderson continued prospecting up the Niukluk River to the mouth of Casa de Paga River. At this point Anderson turned southward and returned to Cheenik, but Hultberg and Libby continued northward and westward over the divide in search of gold, proceeding as far as Teller and Port Clarence Bay where they remained May 5–7.[23] Not until May 20 did Hultberg return to Golovin Bay, and then he left for Council City again on May 22, returning about May 28. He left again about the end of the month, in company with A. E. Karlson,[24] Edwin Englestadt,[25] and Stephen

[20] *Abstract of Record*, p. 330.

[21] Tornensis was one of the seven Lapps brought to the United States in 1894 by the Bureau of Education. These Lapps were imported to instruct the Eskimos how to care for reindeer introduced into Alaska from Siberia in 1891 (Department of Interior Files, P. and M. Division, No. 1326, March 29, 1902; see also Sheldon Jackson, *Report on Introduction of Domestic Reindeer into Alaska [for 1897], with Illustrations*, 55th Cong. 2d sess. [ser. 3590], Senate Doc. No. 30 [1898], pp. 49, 51, 53).

[22] *Abstract of Record*, p. 340. In his testimony before an arbitration commission, Hultberg erroneously refers to Discovery District and Council City District. Council City District was the later and larger area, including Discovery, Eldorado, Bonanza, and other districts.

[23] Jackson, *Report [for 1898]*, 55th Cong., 3d sess. [ser. 3728], Senate Doc. No. 34, pp. 59, 79.

[24] A. E. Karlson, a missionary at Unalaklik, had been a tailor in Sweden, came

Ivanhof,[26] and helped them stake claims on Ophir Creek.

About June 15 the ice in Norton Sound broke up, and people began coming from St. Michael to Golovin Bay and Council City. Hultberg conducted two men, Grant and McCormick, to the new gold discoveries about June 25, and about the first part of July he took Dr. Taylor and Henry L. Porter to Council City.[27]

Ever since January, when Hultberg and Blake made their first trip to Cape Nome, they had planned to return. By June transportation by water was possible, and the following month they were ready to set out. Hultberg supplied two native kayaks, and Blake fitted out a large whaleboat. Hultberg wished to take along two Swedes who had just arrived at Golovin Bay, John Brynteson and John L. Hagelin.[28] To offset these two men, Blake invited Chris Kimber and Henry L. Porter to accompany him.[29]

---

to the United States in 1886, and went to Alaska in 1887 as a missionary for the Svenska Missionsförbundet. (The Swedish Mission Covenant was a non-conformist church, organized in 1878.) In 1889 the Swedish Evangelical Mission Covenant of America assumed the support of Karlson (Theodore Anderson, *Svenska Missionsförbundet, dess uppkomst och femtioåriga verksamhet* [Stockholm, 1928], pp. 12, 37, 38, 39; *Protokoll öfwer Svenska Evangeliska Missions-Förbundets i Amerika, fjerde årsmöte, hållet i Chicago, Ill., 4–12 September, 1888* [Chicago, 1888], p. 27).

[25] Edwin Englestadt was the agent for the Alaska Commercial Company with headquarters at Unalaklik and St. Michael.

[26] Spelled Ivanhof, Ivanoff, Ivanov. He was the son of an Eskimo mother and a Russian father. At Unalaklik he served as an interpreter for the missionaries.

[27] *Abstract of Record*, p. 332.

[28] Brynteson was born in Sweden in 1871, came to the United States in 1887, and was naturalized in 1894. After working in the mines at Ishpeming, Michigan, he decided to go to Alaska. He arrived at St. Michael on July 3, 1898, proceeded to Unalaklik and Cheenik, where he arrived July 21 or 22.

John Hagelin came to Alaska as the agent for the Good Hope Mining Co., an organization of Chicago Swedes. A. E. Karlson, missionary at Unalaklik, had suggested to his superiors that a man be sent up to mine for coal. Hagelin persuaded Brynteson to accompany him, and they went to Alaska together.

[29] There is a difference of views on this matter of inviting men to go on the trip. According to Blake, he invited Kimber and Porter to accompany him, and "this made the little missionary [Hultberg] white with rage, and he acted ugly and spiteful all the way" (Blake, *op. cit.*, p. 2). According to Brynteson, he and Hagelin planned to prospect around Sinuk River; they invited Hultberg, who suggested that Porter, Blake, and Kimber also be included (*Abstract of Record*,

The party of six men left July 31, 1898, for Cape Nome. On August 4 they arrived at Snake River, twelve miles west of Cape Nome. The journey was a rough one, the men were seasick and cold, and the night was approaching. To make matters worse, rain came down heavily, and a gale was in the making. Having kept offshore for several hours in the hope that the sea would go down, the men concluded that their only hope was to make for the shore. Steering into the mouth of the Snake River, Blake almost got inside, but a huge wave broke over the stern and swamped the boat, washed five of the men overboard, and ruined their supplies except the bacon and flour. Another breaker threw the boat up on a gravel bar in the middle of the river.[30] Short of food, without a cheering cup of tea or coffee, and with blankets and clothes soaked in the cold salty water, the men were indeed a forlorn and weary crew. But a large fire and a night's sleep brought refreshment, and the party set out to do some prospecting. Finding the river too shallow for boat travel, they crossed the tundra on foot and reached Anvil Creek at noon.[31] After eating lunch, Porter said, "Blake, let's see some of your gold." Digging a hole two feet deep, Blake washed out the sand gravel and found colors. So did Kimber. Then Hultberg said, "Let me try my luck." Taking the pan and shovel, he went upstream and was gone about two hours. When he saw Blake coming up to look for him, he picked up his pan and shovel and started down the creek. When asked, "Well, what luck?" Hultberg replied in his Swedish accent, "Dey is not any gold up dare."[32] Then Blake suggested that they go up the coast

p. 412). According to Hultberg, he invited Blake, Kimber, and Porter, and he supplied provisions for Hagelin and Brynteson, as well as for Porter (*Abstract of Record*, p. 334).

[30] Blake, *op. cit.*, pp. 3–4.

[31] Anvil Creek is the richest stream in the district. It received its name a month later, from a large mountain rock resembling a blacksmith's anvil (Sam C. Dunham, *The Men Who Blaze the Trail and Other Poems* [New York, 1931], p. 55 n.).

[32] It is this incident which marks the first important find of gold on Anvil Creek. When the party first came to the creek, they were in the tundra, about a half mile from the mouth of the creek and where No. 3 Below was later located. Hultberg probably went up the creek a mile to where Discovery and

to Sinuk Mary's place, get some food, and return to Anvil Creek. Hultberg retorted that he was not going back to Anvil, but suggested that Snake River be further prospected. On arriving at Snake River, about five miles to the west, the party panned and found colors in every pan. Then they set out for their camp at the estuary of the river. Blake, Kimber, and Porter wished to return by the same route they had come, but Hultberg insisted he knew a shorter way. The three Swedes proceeded southward, and the three Americans went eastward. Blake, Kimber, and Porter arrived at camp, became worried that Hultberg and his companions had lost their way, and set out to look for them. About two miles up the river they encountered Brynteson and Hagelin, carrying Hultberg, who was either all played out or shamming illness.[33]

The next morning the party set out for Mary's place, twenty miles westward on the mouth of the Sinuk River.[34] To their surprise, if not secret consternation, they found white men there who had been prospecting for gold in the Kotzebue Sound region.[35] Obtaining supplies, the party started up the Sinuk River,

No. 1 Below are situated. In panning, he obtained 169 colors. He kept secret his find, said there was no gold there, and discouraged Blake and his friends from returning to the place (*Abstract of Record*, pp. 334 f.; Blake, *op. cit.*, p. 4).

It is significant that the first statements about the discovery of gold give Hultberg the main credit (see the letter of Captain E. S. Walker, dated July 13, 1899, to Major P. H. Ray, in National Archives, Department of the Interior, P. and M. Division, 1899, No. 2483, p. 5. Captain Walker says "the first gold discovery in the Cape Nome district was made in August, 1898, on Anvil Creek, Snake River, by N. O. Hultberg"; see also National Archives, War Department Records, Office Chief Quartermaster, Department of the Columbia, No. 2, 1364; and Office of Adjutant General, File No. 268941, August 23, 1899; see also the *Aurora Borealis*, Vol. 2, No. 1, December 31, 1898, a rare typewritten "newspaper" issued at St. Michael, a facsimile of which may be seen in Walter R. Curtin, *Yukon Voyage, Unofficial Log of the Steamer Yukoner* [Caldwell, Idaho, 1938], pp. 112 f.).

[33] *Ibid.*, p. 5.

[34] The Sinuk River is also called the Synrock, Sinook, and Sinrock. Sinuk Mary was a half-breed, married to a reindeer herder whose named was Charlie Antisarlook. Their house was a stopping place between Port Clarence Bay and Cape Nome.

[35] Whalers had brought back quartz from the Kotzebue Sound region in 1897. In 1898 there were 1,254 stampeders to the Kowak River area (called Kobuk

but shortly thereafter Hultberg said he could go no further, "shamming sickness."[36] Porter remained behind with Hultberg, and with a tent, stove, and grub, but the others went on. Blake really believed that Hultberg was sick at the time, but later Blake changed his mind when he wrote:

> Now comes the time when he played me. I had not been gone more than one day when this sly, crafty, avaricious, God-fearing, Eskimo-loving missionary fooled me. He got a boat from some white men at the mouth of Snake River, slipped off in the night, left Porter alone in the tent, and went directly to Golovin Bay, got two more Swedes, Lindblom and Lindeberg, and a small sailboat, and drew a map of the place, told them exactly where we had been and exactly where to go, gave them his power of attorney, and off they started, taking the power of attorney of every Swede missionary in the vicinity and located the whole country.[37]

on some maps). Some of these gold seekers made their way overland or by sea to the Cape Nome and Sinuk River region (Eugene McElwaine, *The Truth About Alaska, the Golden Land of the Midnight Sun* [Chicago, 1901], pp. 83, 85, 88, *et passim*. See also Joseph Grinnell, *Gold Hunting in Alaska*, ed. Elizabeth Grinnel [Elgin, Illinois, 1901]).

[36] It is difficult to know whether Hultberg was "shamming" or not. He had been in Alaska for five years and had found the winters trying. Because of illness he left Alaska for Sweden on August 31, 1898, and returned to Alaska in June, 1899.

[37] Blake, *op. cit.*, p. 5. This statement illustrates Blake's resentment at not being in on the staking of claims on Anvil Creek. There was bickering and disagreement between the Scandinavians and the non-Scandinavians. Hultberg returned to Cheenik with two men, Molligan and Taylor, on a small boat. Caught by a storm in an open boat, tossed about for three days and four nights, Hultberg returned about August 12 to Cheenik, exhausted and sick. On August 31 he left for Sweden, but before he left he urged Brynteson to return to Anvil Creek and he made arrangements with Lindblom to leave his work at Council City and go to Nome.

Blake insinuates that Hultberg divulged the location of secret places. There was no need of this, since Brynteson was a member of the party, and since he was the one who guided Lindblom and Lindeberg to Anvil Creek. Blake's reference to "every Swede missionary" is misleading. Besides Hultberg, the only missionaries in the vicinity were A. E. Karlson of Unalaklik and P. H. Anderson at Cheenik. The statement that these men "located the whole country" must be qualified. Out of some 2,000 claims recorded by June, 1899, Brynteson, Lindblom, and Lindeberg located only ninety for themselves and friends. It would have been correct to say that they located some of the best claims in the whole country.

Blake went up to the headwaters of the Sinuk River, encountered almost continuous rain, caught a severe cold, and remained longer than he intended or his food allowed. Coming back to Sinuk Mary's place, and finding Hultberg "mysteriously" gone, he and his party returned to Golovin Bay, all worn out.[38]

In the latter part of August Brynteson and Hagelin returned to Golovin Bay, then went up to Council City. On August 25 they met Hultberg, who was on his way back to Cheenik. For an hour they discussed the plan of another trip to Nome, and Hultberg urged Bynteson and Hagelin to return to Nome and take Eric Lindblom with them.[39]

On September 6 John Brynteson, Eric O. Lindblom, and Jafet Lindeberg left Council City, and on September 11 they set sail from Cheenik for Cape Nome.[40] Arriving at Snake River on September 15, they proceeded to prospect the creeks of Snake River. On September 16 or 17 they went up to Glacier Creek, on September 17 or 18 to Mountain Creek where they made their first locations, and on September 19 or 20 to Snow Gulch and Glacier Creek.[41] On September 21 they prospected Anvil Creek and found it very rich. The following day they began staking claims. Discovery claim was staked first in the name of all three discoverers. Two willow stakes were driven into the ground on the lower and upper ends of the claim, and a notice was posted, which read: "I claim 1500 feet from this stake and

---

[38] Blake, *op. cit.*, pp. 5 f.

[39] *Abstract of Record*, pp. 335, 342, 351, 356. The records do not reveal whether Brynteson and Hagelin returned alone or with Blake, Kimber, and Porter. It is probable that they all returned together, leaving Sinuk River about August 10–12, and arriving at Golovin Bay about August 18–20. Blake seems to have proceeded to St. Michael, but Brynteson and Hagelin went on to Cheenik, then up the Fish River. Just below Council City they met Hultberg on August 25.

[40] Arthur Frederick Wines, *Cape Nome Mining Region*, 56th Cong., 1st sess. [ser. 3875] Senate Doc. No. 357 (1900), p. 2.

[41] E. S. Harrison, *Nome and Seward Peninsula*, pp. 48, 212. *Abstract of Record*, pp. 409, 410, 417, 418. Cf. Lindeberg's letter in Arthur J. Collier, Frank L. Hess, Philip S. Smith, Alfred H. Brooks, *The Gold Placers of Parts of Seward Peninsula, Alaska, Including Nome, Council, Kougarok, Port Clarence, and Goodhope Precincts*, Bulletin 328, "United States Geological Survey" (Washington, 1908), pp. 16–18 n.

300 feet on either side."[42] Then No. 1 Below Discovery was staked in the name of Jafet Lindeberg, and No. 2 Below, in the name of William A. Kjellman, superintendent of the Teller reindeer station near Port Clarence, by Lindeberg, who had a power of attorney from Kjellman. No. 3 Below was staked by Brynteson for Dr. J. R. Gregory, a government official at St. Michael, and No. 4 Below was staked by Lindeberg for John A. Dexter, trader at Cheenik. No. 1 Above was staked by John Brynteson for himself; No. 2 Above, for P. H. Anderson, by Brynteson; No. 3 Above, for John L. Hagelin, by Brynteson; No. 4 Above, for A. E. Karlson, by Brynteson; No. 5 Above, for Nels O. Hultberg, by Brynteson; and No. 6 Above, for Eric O. Lindblom, by himself.[43]

In addition to these eleven claims on Anvil Creek,[44] the party located one claim on Nakkila Gulch, a tributary of Anvil Creek, for Mikkel J. Nakkila, a Lapp employee in the government reindeer service.[45] Other claims were located on Rock Creek, Snow

[42] *Abstract of Record*, p. 373. This staking was incorrect. The United States mining laws permit lode or quartz mines to be 1,500 by 600 feet, but placer mines are limited to twenty acres (see *U. S. Statutes at Large*, 42nd Cong., 1871–1872, Ch. CLII, Section 2, p. 91). One acre equals 43,560 square feet or 4,047 square meters. Twenty acres equal 871,200 square feet, which is the limit allowed by law. By this first staking of 1,500 by 600 feet, these men had staked 900,000 square feet, or 28,800 square feet too much in each claim. The reason for this mistake very likely was that Brynteson was accustomed to lode mining in Michigan where he had worked before going to Alaska.

[43] Supreme Court of Illinois, December Term, 1905, No. 3912, White Star Mining Company, Appellant, *v.* Nels O. Hultberg *et al.*, Appellees; *Reply for Appellant, White Star Mining Company of Illinois, and Appellees, Claes W. Johnson and Peter H. Anderson, to Argument for Appellees, Nels O. Hultberg and the Swedish Evangelical Mission Covenant of America, in Reply to the Petition for a Rehearing*, p. 12.

[44] There is some evidence for believing that No. 7, No. 8, and No. 9 Above were staked on this trip in September, but this is a moot question. In the legal records, the claims up to and including No. 6 Above were staked on September 22, and No. 7, No. 8, and No. 9, on October 18, 1898. The significance of the point is this: if No. 9 was staked originally for an Eskimo boy, was the restaking intended for P. H. Anderson personally, or as a trustee for the Eskimo boy, or for the mission station? Litigation from 1902 to 1919 developed over this issue.

[45] Mikkel J. Nakkila came to the United States in 1894 as one of the seven Lapps brought by the Bureau of Education to instruct natives in the care of

Creek, Dry Creek, and Quartz Gulch. By September 28 the provisions were running low; and the three men returned to Golovin Bay about October 2.

On September 27 P. H. Anderson had returned to Cheenik with Gabriel W. Price, whom he had met at St. Michael. Price had been in the Kotzebue Sound region in the summer of 1898 and had become discouraged because of his failure to find any traces of gold there. Having secured passage with Captain Frank Osborn on the schooner *Chessan*, to St. Michael, he came over to Cheenik with Blake and Anderson on a small boat, the *Fram*.[46] About October 4 he left for Council City to try his luck there.

Brynteson, Lindblom, and Lindeberg told P. H. Anderson and Dr. A. N. Kittilsen of their trip to Nome, the staking of claims, and their plans for returning to Nome as soon as snowfall made travel with reindeer possible. Two Lapps suggested going up the coast in a large Eskimo umiak. But P. H. Anderson offered the use of the mission's four-ton, two-masted schooner on condition that the men help him build a schoolhouse. The offer was accepted and the schoolhouse was built. By October 11 the men had loaded the boat with provisions furnished mostly by Dr. Kittilsen, but also by Dexter, the trader, and by Anderson from the mission's supplies. On the evening of October 11 Price returned from Council City and was permitted or invited to join the party of six men.

On October 12 Brynteson, Lindblom, and Lindeberg set sail for Nome, accompanied by Dr. Kittilsen, Price, Johan S. Tornensis, and Constantine, an Eskimo. Arriving on October 15, they established camp at the mouth of the Snake River, right on the "Spit."[47]

---

reindeer (National Archives, Department of Interior Files, P. and M. Division, No. 1326, March 29, 1902).

[46] Blake, *op. cit.*, p. 6.

[47] *Abstract of Record*, p. 372. See also Supreme Court of the United States, October Term 1906, No. 647, Claes W. Johnson, Plaintiff in Error, *v.* Nels O. Hultberg, Swedish Evangelical Mission Covenant of America, White Star Mining Company of Illinois, Peter H. Anderson, and the Merchants' Loan and Trust Company, *Transcript of Record*, p. 224.

The party proceeded immediately to rectify the mistakes and omissions of the previous trip. One of the most obvious lacks was an organized district wherein claims could be recorded. With the guidance of Price, who was an experienced miner, the party proceeded to organize a mining district. The following minutes reveal the organization of what proved to be the richest mining district in northern Alaska.

Snake River, Alaska

October 15, 1898.

At a meeting held by the miners of Snake River, October 15, 1898, for the purpose of organizing and creating a new mining district. Dr. A. N. Kittilsen was elected Chairman, G. W. Price was elected Secretary, and the following local laws, rules and regulations were voted upon and adopted:

First. A motion was made by John Brynteson, and seconded by Japhet Linderberg, that the name of the District should be the CAPE NOME MINING DISTRICT, and extend from Cape Nome in a northwesterly direction along the coast for twenty-five miles, and extend twenty-five miles inland, making a district of twenty-five miles square.

Carried.

Second. A motion was made by Eric O. Lindblom, and seconded by John Brynteson, that placer claims should be located thirteen hundred and twenty feet (1,320) by six hundred and sixty feet (660).

Carried.

Third. A motion by Japhet Linderberg, and seconded by J. S. Tornensis, that claims can be located by power of attorney, such power of attorney to be recorded prior to location notice.

Carried.

Fourth. A motion by John Brynteson, and seconded by Eric O. Lindblom, that all claims must be recorded within forty (40) days after the notice is posted.

Carried.

Fifth. A motion by Japhet Linderberg, and seconded by J. S. Tornensis, that water used for mining or otherwise taken from the natural water course must be turned back into the natural water course at the lower end of each claim.

Carried.

Sixth. A motion by Eric O. Lindblom, and seconded by John Brynteson, that Dr. A. N. Kittilsen be elected District Recorder for the term of two years, unless removed for cause, and in case of his absence for more than one week he shall appoint a deputy in his place, and that the fee for recording any and all documents shall be two dollars and fifty cents ($2.50).

Carried.

(Signed) A. N. Kittilsen.
G. W. Price.
John Brynteson.
Japhet Linderberg.
J. S. Tornensis.
Eric O. Lindblom.[48]

On October 17 and 18 the men restaked the claims on Anvil Creek. The dimensions of each claim were reduced to 1,320 by 660 feet; and six stakes were put on the property, one on each corner and one in the middle of each end of the claim. The men then posted notices with names of the owners and claims, together with descriptions of metes and bounds. These notices were prepared by Price and recorded by Dr. Kittilsen, the newly elected recorder, whose office was a tent set up at No. 6 Above. Discovery claim was shortened 180 feet on the upper end; then No. 1 Below was shortened 180 feet on the lower end; and No. 2 Below was shortened 360 feet on the lower end. No. 3 Below was shortened 540 feet on the lower end; and No. 4 Below, 720 feet on the lower end. It was at this time that No. 5 Below was staked for R. T. Lyng, agent for the Alaska Commercial Company at St. Michael, by Dr. Kittilsen; and No. 6 Below, for Thomas T. Lane, by Price.[49]

Proceeding upstream, the men relocated No. 1 to No. 6 Above, inclusive, shortening each claim 180 feet. On October 18 Dr. Kittilsen located No. 7 Above, for himself; Price located No. 8

[48] *Abstract of Record*, pp. 316 f. These minutes are taken from a copy certified by T. M. Reed, U. S. commissioner and recorder ex officio in Nome.

[49] Supreme Court of Illinois, Vacation after October Term, 1905, No. 3912; White Star Mining Company of Illinois, Appellant, *v.* Nels O. Hultberg, The Swedish Evangelical Mission Covenant of America, Claes W. Johnson, Peter H. Anderson, and Merchants' Loan and Trust Company, *Appendix to Petition for Rehearing*, p. 46.

Above, for himself, and No. 9 Above, by a power of attorney, for his brother, R. L. Price.[50] Johan Tornensis located No. 10 Above, for himself, and No. 11 Above, for a relative. No. 12 Above was located for J. C. Widstead, by Dr. Kittilsen, who had a power of attorney.[51]

When the arduous task of staking was completed, the men spent the next two weeks prospecting on their claims. They set up two crude rockers, first on No. 8 Above and then on No. 7 Above. Four or five days of rocking produced about $1,800 worth of gold. On one of these days the men cleaned up $624 after five hours of work.[52] From Snow Creek, with one man shoveling dirt and three men panning, came $76 in dust after three hours' work. The best pan yielded $8.41.[53]

By the end of October it was almost impossible to continue panning or rocking because ice had begun to form in the creeks, and the ground, even near the surface, had begun to freeze. To heat water and soften the earth by fires proved too cumbersome. The men spent a few more days locating new claims and relocating old claims on Rock Creek, Snow Creek, Dry Creek, Nakkila Gulch, Quartz Gulch, Lindblom Creek, and other streams. By the first week in November the men abandond further

[50] No. 9 Above was located by G. W. Price with a power of attorney. There was a previous agreement that Price would sell this claim to P. H. Anderson, and he did convey the claim on November 17, 1898, for a consideration of $20. There is some evidence that No. 9 was intended to benefit two Eskimo boys, Gabriel and Constantine. There is also evidence that No. 8 and No. 9 had been intended for these boys and probably staked for them on the September trip. Questions regarding the alien status of Eskimos and their being under twenty-one years of age evidently prompted the restaking in the name of Price and his brother. Beginning in 1899, Anderson became involved in litigation over No. 9 Above which lasted for twenty years, involved eleven different courts, and went to the Supreme Court of the United States four times. The writer is preparing a separate article on this complex litigation.

[51] Jens C. Widstead was appointed in 1895 to be superintendent of reindeer at the Teller station near Port Clarence Bay and Grantley Harbor (Sheldon Jackson, *Report [for 1895] on Introduction of Domestic Reindeer into Alaska, with Maps and Illustrations*, 54th Cong., 1st sess. [ser. 3350], Senate Doc. No. 111 [Washington, 1896], pp. 15, 93, 94).

[52] *Aurora Borealis*, Vol. 2, No. 1, December 31, 1898.

[53] Letter of P. H. Anderson to N. O. Hultberg, January 1, 1899. A copy of this letter is in the possession of the author.

work; and on November 8 they set sail for Golovin Bay. Encountering considerable drift ice, they found it necessary to return and leave the schooner ice-bound in the Snake River. They hired a native and his dog team to carry their supplies back to Cheenik. About November 11 they encountered P. H. Anderson and Magnus Kjelsberg on the trail with reindeer and sleds, and with their aid the party of nine men returned to Cheenik on November 14 or 15.[54]

The news of the rich strike at Nome was too good to keep. Hardly had the party returned to Cheenik before Price wrote a letter to his friend whom he had left at Council City.

[November 14–16, 1898][55]

John Cooper, *Council City*:

You had better leave Buster to take care of your camp there, and take his power of attorney, and you and Bull [William] Benn start for Nome City. That is where we just came from, and have found very good prospects. Show Mr. Blake this letter, and he may go with you. Several men will start from here soon, among them Eric O. Lindblom, and he will give you all the pointers about where to locate when you get there. Blake has been at the place before, and he will tell you where to go. It is the third river above Cape Nome, and about 10 miles this side of Sledge Island. Take only provisions enough for three weeks, make locations, and return again. . . .

I hope you and Bill, also Mr. Blake, will start at once. Do not make this known too much, but we took $352.60 out of my claim in one day with one rocker, and $1800.00 in five days with two rockers. Blake can let his partners and friends in on it, but I think it advisable for him to go first himself.

Yours, very truly,

G. W. Price

[54] *Abstract of Record*, p. 375. See also E. S. Harrison, *Nome and the Seward Peninsula*, p. 324. Magnus Kjelsberg was a Norwegian from Kaafjord, who came to the United States in 1898 to drive reindeer cross country for the relief of destitute miners on the Yukon. When the expedition proved a failure, Kjelsberg went to the reindeer station near Unalaklik, thence to Golovin Bay and Cheenik, to join Anderson.

[55] The date is not given. But the rush began from Council City on November

In the latter part of November Dr. Kittilsen returned to his home at Unalaklik, and from there proceeded to St. Michael. On the trail he met R. T. Lyng and Edwin Englestadt, agents for the Alaska Commercial Company, on their way to Council City. When they learned of the rich strike they changed their plans and went directly to Cape Nome and Snake River. On November 30 Dr. Kittilsen, William A. Kjellman, superintendent of the reindeer station, and fifteen men, mostly Lapp herders, arrived at St. Michael.[56] At a festive social gathering that same evening Dr. Kittilsen told his friends of the great strike. November 30 was indeed "a red-letter day of the winter '98–'99." Great excitement prevailed.[57] Since everyone wanted to leave immediately, the demand for dogs and sleds was unprecedented. On the very next day, two enterprising parties, having hastily packed their sleds, set out for Nome, one with dogs and one with reindeer. Often two or three parties left St. Michael on the same day, throughout December, and some men made three or four trips. At the height of the rush, one man encountered forty dog teams on one day's travel, and for the rest of the winter at St. Michael a steady departing and returning of sleds was to be seen.[58]

At St. Michael there was a large circus tent that served as Tex Richard's saloon. One evening about the end of November the men were sitting around, playing cards, betting, and arguing. Suddenly the saloon became quiet. A young man, possibly twenty-four years old, swarthy and slender, walked up to the bar and carelessly threw a poke of gold on the disk. Asked who he was and where he came from, he gave his name as Jafet

---

18, 1898. Price returned to Cheenik on November 14 or 15, and in his letter he states that he has just come from Nome City (56th Congress, 1st sess., Senate Doc. No. 441, pp. 8 f. See also L. H. French, *Nome Nuggets*, p. xx).

[56] *Aurora Borealis*, Vol. 2, No. 1, December 31, 1898. Letter of Lenox B. Shephard, U. S. commissioner at St. Michael, June 1, 1899, to C. N. Bliss, Secretary of the Interior (National Archives, Department of the Interior, P. and M. Division, No. 2144).

[57] *Aurora Borealis*, Vol. 2, No. 1, December 31, 1898.

[58] Shephard to Bliss, June 1, 1899, National Archives, Department of the Interior, P. and M. Division, No. 2144.

Lindeberg and said: "I come from Nome, and there you will find more of the same stuff." [59]

From Cheenik, Council City, Unalaklik, and St. Michael the news of Cape Nome spread up the Yukon River from settlement to settlement, from winter camps to mission stations, until Dawson City and the whole Klondike region became aware of a new Bonanza and Eldorado.

Three hundred and fifty miles from the mouth of the Yukon between Andreafski and Anvik, the crew of the steamer *Yukoner* had established their winter headquarters. Five miles below them was the Russian mission where a missionary and a trader named Belkoff lived. The latter left for St. Michael in January, 1899. About February 15 he returned with the news that "everybody is crazy down the river, rushing to the new gold fields." [60] He brought with him a letter from Neil Vawter, United States marshal at St. Michael, who wrote about the gold strike, intimated that it probably was a fake, but thoughtfully enclosed several powers of attorney in case his friends wished to have some claims staked. Acting on this news, Teddy Stravin, chief engineer of the *Yukoner*, and D. H. Volker, first mate, left the ship and set out for Nome within a week after hearing the news. [61]

The news spread from the *Yukoner* to the *Oil City*, another vessel in winter quarters farther up the river. By March the reports had been carried to Fort Yukon and by April or May the

[59] Arvid Höijer och Georg af Forsellers, *Svenske greven av Alaska; guldgrävarliv i Nome, Candle, och Fairbanks* (Stockholm), p. 47. This book is an account of the adventures of a Swedish count, narrated by Mr. Höijer. The book has value for its stories and adventures, but it contains numerous errors of fact, mispellings, and misimpressions. According to this account, Lindeberg threw a poke of gold dust valued at $10,000.00. This is obviously false, since the total output of gold rocked out by the entire party of seven men in 1898 was $1800.00. It has John Blake for H. L. Blake, Hultman for Hultberg, Top Cork for Topkuk, Bruntesson for Brynteson, Rawnock for Roanoke, Katherine Saunders for Katherine Sudden, Neckla for Nakkila, Sidney Lane for Charles D. Lane. Although the mistakes are not grievous, they indicate what happens when memory is unsupported by documents.

[60] Walter R. Curtin, *Yukon Voyage; Unofficial Log of the Steamer Yukoner*, p. 135.

[61] *Ibid.*, pp. 137, 142, 184.

story had been spread around the Klondike region. On May 31, 1899, a small boat, the *W. K. Merwin*, left Dawson for Nome with some 200 passengers, who stood like straphangers on a street car, jammed on the boat and the barge.[62] Early in July the *Rideout* left Dawson with 797 passengers "who fought to get aboard her and her barges." [63]

As the news spread up the Yukon River, it was also carried northward across the Seward Peninsula. In the summer of 1898 some 1,200 to 1,300 men had rushed into the Kotzebue Sound region. Approximately 800 of these men had established winter camps on the Kowak River, but had failed to find gold. The winter had been long and cold, disease and scurvy had set in, and bitterness, despair, and death had been common experiences. To such a group of men rumors of gold strikes had been means of maintaining morale, but the rumors failed to materialize. During the month of April, 1899, the "Flying Dutchman," an enterprising mailman who delivered letters at one dollar each, arrived by dog team from St. Michael at the various camps along the Kowak.[64] He brought news of a big strike on the coast near Sledge Island and Cape Nome, "richer than the Klondike." When the news was confirmed by fearless, enterprising prospectors who hastened overland to Nome,[65] the camps along the Kowak broke up, and the miners proceeded down the river as soon as the ice breakup permitted travel. By July 1 it was

[62] *Ibid.*, p. 291. This small boat was so crowded, and the dining room was so small, that it was necessary to eat in nine different relays — from "the first settin of the first class passengers" down to "the third settin of the third class passengers." This little boat came to an untimely end at 4:00 A. M., August 2, 1900, when it was wrecked in the breakers at Nome (*ibid.*, p. 288).

[63] Mary Lee Davis, *Sourdough Gold, The Log of a Yukon Adventure* (Boston, 1933), p. 162.

[64] Grinnell, *Gold Hunting in Alaska*, p. 73.

[65] George M. Ashford, a civil engineer from Iowa, was on the Kowak, just below Squirrel River, during the winter 1898–1899. Hearing of the strike at Nome, he and two companions set out May 1 over the ice with dog team. On this trip Dr. DeFrance became exhausted and froze to death. The other two men continued, narrowly escaped losing their sled and supplies, and arrived at Sinuk River about May 25, and at Nome May 31, 1899. They found claims staked forty miles west of Nome at this early date before the summer rush (E. S. Harrison, *Nome and Seward Peninsula*, p. 217).

possible to get out of the delta, and to cross Hotham Inlet and Kotzebue Sound. In the latter half of this month, the boats from Kotzebue Sound reached Nome, including the schooner *Penelope*, which arrived July 20 after an eleven-day trip, and the U. S. Revenue Cutter *Bear*, July 26, "bringing eighty victims of scurvy." [66]

The inevitable consequence of the stampede to Cape Nome was the staking of the entire district. By the end of December, 1898 — the first month of the stampede — 300 claims had been recorded and many more had been located.[67] By April 1,200 more claims had been staked, and by July, 1899, approximately 2,000 claims had been recorded with Dr. Kittilsen, recorder for the district.[68] When the Cape Nome Mining District had been staked, new districts were organized and staked, so that by December, 1899, some 4,500 claims had been recorded, and by December, 1900, thirty mining districts had been organized.[69]

It was natural that abuses of many kinds developed in the Cape Nome stampede. The legal right to secure a claim by power of attorney was stretched beyond all reason. Of the original discoverers, Brynteson located five claims for himself and about six for others; Lindeberg located eight for himself and eleven for others; Lindblom located thirty claims for himself

[66] For the story of the *Penelope*, see Joseph Grinnell, *op. cit., passim*. For the arrival of the cutter *Bear*, see Sheldon Jackson, *Ninth Annual Report [for 1899] on Introduction of Domestic Reindeer into Alaska*, 56th Cong., 1st sess. [ser. 3867], Senate Doc. No. 245 (1900), p. 42.

[67] P. H. Anderson to Nels O. Hultberg, January 1, 1899. A copy of this letter is in the possession of the author. Anderson was deputy recorder of the Cape Nome Mining District.

[68] Letter of Captain E. S. Walker, July 13, 1899, in the report of Major P. H. Ray, July 16, 1899, to the Adjutant General, Vancouver Barracks, Washington, National Archives, Department of the Interior, P. and M. Division, 1899, No. 2483, p. 6. See also National Archives, War Department, Office Chief Quartermaster, Department of the Columbia, No. 2, 1364, and Office of Adjutant General, 268941 (received August 23, 1899).

[69] Sam C. Dunham estimates that of the 4,500 claims, about 300 were tundra claims, 275 were beach claims, and 75 quartz or lode claims. That would leave 3,850 placer claims (see his article, "The Yukon and Nome Gold Regions," *Bulletin of the Department of Labor*, V [July, 1900], for an excellent summary of conditions at Nome in 1899). The thirty districts are listed by Eugene McElwaine in *The Truth about Alaska, the Golden Land of the Midnight Sun*, p. 208.

and thirty more by powers of attorney. [70] L. B. Shephard, the United States commissioner at St. Michael, was said to have obtained sixty claims,[71] and Captain E. S. Walker, in charge of troops at Fort St. Michael, was said to have obtained about forty claims.[72]

[70] *Congressional Record, Senate,* April 30, 1900, p. 4841. This information came from Charles H. Caton, who secured his facts from Mr. Whittlesy, an attorney for Charles D. Lane, president of the Wild Goose Mining Co.

Lindblom, Lindeberg, and Brynteson formed the Pioneer Mining Co. In their corporate capacity, it is likely they held other claims besides the ones mentioned.

[71] There is justification in the complaint against Shephard. He was correct in his support of the legality of powers of attorney, but it was difficult for anyone to feel that he was a disinterested judge (National Archives, Department of Justice, File 11479 [1899]. A letter of September 20, 1899, charging Shephard with holding sixty claims, was referred by Attorney General John Griggs to the U. S. district judge for the District of Alaska — C. S. Johnson at Sitka). His main work was not that of a commissioner but that of a general agent for the North American Transportation and Trading Co. Shephard wrote frankly to the Department of Justice that "a commissioner could not maintain himself in this country if he had no other occupation" (Shephard, July 10, 1899, to Robert A. Friedrich, U. S. attorney, Sitka, Alaska; National Archives, Department of Justice Records, File No. 11,620 [1897]). John G. Brady, governor of Alaska, asserted that "the conduct of Commissioner Shephard as St. Michael has been very reprehensible. A special examiner should be ordered to investigate his conduct as an officer. He had many people to declare their intentions before him and gave them their first papers, charging each a fee of three dollars, and generally is accused of being extortionate in demanding fees. If an examiner finds that this man is guilty of a tithe of what he is accused, he should be turned over to the District Attorney and the Grand Jury of the new Court which will open early in the season at St. Michael" (Governor Brady, September 6, 1899, to the Secretary of the Interior, National Archives, Records of the Office of the Secretary of the Interior, P. and M., 1899, No. 2595). Senator Hansbrough of North Dakota received a letter, dated August 5, 1899, which said: "I wish to call your attention to the disgrace to the Republican party in keeping in office the present commissioner at St. Michael's, L. B. Shephard" (*Congressional Record, Senate,* April 30, 1900, p. 4842). Shephard's resignation was sent to the Department of the Interior, July 23, 1900, and a letter of the Secretary of the Interior of August 27, 1900, stated that the resignation was accepted "by direction of the President."

[72] The charge regarding Captain E. S. Walker is in *Congressional Record, Senate,* April 30, 1900, p. 4839. It is also in "Statement of the President of the Law and Order League," *Civil Government for Alaska,* 56th Cong., 1st sess. [ser. 3868], Senate Doc. No. 272 (1900), p. 11. Property owners felt that Walker and Shephard were in the right by defending the established order of things, but it is easy to see how many felt that these two officials were defending their own private interests as well.

The two large transportation companies, The Alaska Commercial Company and the North American Transportation and Trading Company, were accused of hiring Lapps to stake claims at the rate of two dollars a claim. The holdings of these companies extended fifty miles in every direction except toward the sea. On the tundra the companies were said to have owned five hundred claims.[73] Although the law required that mineral be found before locations could be made, men rushed in to stake claims, acting on the theory that the land might contain gold. Hundreds of claims, staked but never prospected, were held for speculative purposes — the owners hoping that a fortunate discovery would enhance the value of an entire section or creek. Many of the claims were of the "hatchet and pencil" variety — staked and recorded although no gold had been discovered and the annual assessment work of $100 which the law required had not been performed. Powers of attorney were forged, and then the claims were conveyed to the forger. By various expedients the land was sequestered from immediate public use along creeks for ten or fifteen miles, by a single individual.[74]

Resentment against the use of fraudulent papers and the abuse of powers of attorney was not slow in making itself felt. The rush to Nome from Council City had begun on November 18,[75] three days after the return of the original discoverers to Cheenik. During the month of December some of the best claims were jumped by men from Council City, resentful of the fact

[73] *Congressional Record, Senate*, April 30, 1900, pp. 4835, 4836, 4839.

[74] A senatorial investigating committee reported that the evidence "shows that in Alaska the land, by means of such expedients, has in some instances been sequestered from immediate public use along creeks for 30 miles by a single individual" (*Mining Laws of the United States*, 56th Cong., 2d sess. [ser. 4067], Senate Report No. 2414, p. I). This charge is probably exaggerated. Snake River is about thirty miles long, Nome River about twenty miles, Sinuk River about forty-five miles long, but no creek in the Cape Nome Mining District is thirty miles in length. In other districts, however, where the divide is farther from the sea, the charge could be true, but it would involve the holding of 120 claims by one man.

[75] L. H. French, *Nome Nuggets, Some of the Experiences of a Party of Gold Seekers in Northwestern Alaska in 1900* (New York, 1901), p. xx.

that they had been outwitted or that they had not been included in the original party. H. L. Blake was furious when he learned that he had missed the opportunity of a lifetime and that others had reaped where he had sown. He demanded to know the meaning of the stakes which men had put up in his valley. Miners caustically inquired where it stood written that this was his valley, and produced registration receipts. Swearing and threatening, Blake left Nome with the promise to return and sue those who had taken his property.[76]

Others were less threatening and more practical. Deciding among themselves that powers of attorney were illegal, they proceeded to jump those claims on Anvil Creek which had been staked for friends. O. Jose Comptois, a French doctor at Council City, jumped No. 2 Above, belonging to P. H. Anderson; J. L. Wilson jumped No. 3 Above, belonging to John L. Hagelin; A. P. Mordaunt jumped No. 5 Above, belonging to N. O. Hultberg. No. 4 Above, belonging to A. E. Karlson, and one claim belonging to Magnus Kjelsberg, were also jumped.[77] These spurious jumpers' claims — recorded in December, 1898 — led to arguments, accusations, and bitter recriminations.

Because of the trouble which had developed over the issue of the legality of powers of attorney, United States Commissioner L. B. Shephard decided to hold a session of court at Cheenik. He asserted that a petition requesting protection had come from the Golovin Bay district, and in response to that petition he had decided to come personally to Cheenik. Lieutenant E. S. Walker caused notices to be posted in the Council City district stating that the special session of the commissioner's court would be held about March 5.[78]

On March 7, 1899, the court was opened at Cheenik by Shephard. Three suits were begun: P. H. Anderson *v.* O. J. Comptois; J. L. Hagelin *v.* J. L. Wilson; N. O. Hultberg *v.* A. P. Mor-

---

[76] Arvid Höijer och Georg av Forselles, *op. cit.,* p. 84.

[77] Letter of P. H. Anderson to N. O. Hultberg, January 1, 1899. A. E. Karlson's claim, No. 4 Above, was jumped but not recorded. Neither the jumper nor the location of Kjelsberg's claim is given in the letter.

[78] *Civil Government for Alaska,* 56th Cong., 1st sess. [ser. 3868], Senate Doc. No. 272 (1900), p. 12.

daunt. The appearance of the defendants was set for March 20, and the trial continued from March 20 to 23. The defendants' request for a jury trial was denied, and their contention that claims located by power of attorney were illegal was set aside. Shephard took the position that where local miners' laws permitted staking by powers of attorney, as they did in the Cape Nome Mining District, such claims were legal. This test case was decided in favor of the plaintiffs on every point, and writs of restitution were issued for the original locators.[79]

Lieutenant O. L. Spaulding, Jr., and Commissioner Shephard sought to impress upon the miners and the defeated litigants the need for law and order and the absence of inflammatory talk. In this they were only partially successful. Two of the men from Council City, Louis F. Melsing and John Watterson, had gone to Nome in February, and had jumped Anvil Creek Claims, No. 10 Above, belonging to Johan S. Tornensis, and No. 11 Above, belonging to Mikkel J. Nakkila, Lapp employees of the Eaton Reindeer Station near Unalaklik. The reason given for this jumping was that Tornensis and Nakkila were not citizens and therefore were ineligible to stake claims.[80] When Lieutenant Spaulding showed Melsing legal papers establishing the fact that the Lapps had declared their intention

[79] Lieutenant Oliver Spaulding, April 13, 1899, to the Adjutant, Fort St. Michael; National Archives, War Department Records, Department of the Columbia 1743 (received July 20, 1899). See also letter of Captain E. S. Walker, May 2, 1899, *ibid.* See also *Congressional Record, Senate,* April 19, 1900, pp. 4416 f., and 56th Congress, 1st sess. [ser. 3868], Senate Doc. No. 272, p. 13.

[80] In 1894 the Bureau of Education of the United States government brought seven Lapps to Alaska to teach the natives the care of reindeer herds. Of these seven, Matthis Eira, Samuel J. Kemi, Per A. Rist, and Aslak L. Somby returned to Lapland in 1897 after completing their three-year term. Three Lapps — Johan S. Tornensis, Mikkel J. Nakkila, and Fredrik Larsen — were prevailed on to remain in Alaska, "with the expectation that they will become herd owners and permanent citizens." Since this decision was made in 1897, a full year before the discovery of gold, it is a distortion of fact to assert, as many miners did, that the Lapps were not interested in becoming American citizens before they got their hands on a gold mine (see National Archives, Department of the Interior, P. and M. Division, No. 1326, March 29, 1902; see also 55th Cong., 2d sess., Senate Doc. No. 30, pp. 10, 48, 49, 51, 53; and Tornensis *v.* Melsing, I, *Alaska Federal Reports,* 645–648, 709, 712, 731; 56th Congress, 1st sess. [ser. 3868], Senate Doc. No. 272, pp. 7–9).

to become citizens, Melsing promised to abandon his claim, but afterward refused to abandon it. He was arrested on March 23, and Watterson was arrested on March 24 for the same reason, both men being taken to jail at St. Michael.[81]

In spite of this decision of the commissioner's court, the issues of powers of attorney and alienage were not settled. In April a "Law and Order League" was organized by fifty-two men, most of whom came from the Council City area. Among the signatories were J. L. Wilson, president, A. P. Mordaunt, secretary, and O. José Comptois — all of them jumpers of claims on Anvil Creek. These men most likely were the moving force behind a formal petition sent to Washington, D. C., entitled, "Statement of the President of the Law and Order League." [82] In the petition a few statements were made about the discovery of gold and the organization of five mining districts. Within these districts, it was alleged, Lieutenant E. S. Walker and United States Commissioner L. B. Shephard held a large number of claims through powers of attorney. It was charged that these two men had conspired to hold a test case at Cheenik in order to justify the holding of claims by powers of attorney. Because of the private interests of these men, it was insinuated, the court session was a farce. The bias of the court was manifest in the fact that the objections of the defendants were overruled, and in the fact that Commissioner Shephard and N. P. R. Hatch, attorney for the plaintiffs, had been the guests of P. H. Anderson, one of the plaintiffs, and had even slept in the same bed with him. The petition concluded with a request for the removal from office of Commissioner Shephard and Lieutenant Walker, and of Lieutenant Spaulding,[83] who had arrested Melsing and Watterson.

The members of the "Law and Order League" were not the only persons dissatisfied with the state of affairs. The little camp

[81] Captain E. S. Walker to the Adjutant General, May 2, 1899, National Archives, Records of the War Department.

[82] Published in 56th Cong., 1st sess. [ser. 3868], Senate Doc. No. 272, pp. 9–15.

[83] Lieutenant Oliver L. Spaulding, Jr., was a son of O. L. Spaulding, undersecretary of the Department of the Treasury.

of 250 men at Nome was being augmented daily by new arrivals in May and June. On May 28 the revenue cutter *Bear* arrived; on June 8 three whalers appeared in the roadstead; and on June 20 the first passenger ship, the *Garonne*, arrived with 150 gold seekers. During the next three weeks people arrived by water and land, from Kotzebue Sound, Golovin Bay, Council City, St. Michael, the Yukon valley, southern Alaska, and "the States," so that the population jumped from about 250 to 2,500 within two months' time.[84]

The great influx of people was bound to cause trouble. From Kotzebue Sound came men who were destitute, suffering from scurvy, and bitterly disappointed over the failure to find gold along the tributaries of the Kowak River. From Dawson City and the Yukon came some of the riffraff, disgusted with the strictness of Canadian law and eager to explore the new American discoveries.[85] When these men arrived and learned that "from sea-beach to sky-line the landscape was staked," they began to curse the prevailing conditions. Less than fifty mines were being worked, hundreds of claims were lying idle, and men were hungry for food and gold. This condition of affairs produced a general mood of resentment which culminated in a decision to call a miners' meeting, throw the whole district open for restaking, and eject the present owners from their claims.[86] It was only the fortunate discovery of gold on the beach that saved Nome from a civil war and afforded new opportunities for the resentful miners.[87]

[84] Samuel C. Dunham, "The Yukon and Nome Gold Regions," *Bulletin of the Department of Labor*, V (July, 1900), 845–847.

[85] Report of Captain E. S. Walker to Major P. H. Ray, July 13, 1899, National Archives, Department of the Interior, P. and M. Division, 1899, No. 2483.

[86] Report of Lieutenant Oliver L. Spaulding, Jr., July 14, 1899, in Major P. H. Ray's report to the Adjutant General, Department of Columbia, July 16, 1899; National Archives, War Department Records, Office of Adjutant General, 268941, Department of the Columbia No. 2, 1364.

[87] The writer is preparing another article on the golden sands of Nome and the developments in the district during the summer of 1899.

Theodore Roosevelt and the Alaska Boundary Settlement

THOMAS A. BAILEY

O f the half dozen or so substantial secondary accounts relating to the Alaska boundary settlement, only one, that by Mr. Henry Pringle, is the result of a systematic survey of the Roosevelt papers; and by limiting himself to three pages on this subject Mr. Pringle has either consciously omitted, or unintentionally overlooked, certain bits of information which, pieced together, throw a somewhat different light on the affair. The object of this study is to review the entire episode as revealed in the Roosevelt papers, while avoiding, in so far as possible, the repetition of familiar details.

The background of the story is briefly this: the Alaska boundary, which had been ambiguously defined in the Anglo-Russian treaty of 1825, seems to have been the object of no particular concern until 1896, when gold was discovered in the Klondike. Desirous of securing a deep-water route through the Alaska panhandle to the gold-fields, the Canadians advanced the claim that the boundary did not follow the sinuosities of the coast but cut through the most important inlets in such a way as to leave their heads in the possession of Canada. The dispute was temporarily adjusted by a *modus vivendi* arranged by Secretary of State John Hay in 1899; and when both British and Canadian high officials evinced an increasing willingness to make a permanent settlement, a convention was signed in 1903 which provided for a tribunal of "six impartial jurists of repute", three to be appointed by the president of the United States and three by his Britannic majesty. Two prominent Canadians, one of whom had had judicial experience, and Lord Alverstone, lord chief justice of England, were chosen to represent Great Britain. Roosevelt appointed Secretary of War Root, Senator Henry Cabot Lodge of Massachusetts, and ex-Senator George Turner of Washington. None of these three men had acquired any considerable "repute" in a judicial capacity, and there were grave doubts as to the impartiality of each one on the Alaska question, particularly so in the case of Senator Lodge, who was not only one of the leading professional Anglophobes in America but had already publicly committed himself against the Canadian claim. The tribunal met in London late in 1903, and by a vote of four to two, Lord Alverstone siding with the Americans, sustained the main contention of the United States, that regarding the inlets. The equal division of four small islands in dispute, as well as the adjustment of the boundary from the 56th parallel to the 141st meridian, strongly suggests that the decision was a compromise rather than a purely judicial award.

Throughout the controversy Roosevelt was unshaken in his conviction that the Canadian allegations did not "have a leg to stand on" and that they were "dangerously near blackmail".[1] In support of his view he asserted in numerous letters that the official British maps, even those presented to the tribunal, up-

[1] *Roosevelt Papers*: Roosevelt to Strachey, July 18, 1902; Roosevelt to Hay, July 10, 1902. Unless otherwise indicated, all correspondence hereafter cited may be found in the Roosevelt collection in the Library of Congress, Washington, D.C.

held the American line. He believed that the Canadians had advanced an extravagant claim in order to extort some substantial concession from the United States by a compromise settlement; and that they were trading upon their loyalty during the recent Boer War to enlist the support of a somewhat unwilling mother country.[2] Roosevelt felt that by consenting to the treaty of 1903 he was giving the Canadians their last chance to emerge gracefully from the bad hole into which they had worked themselves by insistence upon an indefensible claim. He also believed that it would be wise to settle the dispute before the turbulent mining element got out of control and precipitated a crisis.[3]

The joint commission which met at London was not an arbitral tribunal in the generally accepted sense of the term, for the Americans could expect nothing worse than a deadlock and they had an excellent chance of winning. It is clear from Roosevelt's letters that he had no intention of submitting the dispute to artibration, and that he did not regard the Alaska tribunal as an arbitral body at all.[4] He explained his attitude fully to F. W. Holls:

> An arbitration is where some outside body decides the question at issue between two parties. To call a meeting between representatives of two parties in the endeavor to come to an agreement an "arbitration" is in my idea a foolish misuse of words. . . . There is no "proposition for an arbitration", with an uneven or an even number of judges, or under any name, or upon any condition, which ever has received or ever will receive my sanction; and to call the proposed tribunal an "arbitration" is as absurd as to speak of the correspondence that has gone on between the foreign office and the State Department for the last year and a half on the subject by the same name.[5]

[2] Roosevelt to Strachey, July 18, 1902; Roosevelt to Root, Aug. 8, 1903.
[3] Roosevelt to Morley, Dec. 12, 1903.
[4] Roosevelt wrote to Hay, "I have not regarded the question as one open to reasonable doubt, and for that reason have refused to permit any arbitration upon it . . ." (Roosevelt to Hay, Jan. 14, 1903); see also Roosevelt to Ted (Theodore, jr.), Oct. 20, 1903.
[5] Roosevelt to F. W. Holls, Feb. 3, 1903.

But with regard to the four tiny islands in the Portland canal, Roosevelt was willing to admit that the Canadians had a case, and he was even prepared to submit this phase of the question to arbitration.[6]

Lest there be any mistake and the American commissioners regard themselves as judicially-minded arbiters, Roosevelt wrote all three, shortly after their appointment, positive but somewhat contradictory instructions. "You will", he said, "impartially judge the questions that come before you for decision", but "in the principle involved there will of course be no compromise". He declared that he was issuing such instructions because Sir Wilfrid Laurier, the Canadian premier, had recently made a speech in which he had virtually given the two Canadian commissioners a mandate to uphold the Canadian view.[7] It is interesting to observe, however, that nearly a year before, when the question of the joint commission was under discussion, Roosevelt had informed Hay: "I will appoint three commissioners to meet three of their commissioners, if they so desire, but I think I shall instruct our three commissioners when appointed that they are in no case to yield any of our claim." [8]

The British and the Canadians appear to have consented to the treaty of 1903 with the understanding that the three American jurists would be judicially-minded men taken directly from the supreme court or perhaps some lesser tribunal. In view of the fact that Roosevelt was accused of having hoodwinked the British and the Canadians in his appointments, it is only fair to say that he offered, or said that he offered, a place on the tribunal to two of the supreme court justices, presumably Holmes and White, both of whom declined.[9] But even granting that the supreme bench was closed to him, Roosevelt could certainly have found capable and unobjectionable men elsewhere among the federal courts had he intended in good faith to appoint "im-

[6] Roosevelt to Hay, Sept. 15, 1903.

[7] Roosevelt to Lodge, Turner, and Root, March 25, 1903.

[8] Roosevelt to Hay, July 16, 1902; also Roosevelt to Hay, July 10, 1902.

[9] Roosevelt to Arthur Lee, Dec. 7, 1903. Although it cannot be definitely determined that Holmes and White were the two justices, the internal evidence indicates that they were, strongly so in the case of Holmes.

partial jurists of repute". He explained his extraordinary choices by writing to Mr. Justice Holmes that "No man in public life in any position of prominence could have possibly avoided committing himself on the proposition" [10] — which was patently not true. The questions at issue were unusually complicated; and it would probably be fair to say that relatively few men in public life, judicial or political, had either formed any opinion on the question or had committed themselves on it. Even granting that Roosevelt finally decided to appoint commissioners with closed minds who would staunchly defend the American view, he certainly could have chosen men less offensive to the British and Canadians than Senator Lodge and ex-Senator Turner.

A number of years after the event, Senator Lodge wrote that when the Alaska convention came before the senate it encountered strong opposition from those, particularly from the northwest states, who feared that the president might appoint commissioners who would not stand fast on the American contention. Lodge then went to the president and secured from him in confidence the names of the men whom he would choose, whereupon the opposition collapsed and the convention was approved.[11] Assuming that Roosevelt approached the two supreme-court justices before this arrangement with Lodge, the story hangs together remarkably well, and has the added merit of providing what is perhaps the only rational explanation of why Roosevelt could have made such incredibly improper choices. We do know that the convention encountered enough difficulty in the senate to cause Hay considerable worry; and that the opposition suddenly ceased and the agreement was approved almost unanimously.[12] We also know that Hay, in explaining the appointments to Henry White, wrote, "the President thought it was impossible to get the treaty through the Senate without the earnest and devoted assistance of Lodge

[10] Roosevelt to Holmes, July 25, 1903.

[11] C. G. Washburn, "Memoir of Henry Cabot Lodge" (*Massachusetts Historical Society proceedings*, LVIII, 1924–5, 340).

[12] Tyler Dennett, *John Hay* (New York, 1934), 362; New York *Times*, Feb. 6, 1903, 8, col. 1.

and Turner and of the groups which they represented".[13] Probably this is what Hay had reference to when he wrote to Roosevelt, "The Alaska treaty went through beautifully — thanks to your engineering".[14]

As a matter of pure speculation, it is interesting to consider what would have happened had the two supreme-court justices consented to serve. The day after the decision of the London tribunal, Mr. Justice Holmes wrote to Roosevelt: "[Mr. Justice] White, the only person with whom I have talked here except my wife, was saying yesterday that with our judicial scepticism neither of us could have taken so convinced an attitude [as the tribunal?] and we agreed that it was a personal triumph of yours." [15] This interesting statement suggests that if Holmes and White had represented the United States, the Canadians probably would have secured a good deal more. But Roosevelt appears to have thought differently, for six weeks later he wrote to Arthur Lee that if the two supreme-court justices had served, Canada probably would have got nothing.

> You speak of your regret that the Commission was not composed exclusively of judges. I asked two judges of our Supreme Court, whom I thought most fit for the positions, to serve. They both declined; and as I now think, wisely. On this Commission we needed to have jurists who were statesmen. If the decision had been rendered purely judicially, *the Canadians would not have received the two islands which they did receive at the mouth of the Portland Canal*; and one of the judges to whom I offered the appointment has told me that on that account he would have been unable to sign the award. He would have felt that he was sitting purely as a judge, and that judicially the case did not admit of a compromise. Personally, while I think the American case even as regards these islands was the stronger, I yet attach so great importance to having the case settled that I am glad that our commissioners yielded to Lord Alverstone and thus rendered it possible for a decision to be made. But my belief is that if you had had two of our Supreme

[13] Allan Nevins, *Henry White* (New York, 1930), 195.
[14] Hay to Roosevelt, Feb. 11, 1903.
[15] Holmes to Roosevelt, Oct. 21, 1903.

Court judges on the American Commission, they would have stood out steadily for a decision on every point in favor of the American view — a determination which I think would have been technically proper, but in its results most unfortunate.[16]

Assuming that the president was referring to the above-quoted letter of Mr. Justice Holmes, which seems probable, it would appear that his memory was not altogether reliable.

In certain respects the Alaska difficulty is an outstanding example of Roosevelt's big-stick technique. He was determined to secure a settlement in his own way or no settlement at all. In March, 1902, he dispatched orders to the secretary of war to have "additional troops sent as quietly and unostentatiously as possible to Southern Alaska".[17] He wrote numerous letters to Root, Lodge, Hay, and Henry White in which he expressed his determination, if the commission failed, to occupy the disputed area by force, if necessary. Roosevelt's repetition of this theme was so frequent [18] as to suggest that he wanted his views to percolate to British officialdom through these intermediaries. He used a somewhat cruder approach in a remarkable letter to Mr. Justice Holmes, who was then in England. At the outset Roosevelt informed him that he was "entirely at liberty" to tell Joseph Chamberlain, British colonial secretary, "what I say, although of course it must be privately and unofficially". This is the passage that Roosevelt undoubtedly had in mind:

. . . If there is a disagreement I wish it distinctly understood, not only that there will be no arbitration of the matter, but that in my message to Congress I shall take a position which will prevent any possibility of arbitration hereafter; a position, I am inclined to believe, which will render it necessary for Congress to give me the authority to run the line as we claim it, by our own people, without any further regard to the attitude of England and Canada.[19]

---

[16] Roosevelt to Lee, Dec. 7, 1903; italics Roosevelt's.

[17] Henry Pringle, *Theodore Roosevelt* (New York, 1931), 290.

[18] In February, 1903, Roosevelt told the German ambassador substantially the same thing (*Die Grosse Politik*, XVII, 292).

[19] Roosevelt to Holmes, July 25, 1903.

Mr. Justice Holmes showed his letter in confidence to two prominent men whom he met in England, including the chairman of the Canadian Grand Trunk, and then he had an interview with Chamberlain in a purely unofficial capacity. Holmes's report to Roosevelt is both interesting and significant:

> He expressed regret at the attitude and said that so far as he had examined there seemed to him to be a reasonable case on the other side. I said that I knew nothing about the question although experience had led me to regard most things as open to argument. He thought it would have been a step forward for this world [?] if men with wholly open minds had been appointed. As to this particular controversy he did not care much but England had to back up Canada. . . . He was amiable, but considered the implications of your letter as exceedingly grave and to be regretted.[20]

Other attempts to browbeat the British were more subtle. Late in September, 1903, Roosevelt wrote a letter to Henry White, secretary of the American embassy in London, in which he expressed his determination to use strong measures.[21] The president evidently expected White to convey this information to high British officials, which White later testified he did.[22] About the same time Secretary Hay, who had become somewhat alarmed by Roosevelt's bellicose talk, advised White to see that the president's views were conveyed to Prime Minister Balfour. White, presuming on his friendship, had an interview with the prime minister early in October, 1903, and reported that he had "left no doubt upon his [Balfour's] mind as to the importance of the settlement nor as to the result of a failure to agree".[23] Two days after his conversation with White, Balfour was closeted twice with Lord Alverstone, who undoubtedly was informed of the seriousness of the situation. About the same time, Lodge, who knew of Roosevelt's views, also discussed

[20] Holmes to Roosevelt, Oct. 11, 1903.
[21] Roosevelt to White, Sept. 26, 1903.
[22] Nevins, *White*, 199.
[23] *Ibid.*, 200. Probably White read Roosevelt's letter of September 26 to Balfour.

the matter at some length with Balfour.[24] A few days earlier, Ambassador Choate reported that he had had an interview with Lord Lansdowne, British foreign secretary, "in which I pressed upon him very urgently the views of the President as expressed by him in our interview in June . . . ".[25]

Roosevelt evidently believed that his big-stick methods contributed materially to the final result. Shortly after receiving word of the decision he reminded Mr. Justice Holmes: "If you will turn back to the letter I wrote you in July last, and which you showed to Chamberlain, you will notice how exactly the Alaska boundary decision went along the lines I there indicated. I cannot help having a certain feeling that your showing that letter to Chamberlain and others was not without its indirect effect on the decision." [26] But Holmes was not so sure. He replied: "What you say strikes me as extremely probable, although the circumstance will remain among the arcana of history. The English are very touchy about any suggestion of a threat and I said to Mr. C.[hamberlain] that I did not for a moment suppose that it was intended in that sense — although he said and fully realized that the intimation was grave." [27]

Roosevelt undoubtedly over-estimated the effect of the Holmes letter; but his combined efforts, direct and indirect, to bring pressure on high British officials probably were not without effect. It is unthinkable that the colonial secretary, the foreign secretary, or the prime minister could have failed to convey this information to Lord Alverstone, who, faced with the Canadian clamour on the one hand and with the knowledge that an adverse decision might cause Roosevelt to take steps that might lead to war on the other, was in an unenviable position. It is also difficult to believe that Lord Alverstone, who had long known the seamy side of politics before ascending the bench,

[24] *Ibid.*, 200.

[25] A. L. P. Dennis, *Adventures in American diplomacy* (New York, 1928), 154: Choate to Hay, Oct. 20, 1903; also Roosevelt to Hay, June 29, 1903.

[26] Roosevelt to Holmes, Oct. 20, 1903; also Roosevelt to Ted, Oct. 20, 1903.

[27] Holmes to Roosevelt, Oct. 21, 1903.

was entirely immune from such pressure, though he may not consciously have yielded to it.[28] This may in part explain why he signed the final compromise decision, which was unpalatable to a purely judicial mind, and gave way on the southern extremity, where even Roosevelt admitted that the Canadians had a case.

[28] The testimony of the two Canadian commissioners supports the presumption that Lord Alverstone yielded to a compromise settlement (James White, "Henry Cabot Lodge and the Alaska boundary award", *Canadian Historical Review*, VI, Dec., 1925, 345).

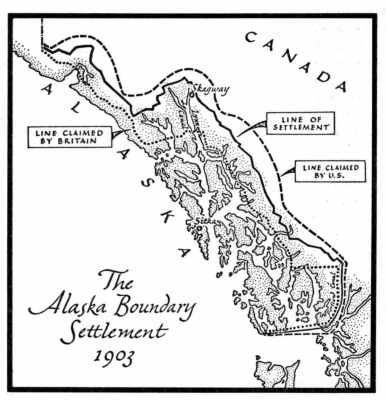

Alaska Boundary Settlement, 1903. Reproduced from A Diplomatic History of the American People, *seventh edition, by Thomas A. Bailey. Copyright © 1954 by Meredith Publishing Company. Reproduced by permission of Appleton-Century-Crofts*

Dr. Tyler Dennett is of the opinion that Roosevelt's handling of the dispute suggests that he was looking for an issue in the campaign of 1904.[29] But Roosevelt's own professions, if they mean anything, indicate that he consented to the final arrangements somewhat reluctantly, and that he did not want this problem unnecessarily aroused on the eve of a presidential election.[30] Nevertheless he was pleased with the advantageous settlement, writing to White: "The Alaska and Panama settlements coming in one year make a very good showing, do they not? I shall get Cuban reciprocity through, too."[31]

As in the case of Panama, Roosevelt got what he wanted by questionable tactics — and at the cost of a neighbour's ill-will.[32] Had he been willing to make haste more slowly, he probably would have secured substantially what he desired in both cases without the accompanying heritage of distrust. And one of the most curious things about the whole Alaska episode is that Roosevelt seems never to have realized how deeply his clumsy tactics hurt the Canadians. As he wrote to Mr. Justice White shortly after the news of the decision, "Our case was ironclad, and the chief need was a mixture of unyielding firmness in essentials and a good-humored courtesy in *everything!*"[33] The result, Roosevelt asserted with perhaps unconscious irony, "furnished a signal proof of the fairness and good will with which two friendly nations can approach and determine issues".[34] Such is not the verdict of history.

[29] Dennett, *Hay*, 359.

[30] Roosevelt to Lodge, July 8, 1903; Roosevelt to Hay, June 29, 1903; Roosevelt to Lodge, June 29, 1903.

[31] Roosevelt to White, Nov. 26, 1903.

[32] Perhaps the intemperance of Roosevelt's language regarding the Canadians is explainable in part by the fact that when the Alaska matter was coming to a head Roosevelt was in a fever over the unwillingness of the "blackmailers of Bogota" to ratify the Panama canal treaty. He even used some of the same vituperative expressions in referring both to the Canadians and to the Colombians. See particularly Roosevelt to Hay, Sept. 21, 1903.

[33] Roosevelt to White, Oct. 19, 1903; italics Roosevelt's.

[34] Annual message to congress, Dec. 7, 1903 (*Congressional record*, 58 cong., 2 sess., 5).

Duane Koenig, a professor of history at the University of Miami, Florida, received his Ph.D. from the University of Wisconsin in 1943. He has taught at the University of Missouri and the University of Alaska. The following episode in the history of Alaskan land transportation first appeared in the Pacific Northwest Quarterly, *XLV (January, 1954), 8–12.*

Ghost Railway in Alaska:
The Story of the
Tanana Valley Railroad

DUANE KOENIG

distinctive tourist attraction of Fairbanks, Alaska, is an old-time wood-burning locomotive on exhibit near the railroad station. Painted on its cab are the letters ARR 1, Alaska Railroad, No. 1. The small and rusting locomotive, fenced by several lengths of chain, is a relic of gold-rush days. Originally ARR 1 belonged to the old Tanana Valley Railroad.[1] This was a narrow gauge carrier with but 45 miles of track, constructed 1905–07. It brought freight and passengers from the Tanana River to the gold camps a few miles north of Fairbanks.[2] While

[1] First called the Tanana Mines Railroad; the name was changed in 1907 to the TVRR.

[2] Falcon Joslin, "Railroad Building in Alaska," *Alaska-Yukon Magazine*, VII (1909), 245.

placer mining prospered, the TVRR prospered. When the gold creeks were worked out, the line had to be sold to the federal government at a mark down from original costs.

During the riverboat months, usually the last of May to early October, the TVRR moved people and goods out of the port of Chena. The town was located directly on the Tanana, and the railroad tracks ran down Chena's Front Street for two-thirds of a mile by warehouses and docks.[3] At other seasons the trains delivered express and passengers arriving in Fairbanks over a sledge stage route from Valdez on Prince William Sound. The Orr and Company horse-drawn sledges took nearly a week to cover the distance of 376 miles.[4] The TVRR, despite mediocre equipment, operated every day of the year, a somewhat strenuous achievement since temperatures along the line could range from −65° in winter to 88° or more in summer.[5]

The organizer of the railroad was a pioneer Fairbanks attorney, Falcon Joslin. Sometimes eulogized by his admirers as "the Harriman of the North," he quickly recognized the need for steel rails to replace the six-horse wagons hauling tools and supplies to the tent and shanty mining camps.[6] Though the automobile was in existence, the wide use of trucks for hauling was scarcely anticipated. The TVRR was incorporated in 1904 under the laws of the state of Maine, only two years after Felix Pedro's lucky strike of gold near Fairbanks.[7] Joslin became president with New York and Chicago businessmen holding the other offices and sitting with Joslin on the board of directors. Three thousand shares of preferred stock and ten thousand shares of common stock were issued.[8]

An opportunity for splendid profit seemed at hand. Teamsters charged $1.00 to $10.00 a ton mile for haulage from Fairbanks to the camps, depending on condition of roads and trails.

[3] Percy Meaker, "The Tanana Valley of Alaska," *ibid.*, IV (1908), 439.
[4] Fairbanks *Sunday Times*, Oct. 18, 1908.
[5] Joslin, "Railroad Building in Alaska," 247.
[6] *Alaska Citizen*, Oct. 14, 1912.
[7] *Railroads in Alaska*, 60th Cong., 2nd Sess., *House Document* No. 1201, p. 11.
[8] *Ibid.*, 11–12.

The rate was $1.00 by sledge in the winter. The TVRR asked eighty-six cents for the same in 1905 and cut this to fifty-eight cents by 1908. Joslin estimated that the TVRR saved the people of the Tanana Valley at least $300,000 a year in freight costs. Passenger fares were thirteen cents a mile in 1908.[9]

The TVRR was built in two stages. In 1905 the road was put in from Chena to Gilmore on Pedro Creek, with a spur of 4.7 miles to Fairbanks. The next year these twenty-six miles of line were considerably improved.[10] The 1907 working season brought extension of the TVRR to Chatanika.[11] The obstacles overcome by Joslin and his associates were considerable: land near Chena was low and subject to periodic floods. Trestle bridges up to 600 feet long were required in the Creeks. [12] Spruce was at hand in suitable quantity and quality for ties and trestles, but rails and equipment had to be transported as much as 6,000 miles and handled as many as eleven times.[13] Six flat cars intended for the TVRR wound up instead at the bottom of the Yukon River.[14] Laborers were paid $7.50 a day and 200 men were sometimes employed in construction.[15]

Offices and shops for the line at first were located at Chena. There were terminal grounds at Chena Junction, Fairbanks, and Gilmore.[16] The amount of money spent on surveys, preliminary work, actual construction, and equipment amounted to

[9] Falcon Joslin, "Possibilities of the Tanana," *Alaska-Yukon Magazine*, IV (1907), 289; and Fairbanks *Sunday Times*, Oct. 18, 1908. But for the financial flurry of 1907, enough money would have been raised to build the TVRR to Richardson, ninety miles up the Tanana Valley.

[10] Joslin, "Possibilities of the Tanana," 289–90; and *Railroads in Alaska*, 11.

[11] *Reports of the Alaska Engineering Commission, Mar. 12, 1914–Dec. 31, 1915*, 64th Cong., 1st Sess., *House Document* No. 610, Part 2, p. 33; and Fairbanks *Daily Times*, Sept. 2, 1908.

[12] Fairbanks *Daily Times*, Sept. 2, 1908. Bridges were occasionally washed out in the spring by high water and accumulated driftwood.

[13] Alfred H. Brooks, *et al.*, *Report on Progress of Investigation of Mineral Resources of Alaska in 1905*, Department of the Interior, U.S. Geological Survey, Bulletin 284, Series A, Economic Geology (Washington, 1906), 112.

[14] *Idem.*

[15] Joslin, "Railroad Building in Alaska," 245; and "Possibilities of the Tanana," 289–90.

[16] Joslin, "Possibilities of the Tanana," 289–90.

$815,969.05.[17] When the TVRR was built in the summer of 1905, a gold spike ceremony took place. Federal district judge James Wickersham made the principal speech of the day.[18] The road was built without any government subsidy except for a five year dispensation from the federal tax of $100 a year for each mile of track.[19] Joslin was quite sensitive on the subject and regularly called for federal aid to Alaska's railroads.[20]

The Klondike and Nome gold strikes had antedated Felix Pedro's discovery of 1902. These areas had, along with Circle City and Rampart, provided many of the initial settlers for Fairbanks.[21] Falcon Joslin, for example, was a prosperous Dawson City lawyer before removing to Fairbanks.[22] At first it was nip and tuck whether Fairbanks or Chena would emerge as the principal supply base for the mining camps. Chena, incorporated in 1904, had the advantage of location at the head of navigation on the Tanana. Fairbanks, incorporated in 1903, was the center of a potentially rich agricultural area. Though Fairbanks suffered a serious flood in 1905 and a devastating fire in 1906, it won out in the race for survival: the early transfer of the

[17] *Railroads in Alaska*, 12.

[18] Ceremony was July 17, 1905.

[19] *Income Tax on Railroads in Alaska*, Hearings before the Committee on the Territories, House of Representatives, 63rd Cong., 2nd Sess., H. R. 9770, Part 1 (Washington, 1912), p. 8.

[20] Joslin, "Possibilities of the Tanana," 292; and Cordova *Daily Alaskan*, Oct. 31, 1912. Of the many proposals submitted to the federal government for developing Alaska, one of the most curious was a 1906 suggestion that Russian Jews who were refugees from Czarist oppression should be settled in the Territory. The theory was that, already being acclimated to cold areas, they would be able to accustom themselves to Alaska without difficulty. Proponent of the scheme was Abe Spring, president of the Tanana Electrical Company. He believed money might be made available from the Baron Hirsch fund for this purpose. See *Railroads in Alaska*, Hearings before the Committee on the Territories, House of Representatives, 59th Cong., 1st Sess. (Washington, 1906), pp. 40–43.

[21] Meaker, *op. cit.*, 437.

[22] Joslin soon became one of Alaska's most enthusiastic publicists and his speeches and articles regularly directed attention to the possibilities of growth for Alaska. He often pointed out that Scandinavia in the same latitude as Alaska had 12,000 miles of railroad track. Why not Alaska? See *Alaska Citizen*, Oct. 14, 1912.

seat of the judicial district to Fairbanks from Eagle being of prime importance.[23]

As Fairbanks grew, Chena declined. By 1908, trains from Chatanika ran through to Fairbanks; by the end of World War I, commuter service to Chena stopped. Shortly afterwards the Chena tracks were pulled up.[24] Yet at the time the line was completed in 1907, Chena was a thriving community of 400 souls. The business district boasted two hotels, two restaurants, a bakery, laundry, flume hose factory, and two general stores.[25] TVRR general manager A. P. Tyson, sometimes called the "genial manager," pondered at his offices in Chena such problems as how to obey an Interstate Commerce Commission ruling that no dynamite or explosives could be carried less than ten car lengths from a locomotive, when his engines normally pulled only four cars.[26]

Chena's population fell to fifty by 1915; the town now had but one general store. When Chena began to slump, the operations of the railroad were transferred to the Garden Island section of Fairbanks.[27] As Chena was depopulated, some settler cabins were moved by sledge to Fairbanks. Other buildings were cannibalized for firewood by the remaining inhabitants. Today only a few foundations give clue to the once booming river port of Chena. This problem of fuel was always serious until the ARR opened up the central Alaska coal fields. As a result of wood shortage, many of the hills around Chena and Ester were denuded of trees at this period.[28]

Fairbanks, on the other hand, reported steady progress. Within five years, what had been a tent city had possibly 5,000

[23] The 1905 flood did about $100,000 damage. The fire of May 22, 1906, razed Front Street of Fairbanks, the business and shopping district.

[24] *Report of the Governor of Alaska to the Secretary of the Interior, 1920*, Department of the Interior (Washington, 1920), 17.

[25] *Polk's Alaska-Yukon Gazetteer and Business Directory, 1907–08* (Seattle, 1907), 143.

[26] *Ibid., 1915–16* (Seattle, 1915), 148; Fairbanks *Daily Times*, Oct. 10 and 18, 1908; and Fairbanks *Daily News-Miner*, Oct. 13, 1912.

[27] *Polk's Alaska-Yukon Gazetteer and Business Directory 1915–16*, 148; and *Reports of the Alaska Engineering Commission, 1914–15*, 33.

[28] *Reports of the Alaska Engineering Commission, 1914–15*, 65.

inhabitants and the usual amenities of community life.[29] There were a book store, two hospitals (St. Joseph's and St. Matthew's), a green house, and two fortune tellers (Mmes Melbourne and Zelpha).[30] A reader of Fairbanks newspapers in 1908 could learn that the TVRR would handle livestock by special arrangement only, but that empty beer kegs and soda bottles would be carried free; that ice and roller rinks and moving pictures were advertising for customers; that "not a single good location can be found for rent and there is a lively demand among those desiring to buy cabins." If he were musically inclined, Sunday concerts featured such original compositions as a "Toast to the Brides of Fairbanks," and the "St. Fairbanks Tickle." Feature stories spoke of the increasing use of cigarettes and "How It Feels to Fly in an Aeroplane." [31]

Two years earlier a commentator had written, "The streets of Fairbanks always present an interesting picture with their handsome store fronts, well dressed men, fashionably gowned women, and happy children going to and from school, and occasional groups of hardy miners and prospectors, horses and buggies, delivery wagons and freight teams."[32] To serve the tastes of the cultivated Fairbanks appetite, the grocery department of the Northern Commercial Company advertised pate de foie gras, crab meat, Russian caviar, and imported anchovies.[33] The TVRR's contribution to this prosperity was a payroll of $25,000 a month, 1907–08.[34]

Though more primitive, the gold creek towns were to some degree reflections of Chena and Fairbanks. They mushroomed as placer operations became profitable and disappeared very often when the easily accessible pay streaks were worked out.

[29] *Report of the Governor of Alaska, 1904* (Washington, 1904), 15; and *Polk's Alaska-Yukon Gazetteer and Business Directory, 1907–08*, 211.

[30] *Polk's Alaska-Yukon Gazetteer and Business Directory, 1907–08*, 211. Fairbanks *Daily Times*, Sept. 3, 1908; and Lafe Eakin Spray, "Fairbanks, Alaska's Golden Heart," *Alaska-Yukon Magazine*, XIII (1912), 143–44.

[31] Fairbanks *Daily Times*, Sept. 13, Oct. 2, 13, 27, and 29, 1908.

[32] Meaker, *op. cit.*, 440.

[33] Fairbanks *Daily Times*, Oct. 30, 1908.

[34] Fairbanks *Sunday Times*, Oct. 18, 1908.

If the schedules of the TVRR are studied over the years, changes will be noted as settlements grew or collapsed. An advertising blurb of the period explained: "The Tanana Valley Railroad supplies placer and quartz mines in the district, and keeps everybody in touch with everybody else with regular train service." [35]

Early equipment included four locomotives, four passenger coaches, and thirty freight cars. An engine and crew were kept at Gilmore to maintain winter service in the event of snow on the divide at Mile 28, 1,496 feet.[36] The schedule of trains was as follows: commuter trains left Chena for Fairbanks at 8:00 A.M. and 1:00 P.M., arriving forty-five minutes later. Return was at 11:00 A.M. and 5:15 P.M. The principal train, the "Gold Stream Special," started from Chatanika so shoppers would have a little time in Fairbanks. It went south at 7:30 A.M. and stopped at Olnes, Ridgetop, Gilmore, Fox, Eldorado, Ester Siding, Chena Junction, and Fairbanks. The trip took four hours and ten minutes. The return trip left Fairbanks at 1:15 P.M. For extra service a gasoline *autocarril* operated twice a day between Fairbanks and Fox. It was also used for TVRR officials and guests.[37] Passenger and freight totals depended on the mining activity. In 1910, 53,248 passengers were moved; this fell to 27,832 by 1914. In 1909, 15,809 tons of freight were transported. This was off a third by 1914.[38]

The present-day traveler who thinks of Cleary as a ski lodge and Chatanika as a gas station finds it hard to recollect the tremendous excitement and activity of fifty years ago. During the acme of the gold frenzy, Fox had 500 people, Gilmore 300,

[35] "The Tanana Magazine," special number, Fairbanks *Daily Times*, December, 1912, p. vii. Agnes Rush Burr, *Alaska* (Boston, 1919), 145, draws a colorful picture of the period, describing sandwiches at $1.00 each, baking powder biscuits at $2.00 a dozen, and Yukon stoves at $45.00.

[36] Fairbanks *Sunday Times*, Oct. 18, 1908; and *Reports of the Alaska Engineering Commission*, 34. Highest grade on the track was 2¼ per cent.

[37] Fairbanks *Daily Times*, Sept. 1, 1908; and Fairbanks *Sunday Times*, Oct. 18, 1908.

[38] *Reports of the Alaska Engineering Commission, 1914–1915.*

Olnes the same, and Chatanika, 650.[39] In some instances populations would be larger if men in the nearby mining camps were included. The towns were in staging and telephone contact with creek camps in the vicinity. As a case in point, freight for Dome or Vault was put off the TVRR near Ridgetop; shipments for Cleary, at Chatanika. Telephone rather than telegraph was used by the railroad for moving its equipment.[40]

Since the TVRR was so intimately associated with the prosperity of mining, it is worth while to note the financial transactions of a typical town. A few banking records are available for the Cleary City branch of the Fairbanks Banking Company.[41] On November 17, 1906, cash on hand in the bank amounted to $18,518.11, most of which was in currency, though $1,330 was in coined gold. There was also $1,648.79 in gold dust. Total bank balance on this date was $101,545.99.[42] The amount of gold dust on hand would vary: on October 27, 1906, it had amounted to $10,987.99.[43] The bank appears to have carried out all the usual banking functions including transfer of funds by wire. At this time Cleary was the trading center for more than 1,000 people.

Stockholders of the TVRR had great hopes for the future. Falcon Joslin spoke freely of building an extension to Circle City and a 600 mile western link to Nome. He hoped for another line up the Tanana Valley, across the Yukon boundary and south down the Chilkat River to a point on the Lynn Canal near Haines. This route would pass for 800 miles through presumably rich gold and copper country. Joslin confidently predicted: "It is believed a station could be established every twenty miles . . . and that gold or copper mines could be opened near every station." [44] He stated that this was geographi-

[39] Fairbanks *Daily Times*, Oct. 21, 1908; *Polk's Alaska-Yukon Gazetteer and Business Directory, 1915–16*, 137–40, 145, 258, 263, and 442; and "The Tanana Magazine," p. ii.

[40] "The Tanana Magazine," p. ii.

[41] On deposit in the School of Mines Library, University of Alaska.

[42] *Ibid.*

[43] *Ibid.*; and Fairbanks *Daily Times*, Sept. 1, 1908.

[44] Joslin, "Railroad Building in Alaska," 247. Section 2 of the Railway Act of May 14, 1898, provided for twenty acres of land for station each ten miles.

cally and commercially the most favorable route for a trunk railroad in Alaska and that it was the only one considered that would entirely cross the territory.[45]

The TVRR kept busy during the halcyon days of placer mining in 1909. Once the gold streams were worked, the recession was swift. Within three years Joslin complained, "Not a foot of railroad construction has been done in Alaska for two years. None is planned. Railroad building has ceased."[46] He went on the record as castigating the government for its illiberal policy towards Alaska carriers: (1) failure to offer grants in aid; (2) reluctance to open coal fields; (3) imposition of a tax of twenty-five cents for each cord of wood harvested from government property (a tax, he alleged, that cost more to collect than it brought in); and (4) the collection of a tax of $100 per mile of track each year from Alaska railroads.[47] The exemption for this last had expired, and it was not until Joslin had personally appeared before a congressional committee in 1914 that it was withdrawn.

There were hopes that quartz lode mining would provide a more substantial basis for the economy of the Fairbanks area than placer operations; these hopes were quickly doomed. In the dozen years after the discovery of gold by Felix Pedro, some $63,000,000 of the yellow metal was produced. Only $900,000 of this came from lode mining. Year of greatest production was 1909 when $9,500,000 was mined. This was off two-thirds by the War of 1914 and down to $350,000 in 1927.[48] Placer mining could be conducted with limited capital, a minimum of equipment, and in a few instances, with substantial return. The

[45] Joslin, "Railroad Building in Alaska," 247. Numerous railroad schemes were discussed during this period. Perhaps the most unusual was that of a Russian promoter named Loecq de Lobel who spoke of a trans-Alaska railroad to Nome, a car ferry to East Cape, Siberia, and a connection to the Trans-Siberian Railroad. See Cordova *Daily Alaskan*, Oct. 31, 1912, and May 26, 1914; and James Wickersham, *Bibliography of Alaskan Literature, 1724–1924*, I (College, Alaska, 1928), 282–87.

[46] "The Tanana Magazine," 12.

[47] *Ibid.*; and Cordova *Daily Alaskan*, Oct. 31, 1912.

[48] Fairbanks *Daily News-Miner*, Feb. 24, 1951; and *Reports of the Alaska Engineering Commission*, 64.

quartz veins in the Fairbanks area were of such character that profits comparable with placer washings were impossible. The lode mining required more machinery and larger investments. Water was highly important, both for placer mining in the valleys and quartz mining on the ridges. Particularly was this true in the former instance. A period of drought could bring mining to a halt. Such a dry spell occurred in 1908. When rains came at the beginning of September, the relief was considerable. Cleary Creek reported the rain "has livened and cheered everyone up." Fairbanks Creek said, "it has put heart into all the people," and Goldstream, "everybody is working everywhere full tilt." [49] People who sought to mine or locate quartz stamping mills without regard to water supply usually suffered the consequences of their folly.[50]

From the standpoint of investment, the TVRR never proved a financial success, though it was able to meet expenses and pay interest on its indebtedness of $666,000.[51] Operating expenses were about 62 per cent of gross earnings.[52] It must not be overlooked that, albeit not a moneymaker, the service of the TVRR to the gold creeks was important. Weekdays the railroad brought passengers, fuel, and supplies. Sometimes on Sundays and holidays excursions were offered at bargain rates for sightseers.[53]

The federal government in 1914 decided to start construction of a through railroad which would extend from Seward to Fairbanks.[54] This would run north and south from the coast to the heart of Alaska and would make coal available to the mi-

---

[49] Fairbanks *Daily Times*, Sept. 4, 1908.

[50] "The Tanana Magazine," 11.

[51] *Reports of the Alaska Engineering Commission, 1914–1915.*

[52] Joslin, "Railroad Building in Alaska," 247.

[53] The writer has seen a broadside of the TVRR offering special train service for July 4, 1913. Excursion rates to Fairbanks, July 2–6, were $4.00 from Chatanika, $3.50 from Olnes, $3.00 from Ridgetop, $2.50 from Gilmore, and $1.75 from Fox. These were round trips. A note added, "No freight of any kind will be handled on the 4th and 5th." Signer was C. W. Joynt, general manager. Broadside is in the possession of Fairbanks Exploration Company. Also, see Meaker, *op. cit.*, 441.

[54] Seattle *Post-Intelligencer*, Sept. 19, 1912; and law of March 12, 1914.

ing camps. Progress was sometimes sporadic, but the ultimate goal was never lost sight of. Falcon Joslin supported the project with enthusiasm, both on the speaker's platform and in print.[55]

The government railroad brought changes for the TVRR. In 1917 the line was first leased and then sold to the government. Considering the bad state of the roadbed and the age of the equipment, the price of $300,000 would appear fair to all concerned.[56] Further, it was patent that until cheap fuel should be available and perhaps the price of gold raised, the mines would never recover. The vitality of the TVRR was tied to mining prosperity. This could be seen from the population charts. Fairbanks, which had 5,000 inhabitants five years after founding, had less than 1,200 by the 1920's.[57]

Under government operation the roadbed of the TVRR was improved, and a temporary narrow-gauge line was built to Nenana.[58] Pending the construction of a bridge over the Tanana at Nenana, freight was brought across the river by ferry and sledge. In 1923 the ARR was at last completed. The Nenana bridge was finished, and in the late spring the Nenana-Fairbanks link was converted to standard gauge. The president himself, Warren G. Harding, visited Alaska in June of 1923 to dedicate the completed ARR.[59] After the introduction of through train service from Seward to Fairbanks, narrow-gauge equipment was once more relegated to the Chatanika run. The line did perform two final services before being abandoned. It transported heavy dredge equipment to Goldstream and Chatanika during the 1920's for mining activities there, and it offered commuter service for students attending the Alaska Agricultural College and School of Mines. The latter had opened its doors in 1923. At this time between Fairbanks and Happy

[55] Law of March 12, 1914.

[56] *Report of the Governor of Alaska, 1917* (Washington, 1917), 48.

[57] *Rand McNally Guide to Alaska and the Yukon* (New York and Chicago, 1922), 158.

[58] *Report of the Governor of Alaska, 1916* (Washington, 1916), 44; and *ibid.*, 1920 (Washington, 1920), 17.

[59] *Report of the Governor of Alaska, 1923* (Washington, 1923), 6.

Station there was a three rail track, able to accommodate the narrow-gauge trains going to Chatanika or the standard-gauge trains heading south. First an electric car and then a gasoline car were used to bring students to the College station. Round-trip tickets from Fairbanks were twenty-five cents. By 1929 bus service was sufficiently developed to threaten the commuter car. In November, 1931, the gasoline car was finally abandoned. Some years later the old College station was moved from its original location to a Fairbanks suburb and converted into a modern dwelling.[60]

Death knell for the Chatanika branch came with the improvement of the highway from Fairbanks to the gold creeks. Narrow-gauge service to Chatanika was discontinued in August, 1930, at a saving to the ARR of $38,362.31 a year.[61] Rails were soon removed and only a few ties and trestles remain to indicate where the line once ran. For the most part the once prosperous gold towns are as derelict as Chena — ghost towns serviced by a ghost railroad. To this page in territorial history ARR No. 1 remains as a permanent monument.

[60] *Report of the Governor of Alaska, 1932* (Washington, 1932), 24. The College station was located between Fairbanks and Chena Junction on the old TVRR right-of-way. For a picture of the old Beach electric car used in bringing students to College station, see *Farthest North Collegian*, Sept. 1, 1931.

[61] *Report of the Governor of Alaska, 1931* (Washington, 1931), 30.

Dr. Hulley received his highest degree from the University of Washington in 1943, and taught for several years at the University of Alaska. His article surveys one of the more fascinating topics in twentieth century Alaskan history. The essay appeared in the Pacific Northwest Quarterly, XL *(October, 1949), 327–40.*

Historical Survey
of the Matanuska Valley
Settlement in Alaska

CLARENCE C. HULLEY

In 1935 Harry Hopkins, Federal Relief Administrator in Washington, D.C., and other federal authorities, took
up the idea of establishing government-assisted colonists in the
most suitable region of Alaska. Such settlement would aid the
growth of the territory, supply agricultural foodstuffs for Alaska,
serve as a step toward the possible defenses of the region, and
above all give a new start to scores of families from among the
millions of farmers who were finding it almost impossible to
make a living in the United States because of prolonged low
prices for agricultural commodities, drought, and other depression ills.

The Matanuska Valley in south-central Alaska, some forty-
five miles northeast of Anchorage, was finally selected by the

federal administrators as the most suitable area for the "New Deal" experiment in colony planting in the Far North. This valley at the head of Knik Arm of Cook Inlet, cupped in by high mountains on three sides, possessed about the most desirable location, soil, and climate for agriculture in Alaska. Back toward Anchorage is the Chugach Range, high enough to ward off part of the rain clouds which drench the Gulf of Alaska coastal lands, yet not high enough to shut off the mild winds that blow from the Pacific Ocean. Northward from the Matanuska Valley lie the Talkeetna Mountains, and beyond these rise the lofty peaks of the Alaska Range. These rugged barriers protect the valley from some of the extreme cold and heat of the interior. The valley climate is a unique mixture of the maritime weather of southern Alaska and the decidedly continental climate of the interior, with coastal characteristics usually dominant. The soil of the Matanuska Valley consists almost entirely of the unconsolidated material deposited by water, wind, or ice during and since the recession of a mighty glacier. This ice mass formerly filled the entire Matanuska Valley to a height of several thousand feet. The present Matanuska and Knik glaciers are two of the best-known existing remnants of the vast ice formation that once filled the whole valley. With a climate moderately mild, a rainfall generous but not heavy, and a soil in a considerable part of the valley better for agriculture than in most of Alaska, the Matanuska region seemed without doubt the best spot in the huge territory to plant the new colony.[1]

The Matanuska Valley was long occupied by the Knik Indians. Relics from the sites of their former villages are found along the shores of the streams flowing into Cook Inlet and Turnagain Arm. The Russians entered Cook Inlet in the times of Baranov, and before the end of the Russian occupation of Alaska had established a trading post at Knik, near the present hamlet of the same name. At Old Harbor and New Kodiak on Kodiak Island, and at Ninilchik on the Kenai Peninsula, the Russians experimented with agriculture, but they made no at-

[1] W. A. Rockie, *Physical Land Conditions in the Matanuska Valley of Alaska,* Federal Government Publication (Washington, 1946), 4.

tempts at farming in the Matanuska Valley. Before 1896 a few trappers, concerning whom little is known, had entered the beautiful valley of the Muddy River, called in the Knik Indian language, Matanuska. In the days of the Yukon gold rush, 1896 to 1902, fortune seekers northward bound for Dawson City, Circle City, or Forty Mile, landed on the shores of Cook Inlet and attempted the overland trip through the Matanuska Valley to the Copper River country and north by the route now followed by the Glenn and Richardson highways. Traces of gold were discovered by these Klondike-bound adventurers in the mountains along the Matanuksa River. Gold is still mined in the mountains that lie on both sides of the Muddy River. A trading post was established at Matanuska about 1900, but settlement attained no importance until after 1915. During the next few years the federal government took up the project of a government railroad from Anchorage to interior Alaska, and several families established themselves on land in the Matanuska Valley. In 1915 the Matanuska Agricultural Experiment Station was established in the valley near the trading post of Matanuska. By 1961 there were about four hundred settlers living in the entire Matanuska region. A greater part of the open and easily accessible land in the valley of the Muddy River was homesteaded during the period 1913 to 1921, while Anchorage was being built as a railroad base, and the Alaska Railroad to Nenana and Fairbanks was under construction. The farming was largely of the subsistence type. Few settlers during that period possessed modern farm machinery; tractors were rarely seen in the valley, and the possession of a team of horses placed any settler among the better equipped. Although clearing and breaking the soil without adequate machinery was most difficult, yet many of these early pioneers in the valley improved their homesteads considerably. However, few attempted to clear or cultivate large pieces of land, but contented themselves rather with working small patches for the growing of vegetables for home consumption. In spite of a few successful attempts, most of the homesteads in the valley were abandoned within a few years. The lure of good jobs "outside" during the boom years of the 1920's caused many of the homesteaders to leave their primitive Alaska farms. Scores of homesteads were abandoned. Alaska homestead laws and the absence of all land tax encouraged settlers to obtain possession of homesteads and then go on extended vacations. The results were most unfortunate. A homesteader might have left for parts unknown years before, yet his claims remained inviolate. And even though he had left Alaska and had not been heard from for years, his homestead could not be legally taken over by anyone else.

A few of these early Matanuska settlers, however, remained in the valley. There was relatively little new settlement or development after 1921 until the beginning of the 1930's, when there was a slight renewed interest in homesteading in the area. During the early 1930's, partly because of the depression in the United States and partly because of the efforts of M. D. Snodgrass, settlement agent for the Alaska Railroad, and Colonel O. F. Ohlson, manager of the Alaska Railroad, a number of families from the United States settled in the Matanuska Valley. In 1934 there were about one hundred families in the whole Matanuska area. Farming methods were still inadequate, patches here and there throughout the valley were under cultivation, abandoned homesteads were scattered from one end of the valley to the other. Roads were poor. Traders at the posts of Wasilla and Matanuska were accused of charging the settlers very high prices for all commodities. Such was the situation when the Roosevelt administration commenced to take steps to plant a government-sponsored colony there in 1934.[2]

In June, 1934, a survey of the Matanuska Valley was made for colonization purposes by agents of the federal government, and when a report was received in January, 1935, the Federal Emergency Relief Administration and the Department of the Interior agreed jointly to undertake the scheme for federal-sponsored settlement. It was supposed by federal agents connected with planning the project that people from the colder northern states would be most likely to survive, prosper, and

[2] Information obtained by the author from Mr. Snodgrass of Palmer in 1947.

increase in the Far North. In March of 1935 branches of the Federal Emergency Relief Administration in the states of Minnesota, Michigan, and Wisconsin were notified to select two hundred families to be sent to colonize the Matanuska Valley. The Social Service Administration in these states was to make investigations of all families to be chosen for the scheme.

The State Emergency Relief Administration then determined the section of each state from which the colonists were to be picked. In instructions sent out from St. Paul by the Supervisor of Field Work, it was stated that the following factors should be taken into consideration in picking out the prospective colonists. The families were to be chosen first from those on the active relief rolls of the county, and second from border-line groups, provided vacancies existed. Settlers of Scandinavian or at least north European origin, presumably better adaptable to cold climates, were to be drawn from farming communities. The age group, twenty-five to thirty-five inclusive, might be extended in the case of applicants with special qualifications. Health and educational factors were to be taken into consideration. Chronic illnesses in any family would debar it from joining the project. A parental educational background showing high school achievement was felt desirable, and elementary school completion was a prerequisite. The relief workers were forbidden to oversell the project and were instructed to place the facts, including possible hardships, before each prospective settler.[3]

According to this directive, the preliminary choice made by the field workers was to include about four times the number of the actual quota of two hundred families. The records of these families were to be carefully checked and their homes revisited to get all additional information possible. It was intended that the actual selection of the families be made in the state offices of the Social Service Division. The federal government would transport the selected families to Alaska, furnish each family with forty acres of land, a house supplied with modern con-

[3] State Emergency Relief Administration, Division of Social Service, Instructions to Field Workers, March 13, 1935.

veniences, and the settlers would be given thirty years on easy terms to pay for it.

In February of 1935 homesteading in the Matanuska Valley was prohibited by Executive Order, No. 6957 (February 4, 1935), which provided that all government-owned lands in the valley were reserved for the colony's needs. The federal administration also took possession of all abandoned homesteads in the area. Advance agents were sent into the valley to select land, arrange transportation from Seward, and make preliminary preparations for the arrival of the settlers.

The proposed project aroused a good deal of controversy in the press and in Congress during the next two or three years. As soon as news of the scheme became known, the critics and enemies of the Roosevelt administration declared the entire plan to be the wildest dream of an insane government. It would be little less than a Siberian exile, they said, to send decent Americans to Alaska, a land which, as they thought, was filled with glaciers, mosquitoes, and cannibalistic natives.[4]

The final selection of the prospective colonists was left to the relief officials in the various counties of Wisconsin, Michigan, and Minnesota. Despite earlier instructions, there seems to have been no uniform or systematic method of selecting the prospective settlers. Some county officials were very exacting, and demanded that the prospective settlers meet all the age, physical, and educational requirements set up by the Social Service Division. In other counties the federal or county officials seem to have selected those families who had been on the local relief rolls for the longest period of time. In other cases persons not on relief applied and were accepted.[5] Some county or state social workers interviewing the prospective colonists painted a very bright, and quite false, picture of conditions in Alaska. Other agents offered the true facts about the climate, handicaps, and difficulties that might be expected in the Far North.[6]

[4] Anchorage *Daily Times*, June 6, 1935.

[5] This information was obtained by the author from the Kerttulas, Sandviks, and other families at Palmer who came in the migration of 1935 to the Matanuska Valley.

[6] Information obtained from the colonists at Palmer.

The Alaska Rural Rehabilitation Corporation was created under the Federal Emergency Relief Administration as a non-profit corporation to administer the colony until such time as it could establish a coöperative organization of its own to manage the colony's affairs. Before a colonist left his home, he signed a contract with the Alaska Rural Rehabilitation Corporation stating the conditions of the migration to Alaska and the commitments to which each party agreed. The transportation of the colonists, their families, and household possessions was to be paid from the point of departure to Palmer in the Matanuska Valley by the Federal Emergency Relief Administration.[7]

The first contingent of Matanuska colonists comprised some sixty-seven families, in all 298 persons. They traveled from St. Paul, where they had been gathered by state organizations, to San Francisco on a special train which became a scene of crying babies and general confusion. Arriving in San Francisco on April 29, the colonists were guests of the city until they sailed for Seward, Alaska, aboard the U.S. Army transport *St. Mihiel*. The ship arrived at Seward on the evening of May 6, but since living quarters for the families had not yet been completed at Palmer, the colonists were kept aboard in Seward until May 10.[8]

About the same time the *St. Mihiel* docked at Seward, the *North Star*, carrying laborers from California, arrived at the same port. These workers were sent at once to Palmer to commence work on temporary tent-houses for the colonists. The *North Star* also carried nearly fifteen hundred tons of cargo, including farm machinery, tools, groceries, food, and household equipment for the settlement.[9]

On the morning of May 10 the first contingent of colonists was crowded into another special train bound for Anchorage. There the settlers were met at the railroad station by a committee of Alaska Railroad officials and Anchorage citizens headed

[7] Information obtained from Mr. and Mrs. O. Kerttula of Palmer.
[8] Information obtained from P. Sandvik of Palmer.
[9] T. C. Feldman, *The Federal Colonization Project in the Matanuska Valley Alaska*, M.A. thesis, University of Washington, 1941, p. 19.

by Colonel O. F. Ohlson. A general holiday was declared by the Anchorage town council, and a banquet was given the colonists in the Community Hall. Colonel Ohlson gave an address, telling the newcomers that President Roosevelt was the person who originated the idea of planting the colony in the Matanuska. Colonel Ohlson neglected to mention that he was perhaps the first one to suggest the idea to the federal government. After the reception and banquet the colonists were taken over the short Matanuska branch of the Alaska Railroad to the new colony center of Palmer, named after an old trader, Joseph Palmer, who had maintained a store in the Matanuska region for years.

About seventy tent-houses, arranged in rows along the railroad track at Palmer, were ready for the settlers on their arrival. Some wells had been dug, and stoves, beds, and other equipment were on hand. Food and household essentials also had been provided, although some badly needed supplies were delayed some months in transit.

Meanwhile, another group of colonists for the settlement gathered at St. Paul, Minnesota, for transportation to Alaska by way of Seattle. These colonists, 135 families, were from the states of Michigan and Wisconsin. Traveling from St. Paul in two special trains, they arrived in Seattle on May 15 and were housed in the Frye Hotel until they embarked for Seward. The *St. Mihiel,* carrying the second detachment of settlers, docked at Seward on the morning of May 22. The men disembarked at once and took the train for Palmer, so that they would be there for the drawing of lots for land. Because shelters were not yet ready, the women and children of this second group of colonists remained on board the *St. Mihiel* at Seward for a few days until temporary dwellings could be constructed.[10]

Before the colonists arrived at Palmer, the Matanuska Valley had been surveyed, and two hundred tracts, each of forty acres in the most desirable sections of the valley, had been marked out. The drawing for these lots or tracts of land, upon which

[10] Anchorage *Daily Times,* May 23, 1935.

each colonist would make his new home, took place on the morning of May 29 at Palmer. There was both excitement and disappointment among the colonists. To encourage satisfaction, they were permitted to trade or exchange tracts with each other if they desired, so that old neighbors and relatives might obtain farms that were in the same sections of the valley.

The Matanuska Valley was still a rolling sea of timber with patches of cleared land here and there. It was raining when the colonists arrived and continued to rain for days. It is usually dry in the springtime in the Matanuska and rainy in the late summer. But nature seemed to scheme to discourage the set-tlers. The tent city of temporary homes which had been put up at Palmer was hardly adequate for such rainy, cold weather. It all seemed a woeful muddle. During late May and June of 1935 it was a somewhat confused and discouraged group of settlers that faced the future in the valley. Rain continued, and there was mud everywhere. An epidemic of colds and other minor ill-nesses spread among the children. Equipment for clearing land and general supplies for the colony, provided by agencies of the federal government, were held up somewhere along the ship-ping route, and there was a considerable delay in their arrival. There was some tardiness, too, in Juneau in preparing the ter-ritorial documents incorporating the Alaska Rural Rehabilita-tion Corporation.[11]

During the months of July, August, and September there was much activity and some discontent among the colonists. A con-siderable number of them were completely unsuited to the con-ditions and soon demanded to be taken back to the United States. Some were the kind who would not succeed anywhere; some had never been out of the area in which they had lived in the Middle West. On the other hand, many were industrious people likely to succeed if given an opportunity.

Construction of permanent homes for the colonists on their individual tracts of land followed several fairly standard plans with some variations. A few of the settlers built temporary log

[11] Information obtained from families in the Palmer district who came there in 1935.

houses, but these were all replaced after a few years with frame houses. Part of the work of construction of the first farm buildings was done by the colonists and part by workers brought in by the federal government. About six hundred transient workers were imported from the "States" during the spring and summer of 1935 to aid with construction work. By the middle of October, 1935, when cold weather commenced, 140 houses were ready for occupancy, and nearly forty others were under construction. Wells, too, had been dug on a number of the occupied tracts of land, although well digging often proved a discouraging task. In some places pipes driven to a depth of forty or forty-five feet brought only salt water.

Most of the settlers brought into the Matanuska Valley by the Roosevelt administration in 1935 were young married couples. During the first two years of the colony's existence over 130 babies were born to the two hundred colonist families. In fact, Dr. Conrad Earl Albrecht, who was physician in the Matanuska Valley from 1935 to 1941, found during those six years that bringing babies into the world made up the major part of his work.

During the first year of the colony's existence the children of school age who lived near Palmer attended classes in railroad box cars. The school-age youngsters who lived close to the old villages of Matanuska and Wasilla attended classes in the rather primitive school buildings already in existence. For the remainder of the colony's school-age children who lived at some distance from Palmer, Wasilla, or Matanuska, a plan was devised for giving some formal instruction. The children of several families gathered one day each week at a centrally located farmhouse and received their weekly instruction. The teachers engaged in this type of work traveled from place to place by car. A central school building was commenced in Palmer during the autumn of 1936. It was a twenty-room structure with library, laboratory, industrial-arts workshop, and gymnasium. It has been added to several times since. Graduates of Palmer High School are now in attendance at the universities of Alaska and Washington, as well as at the State College of Washington and many other institutions of higher learning.

Livestock for the farms in the valley was purchased in the United States and shipped to Palmer for distribution to become the nucleus of future herds. In June, 1935, thirty pigs and 145 cows were distributed among the Matanuska Valley farmers. More cattle arrived in the colony in December of the same year. A shipment of Leghorn chicks arrived at Palmer early in 1936. During the second summer of the colony's existence, six hundred sheep were imported from the state of Washington. Some horses were also imported for the colonists, but the Matanuska Valley farmers soon found that tractors were more economical than horses.

The colonists suffered many difficult times between 1935 and 1941. Some irritations arose from the very nature of the climate and economy of the region, some from maladjustment on the part of the colonists, and some from the administration by federal agents. As early as June, 1935, before the colony was two months old, forty colonists sent telegrams of complaint to President Roosevelt and Governor Troy of Alaska. Patrick Hemmer and Mrs. I. M. Sandvik, who officially represented about forty disaffected colonists, asserted in their telegrams of protest that their homes were not being built according to schedule, that wells were not being dug, that adequate schools were not being provided, that prices at the government commissary were higher than those charged by privately owned stores in Palmer, Matanuska, and Wasilla.[12] Mrs. Sandvik had a large family, and one can well understand her concern about adequate schools.

This complaint and others were given considerable publicity by newspapers in the United States. Certain members of the Senate became concerned and asked Harry Hopkins to give a report on the conditions in the far-away Alaska colony. Mr. Hopkins stated in his report to the Senate late in June, 1935, that facilities providing for safe and reasonably comfortable living conditions would be completed before winter commenced

[12] Anchorage *Daily Times*, June 19, 1935.

in the valley. The Federal Relief Administrator admitted that construction work in the colony was far behind schedule. Eugene Carr was dispatched to Palmer as a special representative of the Federal Emergency Relief Administration to investigate conditions and to make on-the-spot decisions. One of the first changes made was an adjustment of prices at the commissary.[13]

The soils of the Matanuska Valley vary greatly.[14] Because of the action of glaciers and winds, the distribution of the deep permeable soils needed for agriculture is very uneven. A great part of the valley consists of a few inches of silty, sandy loam over underlying gravel. Certain sections have deep top soil of high agricultural value, but in many other places are gravel outcroppings. However, no two farms have quite the same soil conditions, and each colonist had to learn how to fertilize and cultivate his own land to the best advantage.

Drainage, too, was a major problem on many farms. Glaciers left kettles, and surface drainage was far from complete. Settlers had to wrestle with problems quite unknown in the Middle West.

Climatic conditions, while more favorable than in most of Alaska, were nevertheless quite different from what the colonists had known back in former homes. Throughout the valley the summer is cooler than in any agricultural region in continental United States, while the autumn and winter are milder than in most of the north-central region of the "States." Spring is cool, and summer is marked by very long days. Spring and early summer are frequently very dry, while late summer and early autumn are usually too wet for easy harvesting of any crop. Some sections of the valley are subject to summer frosts, while other sections rarely ever have them. Certain sections of the valley are subject to very severe windstorms, known as the "Matanuska wind" and the "Knik wind," from the two valleys out of which they blow. The "Matanuska wind" enters the

[13] 74th Congress, 1st Session, *Congressional Record*, Vol. 79, Part 9, June 27, 1935, p. 10284; Anchorage *Daily Times*, June 28, 1935.

[14] For a complete discussion of the soils of the Matanuska Valley, see Rockie, *op. cit.*

valley from the northeast, usually in winter and spring, and blows with considerable violence for several days in the region north and east of Palmer. In some places trees lean to the west or southwest as a result of the force of these spring winds. The "Knik winds" blow from the southeast; it is a warm wind and frequently brings in a dust storm. In certain sections of the valley a gale of great violence may be blowing, and in other sections within a mile or two, but out of the path of one of these valley winds, the air may be still.

In temperature and precipitation the climate is more moderate than might be expected. Summer temperatures are never oppressive, the mean temperature being 52.8 degrees, and the thermometer rarely registers as low as 10 degrees below zero during the months of December, January, and February. The growing season at Palmer averages about 110 days, and from the middle of June until late in July there is practically no darkness. About fifteen inches is the average precipitation in the valley. Humidity is usually high, and as a rule, evaporation is low. Plowing and sowing of crops usually commence between April 25 and May 1.

To make ready for cultivation the greater portion of the valley land required clearing of timber and undergrowth. This was laborious and costly. Dairying and truck farming were the types of agriculture most likely to prove profitable. Both required much careful and hard work, and cheap hired labor was not available. For seven months of each year livestock had to be fed and housed in barns. Many of the settlers were accustomed to the grain-growing types of agriculture of the Middle West and scorned truck gardening and dairying, and they soon became depressed by the long dark winters and the cold windy springs and discouraged by the continuous hard work that was required of them.

Not all the Alaskan markets were open to products from the Matanuska region. Freight rates and the competitive prices of agricultural products from the United States prevented shipment of the Matanuska products to southeastern Alaska and other distant parts of the territory. The Anchorage market was limited and soon became oversupplied with certain commodities which were produced more cheaply in the United States where costs of labor were less. Commercial interests that were already supplying Alaska from Seattle had no intention of losing the profits of the trade and did their best to hold the business. Stories were spread that Matanuska vegetables were without taste and food value, because they had grown too rapidly.

Many settlers abandoned the colony. As early as June 28, 1935, six families requested to be returned to the United States. The federal government paid their return transportation. Within another month twenty more families had packed their belongings and departed for the "States." Several colonists left the project to become associated with other work in Alaska. By July of 1940, 106 of the original colonists had returned to the United States or had left the colony to find other employment in Alaska. As these families left Matanuska, others were recruited by federal agents to take their places. Several Alaskan families joined the colony, subject to the same regulations.[15] Other new colonists came from the "States."

Construction of the community went forward steadily. The colonists teamed together to finish the building of a community center, warehouse, dormitory, power plant, school, and hospital in Palmer. Work on the hospital had been commenced in July, 1935, following an outbreak of a series of epidemics of scarlet fever, measles, and other communicable diseases among the younger colonists. Palmer Hospital was later taken over by the Seventh Day Adventists and has been managed by this group for several years. By the autumn of 1937 Palmer, although not incorporated, was permanently established as a town. By 1940 about 150 tracts were occupied. According to the Anchorage *Daily Times*, the federal government had put $4,169,370 [16] into the project.

The Federal Emergency Relief Administration had charge of the colony during 1935 when the basic construction work was under way. Later the federal government placed the Matanuska

[15] Feldman, *op. cit.*, 30–32.
[16] Anchorage *Daily Times*, July 9, 1940.

Valley project under the control of the Department of the Interior. Don Louis Irwin, who had been superintendent of the Agricultural Experiment Station at Fairbanks during 1934-1935, became the first general manager of the project. The financing of the individual purchases of farms and equipment was carried out through the Alaska Rural Rehabilitation Corporation of Palmer, which was incorporated under Alaskan territorial law. The administration of the colony's business was taken over by the Alaska Rural Rehabilitation Corporation in October, 1936. Governor Troy of Alaska appointed the board of directors, which took over its duties on October 31, 1935. The board included Colonel Ohlson, Luther C. Hess, E. R. Tarwater, A. H. McDonald, and several colonists.[17]

In June of 1935 the colonists set up a community council to meet with the general manager. Each of the nine camps into which the colonists were divided selected a man and a woman representative to be members of this council. The body met once a week with the general manager to discuss problems of the colony. Out of this community council grew the Matanuska Valley Civic Association, organized in 1938 to guide civil and social development in the colony. During the first year the task of distributing farm machinery among the colonists was handled by this organization. It was instrumental in founding the *Valley Settler* (a local newspaper published by the colonists), in getting fire-fighting equipment, and in securing the services of a public nurse for the colony.[18]

The Matanuska Valley Farmers Coöperative was created in the autumn of 1937. The Works Progress Administration in the federal capital drafted the plans for this coöperative organization, and it was incorporated under Alaskan territorial law. A contract was made whereby the Alaska Rural Rehabilitation Corporation acted as managing agent for the coöperative until it was able to handle its own business. This arrangement was in effect for two years. Other colonists and old settlers became members of the coöperative. Plans were laid for the association

---

[17] Feldman, *op. cit.*, 33–34.
[18] *Valley Settler*, January 27, 1938.

to take over all businesses related to management of the store, creamery, and hatchery, as well as the marketing of the products of the colony. Every farmer was given an opportunity to purchase his quota of shares in the coöperative. L. C. Stock was engaged as the first general manager of the Matanuska Valley Farmers Coöperative.

During the winter of 1935 a branch of the National Grange was organized in Palmer, Northland Grange No. 1. The Palmer Grange devoted its efforts to attempting to provide rural electric power for the valley, better roads, lower freight rates, and farm legislation.

Other organizations instituted during the first half-dozen years of the colony's existence included a 4-H club, a Poultry Growers Association, and a Home Demonstration club, organized through the Extension Service of the University of Alaska. Churches were active in the community. The Lutheran and the Roman Catholic denominations were the strongest. In Father J. Snead of Portland, who became pastor at Palmer, the Roman Catholics found a young, energetic, and broad-minded leader. The Adventists and other groups also had considerable strength.

In 1940 the holdings of the Alaska Rural Rehabilitation Corporation, the federal-government owned and controlled agency, were sold to the Matanuska Valley Farmers Coöperative Association. This action of January, 1940, brought the creamery, hatchery, cannery, garage, trading post, power plant, hospital, dormitory, and staff houses at Palmer under the coöperative, although actual control of these projects was not transferred until 1941. Since 1941 the cooperative has added other facilities, such as a potato-storage plant, a products-processing plant, and a slaughter house. The coöperative has about 165 members and is a nonprofit corporation. It functions as an independent organization, purchasing farmers' needs and marketing farmers' products. It is under the watchful eye of the federal-government agencies which hold mortgages totaling a good part of the entire assets of the Matanuska Valley Farmers Coöperative Association.[19]

The federal government, through its official agency at the time that the Matanuska colony was established, loaned the colonists the money to set up their farms and aided them to get established. The loans were to be repayable over a thirty-year period. The colonists have been paying for their lands, buildings, and equipment ever since. There have been various difficulties and many dissatisfied colonists. Forty acres proved to be too small a holding from which to make a living in the Matanuska Valley. Most of the farmers who have remained have acquired considerably larger acreages.

Until 1938 the colonists were given credit for cash payments each month for work done on the improvement of farms. In April, 1938, the general manager announced that this work-credit system would end on the first of October, 1938. After that date the colonists would be treated as self-supporting.

Besides the problems arising from climate, soil, drainage, and marketing, other difficulties faced the colony. In 1936 the warehouse and offices at Palmer were destroyed by fire, and some of the records were burned. Gossip created vicious tales as to how and why the fire occurred. A near disaster befell the colony in October, 1939, when an unusually early snowfall buried about 80 per cent of the crops. There was an ever-present tension between the laissez-faire type of enterprise, long characteristic of American economic life, and collectivism under government sponsorship. Bickering developed between the Farmers Coöperative members and the Alaska Rural Rehabilitation Corporation, and factions developed within the coöperative itself. There were rumors of loss and inefficiency in the management of the coöperative store and other coöperative ventures, and managers followed each other in rapid succession. Private enterprises opened businesses in Palmer in competition with the Farmers Coöperative projects. Many of the colonists pre-

[19] Information obtained at Palmer from personal contacts and discussions during 1947 and 1948.

ferred to deal with these competitive businesses rather than support their own establishments. The settlers brought in by the government in 1935, working under government sponsorship and subsidies, entered into competition with the older settlers who had established themselves by their own unaided efforts. Some of the older settlers joined the coöperative colony, but others continued to denounce it.

The colony struggled on through the hard years from 1935 to 1940. The turn of the tide came when, in 1940, the federal government commenced construction of the Fort Richardson army base near Anchorage. By 1943 there were over 50,000 men at this base. Then the colony entered upon a period of wartime prosperity. Everything that could be produced from the earth was needed for the army and the thousands of civilians brought by the war into Alaska. An acre of lettuce, cabbage, or celery brought a return of thousands of dollars. Moreover, there were many well-paid jobs to be obtained within forty miles of the colony. Thus the Matanuska Valley colonists did exceptionally well during the years from 1941 to 1945. The actual income of most of the farmers in the colony was increased by three or four times that of the earnings of 1937–1938.

The Matanuska colony is now nearly fifteen years old. Despite all handicaps, internal difficulties, and adverse criticism, much has been accomplished. There are now about 2,000 people in the Matanuska Valley, including the inhabitants of the towns of Palmer and Wasilla. Palmer has not yet been incorporated by Alaskan law, but it is, nevertheless, a busy and thriving country town of three hundred inhabitants. There are 8,500 to 9,000 acres of land under cultivation in the valley. The colonists own more than 800 cows, chiefly of the Holstein and Guernsey breeds, and dairying has become the most dependable type of agriculture in the valley. Besides the dairy cattle there are between 700 and 800 pigs, some 1,300 head of sheep, and 200 to 250 head of beef or younger cattle (figures given are for 1948; there has been some increase since then). Vegetable crops, expecially celery, cauliflower, lettuce, cabbage, peas, and potatoes have been grown profitably. Grains, including wheat, oats, barley, and rye, have also paid well. Berries are grown in limited quantities for the local market and for home use. At times potatoes and some of the other vegetables have been a "drug on the market," owing to local overproduction, poor transportation facilities, outside competition, etc.

In 1941 the Matanuska Valley Electric Association was created with Walter Mau as manager. The electrification of the valley went forward rapidly, and now almost all settlers are supplied with electrical power. Telephone service is being supplied to the valley farmers by a coöperative at reasonable rates. Additions have been made to the school building twice since it was built in 1936. During 1936–1937, 332 pupils were in attendance, 15 teachers were employed, and school-bus routes established. Today the school has grown considerably larger and is considered one of the better-equipped schools in the territory.

The Matanuska colony scheme cost the federal government between five and six million dollars, but this included over one million dollars for roads and school. It appears that about a dozen of the original settlers of 1935 have paid off their original $7,000 or $8,000 debt, plus interest, which was the average indebtedness of each farmer brought in by the Roosevelt administration. The settlers have a period of thirty years in which to pay off their indebtedness, and as the annual payments are small and the interest rate comparatively low, some prefer to take the full period to pay off the sum rather than hasten to complete it earlier. About forty of the original two hundred families who were brought in by the "New Deal" in 1935 still reside in the Matanuska Valley. Many of these have paid off a sizable amount of the original debt, and most have at least kept up their annual payment.[20]

Colonies and colonization schemes must be judged by long-term results. Even success is hard to measure. One is safe in saying that, despite all stories, criticisms, and reports of failure, the Matanuska colony has been at least a limited success. A visitor today will see in the Matanuska Valley small farms as

[20] This information was obtained from the office of the general manager, Alaska Rural Rehabilitation Corporation, Palmer, Alaska, in 1948.

prosperous looking as any in continental United States, and the colony is only fifteen years old. In the westward expansion of the American people across the United States, the lure of cheap land was sufficient to entice settlers to new regions; however, today, and especially in Alaska, the situation is very different. Alaska at its best is a marginal agricultural region. The long winters, the difficult springs, and the distance from populated centers, all discourage settlers. Likewise, the great age of individual laissez-faire enterprise is, it appears, on the wane. All manner of projects throughout the world are now being promoted by government assistance. If the United States desires to develop the limited possibilities of Alaskan agriculture, it may have to continue some form of government aid and encouragement to settlers in the huge territory of the North.

Senator Gruening has had the most varied career of any author in the anthology. He received his bachelor's degree and his M.D. from Harvard University. Turning from medicine to journalism, he edited The Nation *and the New York* Post. *One of his books,* Mexico and Its Heritage, *was published in 1928. In 1933 he became a principal New Deal adviser on Latin American affairs. He was head of the Interior Department's Division of Territories and Island Possessions from 1934 to 1939. President Franklin Roosevelt appointed him governor of the Territory of Alaska in 1939. When the Territory achieved statehood, he was elected one of the new state's first senators. As author of* The State of Alaska (1954), *Gruening is both an historian of Alaska and an Alaskan historical figure.*

The following paper, which appeared in Scientific Monthly, *LXXVII (July, 1953), 3–12, was presented at the Third Alaskan Science Conference, in 1952. Though some of the information is dated, the reader can study how Senator Gruening uses historical analysis to understand contemporary problems.*

Alaska: Progress and Problems

ERNEST GRUENING

It is difficult to dissociate a discussion of Alaska's progress and problems from its previous history. Perhaps the word "progress" should be defined first, because there may be divergent views about what constitutes progress.

There was, and perhaps still is, a school of thought in the United States that believed the best use of Alaska was to keep it a wilderness area and lock up its resources indefinitely, reserving them for use in some far-distant future. There is still another that, concerned with the preservation of a particular resource, fears the advancing march of modernity and would hold it in check to safeguard that resource at any price. There was until very recently a school of thought in the Office of Indian Affairs that believed it desirable to preserve aboriginal custom and manners unchanged, to try to enclose its human exemplars as hermetically as possible, and to insulate them from the penetration and contamination of the white man's civilization. Such ideas are perhaps entitled to respectful attention, but for the purpose of this discussion I shall try to outline my conception of progress for Alaska.

World population is increasing at an unprecedented rate. Many areas are overcrowded, and sparsely settled areas, if habitable, naturally invite settlement. Considerations of special importance relating to national defense call for the populating of Alaska and for the creation of conditions there that will tend to insure the permanence of such population. Apart from all this, the westward trek of peoples, in search of greater freedom and greater economic opportunity, is undoubtedly the oldest American tradition. It is a tradition that antedated the founding of our republic and indeed was inseparably connected with its origins. It brought the Jamestown colonists, the Pilgrims, the Dutch, and the great variety of European emigrants across the Atlantic in the seventeenth and eighteenth centuries. It led them to cross the Appalachians toward the close of the eighteenth century. It carried them across the plains, over the Rockies and to the Pacific coast in the nineteenth century. It is bringing them to Alaska *now* in the middle of the twentieth century. This contemporary westward migration of Americans to Alaska is in a sense a final chapter in a great episode. This chapter gives new vitality and meaning to the phrase long used to describe Alaska, "the last frontier."

If we accept this interpretation of what is now taking place, it follows naturally that, to whatever extent immigration to Alaska has been achieved, it may be considered progress, particularly if the evidence indicates that the settlement is probably permanent. So we may set down the following as the first item under the head of progress: The population of Alaska *is* increasing very rapidly, and the increase has aspects of greater permanence than previous migrations.

The first Alaska census, taken in 1880, showed a population of 33,426. The next census, 1890, showed the population to be 32,052. This slight decrease need not be considered significant, as it is known that the first census in 1880, taken under great difficulties, was not too reliable. But certain it is that in the ninth decade of the nineteenth century, when the population of the

United States increased by over 12,000,000, the population of Alaska did not increase. The census of 1900, reflecting the great gold rush, showed a population of 63,592, or an increase of almost 100 per cent. This impulse carried over to 1910, with the gold strikes in the Tanana Valley, the Iditarod, and Nome following those in the Klondike. The somewhat temporary nature of this influx, coinciding with the diminishing productivity of the gold fields, was reflected in the drop in population to 55,036 in 1920. World War I certainly contributed to that decrease because there was little in the way of economic opportunity in Alaska to induce the young men who had gone to war to return to Alaska. The increase in the third decade to 59,278, or some 7 per cent, indicated no great change. Actually, if Alaska's population figures for the first three decades of this century are contrasted with those of the United States, it will be plain that Alaska, viewed politically, economically, and socially, was static and stagnant. In those same thirty years the population of the United States increased by 45,000,000. But in Alaska there was a decrease, from 1900 to 1930, of 4314, or over 6 per cent. The accidental discovery of gold that brought a rush of prospectors to Alaska at the turn of the century had doubled the population, and by and large that figure was retained for the next thirty years. But throughout the first third of this century Alaska experienced none of the normal growth, either through excess of births over deaths, or through immigration, which was characteristic of the United States as a whole, and which was particularly related to the westward movement of population.

In Alaska the real change began in the 1930's. The 1940 census showed that Alaska's population had reached 72,524. This was an all-time high for Alaska; it showed an increase of 22.3 per cent, a percentage of increase in the preceding decade that was exceeded in that same decade by only two states in the Union. Thus Alaska in the fourth decade of this century — from 1930 to 1940 — showed a percentage of increase greater than that shown by forty-six states. The Alaskan increase of 22.3 per cent contrasted with a 7.2 per cent increase for the United States as a whole.

In the fifth decade, however, the increase and the acceleration were even greater. The 1950 census showed a population of 128,643, or approximately 77 per cent in the last decade, an increase greater, percentagewise, than that of any state or territory, and a population which had more than doubled in 20 years. Today Alaska's population may be conservatively estimated at over 165,000, and its increase is not only continuing but continuing at an accelerating rate. We may conservatively forecast a population of 200,000 in 1955, and of 300,000 in 1960.* The really important aspect of this growth is that it contains many elements of permanence formerly lacking. Until recently, until this present growth got under way, Alaska differed substantially from the previous frontiers in American history. Whereas the westward march from the Atlantic to the Pacific contained a large proportion of would-be settlers, individuals who hoped to establish themselves permanently in new surroundings, no such purpose actuated the overwhelming majority of those who came to Alaska from the time of the first population increase in the late 1890's until the early 1930's. They came rather as the Spanish and Portuguese came to Central and South America, not to take up permanent residence in the New World but to get gold and take it back with them to the mother country. Obviously, with that motivation there could be no permanence but only transience. Desire to improve the environment was lacking, and the resulting lack of improvements perpetuated the transience. It was a kind of vicious cycle. Those who came to get rich quickly — if possible — and get out found little here to make permanent residence attractive, and, their intentions being what they were, they did little to make the environment better. This, of course, was by no means true of a small minority who stayed on, but by and large the pattern was set by those whose stay was purposefully temporary. This attitude was reflected in the relative inaction of successive territorial legislatures. And the Federal Government continued its course of indifference and lack of interest.

What, then, are the factors that have contributed to this popu-

*In 1960, the population of Alaska was 226,167. — Ed. Note.

lation increase and to its presumed permanence? The answer lies in part in a fundamental change in Federal attitude which has been reflected in Federal policy and action. An important motivation for this change may be found in international events. In the first three decades only two significant *Federal* actions contributed to Alaska's development. One was the construction of the Alaska Railroad, begun in 1915 by the Wilson administration and completed in 1924. The second was the establishment of a land-grant college — the Alaska Agricultural College and School of Mines, authorized in 1915 and opened in 1922, which in 1935 became the University of Alaska.

In the 1930's there were several such actions. First was the increase in September, 1933, of the price of gold from $20.67 to $35 an ounce. This gave Alaska's second industry, mining, a great lift, which continued for the rest of that decade. Second was the Matanuska colonization project in 1935, which brought 200 families into the Valley, gave agriculture in Alaska an impetus, and widely publicized Alaska as an area of potential settlement. Third was the extension of social security to Alaska in 1937 by action of the Alaska legislature after a request from the Federal authorities.

In the 1940's international events and the Federal actions resulting therefrom stimulated population growth. Preparations for defense, totally lacking previously, brought in thousands of construction workers and G.I.'s. Not a few of the G.I.'s settled in Alaska at the end of hostilities.

The defense program for World War II brought the first major airports and radio range stations to Alaska. They made possible commercial air service between the States and Alaska, which was initiated in 1940 and amplified in 1945 by certification of additional carriers and additional routes by the Civil Aeronautics Board.

The defense program also brought the Alaska Highway in 1942 (although a highway over a different route had been recommended three years earlier by an American commission), and the Glenn Highway and with it the beginnings of a territorial highway system.

The World War II defense program established three permanent bases in Alaska (not counting the Aleutians) whose existence has benefitted the economies of their areas: Fort Richardson near Anchorage, Ladd Field near Fairbanks, the naval station at Kodiak. It established a scattering of CAA stations throughout Alaska. It made a Coast Guard District of Alaska.

These were the material contributions incidental to defense when hostilities ended in 1945. They were substantial. They aided the economy of Alaska, created some permanent and needed improvements, and established a great new interest in Alaska in the States as a new frontier of promise and opportunity. The last contribution was of great importance.

The years since 1945 have seen a great amplification and intensification of the process. The "Cold War" and defensive preparations to avert a third world war have brought extensive housing, the first highway program in Alaska in the interior (though not in southeastern Alaska), great airports at Anchorage and Fairbanks; a public works program on a fifty-fifty matching basis which is helping to provide schools and utilities for our towns; the beginnings of an electrification program by the United States Reclamation Service at Eklutna; a program of agricultural research; a new interest in the mining of strategic minerals; the erection of the Geophysical Institute at the University of Alaska.

No less significant, however, have been the territorial changes in attitude and performance. The Territory was becoming conscious of its responsibilities and its destiny. It established a full-time health program in 1945; a territorial housing authority; a territorial Department of Agriculture; a development board. In 1946 it passed a Veterans' Act under which several thousand Alaska veterans were loaned funds to buy or build homes or to acquire farms or businesses.

In 1949 the legislature established a territorial Department of Fisheries. It set up a Department of Aviation, and under it, with funds from aviation gasoline and some Federal matching, brought about the construction or improvement of a hundred airports and seaplane facilities. In 1951 the legislature enacted

legislation to promote the tourist industry on a fifty-fifty matching basis with private subscriptions. A most constructive step
was also taken in banning billboard advertising.

Most significant of all was the enactment in 1949 of a comprehensive revenue program. Previously taxes had been negligible, and whole categories of businesses and individuals de-
riving substantial profits and income from Alaska had paid no
taxes whatever. The result was that the revenues were insufficient to support essential public services. Great wealth was extracted from the Territory, but next to none stayed here for its
development. That has now been fully remedied by an inclusive yet moderate tax structure. The Territory will not only balance its budget at the end of this biennium but will also emerge
with a surplus of several million dollars. The Territory has no
indebtedness. By being financially strong and sound, it is able,
and will increasingly be able, to render the services — schooling, health, welfare — which the American people properly expect as part of their way of life.

So far the record of progress relates chiefly to governmental
action, Federal and territorial. But private industry is coming
to Alaska. In this very year the first pulp plant in Alaska is under construction near Ketchikan to utilize the long-unutilized
forests; a plywood mill is under way at Juneau; the Aluminum
Company of America is making gigantic plans for processing
at Dyea; extensive private oil drilling is scheduled for the coming season in the Katalla-Yakataga area; new tin and coal mines
have been opened — all undertakings of private capital, which
is entitled to every legitimate encouragement and assistance,
particularly since so large a part of Alaska's economy has been,
and will for some time continue to be, based on government
spending.

These, then, are some of the factors that account for Alaska's
recent and accelerating growth and progress.

At this point the above rather limited identification of *progress* with *growth of population* should be supplemented by sug-
gesting the goal to which that progress is or should be directed.
This goal, in the process of its attainment, predicates a highly

important role for Alaska. Given its unique geographical position — its location in far northern latitudes, its fronting on the Arctic Ocean, its extension into the Eastern Hemisphere, its juxtaposition to the Soviet imperialism — all characteristics which no other area under our flag possesses, Alaska's destiny must be envisioned and shaped on the cosmic scale to which its great size, position, and potentialities invite our national enterprise.

In short, the destiny of Alaska is to be not merely militarily a bulwark of defense (and, if necessary, of offense) for this continent — and hence for the free world — the strategic assignment Billy Mitchell so brilliantly forecast, but, concomitantly, a no less vital outpost for the American idea and therefore a living demonstration of all that is best in an American society. That is a major role in national and world affairs, but it requires no great imagination to appreciate its desirability and value. It is a challenge only to our powers of performance.

To date, the cultures of only two peoples have established themselves permanently this far north. They are the Scandinavians (and Finns), who have erected a high civilization and a stable economy in these latitudes and whose concepts of freedom are similar to ours; and they are the Russians who, under the present rulers in the Kremlin, have established at our doors a militant society whose concepts are antithetical to ours and menace freedom wherever it may be found or hoped for on earth. Therefore the *national* stake in the attainment of Alaska's destiny is emphasized here, and the suggestion is made that it be constantly borne in mind as we discuss Alaska's problems.

The most essential step toward this major objective is statehood. This is not the place for a detailed presentation of the cogent arguments for it, but here are a few salient points:

1) The people of Alaska asked for statehood in a referendum six years ago.

2) Public opinion in the United States overwhelmingly supports statehood for Alaska.

3) Every Congressional committee to which the issue has been referred has, after study, reported favorably upon it.

4) No arguments have been advanced against statehood which are not in essence identical with those presented against the admission of states previously admitted.

5) The minority opposition in Alaska has dwindled almost wholly to contention about the statehood bill itself — introduced in the last Congress — with regard to whether it was generous enough.

6) The national interest will be greatly served by statehood and disserved by its continuing denial.

Statehood will go far to provide a solution, or at the very least will facilitate a solution, of many of Alaska's problems. All these problems are related directly or indirectly to the issue of continuing growth in population and of its permanence.

Among the most pressing are land problems. Alaska is a very sparsely settled part of the world. It has about one person for every 3½ square miles, in contrast to the United States with about fifty per square mile. Among the obstacles to settlement are the Federal land laws. In general, these are the laws adopted decades ago for the forty-eight states. They are obsolete, inappropriate for Alaska, and to a degree unworkable. Poor as they are, their application is further handicapped by the failure of Congress to appropriate adequate funds for surveys, and likewise by red tape in their administration. This is a field in which Alaskans are estopped by law from helping themselves.

Over 99 per cent of Alaska is Federal land — either public domain controlled by the Department of the Interior, or reserved or withdrawn by some other Federal department. The Organic Act for Alaska passed by Congress in 1912, likewise an obsolete and outworn instrument — against whose limitations of territorial autonomy every governor since its enactment has protested — leaves the businesss of basic land legislation in the hands of Congress. Congress has done little to improve the situation.

The first Alaska legislature created by the Organic Act, meeting in 1913, memorialized Congress on various basic issues which the Organic Act specifically forbade the territorial legislators to do anything about. Its memorials on the subject of land were fourfold. *One* asked that the land laws be revised and simplified to promote settlement. A *second* asked that an end be put to reservations and withdrawals, and that some of those already made be restored for public entry. A *third* asked that an end be put to shore-space reservations. A *fourth* dealt with still other aspects. Not only has Congress paid no heed, but the reservation and withdrawal policy has continued without let or hindrance so that today approximately one-fourth of Alaska, some 94,000,000 acres or 147,000 square miles, is in some form of withdrawal or other. This is an area larger than our third largest state, Montana. It is an area larger than the total areas of eleven smaller states — the six New England States and New Jersey, Delaware, Maryland, South Carolina, and West Virginia. This does not mean that some of these withdrawals have not been for a good purpose. But the withdrawal process has become so tangled, haphazard, and confused, with withdrawals overlapping and with their original purpose long since forgotten and invalid, that it has taken the Department of the Interior two years to find out what and where these withdrawals are. The question of returning such withdrawals, whose present use is not clearly essential, still lies ahead. A subcommittee of the House Committee on Interior and Insular Affairs is coming to Alaska this week to address itself particularly to the problems of the revision of our land laws. But experience has shown that there is often a long gap between Congressional investigation and favorable action.

What is needed is a thorough overhauling of our land laws relating to Alaska. Their objective should be to promote settlement. One of the arguments repeatedly used by the Congressional opponents of statehood is that only a small fraction of land in Alaska has passed from Federal to private ownership. Yet Congress itself has held the keys and has persistently refused to unlock the door.

The statehood bill, which lost by a margin of one vote in the last Senate, would give the State of Alaska some 23,000,000 acres of land to be chosen by the authorities of the new state. Reserved land is, of course, excluded from this offer which would, nevertheless, give the State of Alaska an area as large as New England or, to put it in another way, give Alaska more land for its use or disposal than is now possessed by four public land states, namely, Arizona, Idaho, Utah, and Nevada which have, respectively, 19,327,927, 19,269,006, 14,803,363, and 8,894,920 acres not in public domain. The *percentage* of this proposed grant to the new state of Alaska is, of course, smaller than that given to the public land states, leaving some 93 per cent of Alaska's total area in public lands, as compared with Nevada's 87 per cent, Arizona's 73 per cent, Utah's 72 per cent, and Idaho's 67 per cent. But here the percentages are less important than the actual amount of land — the best unreserved land — the new state would receive.

But statehood is introduced here again in this discussion merely to point out its remedial benefits, which are probably not otherwise obtainable. The process of revision of the land laws — as distinct from the question of land grant to the new state — would be speeded by statehood to the extent that the addition of two senators and a representative with a vote would aid the process.

There is another aspect of land law revision which requires attention. Two important geographic areas are now in national forest reserves. They are the Tongass National Forest, which roughly coincides with all southeastern Alaska, an area of some 16,000,000 acres, and the Chugach National Forest of some 4,000,000 acres, which includes the next habitable coastal area to the westward. These two areas include seven of the fourteen principal towns in Alaska: the capital, Juneau, and Ketchikan, which ranked respectively second and third in the last census, Sitka, Petersburg, Wrangell, Cordova, and Seward.

The forestry resource is extremely important to Alaska. Its utilization on a major scale is just beginning with the construction of Alaska's first pulp plant near Ketchikan. Its functioning should in no wise be impaired. But there is an aspect of these two national forest reserves, unrelated to the forestry function, which is unique. Nowhere else under the flag do national forests blanket a whole economic area or include and circumscribe a state's principal urban centers. The situation would be analogous to having the national forests occupy the total western fourth of Washington and Oregon and surround the cities of Seattle, Tacoma, and Portland. Recently a small beginning has been made in southeastern Alaska by excluding from the forest reserve, and returning to public domain for disposal under laws and regulations applicable to it, limited areas surrounding these towns. The objective is to enable these towns to develop suburbs and to achieve the normal development of other American cities. But, apart from the fact that even this move, while in the right direction, has only begun, uncertain as to issue and insufficient in scope, one great obstacle to normal development remains. That is that the highway construction policies in these important areas, which include half the principal urban centers of Alaska, are not in the hands of road-building agencies whose mandate and purpose it is to develop highway communications. The control rests in the hands of the regional forester, whose mandate is forest conservation and utilization, and not commercial, industrial, or urban development. The consequence of this anomaly is that, while the interior of Alaska is developing a fine highway *system*, linked to the continental highway system, southeastern Alaska's insignificant road mileage consists of mere short stretches of highway leading only a very slight distance out of each town and connecting with no other community.

The remedy is to exclude from the forest areas the *rights-of-way* for proposed and needed through highways and permit such arteries to be included in the construction program which is rapidly speeding the development of interior Alaska. Such a reform would in no wise interfere with the forestry function but would promote growth, settlement, and other development. Desirable sites within the forest areas should likewise be made easily available on a fee simple basis for the development of tourist lodges.

So much for the basic land problem.

Since its discussion has brought us to the subject of highways, it will be well to continue with it. Highways are indispensable to development and settlement. One has only to observe the springing up of lodges, tourist cabins, and homes taking place in Alaska whenever and wherever a highway cuts through the wilderness to be aware of this visible result. Among the memorials to Congress adopted by the first legislature in 1913 was a request for highway construction. Except for the Richardson Highway built in the second decade as a low standard road, Congress did nothing (until three years ago), but discriminated grossly and uniquely against Alaska by failing to include Alaska in the Federal Highway Act — except for a limited participation in forest areas. No other territory suffered this discrimination. Alaska's share of Federal funds in the twenty-nine years since the passage of this act has been estimated at $350,000,000. Fractional matching on some formula would have been required, but Congress declined to sanction any formula. World War II's exigencies, however, brought the Glenn Highway, connecting Anchorage with Fairbanks and Valdez by means of the Richardson Highway, and also that part of the Alaska Highway between the Yukon boundary and Fairbanks as well as the Tok cut-off. Three years ago, in consequence of the Soviet threat, Congress authorized a road-building program with an annual appropriation of between 20 and 25 million dollars which includes black-topping the principal highways. Under this program a highway starting at Homer and connecting the Kenai Peninsula has been completed; Seward has been connected with the system. A road into the Forty-mile and to the Yukon at Eagle near the Canadian boundary and a connection with Dawson have been completed. Two other major projects have been begun, namely, a road to Mt. McKinley Park from the Richardson Highway and a highway from Cordova to Chitina over the old Copper River and Northwestern Railway right-of-way.

In addition, numerous shorter farm and access roads have been built. This is a fine beginning, but it should be considered only a beginning. It is fair to consider that Alaska's road-building program came a quarter of a century after the Federal Government had started its cooperative highway aid program with the forty-eight states and other territories. Indeed, the present Federal highway program, although most ably administered in Alaska, is already demonstrating its insufficiency, for surfacing and maintenance are consuming an increasing share of the budget. Thus the Paxson-McKinley Park Highway, begun two years ago, has had its current fiscal year allocation cut to $500,000, and the Cordova-Copper River Highway, which would link the one as yet unconnected city in central Alaska with the territorial and continental highways system, starts with an appropriation of only $650,000, although the cost of the project is estimated at $12,000,000. If the road program is to be effective in building up Alaska and serving its pressing needs, it must expand, and the annual Congressional appropriation — some $20,000,000 for the coming fiscal year — must at least be doubled for the next ten years; at the end of that period this would approximate in appropriation what would have been Alaska's rightful share had not Congress after Congress discriminated against Alaska by failure to include it in the Federal Highway Act. But more pertinent than the argument based on atonement is the fact that Alaska will require, at the very least, the mileage that an annual appropriation of $40,000,000 for the next ten years will construct. A hundred-million-dollar annual program would be even sounder. This is clearly a Federal function, although the Territory which now builds and maintains some smaller road and harbor projects could properly be expected to bring its present two-cent gasoline tax up to the national average, which is about six cents.

The need for harbor projects presents another problem. For years this has been the function of the Army Engineers, but in recent years they have all but ceased to construct in Alaska. The responsibility is, of course, the Congress's. The engineers have studied, surveyed, and recommended many needed projects for small boat harbors to take care of Alaska's fishing fleets, for flood control and much else. These projects remain pigeonholed. In recent years there has been a tendency to stigmatize such river and harbor projects as pork-barrel projects. That is not the case in Alaska. These are sorely needed projects that have hitherto been beyond the financial means of the Territory and local communities. But the need remains. The failure to provide them checks growth that would otherwise take place.

In a related category is power development. The recent announcement of Alcoa's plan to harness the upper Yukon and to drop some of its waters onto Alaskan territory at Dyea in order to process alumina is epoch-making. Its coming will be the most important single event in the history of Alaska's development. It has several unique aspects.

First is its magnitude. It will call for an initial investment of $400,000,000. It was reported recently in a national magazine that this is the second largest investment ever made in a single plant, being topped only by a steel plant in Pennsylvania which cost $421,000,000. Actually Alcoa's investment will go well beyond $421,000,000 and will be, not the second largest, but the largest investment by a private industry under the flag. It will employ some 4000 people 365 days a year and will have an annual payroll of about $25,000,000. These people will require a town housing 20,000 persons to be built in the Dyea Valley. At least 10,000 more can be expected in neighboring Skagway. The beneficial economic consequences, direct and indirect, to Alaska stagger the imagination. In itself it will increase Alaska's present population by nearly 20 per cent. By itself this plant will supply the most important ingredient hitherto missing from Alaska's economy — a large year-round non-governmental payroll.

Second is the fact that the power to be utilized originates in Canada in the headwaters of the Yukon and adjacent lakes. It is now running to waste and will continue to do so unless harnessed by the force of gravity which the 2500-foot drop to sea level on the Alaskan side of the boundary provides.

Third, the project utilizes a raw material, bauxite, which as far as is now known does not exist in Alaska but will be brought here from Surinam in South American and be partly processed in the States before arrival here. The land on which this development will take place has not been found of any value and has likewise been unutilized, although known and accessible since the days of '98. Thus this project is unique on several counts, and it represents the antithesis of exploitation and wastage of natural resources. The hydroelectric development is essential to this industry, for large quantities of cheap power are indispensable to the manufacture of aluminum.*

This very fact calls attention to the urgent need of developing cheap power elsewhere in Alaska to attract industry. Alaska and adjacent Canada have in all probability the greatest undeveloped power potentials on the North American continent. But private industry is seldom in a position to finance such power development. In the diversification of Alaska's economy, which has hitherto been highly limited by seasonal factors, its only principal industries, fisheries and placer mining, operated only in the summer months, and more year-round payrolls are needed. Cheap and abundant power alone will attract them.

The answer — in the absence of private enterprise, able, willing, and ready to undertake the great cost of power production — is governmental development. One project, the harnessing of Lake Eklutna to supply the greater Anchorage area, is under development. It will cost about $30,000,000, supply 30,000 kilowatts. All this is, of course not a grant or a gift, but a loan fully repayable with interest by the users — the City of Anchorage, the Chugach and Matanuska electric cooperative, and the Army. It is an interesting commentary on Alaska's great power needs that some two years before this project's completion the entire output is already preempted. When completed, it will not satisfy the current demand — to say nothing of the expanding demand of the greater Anchorage area. The need is for more power projects, the most promising of which is now the harnessing of the Susitna River. This project, which has been under study by the Bureau of Reclamation, will supply an estimated 400,000 kilowatts, or thirteen times as much as Eklutna. It would generate power at less than ten mills and

*The Dyea project has not yet materialized. Some other specific problems mentioned here have been resolved since this article was written, including, of course, the achievement of statehood. — ED. NOTE.

make it available for 200 miles on either side of the rail belt. The problem is how to get authorization and appropriation for such a project, which, let it be emphasized again, is not a gift or grant but the soundest kind of investment by the government in behalf of private enterprise, and repayable with interest. But how to get it? Congress was, with the greatest of difficulty, even with the potent cooperation of the military and the support of numerous public and private agencies, persuaded to authorize the Eklutna project. A reactionary administration would in all likelihood view other public power developments coldly, even though private capital was unavailable for the purpose. Both the executive and the legislative branches will have to be persuaded. The benefits, let it be ever borne in mind, would be national as well as Alaskan. The representation of two senators and a voting representative would greatly improve the chances of realizing such a project.

It will be seen at this point, and it becomes increasingly clear, that Alaska is largely dependent on the vision and understanding of the Congress, on the whole a distant body with little firsthand knowledge of Alaska's needs and problems and of their intimate relation to the national interest.

And that brings us to another problem — or rather a whole series of problems — one of our greatest problems in Alaska, lack of knowledge. Very little is really known about Alaska and its resources. Research — intensified research, enlarged research, continuing research — is essential.

Yet it is an ironic fact that, while private industry has learned the importance of research, government, on the level where the means for research are provided, has not. When Congress engages in its periodic retrenchment drives, research is likely to be the first victim. Possibly an exception is made of research in the field of national defense, where Congress has responded well. But, in Alaska, defense and economic development, defense and population growth are almost inseparable.

It would be superfluous to stress the importance of agriculture. It is the most basic of all economic pursuits. It is the greatest stabilizer of population. Yet, despite the fact that thirty years

ago a land-grant college was established in Alaska, as a result
of which it was entitled to certain annual appropriations for research and extension work under a variety of Congressional enactments, Congress persistently refused to appropriate the legally authorized funds. Year after year our voteless delegates
would plead eloquently but in vain. The appropriations that
were made were negligible, far below the sums legally Alaska's,
and wholly inadequate. It should have been clear that Alaskan
latitudes, with their unstudied climatic, soil, and entomological
factors, required specific research of their own. Nothing was
done about it until — as with so many recent Alaskan developments — word of intensive and successful agricultural activity
in comparable latitudes in Soviet Siberia reached the Congress.
Then for the first time a cooperative program of research under
the joint auspices of the federal Department of Agriculture, the
University of Alaska, and the Territory was provided. It was
begun most auspiciously three years ago, even though on a relatively modest scale. But even now it is already menaced by
Congressional retrenchment, which will force suspension of
some important research already undertaken. Such curtailment
is a constantly impending threat which in itself impairs the
morale and effectiveness of those engaged in this essential undertaking.

In the field of fisheries, which involves Alaska's greatest natural resource, the Pacific salmon — a field Congress and the
Department of the Interior insist on retaining under Federal
control — appropriations for research have been almost totally
lacking, and funds for enforcement of presumably sound conservation measures always insufficient. In consequence the annual
salmon runs are slowly but surely diminishing. The Territory
has attempted to alleviate the situation by setting up its own
Department of Fisheries, engaging in research, experimenting
in the expansion of salmon spawning areas, and even contributing stream guards; but the problem basically is lack of adequate sustenance by long-range governmental planning.

In the field of health it has long been clear that adequate
knowledge of arctic and subarctic physiology and pathology

were lacking. The question is intimately related to national defense in Alaska. Soviet knowledge in this field, based on long experience in arctic and subarctic latitudes, appears greatly to exceed ours, although since the lowering of iron curtains our information on the subject is largely presumptive. For years the establishment of an Arctic Institute of Health at the University of Alaska or elsewhere in our Territory has been urged upon the United States Public Health Service, the Bureau of the Budget, and the Congress. Nothing has resulted thus far.

In many of Alaska's other problems the Federal Government plays a controlling part. The question of aboriginal or possessory rights or claims requires settlement. Five years ago Congress finally gave evidence of its recognition of the problem by passing the Alaska Timber Sales Act, which froze the fees collectable for stumpage in escrow pending legislation to dispose of the problem. An excellent bill sponsored by Alaska's delegate and endorsed by the Office of Indian Affairs in Washington still awaits action by the Congress.

The judiciary and law enforcement were specifically retained for the Federal authorities under the Organic Act of 1912 — except within municipalities. The Organic Act of 1884 provided one Federal judge and four lower court judges, called United States commissioners. Congress provided no salaries for them but arranged that they subsist on the fees they collect for probate and other services from the public. The number of commissioners has grown, and there are now more than fifty, but they are still unsalaried despite repeated efforts to get Congress to remedy this disgraceful state of affairs. Except in the four or five principal cities, these fees, which are expected to furnish the commissioners' livelihood, are insufficient to keep body and soul together. The four Federal district judges who appoint the commissioners have a serious problem in finding competent and worthy commissioners in the smaller communities. The administration of justice — cornerstone of the free society — suffers. Under statehood Alaska would have its own judiciary, and, needless to say it, it would be paid.

The police power — outside the incorporated towns — is likewise vested by the Federal Government in the four United States marshals and their deputies. But appropriation to provide an adequate number of deputies is never made. Congress has grossly failed in carrying out its responsibility for law enforcement in the Territory which nevertheless it has insisted on retaining. A visible symbol of the Federal failure in this field is the Anchorage jail — a Federal institution — whose foulness has been the subject of repeated protests.

The Territory, however, has made an excellent entry into the field of law enforcement by creating an efficient highway patrol, now numbering over forty officers and men, in an endeavor not merely to enforce traffic regulations but also to supplement the Federal Government's feeble efforts. The gap, however, has not yet closed, and the responsibility, as long as Alaska remains a Territory shackled to the Organic Act of 1912, is still the Federal Government's.

Progress in Alaska has, of course, brought its problems. It is gratifying that they are the problems of growth and not of shrinkage. But basic to an adequate solution of these problems should be the understanding that Alaska's growth and development are and should be of great national concern, and that their rapid attainment is in the national interest. The need for better and fuller Federal cooperation is emphasized not merely by that concept, but also by the long years of neglect, by the continuation of many Federal practices of omission and commission that are unjustifiable, and by the vital importance of Alaska in the face of international events.

If it be urged that Congress raise its sights and increase its appropriations for essential objectives in Alaska, there should be no disposition to evade any responsibility or participation that can properly be borne or shared by the 165,000 people now resident in Alaska. As of today they are, by and large, doing their part. They can without difficulty today support *a* state. But Alaska, from the standpoint of national interest, should be viewed as something more than just another state, be it the forty-ninth or the fiftieth.

Federal policy should keep as its objective not merely economic development of Alaska, but also parallel political development and social development which require the fullest measure of self-government obtainable under our American system.

However, given the need of fulfilling Alaska's destiny as a *national* objective, statehood should not and cannot write *finis* to substantial federal assistance in achieving that goal. Nor is this postulate inconsistent with the demand for the full political equality of statehood. Actually statehood may be considered a helpful and indeed an indispensable instrument in helping the nation obtain its goal in Alaska. Politically, Alaska may be just another state when Congress acts and the necessary preliminaries have been complied with by Alaskans. But materially and ideologically the nation can have incorporated in its design and resource a great northern domain, in essence a new domain in its developed potency, militancy, and resourcefulness. That domain can embody all that is best in the American way of life and advance the front of democracy farther west and farther north than it ever has been.

Contributors' Bibliography

A SELECTIVE LIST OF ARTICLES AND BOOKS
RELATING TO ALASKAN HISTORY

ANDREWS, C. L., "Alaska under the Russians — Baranof the Builder," *Washington Historical Quarterly*, VII (July, 1916), 202–16.

———, "Alaska under the Russians — Industry, Trade and Social Life," *Washington Historical Quarterly*, VII (October, 1916), 278–95.

———, "Alaska Whaling," *Washington Historical Quarterly*, IX (January, 1918), 3–10.

———, "Biographical Sketch of Capt. William Moore," *Washington Historical Quarterly*, XXI (July, 1930), 195–203. Continued in, XXI (October, 1930), 271–80; and, XXII (January, 1931), 32–41.

———, "Driving Reindeer in Alaska," *Washington Historical Quarterly*, XXVI (April, 1935), 90–93.

———, *The Eskimo and His Reindeer* (Caldwell, Idaho: Caxton Printers, 1939).

———, "Historical Russian Library of Alaska," *Pacific Northwest Quarterly*, XXIX (April, 1938), 201–04.

———, "Marine Disasters of the Alaska Route," *Washington Historical Quarterly*, VII (January, 1916), 21–37.

———, "Reindeer in the Arctic," *Washington Historical Quarterly*, XVII (January, 1926), 14–17.

———, "Russian Plans for American Dominion," *Washington Historical Quarterly*, XVIII (April, 1927), 83–92.

———, "Russian Shipbuilding in the American Colonies," *Washington Historical Quarterly*, XXV (January, 1934), 3–10.

———, "The Salmon of Alaska," *Washington Historical Quarterly*, IX (October, 1918), 243–54.

———, "Some Notes on the Yukon by Stewart Menzies," *Pacific Northwest Quarterly*, XXXII (April, 1941), 197–202.

———, "Some Russian Books on Alaskan History," *Pacific Northwest Quarterly*, XXVIII (January, 1937), 75–87.

———, *The Story of Alaska* (Caldwell, Idaho: Caxton Printers, 1938; several later printings).

BAILEY, THOMAS A., *America Faces Russia* (Ithaca, N.Y.: Cornell University Press, 1950; reprinted in 1964 by Peter Smith, Gloucester, Mass.).

———, *A Diplomatic History of the American People* (New York: F. S. Crofts, 1940; several later editions).

———, "Why the United States Purchased Alaska," *Pacific Historical Review*, III (March, 1934), 39–49.

BROOKS, A. H., *Blazing Alaska's Trails* (Caldwell, Idaho: University of Alaska and Arctic Institute of North America, 1953).

———, "The Development of Alaska by Government Railroads," *Quarterly Journal of Economics*, XXVIII (May, 1914), 586–96.

———, "History of Mining in Alaska," *Alaska-Yukon Magazine*, VIII (May, 1909), 149–52.

———, "The Influence of Geography on the Exploration and Settlement of Alaska," *Bulletin of the American Geographical Society*, XXXVIII (February, 1906), 102–05.

———, "The Mining Industry of Alaska," *Engineering and Mining Journal*, LXXVII (January 14, 1904), 75–78.

———, *The Mount McKinley Region, Alaska* (Washington: USGS Professional Paper No. 70, 1911).

———, "A Reconnaissance from Pyramid Harbor to Eagle City, Alaska, including a Description of the Copper Deposits of the Upper White and Tanana Rivers," *Twenty-first Annual Report of the USGS, 1899–1900*, Part II, 331–91.

———, "A Reconnaissance in the White and Tanana River Basins, Alaska, in 1898," *Twentieth Annual Report of the USGS, 1898–99*, Part VII, 425–94.

———, "The Value of Alaska," *Geographical Review*, XV (January, 1925), 25–50.

BURPEE, L. J., editor, *An Historical Atlas of Canada* (Toronto and New York: Thomas Nelson & Sons, 1927).

————, editor, *Journal of the Yukon, 1847–48*, by Alexander Hunter Murray (Ottawa: Government Printing Office, 1910).

————, *The Search for the Western Sea* (Toronto: Macmillan, 1935; two vols.).

CAMPBELL, C. S., *Anglo-American Understanding, 1898–1903* (Baltimore: The Johns Hopkins University Press, 1957).

————, "The Bering Sea Settlements of 1892," *Pacific Historical Review*, XXXII (November, 1963), 347–66.

CARLSON, L. H., *An Alaskan Gold Mine: The Story of No. 9 Above* (Evanston, Ill.: Northwestern University Press, 1951). The book is a revised version of five articles which appeared in *The Covenant Quarterly*: "Part I, 1898–1901 – The Story of No. 9 Above," VII (November, 1947), 193–237; "Part II, The Eskimo Lawsuit," VII (November, 1947), 238–69; "Part III, The Arbitration Commission of 1904," VIII (February, 1948), 21–47; "Part IV, The Appeal to the Courts," VIII (August, 1948), 157–85; "Part V, Ramifications and Conclusions," VIII (November, 1948), 229–55.

————, "The First Mining Season at Nome, Alaska, 1899," *Pacific Historical Review*, XVI (May, 1947), 163–75.

————, "Nome: From Mining Camp to Civilized Community," *Pacific Northwest Quarterly*, XXXVIII (July, 1947), 233–42.

————, "Swedish Pioneers and the Discovery of Gold in Alaska," *American Swedish Historical Foundation Year Book, 1948* (Philadelphia, 1948), 63–81.

CHEVIGNY, HECTOR, *Lord of Alaska* (New York: The Viking Press, 1942; several later printings).

————, *Lost Empire* (New York: The Viking Press, 1937; later printings).

GILBERT, B. F., "The Alaska Purchase," *Journal of the West*, III (April, 1964), 163–74.

————, "Arts and Sciences in Alaska: 1784–1910," *Journal of the West*, I (October, 1962), 135–48.

————, "Economic Developments in Alaska, 1867–1910," *Journal of the West*, IV (October, 1965), 504–21.

GOLDER, F. A., "The Attitude of the Russian Government Toward Alaska," in *The Pacific Ocean in History*, edited by H. M. Stephens and H. E. Bolton (New York: Macmillan, 1917).

————, *Bering's Voyages* (New York: American Geographical Society, 1922–1925; two vols.).

————, *Guide to Materials for American History in Russian Archives* (Washington: Carnegie Institution, 1917–1937; two vols.).

————, "The Purchase of Alaska," *American Historical Review*, XXV (April, 1920), 411–25.

————, "Russian-American Relations during the Crimean War," *American Historical Review*, XXXI (April, 1926), 462–76.

————, *Russian Expansion on the Pacific, 1641–1850* (Cleveland: Arthur H. Clark, 1914).

————, "The Russian Fleet and the Civil War," *American Historical Review*, XX (July, 1915), 801–12.

————, "Russia and Russian Alaska," in A. P. Taylor, ed., *The Hawaiian Islands* (Honolulu: Printshop Co., 1930).

————, "A Survey of Alaska," *Washington Historical Quarterly*, IV (April, 1913), 83–95.

GRUENING, ERNEST, "The Political Ecology of Alaska," *Scientific Monthly*, LXXIII (December, 1951), 376–86.

————, *The State of Alaska* (New York: Random House, 1954).

HINCKLEY, TED C., "Excerpts from the Letters of Dr. Clarence Thwing, Presbyterian Missionary to Wrangell, Alaska During the Mid-1890's," *Journal of Presbyterian History*, XLI (March, 1963), 37–55.

————, "The Inside Passage: A Popular Gilded Age Tour," *Pacific Northwest Quarterly*, LVI (April, 1965), 67–74.

————, "The Presbyterian Leadership in Pioneer Alaska," *Journal of American History*, LII (March, 1966), 742–56.

————, "Prospectors, Profits and Prejudice," *The American West*, II (Spring, 1965), 59–65.

————, "Publicist of the Forgotten Frontier," *Journal of the West*, IV (January, 1965), 27–40.

————, "Punitive Action at Angoon," *Alaska Sportsman*, XXIX (January, 1963), 8, 9, 43–45; concluded, XXIX (February, 1963), 14, 15, 40–42.

————, "Rustlers of the North Pacific," *Journal of the West*, II (January, 1963), 22–30.

————, "Sheldon Jackson, Presbyterian Lobbyist for the Great Land of Alaska," *Journal of Presbyterian History*, XL (March, 1962), 3–23.

————, "Sheldon Jackson as Preserver of Alaska's Native Culture," *Pacific Historical Review*, XXXIII (November, 1964), 411–24.

HULLEY, C. C., *Alaska: Past and Present* (Portland, Ore.: Binfords & Mort, 1958; revised edition).

KEITHAHN, E. L., *Eskimo Adventure* (Seattle: Superior Publishing Co., 1963).

———, *Igloo Tales* (Washington, 1945).

———, *Monuments in Cedar* (Ketchikan: Roy Anderson, 1945; revised 1963).

———, "The Petroglyphs of Southeastern Alaska," *American Antiquity*, VI (October, 1940), 123–32.

———, "Stone Artifacts of Southeastern Alaska," *American Antiquity*, XXVIII (July, 1962), 66–77.

KERNER, ROBERT J., *Russian Expansion to America: Its Bibliographical Foundations* (Papers of the Bibliographical Society of America, Volume XXV, 1931).

———, *The Urge to the Sea* (Berkeley and Los Angeles: University of California Press, 1942).

KOENIG, DUANE, "The World's Most Northern University," *Bulletin of Association of American Colleges*, XLIII (October, 1957), 419–21.

MAZOUR, A. G., "Dimitry Zavalishin: Dreamer of a Russian-American Empire," *Pacific Historical Review*, V (March, 1936), 26–37.

———, "Doctor Yegor Scheffer: Dreamer of a Russian Empire in the Pacific," *Pacific Historical Review*, VI (March, 1937), 15–20.

———, "The Russian-American and Anglo-Russian Convention, 1824–1825: An Interpretation," *Pacific Historical Review*, XIV (September, 1945), 303–10.

———, "The Russian-American Company: Private or Government Enterprise," *Pacific Historical Review*, XIII (June, 1944), 168–73.

———, *Russia: Tsarist and Communist* (New York: Van Nostrand, 1962).

NICHOLS, J. P., *Alaska: A History of Its Administration, Exploitation, and Industrial Development during Its First Half Century under the Rule of the United States* (Cleveland: Arthur H. Clark, 1924; later printing).

———, "Wreck of the St. Nicholas," *Washington Historical Quarterly*, XIII (January, 1922), 27–31.

PIERCE, R. A., "A Note on Ivan Petroff and the Far Northwest," *Journal of the West*, III (October, 1964), 436–39.

————, *Russia's Hawaiian Adventure, 1815–1817* (Berkeley and Los Angeles: University of California Press, 1965).

SHENITZ, H. A., "Baranov, Empire Builder," *Alaska Sportsman*, XXVII (July, 1961), 10–13, 43, 44.

————, "Vestiges of Old Russia in Alaska," *Russian Review*, XIV (January, 1955), 55–59.

SHERWOOD, M. B., "Ardent Spirits: Hooch and the *Osprey* Affair at Sitka," *Journal of the West*, IV (July, 1965), 301–44.

————, *Exploration of Alaska, 1865–1900* (New Haven and London: Yale University Press, 1965).

————, "Ivan Petroff and the Far Northwest," *Journal of the West*, II (July, 1963), 305–15. The article is substantially the same as Chapter 4 in *Exploration of Alaska, 1865–1900*.

————, "A Pioneer Scientist in the Far North," *Pacific Northwest Quarterly*, LIII (April, 1962), 77–80.

TOMPKINS, S. R., "After Bering: Mapping the North Pacific," *British Columbia Historical Quarterly*, XIX (January–April, 1955), 1–55.

————, *Alaska: Promyshlennik and Sourdough* (Norman: University of Oklahoma Press, 1945; later printing).

————, *The Russian Mind: From Peter the Great Through the Enlightenment* (Norman: University of Oklahoma Press, 1953).

————, *Russia Through the Ages* (Englewood Cliffs, N.J.: Prentice-Hall, 1940).

VEVIER, CHARLES, "American Continentalism: An Idea of Expansion, 1845–1910," *American Historical Review*, LXV (January, 1960), 323–35.

————, editor, *Siberian Journey: Down the Amur to the Pacific, 1856–57* (Madison: University of Wisconsin Press, 1962).

Index

(When convenient, modern Russian transliteration is used in the key entry.)